THE Untold

EXPLORING THE HUMAN SIDE OF WAR

CIVIL WAR

JAMES ROBERTSON

EDITED BY NEIL KAGAN

NATIONAL GEOGRAPHIC

WASHINGTON, D.C.

CONTENTS

THE HUMAN SIDE OF WAR
18

THE LIFE OF SOLDIERS
86

RESOURCES, RESOLVE, & INGENUITY
150

4
A WAR
OF FIRSTS
190

5
WARRIORS, POETS,
& SCOUNDRELS
256

6
AFTERMATH
314

Untold Stories *This volume is dedicated to all of the unidentified soldiers and civilians who were eyewitnesses to the most tumultuous event in American history. Their stories are etched in their faces and in the language of their bodies, including the young fifer and drummer boys, page 1; bugler on horseback, page 2; and soldier and sweetheart, page 7.*

PORTRAYING THE HUMAN DRAMA

To commemorate the 150th anniversary of the Civil War, the National Geographic Society has invited award-winning historian James Robertson to share with readers his intimate knowledge of the subject, acquired over many years as a teacher, scholar, and consummate storyteller. The result is *The Untold Civil War,* a unique collection of true stories that dramatize something often left untold in accounts of campaigns and battles—the human side of war. Revealed here are the hopes, fears, foibles, and ideals of Americans of all descriptions, caught up in a great historic epic that defined this nation.

Robertson brings the Civil War to life here by focusing on telling details that personalize the conflict. He makes the remote Stonewall Jackson distinctly human, for example, by relating how the general indulged his favorite horse, Little Sorrel: "When the army went into bivouac late in the day, the horse had the peculiar habit of lying down like a dog—sometimes on his back. The normally stern Jackson made a pet of the animal, and often fed it apples when he thought no one was looking." The deadly perils soldiers faced when not in battle are summed up vividly by the author with these few instances: "Lt. Silas Beck died after eating a poisoned apple. Musician Thomas Ballard was mistaken for a bear and shot dead while brushing his teeth in a moonlit creek. Cpl. Thomas Cabe was captured and went insane amid the squalor of Camp Douglas Prison."

The Civil War was always a part of Robertson's life. Raised in Danville, Virginia, he is the great-grandson of a Virginian who survived Pickett's Charge at Gettysburg. He was just 31 when President John F. Kennedy appointed him Executive Director of the U.S. Civil War Centennial Commission. He recently retired as Virginia Tech Alumni Distinguished Professor in History and Executive Director of the Virginia Center for Civil War Studies. Throughout his career, Robertson has brought to light the experiences of common soldiers and civilians, like the unidentified Union couple at right, telling of their ordeals and triumphs. He is the acclaimed author of more than 20 books, including *Stonewall Jackson: The Man, the Soldier, the Legend,* and the well-known voice of weekly talks about little-known people and events of the Civil War, which aired for 15 years on National Public Radio.

It was my pleasure as editor of this book to work closely with James Robertson. I pored over thousands of Civil War photographs, sketches, and artifacts, selecting images to highlight his stories, which I have organized here in chapters thematically. Readers will find an overview of the war's major events on the following pages. The remainder of the book offers something no survey can provide—an unforgettable human drama, drawn from history.

NEIL KAGAN, EDITOR

MILESTONES AND TURNING POINTS

John Brown never finished anything he started. Born in Connecticut and raised in Ohio, he failed at more than a dozen business ventures in six states. Although he fathered 20 children by two wives, he did little to control those broods. Slavery was the worst of evils, he thought, and hatred for it consumed him. Brown was an avid reader of Scripture. His favorite passage was "Without the shedding of blood there is no remission of sins."

His slaughter of five pro-slavery men in the dead of night in 1856 was among the deeds that turned a budding Western territory into "Bleeding Kansas." Leaving that land in turmoil, Brown went back east to pursue a new scheme—seizing the federal arsenal at Harpers Ferry, Virginia, in hopes of starting a slave insurrection. He failed at that as well and went to the gallows in 1859. Brown's one lasting accomplishment was posthumous.

His raid helped propel a nation that had been quarreling bitterly over slavery for decades toward a bloody reckoning he would have welcomed. During the presidential campaign of 1860, pro-slavery Southern Democrats split with Northern Democrats and their compromise candidate, Illinois senator Stephen Douglas. That helped Republican Abraham Lincoln, an antislavery candidate, snare a victory that left many Southerners seething. At year's end, South Carolina became the first state to secede from the Union.

Bodily Punishment
Braided leather whips like the one shown here were commonly used on slaves who attempted to flee.

1861: OPENING SHOTS

By February 1861, six states in the Deep South had joined South Carolina in the emerging Confederacy. States that lay closer to the North held back, despite appeals from fire-eaters like Roger Pryor, a hotheaded ex-congressman who assured his fellow Virginians that Northerners would not dare attack them if they seceded. At one meeting, Pryor shook

PRELUDE TO WAR

1861

May 1854 The Kansas-Nebraska Act becomes law, leading to armed conflict in Kansas between pro-slavery and antislavery forces and the formation of the Republican Party.

October 1859 John Brown raids the Federal arsenal at Harpers Ferry, Virginia, in a failed attempt to initiate a slave insurrection.

December 20, 1860 South Carolina becomes the first Southern state to secede from the Union.

September 1850 The Compromise of 1850 passes Congress. Intended to settle the debate over slavery, the legislation instead causes greater controversy.

March 1857 The U.S. Supreme Court in the *Dred Scott* decision rules that slaves are the property of their owners.

August–October, 1858 Abraham Lincoln gains attention for his antislavery views in debates with Stephen Douglas in an Illinois senatorial campaign.

November 6, 1860 Republican Abraham Lincoln wins the presidential election with no support from the South.

February 4, 1861 Representatives from seven Southern states meet in Montgomery, Alabama, to form the Confederate States of America.

a handkerchief at the crowd and declared that he could wipe up with it "every drop of blood shed in a war by the secession of the South."

Some Northerners believed that the South should be allowed to leave the Union peacefully. One man who did not feel that way was Abraham Lincoln. Any nation that could stand by and watch itself disintegrate, the new President stated, was unworthy of the name. Lincoln believed that war was inevitable but preferred to let Confederate President Jefferson Davis bear the burden of starting it. By resupplying Fort Sumter, a beleaguered Union garrison in Charleston harbor, he left Confederates the choice of attacking the post or backing down.

The Civil War began before dawn on April 12 when the first shots were fired at Fort Sumter, which fell two days later. Lincoln responded by calling for 75,000 troops to squelch the Southern uprising, which soon grew to include 11 states as Virginia, North Carolina, Tennessee, and Arkansas joined the Confederacy. The South was fighting for independence, the North to restore the Union. Confederates and Unionists alike expected to wage a quick war culminating in one grand, climactic battle. Many of the first volunteers enlisted for 90-day terms.

In July, two armed mobs that were not yet armies converged at Manassas Junction, Virginia. The all-day struggle contained equal shares of courage and chaos. One of the 60,000 green recruits there was Richmond merchant Frank Potts, who told of killing his first man—a Union soldier within 70 yards of him. "I could not miss," Potts wrote. "Aiming at his heart, I fired. I saw him no more. God have mercy on him." The Virginian then added: "I was fighting for my home, and he had no business being there."

The Union defeat at Manassas did more to rouse Northerners than to embolden Southerners. The Confederacy rested on its laurels and awaited peace overtures. South Carolina diarist Mary Chesnut predicted: "We will dilly-dally, and Congress orate, and generals parade, until they in the North get up an army three times as large." She was right. A stunned North began to prepare for a long war, drawing on its

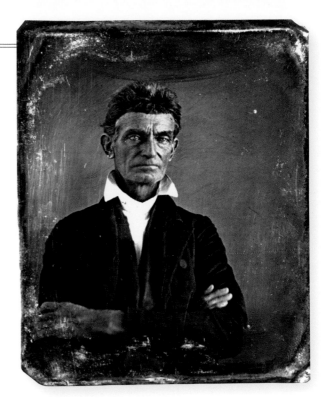

Fierce Abolitionist
John Brown posed for this photograph in Kansas in 1856 not long after his deadly attack on pro-slavery settlers there.

February 18, 1861 Mississippian Jefferson Davis inaugurated provisional President of the Confederacy.

April 12, 1861 The Civil War begins as Confederates bombard Fort Sumter, which falls two days later.

April 17, 1861 Virginia state convention votes to leave the Union. Three other border states will soon join Virginia and the seven original Confederate states.

June 10, 1861 A detachment of Union soldiers stationed at Fort Monroe makes an advance up the Virginia Peninsula but is repulsed at Big Bethel, near Hampton.

September 4, 1861 Confederates occupy Columbus, Kentucky, in defiance of that state's neutrality.

March 4, 1861 Abraham Lincoln is inaugurated 16th President of the United States and pledges to preserve the Union.

April 15, 1861 Lincoln calls on states to supply 75,000 volunteer soldiers to meet the Southern "insurrection."

May 24, 1861 Lincoln orders Union troops to cross the Potomac and occupy both Alexandria and Arlington Heights, Virginia.

April 19, 1861 Lincoln imposes a naval blockade on the Confederacy.

July 21, 1861 In the first pitched battle of the war, Union forces attack Confederates at Manassas along Bull Run and are routed in late afternoon.

October 21, 1861 Federals are routed at Ball's Bluff after crossing the Potomac into Virginia upriver from Washington.

superiority in manpower, sea power, and industrial might. A Federal blockade of Southern ports along the Atlantic and Gulf coasts slowly took effect. Out west, the first fleet of ironclads ever to wage war was built to support forthcoming Union advances along the Mississippi, Ohio, Tennessee, and Cumberland Rivers. Northern morale received a boost that autumn when New Englander Julia Ward Howe transformed an abolitionist anthem hailing the martyrdom of John Brown into the stirring "Battle Hymn of the Republic."

As winter closed in, Southerners battened down the hatches and prepared for a long, rough voyage. The contest at Manassas on which they had pinned their hopes would soon seem like a quaint relic of the past, resembling an engagement in the War of 1812. The slow, punishing siege of Petersburg that ultimately decided the Civil War would be more like the murderous trench warfare of World War I.

Yankee Gunners
Men of the First New York Light Artillery man their guns in Fort Richardson, erected by General McClellan's forces near Richmond, Virginia, following the Battle of Seven Pines in June 1862.

1862: A Deepening Storm

"As far as the eye could reach, in every direction," Union soldier Wilbur Hyman observed, "lay the silent forms of those who went down in the storm of battle." It was the morning after two days of intense fight-

ing at Shiloh in southwestern Tennessee. The battle had begun early on April 6, 1862, with a surprise attack by Confederates on Federals led by Ulysses S. Grant. It ended the following evening with the two sides back where they started. An Iowa soldier remarked afterward: "In places dead men lay so closely that a person could walk over two acres of ground and not step off the bodies." Dead and dying horses lay amid wrecked wagons and abandoned guns.

This catastrophe was the largest battle yet fought in the Western Hemisphere. Total casualties were more than 23,000 men, which exceeded the losses in all of America's previous wars combined. One of the fatalities was Pvt. William Pope of Kentucky. With both legs shot off and no hope of recovery, Pope asked a compatriot: "Johnny, if a boy dies for his country, the glory is his forever, isn't it?"

1862

February 16 U. S. Grant seizes Fort Donelson on the Cumberland River and gains the nickname "Unconditional Surrender."

April 6–7 Battle of Shiloh in Tennessee claims more than 23,000 casualties.

June 2 Robert E. Lee replaces the wounded Joseph E. Johnston as commander of the Army of Northern Virginia.

June 12–13 Confederate Cavalry leader J. E. B. "Jeb" Stuart rides completely around the Union army near Richmond.

February 6 Union forces capture Fort Henry on the Tennessee River.

March 9 History's first battle between ironclads occurs between U.S.S. *Monitor* and C.S.S. *Virginia* at Hampton Roads, Virginia.

June 1 George McClellan's massive Union army is stopped nine miles from Richmond at Seven Pines.

April 25 A Union fleet under David Farragut receives the surrender of New Orleans, the South's largest seaport.

June 9 With victory at Port Republic, Confederate Gen. Thomas "Stonewall" Jackson concludes his triumphant Shenandoah Valley Campaign.

In 1862, the short, glorious contest many envisioned when the war began became a nightmare without end. The human costs surpassed all expectations. The advent of the rifle, with four times the range of the smoothbore musket, changed warfare fundamentally and gave well-prepared defenders a huge advantage over exposed attackers. At Shiloh and some other battlefields, however, defenders too were caught in exposed positions, resulting in dreadful losses on both sides—and horrific scenes afterward. Dead men putrefied and swelled in the heat and were dumped into hastily dug trenches, filled with hundreds of unidentified corpses. Dead and dying animals were cremated in huge fires that left acrid smoke hanging over the countryside.

Shiloh was a setback for Grant, who had won renown by capturing Forts Henry and Donelson in February. His swift rise to fame aroused jealousy and skepticism among superiors, who faulted him for being caught off guard, suspected that he was an alcoholic, and urged the President to sack him. "I can't spare this man," Lincoln replied. "He fights."

Stroke of Luck
This Federal belt plate, recovered from the battlefield at Fredericksburg, Virginia, was struck by a .58-caliber rifle bullet and probably saved a soldier's life there.

The Confederates lost their top commander in the Western theater (the vast region beyond the Appalachians) when Albert Sidney Johnston died at Shiloh. He was followed by the inept P. G. T. Beauregard and the erratic Braxton Bragg, whose bid to reclaim Kentucky for the South ended in defeat at Perryville that October. By late 1862, Union forces had captured New Orleans, Baton Rouge, and Memphis on the Mississippi River, further eroding Confederate territory, strength, and confidence.

In the East, meanwhile, Lincoln was struggling to find an army commander who would fight. George B. McClellan molded the Union Army of the Potomac into a huge, well-trained force but faltered in his springtime advance up the Virginia Peninsula toward Richmond, the Confederate capital. Robert E. Lee assumed command of the Confederate Army of Northern Virginia there in June and repulsed the invaders. He then took the offensive, won a smashing victory at the Second Battle of Manassas in late August, and boldly crossed the Potomac River into Maryland.

Lee's troops were badly outnumbered when they clashed with Union forces at Antietam on September 17 in what proved to be the bloodiest day of combat in American history. The cautious McClellan lost

June 25–July 1 Lee's counteroffensive, known as the Seven Days' Campaign, forces McClellan to withdraw from Richmond.

August 28–30 Lee's army wins the Second Battle of Manassas.

September 22 Lincoln issues his preliminary Emancipation Proclamation.

October 8 Braxton Bragg's Confederate invasion of Kentucky comes to an end at the Battle of Perryville.

December 29 Confederates at Chickasaw Bluffs, near Vicksburg, repulse Union troops led by William T. Sherman, who reports that he "landed, assaulted, and failed."

August 9 Stonewall Jackson thwarts a new Federal offensive in Virginia with victory at Cedar Mountain.

September 17 Battle of Antietam results in America's bloodiest day and impels Lee to end his invasion of Maryland.

October 3–4 Confederates fail to dislodge Federals holding the rail junction of Corinth, Mississippi.

December 13 Battle of Fredericksburg ends in a costly defeat for Federals attacking Lee's stout defenses.

his chance for a decisive victory there. He then let Lee's army withdraw unimpeded to Virginia and was later sacked by Lincoln. His successor, Ambrose Burnside, launched a disastrous December attack at Fredericksburg, where Lee's well-prepared defenders bludgeoned the Union army. "If there is a worse place than hell," Lincoln said afterward, "I am in it."

When soldiers settled into winter camps at the end of this trying year, their sufferings were far from over. Homesickness and loneliness vied with physical maladies such as diarrhea, typhoid fever, pneumonia, scarlet fever, measles, and other scourges that together claimed twice as many lives as were lost in combat. Those who survived became hardened veterans. They grew accustomed to the bitter taste of gunpowder, the choking smoke, and the roar of cannon fire, and somehow kept their wits about them amid the chaos of battle. A soldier of the 104th New York wrote his wife after one such contest: "Probably 50 bullets come in a few inches of me while my comrades fell right and left. I was not a bit afraid in battle but now the battle is over and I look back and see the many chances I had, it almost makes me tremble now. A man feels and acts strange in battle, when the danger is the most his fear is the least."

1863: THE PIVOTAL YEAR

The war entered its decisive phase in 1863 as the Union brought its might to bear. The new year began dismally for the Confederates, who fumbled away a chance for victory in a three-day battle at Stones River in Tennessee. A semiliterate soldier of the 34th Alabama in Bragg's army described the aftermath of that struggle to his wife: "I can inform you that I have Seen the Monkey Show at last and I don't Waunt to see it no more . . . Som had their hedes shot of and some ther armes and leges . . . I can tell you that I am tirde of Ware." Many Southern soldiers and civilians would come to share that war-weariness as their fortunes declined during 1863. The Confederate government had to impose conscription to meet manpower shortages, a measure some saw as a violation of states' rights.

Fire Zouave *This tinted photograph shows a soldier of the 72nd Pennsylvania, also known as Baxter's Fire Zouaves, who were recruited from Philadelphia fire companies and fought at Gettysburg.*

1863

April 2 Mob in Richmond composed largely of destitute women engages in a bread riot, looting stores.

June 9 Federal cavalrymen battle Jeb Stuart's troopers at Brandy Station, Virginia.

June 24 Lee's forces advance from Maryland into Pennsylvania.

January 1 Lincoln's Emancipation Proclamation becomes law; the Union prepares to recruit black troops.

January 2 Battle of Stones River in Tennessee ends inconclusively but leaves Bragg's Confederate forces depleted.

May 16 Union forces under Grant gain victory at Champion Hill in Mississippi and close in on Vicksburg.

May 1–4 Lee wins Battle of Chancellorsville in Virginia but loses Stonewall Jackson, who is mortally wounded and dies on May 10.

July 1–3 Battle of Gettysburg, the war's costliest struggle, ends with Pickett's Charge, a brutal setback for Lee that causes him to withdraw to Virginia.

The Union instituted conscription as well, igniting deadly draft riots in New York and disturbances in other cities. Yet the North had a much deeper reservoir of manpower. Lincoln's Emancipation Proclamation opened the door for blacks to enlist and eventually added 180,000 men to Federal rolls. Support for the President's war effort, which eroded in 1862, rebounded in 1863 as the Union repulsed a second onslaught by Lee's army and made great strides in the West.

Lincoln's faith in Grant was rewarded when the general overcame initial setbacks at Vicksburg and laid siege to that stronghold on the Mississippi. On July 4, the city and its nearly 30,000 defenders surrendered. The fall of Vicksburg and nearby Port Hudson, Louisiana, gave the Union control of the Mississippi and caused Lincoln to exclaim: "Grant is my man, and I am his the rest of the war."

Terror in New York
Lynchings like the one portrayed here occurred during the New York City draft riots in July 1863 as mobs opposed to conscription and waging a war to end slavery lashed out at black victims.

Grant's breakthrough coincided with Lee's defeat at Gettysburg, which came just two months after his Confederates won a stunning victory at Chancellorsville. That triumph encouraged Lee to advance northward into Pennsylvania. His purpose was not to seize and hold Union territory but to take the fight to the enemy and win a victory that might cause war-weary Northerners to demand an end to the war.

His gamble failed when the opposing forces collided at Gettysburg. Lee was drawn into battle before he was ready for it and had to attack strong Union defenses on high ground. He was hampered because his best fighting general, Thomas "Stonewall" Jackson, had been fatally wounded at Chancellorsville, and his cavalry leader, J. E. B. "Jeb" Stuart, was nowhere in sight. Three days of heavy fighting cost each side more than 20,000 casualties but took a heavier toll on the Confederates, who could not make up such losses. Union forces failed to stop Lee from withdrawing into Virginia, but his aura of invincibility was gone.

Confederate hopes revived briefly in September when Bragg's forces smashed through enemy lines at Chickamauga in northern Georgia. Much of the Union army fled in disarray, but Gen. George Thomas—a Virginian whose family disowned him for siding with the North—held out long enough to allow Federals

July 9 Port Hudson, Louisiana, falls to the Federals, bringing the entire Mississippi River under Union control.

July 18 The 54th Massachusetts, an all-black regiment, takes part in a valiant but futile assault on Fort Wagner in South Carolina.

November 19 Lincoln journeys to Gettysburg to dedicate a soldiers' cemetery and makes "a few appropriate remarks," known to posterity as the Gettysburg Address.

December 1 Lee's Confederates hold their line in Virginia after clashes around Mine Run.

July 4 Grant captures Vicksburg after laying siege to the town.

July 13–16 New York City draft riots begin as a protest against conscription and escalate to include deadly attacks on blacks.

September 19–20 Confederates win the Battle of Chickamauga in Georgia, forcing Federals to retreat to Chattanooga, Tennessee.

November 24–25 Grant's forces seize Lookout Mountain and Missionary Ridge, overlooking Chattanooga, and force Bragg's Army of Tennessee to retreat in disarray.

to regroup at Chattanooga, Tennessee. Thanks to Thomas, hailed as the Rock of Chickamauga, what could have been a devastating Union defeat became the prelude to victory. Grant reached Chattanooga in October, brought in reinforcements, and swept Bragg's forces off Missionary Ridge and Lookout Mountain in November. It was a bitter setback for Confederates that left their foes poised to advance on Atlanta. Diarist Mary Chesnut spoke for many in the South when she wrote at year's end: "God help my country."

1864: A WAR OF ATTRITION

One of Many

This dead Confederate was among thousands of men killed in several days of fierce fighting near Spotsylvania Court House, Virginia, in May 1864.

"Nothing can describe the confusion, the savage blood-curdling yells, the murderous faces, the awful curses, and the grisly horror of the melee." Thus did one soldier evoke the fearful Battle of Spotsylvania in May 1864. Union soldiers assaulted fortified Confederates there for 18 hours in a steady rain. For hundreds of yards, only the width of the earthworks separated the two armies. More than 10,000 men fell dead or wounded amid a "seething, bubbling, roaring hell of hate and murder." By day's end, corpses lay five deep in the Virginia mud, many reduced to little more than torn bits of rag and bone.

This bloodbath was one of many costly battles waged in 1864 as Union forces fought a war of attrition aimed at wearing down the Confederates, who had fewer men to spare. U. S. Grant, appointed general-in-chief of all Union forces in early 1864, believed that in the past, Federal armies had "acted independently and without concert," like a balky team of mules, with "no two ever pulling together." This time, Grant would lead a relentless drive against Lee's army in Virginia while William T. Sherman, Grant's trusted subordinate, would advance simultaneously from Chattanooga toward Atlanta, a vital supply depot and rail junction. The combined Union offensives would take a steep toll in Union lives as well, because tactics had changed during the course of the war. Soldiers who once scoffed at fortifying their positions were now adept at digging trenches and raising earthworks that shielded them against attack and left their foes dreadfully exposed.

April 12 Nathan Bedford Forrest's Confederate cavalry attack Fort Pillow in Tennessee, on the Mississippi River, leading to a massacre of black troops.

May 11 Jeb Stuart falls mortally wounded at Yellow Tavern, near Richmond, in a battle with Philip Sheridan's Union troopers.

June 3 Grant suffers his worst setback in a head-on assault on Lee's fortified troops at Cold Harbor.

February 17 Confederate experimental submarine C.S.S. *H. L. Hunley* goes down after sinking the U.S.S. *Housatonic*, a frigate blockading Charleston Harbor.

March 9 Grant becomes general-in-chief of all Union armies.

May 5–6 Battle of the Wilderness in Virginia launches a prolonged struggle between Grant and Lee.

May 12 Grant and Lee grapple again at Spotsylvania in one of the war's most vicious battles.

June 15 Grant's troops reach Petersburg, Virginia, where they will besiege Lee's army.

Confederates would rely increasingly on such fortifications to hold back numerically superior Federal forces.

Early in May, Grant advanced against Lee, defending Richmond. "We must destroy this army of Grant's before he gets to the James River," Lee declared. "If he gets there, it will become a siege, and then it will be a mere question of time." Lee surprised Grant by attacking his forces soon after they entered the tangled Wilderness. Two days of savage combat there cost Grant dearly, but he did not retreat as his predecessors had. Forging ahead, he compelled Lee to fall back step by step, keeping himself between Grant and Richmond. Union troops smashed into fortified Confederates at Spotsylvania, and later along the North Anna River and at Cold Harbor, where Grant attacked "without stealth or deception," one observer reported, and suffered a "colossal, bloody defeat."

Union casualties had exceeded 50,000 men in a month of fighting. Grant had reduced Lee's smaller army substantially, however, and he now adroitly shifted course. Instead of advancing directly on Richmond, he crossed the James River and made for Petersburg, hoping to sever the rail line on which Richmond depended for supplies. Lee reached Petersburg in time to defend the town and protect Richmond, but his greatest fears were now realized. His entrenched army was under siege. Grant would continue to snipe at his forces and launch sporadic attacks while hunger, disease, and lack of supplies and reinforcements further weakened the once formidable army on which Richmond depended.

Meanwhile, Sherman was advancing on Atlanta with 100,000 men against an army half that size. His Confederate opponent, Joseph Johnston, fell back to conserve his forces and was replaced by the aggressive John Bell Hood, who launched costly attacks that left Confederates stretched too thin to hold the ring of fortifications around Atlanta. On September 2, Sherman announced proudly: "Atlanta is ours, and fairly won." Northern elation over Sherman's feat came shortly before national elections and assured Lincoln a second term as President. Yet Sherman, a stern practitioner of war, was not finished. The South would not yield, he concluded, until it was brought to its knees.

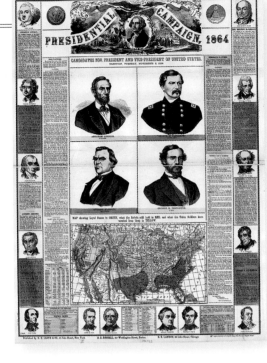

Mapping the Election
This 1864 campaign broadside portrays President Lincoln and his Democratic opponent, George McClellan, along with their running mates. The map shows Union territory in green, Confederate territory in red, and territory "the Union Soldiers have wrested from them" in yellow.

June 19 Confederate merchant raider Raphael Semmes loses his ship, C.S.S. *Alabama,* to the U.S.S. *Kearsarge* off Cherbourg, France.

July 30 Union forces blow a gaping hole in Confederate defenses at Petersburg but lose the ensuing Battle of the Crater.

September 2 Sherman takes Atlanta.

October 19 Battle of Cedar Creek in Virginia ends in victory for Sheridan's Federals and gives him control of the Shenandoah Valley.

December 21 Sherman's soldiers march triumphantly into Savannah, cutting the Confederacy in half.

July 20–22 Confederates under John Bell Hood suffer costly defeats by William Sherman's troops in the Battles of Peachtree Creek and Atlanta.

August 5 Adm. David G. Farragut's armada fights its way into Mobile Bay, Alabama. Warned of mines in the channel, Farragut shouts: "Damn the torpedoes! Full speed ahead!"

November 16 Sherman leaves Atlanta in flames and heads toward Savannah on his punishing march through Georgia.

November 8 Lincoln wins reelection with strong support from Union troops.

December 15–16 George H. Thomas's Federal army shatters Hood's Army of Tennessee in the Battle of Nashville.

Federal troops set fires in Atlanta, leaving 2,000 buildings in ruins. After sending part of his army north to defeat Hood's depleted forces, Sherman led 60,000 men across Georgia to Savannah. They destroyed everything of value they encountered. "Pillage became wanton," one soldier confessed. A Union officer felt ashamed: "Dante's Inferno could not furnish a more horrible and depressing picture."

Three days before Christmas, Sherman presented Savannah to President Lincoln as a yuletide gift. He had cut the Southern nation in two. Slavery was doomed. The Confederacy was dying—and would soon be put out of its misery.

1865: Defeat and Triumph

The winter of 1864–65 was the severest of the war, and immeasurably so for the beleaguered, impoverished South. From the trenches at Petersburg, a North Carolina soldier wrote his wife: "George Gill had his brains shot out yesterday and Jack Gibbons' son and three others were torn all to pieces with a shell, but I thank God they haven't hit me yet . . . I was sorry to hear that you didn't have enough to eat and the children were crying for bread, but you must be brave, little woman, and do the best you can . . . I know the good God will not let you suffer more than you are able to bear."

The suffering was not quite over. In February, Sherman and his army marched northward from Savannah and scourged South Carolina, which had given birth to secession. Columbia, the state capital, went up in flames. Charleston surrendered after a two-year holdout. Confederates could not stop Sherman's relentless advance through the Carolinas.

Grant waited for warm weather and dry roads before assaulting Lee's dwindling army. The Union

Lincoln's Last Seat

President Lincoln was seated in this rocking chair in the presidential box at Ford's Theatre on the night he was shot. The chair's crimson velvet is stained with his blood.

1865

January 19 Sherman orders his army to advance northward into the Carolinas.

February 17 Outflanked Confederates abandon Charleston, South Carolina; Federal-occupied Columbia, South Carolina, erupts in flames.

March 4 Lincoln delivers his Second Inaugural Address, urging "malice toward none."

January 15 Union army and naval forces overwhelm Fort Fisher in North Carolina, closing off the Cape Fear River and Wilmington, the last Confederate port open to the outside world.

January 31 Jefferson Davis bows to pressure from those dissatisfied with his performance as commander-in-chief and names Lee as general-in-chief of all Southern armies.

February 25 Joseph E. Johnston takes command of Confederate troops in the Carolinas but can do little to halt the advance of Sherman's superior forces.

February 22 Federals seize Wilmington, North Carolina.

April 2 Grant's army shatters Lee's thin defenses on the Richmond–Petersburg line; Confederates retreat westward, leaving the Confederate capital defenseless.

line on the Richmond-Petersburg front extended far beyond Lee's capacity for adequate defense. On April 2, the long-awaited onslaught swept over the Confederate works like a tidal wave. Lee and his remnant withdrew westward. Richmond fell the next day.

On Palm Sunday, April 9, Lee met Grant at Appomattox Court House to surrender. Both men displayed magnanimity. Early that day, Lee had vetoed a proposal that his army scatter and wage guerrilla warfare. Grant, who in earlier years had known failures so deep as to be called defeats, displayed no vindictiveness toward his vanquished foes. He offered them parole rather than imprisonment and allowed them to return home, "not to be disturbed by United States authority" so long as they kept the peace.

Those first steps toward reconciliation were earnest, but the wounds of a fractured nation would not soon heal. Less than a week after Lee surrendered, Abraham Lincoln was assassinated by Confederate sympathizer John Wilkes Booth. Lincoln's tragic death ushered in the tumultuous era known as Reconstruction, when the bitter legacy of slavery and disunion would continue to haunt the nation. It would be some time before Union and Confederate veterans would meet on old battlefields and join hands in peace. When they did, Americans would recognize how much those soldiers on opposing sides had in common. One old Confederate, Capt. Givens B. Strickler of Virginia, wrote of his long-suffering comrades in Lee's army in terms that applied equally to their foes: "Time will not suffice to tell in detail the story of the services bravely rendered, and sufferings cheerfully borne in battle, in bivouac, and upon the toilsome march—in summer's heat and dust, in winter's cold, mud and snow. That story must some day be written by some pen inspired by truth and love." It would be a tale of which any country would be proud, he added, "a story of dauntless courage, of unselfish devotion to duty, of suffering endured without a murmur, and death encountered without a qualm." ✶

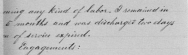

Overcoming Adversity *Cpl. J. S. Pendergast of the 24th Massachusetts, who lost his right arm in battle in 1864, won $20 for this submission to a left-handed penmanship contest, promoted by William Bourne, editor of the journal* The Soldier's Friend.

April 9 Lee surrenders to Grant at Appomattox.

April 26 Joseph Johnston surrenders the remnant of his army to Sherman in North Carolina.

April 14 John Wilkes Booth shoots Lincoln at Ford's Theatre in Washington, D.C.; the President dies early the following morning.

May 10 Jefferson Davis and a small entourage are captured near Irwinville, Georgia; two years of imprisonment ensue for the former Confederate president.

May 4 Lincoln is buried in Springfield, Illinois, after his body was carried there on a funeral train past throngs of mourners.

May 23–24 In one of the largest spectacles ever seen in Washington, more than 100,000 Union soldiers stage a grand review to celebrate their victory.

July 7 Four people convicted of conspiring with Lincoln's assassin, Booth, are hanged in Washington; among the four is Mary Surratt, the first woman ever executed by the U.S. government.

November 10 Former Andersonville Prison commandant Henry Wirz becomes the only Confederate officer executed for wartime crimes.

December 18 The 13th Amendment is ratified, abolishing slavery.

Decision in a Churchyard *Displaced church pews serve as a makeshift headquarters for the Army of the Potomac's high command at Massaponax Church, Virginia, on May 21, 1864. Gen. Ulysses S. Grant leans over a pew in conversation with Gen. George Meade (holding map).*

THE HUMAN SIDE OF WAR

R ed and blue lines on battle maps tell us where armies clashed but leave out the most important factor in war: the human element. Strategy and tactics reveal nothing of the emotions
of men within the ranks. Three million individuals served in the opposing armies during
the Civil War. Ten times that number remained behind the lines as civilians and faced the anxieties,
cares, and dangers of this all-American conflict, waged on home ground. A decade after the fighting
ended, Walt Whitman declared that the Civil War "was not a quadrille in a ball-room. The interior
history will not only never be written—its practicality, minutiae of details, and passions will never
even be suggested." The poet was mistaken. Many accounts of this great human struggle survive.
Taken together, they cast new light on the interior history of the nation's bloodiest years.

ULYSSES S. GRANT

Grant had his peculiarities. His breakfast usually
consisted of a cup of coffee and sliced cucumbers in
vinegar. When he ate meat, it had to be cooked until
it was black. Grant, the author of so much bloodshed,
detested the sight of blood, and red meat made him
queasy. Each morning he stored a dozen cigars in
various pockets. These he smoked during the course
of the day. He seldom expressed emotion, win or
lose, but regretted one bitter defeat for the rest of his
life. (See "Carnage at Cold Harbor," pages 74-7.)

ROBERT E. LEE

He was 54 when the Civil War began. Two of his uncles were signers of the Declaration of Independence. His father, "Light Horse Harry" Lee, fought beside George Washington. Gen. Winfield Scott called Lee the most handsome man ever to wear the uniform of a soldier. This distinguished Virginian weighed 175 pounds and stood 5 feet, 11 inches tall, but he had the dainty feet of a boy. (See "Civil War Oddities," pages 78-9.)

ABRAHAM LINCOLN

The war weighed heavily on Abraham Lincoln. On hearing of the terrible losses suffered by Union troops at Fredericksburg in December 1862, he declared: "If there is a worse place than Hell, I am in it." Author Harriet Beecher Stowe, who visited him the following year, described him as consumed by "a dry, weary, patient pain." The soothing medicine that helped him endure the pains of his Presidency was laughter. "I laugh because I must not weep," he explained. (See "The Wit of Abraham Lincoln," pages 68-9.)

A Brothers' War

The Civil War has often been called "a brothers' war," and for good reason. Hostilities between North and South split states apart and fractured families by pitting father against son and brother against brother, often with tragic consequences. A family in Baltimore was a case in point.

Two brothers, Clifton and William Prentiss, became estranged in 1857 over the slavery question. They parted ways in anger, as did many of their fellow Marylanders. When war came, 25-year-old Clifton Prentiss joined the Sixth Maryland (Union) Regiment. William, three years younger, enlisted in the Second Maryland (Confederate) Regiment. The schism between the two seemed permanent.

For four years, William fought wherever the Confederate Army of Northern Virginia campaigned. Clifton saw action with the opposing Federal Army of the Potomac. Early on the morning of April 2, 1865, Gen. Ulysses S. Grant launched a massive attack on Gen. Robert E. Lee's lines at Petersburg. Taking part in that grand assault was Maj. Clifton Prentiss, who led Federals of the Sixth Maryland over the Confederate works. Prentiss was urging his men forward in pursuit of their foes, who were pulling back, when a bullet struck him in the chest and tore away most of his sternum. Two soldiers bore him to an improvised field hospital nearby. Others in his regiment scoured the battleground to separate the wounded from the dead.

They came upon a Confederate soldier with a horribly mangled leg. Federals sought to make the man comfortable. To their surprise, he asked if the Sixth Maryland was close by. "We belong to that regiment," one Federal answered.

"I have a brother in that regiment," the Confederate replied, "Captain Clifton Prentiss. I am William Prentiss of the 2nd Maryland."

"Why, Captain Prentiss is our major now, and he is lying over yonder wounded."

With pain from the shattered leg almost blinding him, William Prentiss managed to say: "I would like to see him."

A soldier ran to where Clifton Prentiss lay injured and told him of William's request. The Union major shook his head and declared: "I want to see no man who fired at my country's flag."

When the colonel of the Sixth Maryland learned of the situation, he ordered the stricken Confederate brought over and placed on a blanket alongside the injured Federal. Clifton Prentiss glared at his younger brother. William Prentiss looked at him through a haze of pain and smiled.

That look of affection smothered the hurt and wiped away the anger. As their hands joined, an eight-year separation and four years on opposing sides of the conflict ended in a tearful reconciliation on a torn piece of ground at Petersburg.

The reunion was short-lived. Surgeons amputated William's leg, but the operation did not save him. He lingered for weeks until his death on June 20, 1865. The gaping lesion in Clifton Prentiss's chest would not heal. He died two months after William's passing.

It would be comforting to say that Clifton and William Prentiss lie side by side today. They do not. Yet for a brief moment in the aftermath of battle, this cruel brothers' war gave way mercifully to brotherly love. ✵

> "I WANT TO SEE NO MAN WHO FIRED AT MY COUNTRY'S FLAG."
>
> **MAJ. CLIFTON PRENTISS**

A House Divided *A Union artilleryman, armed with saber and revolver, displays the same grim determination as the Confederate foot soldier shown brandishing a huge bowie knife.*

Lincoln's Beard

Abraham Lincoln was never as old as he looked. He was a generation younger than his predecessor, James Buchanan. The nation was suffering severe growing pains and found comfort in leaders who seemed old and wise. One feature that surely added years to Lincoln's appearance was his beard. He was the first American President to wear chin whiskers.

In the mid-1800s, facial hair came into vogue. Lincoln's beard was a product of the 1860 presidential election. In October of that year, a New York City Republican delegation sent him a letter, advising him candidly that he would be much improved in appearance if he would "cultivate whiskers and wear standing collars. We really fear voters will be lost to 'the cause' unless our 'gentle hints' are attended to."

A few days later, Lincoln received a note from 11-year-old Grace Bedell of Westfield, New York. He would look a great deal better with a beard, she told him, "for your face is so thin." The shrewd child went on to appeal to his political instincts: "All the ladies like whiskers and they would tease their husbands to vote for you and then you would be President." Grace closed her communiqué by promising to get her brothers to vote for Lincoln if he let his beard grow.

An amused Lincoln wrote in response: "As to whiskers, having never worn any, do you not think people would call it a piece of silly affectation if I were to begin it now?"

Lincoln soon answered his own question. By the end of November, he was growing a beard. He was on his way to Washington as President-elect when his train stopped at Westfield. Grace Bedell was in the crowd that greeted him.

Signature Beard *Clean-shaven until the closing weeks of the 1860 presidential campaign, Lincoln sported a beard when he arrived in Washington in February 1861.*

Lincoln called for the child to come up on the platform of the car where he was standing. "You see," he told Grace, "I have let these whiskers grow for you."

The lanky President-to-be leaned over and kissed the girl, then introduced her to the crowd as the one who had advised him to grow a beard. The press gave the story national coverage. "Her advice has not been thrown away upon the rugged chieftain," the *New York Herald* stated. "The young girl's peachy cheek must have been tickled with a stiff whisker," for which she was "heavily responsible."

Lincoln initially kept the beard closely cropped, but it seemed to become bushier as the Civil War dragged on. Why he really grew it remained a matter of conjecture. Perhaps, critics charged, Lincoln was hiding his face because he knew he was not ready to be President. Or maybe the whiskers demonstrated the supreme self-confidence of a man who was willing to risk the inevitable puns that followed. "Old Abe is putting on (h)airs," one journal quipped. Another accused Lincoln of using an ointment to stimulate the growth of his "manly adornment." Some publications, caught off guard by word of the new whiskers, solved the problem by adding fake beards to earlier likenesses of Lincoln.

Quite possibly, the new chief executive wanted to present a new face to the public—a face more authoritative and elderly. The beard did not make the man, but it helped define and distinguish him in the eyes of admirers, who thought of him fondly as "Old Abe" or "Father Abraham."

Lincoln carried the Grace Bedell letter with him for years and often showed it to friends. It demonstrated that he was never too old to heed sound advice from a youngster. ✶

93

Westfield Chatauque Co N.Y.
Oct 15. 1860

Hon A B Lincoln

Dear Sir

My father has just come home from the fair and brought home your picture and Mrs. Hamlin's. I am a little girl only eleven years old, but want you should be President of the United States very much so I hope you wont think me very bold to write to such a great man as you are. Have you any little girls about as large as I am if so give them my love and tell her to write to me if you cannot answer this letter. I have got 4 brothers and part of them will vote for you any way and if you will let your whiskers grow I will try and get the rest of them to vote for you you would look a great deal better for your face is so thin. All the ladies like whiskers and they would tease

...d's to vote for you and then you ...resident. My father is a going to ... and if I was a man I would ...n to but I will try and get ... vote for you that I can I think ...nce around your picture makes it ...retty. I have just got a little baby ... weeks old and is just as cunning as can be. When you direct your letter direct to Grace Bedell Westfield Chatauque County New York I must not write any more answer this letter right off Good bye

Grace Bedell

"ALL THE LADIES LIKE WHISKERS AND THEY WOULD TEASE THEIR HUSBANDS TO VOTE FOR YOU AND THEN YOU WOULD BE PRESIDENT."
11-YEAR-OLD GRACE BEDELL

Improved Appearance *After seeing an image of Abraham Lincoln's gaunt features, 11-year-old New Yorker Grace Bedell wrote this letter to the presidential candidate advising that he grow a beard. "My father is going to vote for you," she added, "and if I was a man I would vote for you."*

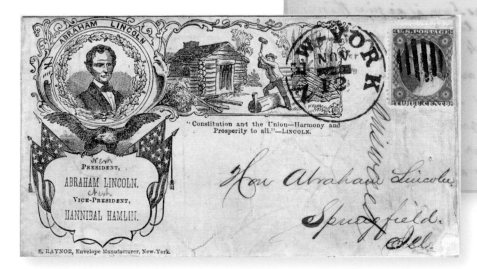

ABRAHAM LINCOLN

"Constitution and the Union—Harmony and Prosperity to all."—LINCOLN.

NEW PRESIDENT,
ABRAHAM LINCOLN.
And
VICE-PRESIDENT,
HANNIBAL HAMLIN.

S. RAYNOR, Envelope Manufacturer, New-York.

Hon Abraham Lincoln
Springfield.
Ills.

Plight of the Runaway

The Fugitive Slave Act of 1850 stirred passions that grew hotter as the decade unfolded and helped ignite the Civil War. The number of slaves fleeing northward was small in comparison with the total slave population. Few owners hired slave catchers because of the cost and uncertainty of tracking down runaways. Yet this new federal law helped slaveholders reclaim their human "property" and made aiding fugitives a crime. It was as drastic as it was one-sided.

The act required federal marshals to arrest suspected fugitives and led to flagrant abuses by professional slave catchers who were little more than kidnappers, searching for any black men they could find to drag into slavery. Once apprehended, fugitives were not allowed to appeal to a jury. Commissioners heard "evidence," which usually was only a sworn statement of ownership, and received twice the fee for returning a slave to his supposed owner as they did for denying the warrant. Owners could reclaim fugitives no matter how long they had been at liberty. In February 1851, a man named Mitchum was taken from his wife and children in Indiana and returned to a plantation owner who swore that Mitchum had absconded 19 years earlier.

Northerners recoiled at an act that forced people who were free back into bondage. Ralph Waldo Emerson called it "a filthy law" that no one could obey "without loss of self-respect." Many states sought to nullify the legislation by enacting laws shielding runaways. The most extreme act of nullification was passed in Massachusetts, making it illegal for any state official to enforce the Fugitive Slave Act. Authorities there who were asked to return slaves to their owners were damned if they did and damned if they didn't.

The Fugitive Slave Act did not halt the fabled Underground Railroad, a loose-knit network of abolitionists who helped escaped slaves reach freedom. "Conductors" like escaped slave Harriet Tubman continued to make perilous trips into the South to help deliver people from bondage. Whites and free blacks continued to shelter runaways at way stations as they journeyed through border states to the so-called free states, where compassion for their plight was not universal. Many fugitives received little help from sympathizers and relied largely on their own courage and skill to reach the North, where they remained prey to slave catchers.

The quest for freedom sometimes ended tragically. In January 1856, slave Margaret Garner fled a Kentucky plantation with her four children, crossed the frozen Ohio River, and went into hiding in the Cincinnati area. The owner traced them and obtained a warrant for their arrest. As mounted men were about to seize the family, she grew desperate and tried to kill her offspring to prevent their return to slavery. She cut her daughter's throat but was stopped before she could do the same to her three sons. Officials in Ohio wanted to try her for murder, but a federal commissioner ordered her and her family returned to their owner, who had them shipped to New Orleans to be held there in slave pens and sold to the highest bidder.

One of Mrs. Garner's sons drowned in a boat collision on the Mississippi River. She and her two surviving sons were separated at auction. Margaret Garner died a slave in 1858. ✶

Fugitives in Peril *A poster warns black residents of Boston of the dangers resulting from the Fugitive Slave Act of 1850. Shackles like those above were used to bind slaves.*

"THE FADED FACES OF THE NEGRO CHILDREN
TELL TOO PLAINLY TO WHAT DEGRADATION THE FEMALE
SLAVES SUBMIT. RATHER THAN GIVE HER DAUGHTER
TO THAT LIFE, SHE KILLED IT. IF IN HER DEEP MATERNAL LOVE
SHE FELT THE IMPULSE TO SEND HER CHILD BACK TO GOD,
TO SAVE IT FROM COMING WOE,
WHO SHALL SAY SHE HAD NO RIGHT TO DO SO?"

ANTISLAVERY ACTIVIST LUCY STONE, ON MARGARET GARNER

Act of Desperation *Artist Thomas Satterwhite Noble immortalized the tragedy of runaway Margaret Garner and her children in his 1867 painting "The Modern Medea." Garner killed her daughter and attempted to kill her sons rather than see them returned to bondage.*

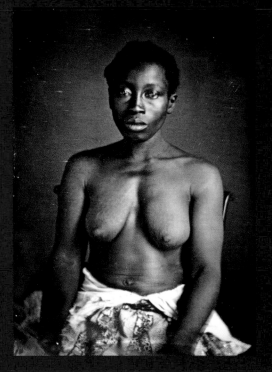

The Face of Slavery *This daguerreotype was one of a collection of photographs of enslaved Africans, part of an 1850 study of racial traits conducted by Harvard scientist Louis Agassiz. The subject's resigned expression suggests that she has little hope of a better future.*

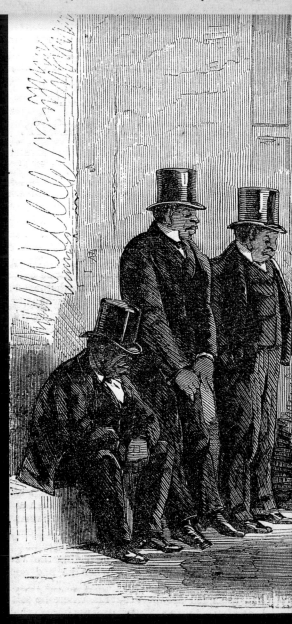

NEW ORLEANS
SLAVE DEPOT
No. 15 Perdido street—near St. Charle
J. W. BOAZMAN,
Will keep constantly on hand a large and well selected lot of SLA
FOR SALE.   Negroes also Bought and Sold on Commiss

☞I have on hand a number of NEGROES TO HIRE BY
MONTH, among them are men, boys, house servants, cooks, w
and ironers, nurses, &c.

REFER TO { Wright, Williams & Co.   Moon, Titus & Co
Williams, Phillips & Co.   S. O. Nelson & Co
Moses Greenwood.   E. W. Diggs.

Hard Labor *Slave children, not yet in their teens, worked alongside adults during harvesttime in cotton fields like this one on a Southern plantation.*

"ONE OF MRS. GARNER'S SONS DROWNED
IN A BOAT COLLISION ON THE MISSISSIPPI RIVER.
SHE AND HER TWO SURVIVING SONS
WERE SEPARATED AT AUCTION.
MARGARET GARNER DIED A SLAVE IN 1858."

Human Chattel *An 1863 issue of* Harper's Weekly *(below) shows slaves for sale in New Orleans dressed in livery, perhaps to increase their value as "house" servants. A broadside (left) advertises "negroes" for sale and hire.*

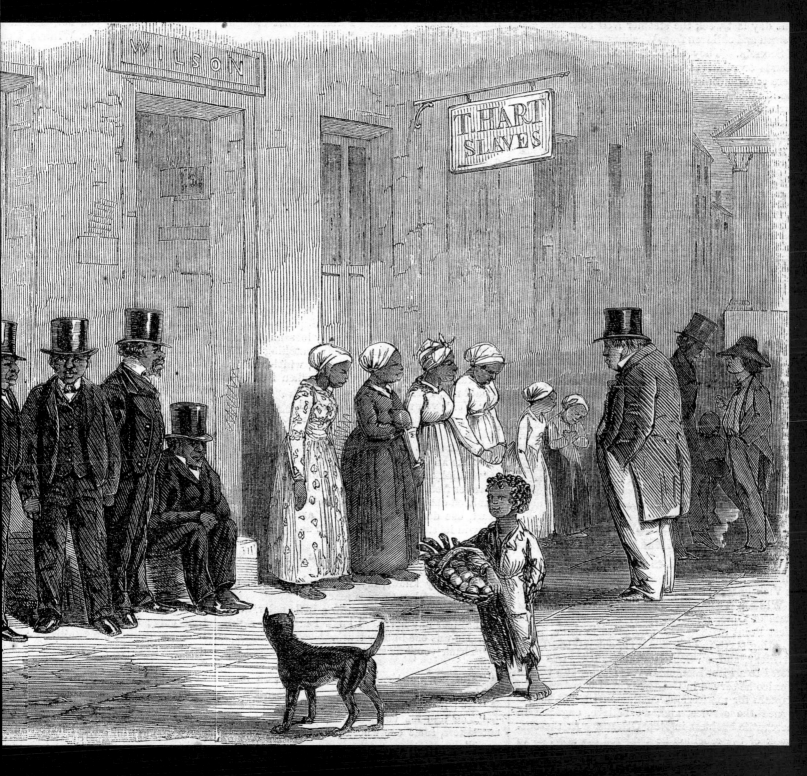

Lincoln's Somber Debut

Presidential inaugurations are meant to be festive occasions, but the swearing-in of Abraham Lincoln on March 4, 1861, felt more like a funeral. It was a raw, windy day. This was no time for Americans to celebrate, for seven states had left the Union and civil war seemed imminent. Three of every five voters had cast ballots for someone other than Lincoln, whose political experience on the national level consisted of a single term in the House of Representatives. There were some who hoped his first day in office would be his last. Before departing for Washington, Lincoln had received a note from "one of a sworn band of 10, who have resolved to shoot you in the inaugural procession."

He rode to the Capitol in an open carriage with outgoing failure James Buchanan, who sat in mournful silence. The city seemed depressed. There was little enthusiasm from those packing the sidewalks. Soldiers so densely surrounded the carriage that the occupants could hardly be seen.

The largest Inaugural crowd in the history of the young Republic waited solemnly on Capitol Hill. Shortly after 1 p.m., Lincoln emerged on the platform. He looked, wrote one reporter, "as grave and impassive as an Indian martyr." The elaborate trappings around the speaker's stand seemed out of keeping with the tall, gaunt, rough-hewn frontiersman. A New Englander commented: "It's as if one wanted to inaugurate a Quaker in a basilica."

At that time, the Inaugural Address preceded the oath of office. A faint ripple of cheers greeted Lincoln as he made his way to the rickety little table provided for his speech. The address lasted 30 minutes. First came reassurance. Lincoln

Trademark Headgear *President-elect Abraham Lincoln wore this stovepipe hat during the 1861 Inaugural ceremonies (seen at right), held on the east front of the United States Capitol. A new dome was under construction at the time.*

told the unhappy South that it had no cause for alarm. He would not interfere with slavery in areas where it existed. However, he added, the Union is perpetual. No state by its own action can abandon it. Then he issued a stern warning to secessionists: "In your hands, my dissatisfied countrymen, and not in mine, is the momentous issue of civil war ... You have no oath registered in Heaven to destroy the government, while I have the most solemn one to 'preserve, protect, and defend' the Constitution."

Lincoln closed his address with a poetic appeal for unity and goodwill. Recalling the American Revolution, when Northerners and Southerners joined in fighting for liberty, he declared: "The mystic chords of memory, stretching from every battlefield and patriot grave, to every living heart and hearthstone all over this broad land, will yet swell the chorus of the Union, when again touched, as surely they will be, by the better angels of our nature."

Lincoln's voice cracked on that last sentence, and many who were close enough to hear what he said reached for their handkerchiefs, stirred by hopes that those better angels might yet prevail over the angels of death and destruction. But the mood turned somber when Chief Justice Roger Taney, described by one observer as "a cadaver in black silk," tottered forward to administer the oath of office. Taney was a Maryland slaveholder, whose sweeping defense of slavery in the Dred Scott decision moved the nation a step closer to war.

Among the victims of that bitter struggle would be Lincoln himself, slain by a man who stood there in 1861 amid the Inaugural crowd—an erratic actor with secessionist sympathies named John Wilkes Booth. ✶

Chief Justice
Roger B. Taney

"THE MOOD TURNED SOMBER
WHEN CHIEF JUSTICE ROGER TANEY,
DESCRIBED BY ONE OBSERVER
AS 'A CADAVER IN BLACK SILK,'
TOTTERED FORWARD TO ADMINISTER
THE OATH OF OFFICE."

Bad Day at Fort Sumter

Roger Pryor had a chance to fire the war's first shot. Instead, he nearly became its first victim. No one ever accused Pryor of modesty. A young and impetuous secessionist from Petersburg, Virginia, he resigned from the U.S. Congress in early 1861 when his native state held back from seceding. He gravitated to Charleston, where a showdown loomed between hotheaded South Carolinians and a small Union garrison, besieged at Fort Sumter in the middle of the harbor. "Strike a blow!" Pryor urged the Carolinians, promising them that once blood was shed, "Old Virginia will make common cause with her sisters of the South."

In the predawn hours of April 12, 1861, Confederates offered Pryor the honor of launching the bombardment of Fort Sumter by pulling the lanyard of the signal cannon. But this fire-eater whose words had helped prime the conflict was not ready to ignite it. "I cannot fire the first gun of the war," he said in a voice husky with emotion.

Hundreds of impatient Southerners were ready to fire and did. Fort Sumter at the time was still under construction. It stood on two and a half acres of land and contained five million bricks. Its walls were 50 feet high and up to 5 feet thick. For 34 hours, Confederates sent more than 3,000 shells exploding over or into the fort. By noon the following day, fires inside Sumter were out of control, and no help was in sight. Maj. Robert Anderson, the fort's commander, saw nothing left to defend but honor itself. The Federal garrison of fewer than 80 men raised the white flag.

Confederate Gen. P. G. T. Beauregard sent Pryor and three other aides out to accept the fort's surrender. Pryor took no part in the proceedings. His Virginia was still in the Union. While opposing officers completed details, Pryor sauntered to a casemate doubling as the surgeon's quarters. It was hot, stuffy, and tense. He needed a drink and groped about in the dark room for some medicinal whiskey. An alluring black bottle and tumbler were on the table. Without checking the label on the bottle, Pryor poured himself three fingers and tossed it off in a couple of gulps.

The unpalatable liquid was, in fact, iodide of potassium, a lethal drug. Pryor let out a scream that brought Dr. Samuel Crawford, the fort's surgeon, to the room. Pryor confessed what he had done. "If you have taken the amount of that solution that you think you have," Crawford said, "you have likely poisoned yourself." A pale, horrified Pryor begged for aid. Crawford helped him past the lines of Federal casualties to the improvised dispensary, where he pumped his stomach. Pryor narrowly escaped being the first fatality of the Civil War.

Crawford came under fire for helping Pryor. "Some of us questioned the doctor's right to interpose himself in a case of this kind," Union Capt. Abner Doubleday declared. If a Rebel chose to poison himself, they reasoned, a Union physician had no business rescuing him. Crawford had a neat rejoinder. "I am responsible for all of my medicine because it is federal government property. I could not permit Pryor to carry any of it away." Pryor later lived up to his fighting words by serving as a Confederate brigadier general. But he would be best remembered as a fitful fire-eater who hungered for war beforehand but found it hard to swallow when it came. ✮

> "STRIKE A BLOW!
> THE VERY MOMENT
> THAT BLOOD IS SHED,
> OLD VIRGINIA WILL
> MAKE COMMON CAUSE
> WITH HER SISTERS
> OF THE SOUTH."
>
> **ROGER PRYOR**

Healing Potions *Medical bottles such as these were part of a surgeon's supplies in the 1860s.*

Change of Flags *This map by Northern soldier-artist Robert Knox Sneden graphically illustrates the massive fire-power brought to bear on Fort Sumter by the surrounding Southern artillery batteries. After the surrender, Confederates gathered in the damaged parade ground (below) and raised their Stars and Bars national flag in place of the Stars and Stripes.*

Roger Pryor

A General and His Horse

Few people who gaze at equestrian statues of Civil War heroes give much attention to their horses. But those mounts were not mere accessories, like an officer's sword or hat. Every major Civil War commander had a favorite horse.

Gen. George McClellan's swaggering black steed, Daniel Webster, and Robert E. Lee's beloved gray stallion, Traveller, were stately animals that looked perfectly suited for their distinguished masters. Stonewall Jackson's favorite horse, Little Sorrel, was another matter entirely. That animal was as small as his master was tall. The two made an odd and unique couple.

When Jackson took command at Harpers Ferry in late April of 1861, he found large numbers of horses, left behind when Federals abandoned the town. Jackson purchased two of the animals. The smaller one, at least ten years old at the time, he called Fancy. Jackson intended to give it to his wife but changed his mind when he rode the animal. An immediate bond developed between them. Fancy was known thereafter as Little Sorrel and became the most trusted and treasured of the four mounts Jackson possessed.

Sculptors and artists ever since have refused to accept the plain fact that Little Sorrel was little. Reddish brown in color, well formed, and compactly built, the horse was so small in stature that when Jackson's legs extended from the saddle, the general's huge feet were only inches from the ground.

Little Sorrel was seemingly incapable of fatigue. He usually did a mile in a little over two and a half minutes—a feat that left Jackson's mounted aides lagging far behind. Once, when the animal became momentarily lost, the staff cheered.

> "IN BATTLE, LITTLE SORREL'S NORMALLY SOFT EYES BLAZED LIKE HIS MASTER'S. YET WHEN THE ARMY WENT INTO BIVOUAC LATE IN THE DAY, THE HORSE HAD THE PECULIAR HABIT OF LYING DOWN LIKE A DOG—SOMETIMES ON HIS BACK."

Stonewall Jackson's VMI forage cap

Nevertheless, Jackson found the horse's gait "as easy as the rocking of a cradle."

In battle, Little Sorrel's normally soft eyes blazed like his master's. Yet when the army went into bivouac late in the day, the horse had the peculiar habit of lying down like a dog—sometimes on his back. The normally stern Jackson made a pet of the animal, and often fed it apples when he thought no one was looking.

Only once during the Civil War did Little Sorrel bolt in combat. That came in 1863 when Jackson was mortally wounded by gunfire from his own men in the darkened woods of Chancellorsville.

For several years afterward, the horse lived with Mrs. Jackson in North Carolina. Little Sorrel spent his last years at the Virginia Military Institute. Faculty and students imbued with the Jackson legend accorded the animal great respect and affection.

One cadet remembered that whenever artillery practice began, the aging horse "would come running stiff-legged onto the parade ground, sniffing the air and snorting loudly, head and tail up, limping up and down in front of the line, enjoying the noise and smoke, a comical and pathetic sight, though heart-appealing in the extreme."

When Little Sorrel died in 1886, the flags at VMI went to half-mast. The horse had lived 36 years, only three years less than General Jackson did.

Little Sorrel was preserved and displayed at the VMI Museum. He stands there today, straight, determined, and ready to do as ordered—much like Jackson himself.

"Old Jack" and Little Sorrel were more than a man and his horse. They gave each other care and companionship. The little horse also gave something else—pure devotion—and received as much in return. ★

Faithful Companion

Stonewall Jackson sits astride his warhorse, Little Sorrel, before launching his flank attack at Chancellorsville on May 2, 1863. Jackson was mortally wounded that evening while conducting a reconnaissance. Little Sorrel, pictured at left after the war, became a mascot on the VMI campus.

The Widow Henry

Every war has its casualties. So often the innocent suffer as much as the guilty. Such was the fate of Judith Henry.

She was a descendant of Robert "King" Carter, an aristocratic planter whose holdings embraced 300,000 acres in northern Virginia. Judith Carter grew up in luxurious splendor. In 1801, she married Dr. Isaac Henry, one of the U.S. Navy's first surgeons. The couple settled in a home on 330 acres in fertile Prince William County.

Following Dr. Henry's death in 1829, his widow remained in the Henry home. The two-story log house stood near the top of a dominant hill overlooking a stream called Bull Run. The property was mostly open country, dotted here and there by cedars and pines. The farm slowly went into disrepair.

By the summer of 1861, the elderly Mrs. Henry was confined to her bed. Two invalid sons, a daughter, and a black servant lived there quietly with her. Then on Sunday morning, July 21, the first major battle of the Civil War exploded around the Henry farm.

Confederate cannon south of the home opened fire at Union batteries north of the Warrenton Turnpike. Shells whistled over the house from opposite directions. The two sons attempted to move their mother to safety by placing her on a mattress and starting toward a neighbor's home. Yet the shell fire was so heavy, and Mrs. Henry so frightened, that they bowed to her wishes and took her back inside the house.

Soon the Henry home was shrouded in smoke and the fighting around it so intense that its occupants were trapped. The widow Henry was upstairs in her bed, being attended by servant Lucy Griffith. Not long after noon, Union Capt. James Ricketts moved a battery of cannon halfway up the slope of Henry Hill and no more than 300 yards from the home. After Ricketts got his guns in line, several of his men began dropping from bullet wounds. He concluded that the shots came from Confederate snipers using the Henry home for cover. Ricketts trained his guns on the house and fired.

One of the first shells pierced the upper level of the home, shattered Mrs. Henry's bed, and sent wooden splinters flying through the room. Lucy Griffith, who had taken cover underneath the bed, was badly wounded in the heel and permanently crippled. Mrs. Henry had a foot nearly severed and suffered additional wounds in the neck and side.

Through the remainder of the battle, the critically injured widow, her wounded servant, shell-shocked daughter, and helpless sons sought to console one another as the home was shot to pieces. Mrs. Henry died near sundown as the beaten Federals retreated to Washington. One of her sons rushed from the home, lay down in the yard, and sobbed: "They've killed my mother!"

The next day, Confederate soldiers buried 85-year-old Judith Henry in the small family cemetery a few yards from the house. Several years later, a frame home was built on the site of the log structure where the Henry family had known many years of peace.

Judith Henry was rescued from historical obscurity when the site of her death was preserved as a prominent landmark within the Manassas National Battlefield Park. The aged widow suffered the misfortune of being in the wrong place at the wrong time. She was the only known civilian to die in the battle. ★

Civil War–era Parrott rifled 10-pounder gun

"THEY'VE KILLED MY MOTHER!"

THE INVALID SON
OF MRS. JUDITH HENRY

Victim of Battle *Union soldiers, photographed in 1862, view the remains of the Henry House on the Manassas battlefield. The house, depicted at the center of the map (right), was located on high ground and became a focal point of the fighting in 1861.*

Jackson Becomes Intoxicated

Biography is the most popular and dramatic form of history, and no event in the nation's past offers a more intriguing cast of characters for biographers than the Civil War. The escapades of its leading figures are legion and show that this great American tragedy was often leavened with comedy. Even the pious and abstemious Stonewall Jackson once provided his aides with comic relief by getting conspicuously drunk.

Jackson suffered from a number of physical maladies. He was also a man who practiced abstinence religiously. This was evident one chilly night in the war's first autumn. Surgeon Hunter McGuire, Jackson's personal physician, insisted that the general take a drink of whiskey as a stimulant. Jackson swallowed the liquid and made a distorted expression.

"Isn't the whiskey good?" McGuire asked.

"Yes, very," Jackson answered. "I like it, and that's the reason I don't drink it."

On New Year's Day, 1862, while most armies were in winter camp, Jackson led his forces on a grueling march toward the Federal stronghold at Romney in what is now West Virginia. The weather soon turned nasty. Sleet alternated with snow and hampered his men at every step. By the second day, even the determined Jackson began to suffer from the elements. The temperature was in the low 20s, and chill winds made the snow blinding.

A friend at Winchester gave Dr. McGuire a bottle of smooth but very powerful brandy before the army left that town and resumed its ordeal. Jackson called a midday halt in the march. He and his staff gathered in an abandoned log cabin and ate a meager lunch.

Surgeon McGuire noticed that Jackson was shivering in the cold and pointed to the bottle of brandy that he had placed on the table. "General," he said, "you had better take some of this. It will be good for you."

"Do you think so, sir?" Jackson replied. "If you tell me I need it, of course I will take some." He evidently had no idea what was in the bottle.

While the staff watched in wonder, the unsuspecting Jackson filled a large tumbler to the brim and drank it down without removing the glass from his lips. He resumed his meal and, as was his custom, said little.

General and staff then remounted and continued the journey. Jackson soon took a handkerchief from his pocket and began wiping perspiration from his forehead. The party rode in silence through the snow for a short distance. Jackson then turned to an aide and said he was glad to see that the temperature was moderating: "The troops will not suffer much."

With that, Jackson unbuttoned his overcoat. The lieutenant, chilled to the bone and well aware that the temperature had not risen, answered dutifully: "Yes, sir."

Another mile or two passed in silence. Jackson then opened his coat and loosened his collar. "Lieutenant," he stated, "I don't think that I ever noticed such a remarkable change in temperature in such a short time."

Staff members watched their stern general swaying in the saddle and continuing to unbutton while wind and snow lashed the countryside. Jackson's aides could hardly suppress laughter at the sight of their Calvinistic leader undergoing what were for him the strange effects of liquor, warming his innards like hellfire.

Jackson soon cooled down. He never mentioned the incident. No member of his staff dared do so until years after the war. ✯

Strong Brew *Distilled from wine, brandy in the Civil War era could be very potent, particularly when taken fast in large quantities. Stonewall Jackson, portrayed at right as he appeared in 1862, proved quite susceptible to the liquor's effects.*

"I LIKE IT,
AND THAT'S THE REASON
I DON'T DRINK IT."
GEN. STONEWALL JACKSON

The Great Railroad Chase

The incident was so thrilling that Hollywood twice made a movie on the subject. But no dramatization could match the suspense of this great chase, which was truly a matter of life or death.

It happened in the spring of 1862. Union Gen. Ormsby Mitchel was preparing to seize Huntsville, Alabama, a vital rail junction. If all went well, he would then move northeastward along the Memphis & Charleston Railroad and take Chattanooga, which was linked to Atlanta by the Western & Atlantic Railroad. To sever that supply line and cut Chattanooga off from Atlanta, Mitchel sent Union raider James J. Andrews with a small band of men into Georgia to hijack a train on the Western & Atlantic and wreck track, burn bridges, and cut telegraph wires as the train moved north.

Andrews and another civilian were joined by some 20 soldier-volunteers, including Samuel Slavens of the 33rd Ohio, who wrote his wife beforehand: "If anything happens to me that we never meet again on earth, I hope we will meet in heaven. Life is uncertain in a war."

The raiders made their way through enemy lines in plain dress to Marietta, Georgia, where they boarded as passengers a northbound train pulled by the locomotive *General*. Several miles up the track, everyone disembarked for breakfast except Andrews's men, who seized the locomotive and three boxcars. With a jerk that sent men sprawling, "the little train darted away," recalled William Pittenger of the Second Ohio, leaving those at the station "in the wildest uproar and confusion."

Conductor William Fuller and two other men gave chase. On foot, by hand car, and soon by locomotive, they followed

Mutual Determination *Union raider James Andrews (left) was as intent on using the locomotive and cars he captured as conductor William Fuller (right) was on retrieving his stolen train.*

the hijacked train, which stopped several times so that raiders could cut telegraph lines and tear up some track, a slow task for which they were ill equipped. The broken track did not deter the pursuers, who changed locomotives and boarded the swift *Texas* in Adairsville. It was headed south but shifted into reverse and went after the *General* at a breakneck pace, approaching 60 miles an hour—twice the usual rail speed of that day. When the raiders looked back, Pittenger related, they could see smoke billowing in the distance from the oncoming engine: "The shrill whistle was like the scream of a bird of prey." With the *Texas* on their tail, they no longer had time to destroy track. Andrews set fire to two boxcars and cut them loose. The *Texas* pushed the burning cars onto a sidetrack and kept up the chase, which continued for more than 80 miles. Two miles north of Ringgold, with no fuel left, the *General* wheezed to a stop. The raiders scattered but were soon captured. They had not done much damage to the railroad, and General Mitchel pulled back from Chattanooga.

Because the raiders were in civilian attire, they faced charges of espionage. In June, Andrews and seven of his men went to the gallows in Atlanta. Samuel Slavens was hanged twice. The first time, the rope around his neck broke. He was given a drink of water but no reprieve and died the next time.

Other raiders survived the ordeal. Several managed to escape from a local jail, and Pittenger and five fellow Union soldiers were exchanged as prisoners of war. They became the first recipients of a new congressional award: the Medal of Honor. Slavens, who knew that nothing in life was certain, received the award posthumously. ✶

"IN JUNE, ANDREWS AND SEVEN OF HIS MEN WENT TO THE GALLOWS IN ATLANTA. SAMUEL SLAVENS WAS HANGED TWICE. THE FIRST TIME, THE ROPE AROUND HIS NECK BROKE. HE WAS GIVEN A DRINK OF WATER BUT NO REPRIEVE AND DIED THE NEXT TIME."

Samuel Slavens

End of the Line *Out of fuel and unable to escape the rapidly approaching* Texas, *Andrews's raiders hastily abandon the* General, *which they seized in Marietta, Georgia, on April 12, 1862, and left near the Tennessee border.*

The Burial of Latané

William Latané practiced medicine and managed his family's estate in the Tidewater Virginia town of Tappahannock. He was 29 when war erupted. Latané became a captain in the Ninth Virginia Cavalry Regiment. One trooper described him as "a man of small stature and quiet demeanor, but quick to perceive a wrong and very assertive in his opposition to it."

On June 12, 1862, he was among 1,200 Confederate cavalrymen who rode quietly out of Richmond under the dashing and flamboyant Gen. James Ewell Brown "Jeb" Stuart. A huge Federal army lurked near the capital, on either side of the Chickahominy River. Stuart's mission from new army chief Robert E. Lee was to pinpoint how far the enemy's right flank extended northwest of Richmond.

Stuart located the end of the Union line—then returned to Lee in Richmond by riding completely around the largest American fighting force ever assembled. His epic reconnaissance covered 100 miles in three days, caused Federals considerable damage and wounded their pride, and raised spirits in beleaguered Richmond and throughout the South.

All of this came at the cost of one Confederate soldier. On the second day, a few miles east of Hanover Court House, Stuart had his first encounter with Union cavalry—100 or so dismounted horsemen, arrayed in battle position atop a small hill. Stuart rose to the challenge. Captain Latané galloped forward in the lead, shouting: "On to them, boys!"

Latané slashed a Union officer with his saber before he fell dead, pierced by five bullets. His younger brother John, a sergeant in the company, remained with William's body while Stuart's force, which had dispersed the enemy, resumed its journey.

Confederate cavalry hat

"GENTLY THEY LAID HIM UNDERNEATH THE SOD AND LEFT HIM WITH HIS FAME, HIS COUNTRY, AND HIS GOD . . . "

POET JOHN THOMPSON

A few hours later, a slave called Uncle Aaron came down the road pushing a mill cart full of corn and saw the two soldiers in the field. He dumped out his corn and with John's help loaded the dead captain into the cart and started for home—the Brockenbrough plantation, known as Westwood.

It was a slow, two-mile journey. At Westwood, the only family member present was Mrs. Catherine Brockenbrough. Sergeant Latané could not linger because Union patrols were in the area. He asked her if she would bury his brother. "At the risk of my life," she promised.

Mrs. Brockenbrough went to the adjacent estate, Summer Hill, home of her niece, Mrs. Mary Newton, and Mary's sister-in-law, Alice Newton. That night the women prepared the body for burial while Uncle Aaron made a coffin. The next morning he dug a grave in the Newton family cemetery.

Union pickets prevented a minister from passing through the lines to conduct the funeral service. So Alice Newton presided over the ceremony by reading from the Episcopal Book of Common Prayer.

Poet John Thompson heard of the incident and eulogized Latané in the *Southern Literary Messenger:* "Gently they laid him underneath the sod / and left him with his fame, his country, and his God." Inspired by the lines, artist William Washington painted a huge canvas entitled "The Burial of Latané." Hundreds of copies hung in Southern homes well into the 20th century. The dominant figure in the painting is Alice Newton, reading the service. Standing in the foreground, leaning on his shovel, is Uncle Aaron.

Strange it is that a woman and a slave dominate this famous painting of a Confederate burial, memorializing a war launched by men intent on perpetuating slavery. ✶

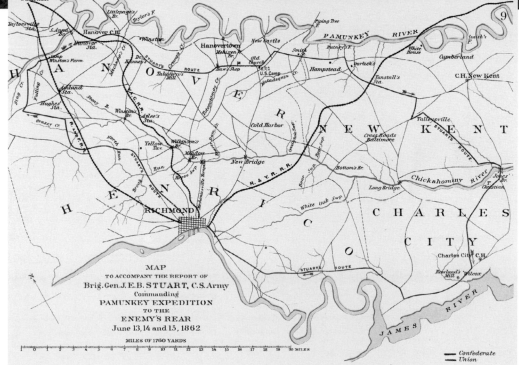

Painter of the Lost Cause
Virginia artist William D. Washington's oil painting of Captain Latané's burial, painted in 1864, became immensely popular in the postwar South. The canvas was reproduced as a steel engraving and was displayed in many households. The inset map traces the route of Stuart's "Ride Around McClellan."

Kate Chase Sprague

The most prominent woman in wartime Washington was not Mary Todd Lincoln. She was upstaged by Katherine Chase, a bright, beautiful rival young enough to be her daughter. Kate shared a driving ambition with her widowed father, Treasury Secretary Salmon P. Chase—he to be President of the United States, she to be the First Lady of the land.

She was 21 when war began. Her father had weathered the deaths of three wives, and Kate was his greatest pride and sincerest idolater. Having acted as hostess when he was governor of Ohio and a U.S. senator, she did the same when he entered Lincoln's Cabinet.

Kate was stunning, and she knew it. Tall and shapely, with golden-reddish hair, hazel eyes, and fair skin, she combined a girlish charm with the nerve and wit of a woman twice her age, holding her own in the masculine arena of political conversation and intrigue. After her father failed to gain the 1860 Republican presidential nomination, she disdained the Lincolns. Viewing them as impostors in the White House, she acted as Washington's First Lady-to-be, confident that her father would succeed his boss as chief executive sooner or later.

At the first state dinner of the new administration, Mary Todd Lincoln nervously fluttered her fan as she welcomed guests to the White House. When the Chases arrived, she told Kate: "I shall be glad to see you any time, Miss Chase."

"Mrs. Lincoln," her young rival replied, "I shall be glad to have *you* call on *me* at any time."

In 1862, with Mrs. Lincoln deeply in mourning for her beloved son Willie, Kate Chase became Washington's leading hostess. The *New York Times* declared that "she wielded her power and the influence of her high social station as no other woman in this country has ever wielded such forces." Certainly, no one could overlook her splendid entertainments and her beautiful gowns and jewels.

Kate visited army camps to cheer the soldiers, all the while maintaining a busy social schedule. She was courted by Governor William Sprague of Rhode Island, soon to become a U.S. senator. Kate was stronger, shrewder, and more sober than Sprague. But he was wealthier than her father, and Salmon Chase needed his financial backing and political support to challenge Lincoln for the Presidency in 1864. He heartily endorsed Sprague's attentions to his daughter.

Their marriage in November 1863 was Washington's biggest social event that year. Her father had to sell property in Ohio to pay for the wedding. One writer characterized the affair in verse: "Deck, O flowers, this bride so rare / Come with beauty, blush and scent / Roses twine her silken hair / Queen of all the continent."

But Kate was never to be queen, or First Lady, which was as close as any woman could come to power in Washington at a time when only men were able to vote and hold high office. In 1864, her father abandoned his quest for the Presidency and accepted a Supreme Court appointment from Lincoln. Her marriage produced four children and little else of lasting value. William Sprague proved to be an alcoholic and womanizer, while Kate continued to have a host of male admirers. The death of her father in 1873 was a devastating blow. A financial panic later that year swept away the Sprague fortune.

In time, gossip told of an affair between Kate and New York Senator Roscoe Conkling, who was assailed by her jealous husband. The Spragues divorced in 1882. Much like her old rival, Mary Todd Lincoln, Kate languished in her later years. She traveled abroad, descended into poverty, and died all but forgotten by a society she once dominated as nearly as any woman could. ★

> "I SHALL BE GLAD TO SEE YOU ANY TIME, MISS CHASE."
> **MARY LINCOLN**

> "MRS. LINCOLN, I SHALL BE GLAD TO HAVE *YOU* CALL ON *ME* AT ANY TIME."
> **KATE CHASE**

Queen of Society
A young Kate Chase shows the promise of her future beauty in this 1850s image. During the Civil War, she presided over Washington society, eclipsing First Lady Mary Todd Lincoln (inset). British reporter William Howard Russell recalled that she always had "a faint, almost disdainful smile upon her face, as if she were a titled English lady posing in a formal garden for Gainsborough or Reynolds."

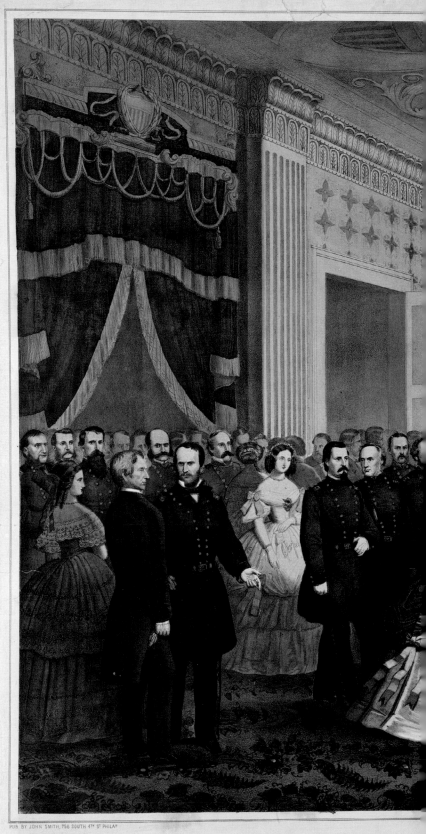

Capital Events *Salmon P. Chase, seen in this portrait taken at Mathew Brady's studio, served as a U.S. senator and as Chief Justice of the Supreme Court and was present at numerous White House events such as the reception for Gen. and Mrs. Ulysses S. Grant, portrayed at right in a color lithograph by Anton Hohenstein.*

PUB. BY JOHN SMITH, 756 SOUTH 4TH ST PHILAD

ABRAHAM LI

RESPECTFU

LN'S ⬥ LAST RECEPTION.

TED TO THE ⬥ PEOPLE OF THE UNITED STATES

Chantilly

Urban sprawl has obliterated many Civil War battlefields and reduced others to tiny plots of hallowed ground, hemmed in by housing developments and shopping centers. One such lonely remnant is Ox Hill Battlefield Park in Fairfax County, Virginia, near the nation's capital. A small green space surrounded by steel, glass, and concrete, it contains a pair of weather-beaten stones commemorating the death of two Union generals who fought here at the Battle of Chantilly. That engagement is often treated as a mere footnote to the Second Battle of Manassas, or Bull Run. Yet what happened at Chantilly is dramatic, memorable, and worth preserving.

Opposing forces converged at this spot amid gathering storm clouds on September 1, 1862, following several blazing-hot days of fighting at nearby Manassas. The battle there had culminated on August 30, when Robert E. Lee's Confederates gained a smashing victory over John Pope's Army of the Potomac. On August 31, Lee dispatched Stonewall Jackson and his veterans to sweep around Pope's columns as they retreated toward Washington and block the way. Pope learned of Jackson's maneuver and sent forces to intercept him.

On September 1, Jackson's vanguard encountered those Federals at Ox Hill, near a mansion called Chantilly. Jackson paused to consolidate his forces before attacking. For once, he was beaten to the punch by a foe as combative as he was—Union Gen. Isaac Stevens, who had graduated first in his class at West Point and served as governor of Washington Territory. Stevens smarted over the recent defeat at Manassas. As thunder rumbled, he threw his division into battle.

> "THE ONE-ARMED GENERAL, SWORD IN HIS HAND AND BRIDLE IN HIS TEETH CONDUCTED HIS OWN RECONNAISSANCE AND CAME UP AGAINST A REGIMENT OF GEORGIANS. THEY SHOUTED AT HIM TO SURRENDER, BUT HE WHIPPED HIS HORSE AROUND AND MADE A DASH FOR IT,"

1840 Heavy Cavalry Saber— the "Old Wristbreaker"

The fighting began around 5 p.m. amid what one soldier called "one of the wildest rainstorms I ever witnessed." Lightning split the sky and rain fell in torrents, nearly drowning out the din of battle. Stevens grasped the flag of his old regiment, the 79th New York Highlanders, and led troops through a cornfield toward Confederates waiting behind a rail fence. He made a conspicuous target and was shot dead. The attack faltered, and his disheartened men fell back.

Nearby, New Jersey's finest soldier was mounting another charge. Gen. Philip Kearny was a battle-scarred veteran of the Mexican War. He had said he would give an arm to lead a cavalry charge there, and he did just that. Gen. in Chief Winfield Scott called him "the bravest man I ever saw, and a perfect soldier."

Kearny's division was locked in hand-to-hand fighting near the cornfield. He spotted remnants of Stevens's division off to one side and ordered them back into action. They hesitated, fearing that Confederates were lurking amid the stalks. The one-armed general, sword in his hand and bridle in his teeth, conducted his own reconnaissance and came up against a regiment of Georgians. They shouted at him to surrender, but he whipped his horse around and made a dash for it before collapsing under a lethal hail of bullets not far from where Stevens fell.

The Battle of Chantilly ended at dusk after 90 minutes of thunderous combat that left 500 Confederates and 700 Federals dead or wounded. The standoff here allowed the remainder of the Army of the Potomac to withdraw unmolested within Washington's defenses. Since then, the city and its suburbs have expanded relentlessly, obliterating all of the battlefield except for a few precious acres, where two of the Union's best fighting generals died for their country. ✫

Desperate Moment *Holding his reins in his teeth, one-armed Gen. Philip Kearny leads his men against Confederates in this 1867 lithograph by Augustus Tholey dramatizing Kearny's last moments.*

Where Generals Fell *A map by veteran Robert Knox Sneden shows the main battle lines at Chantilly on the afternoon of September 1, 1862.*

An Unquotable Quartermaster

Of the thousands of men who served under Stonewall Jackson, none was more of a character than Maj. John Harman. He was one of five brothers who joined the Confederate army. He was also the only officer who dared to curse in Jackson's presence. The fact that he could not control his temper made him one of the best quartermasters on either side.

A man of rough background and equally rough personality, Harman was born in 1824 on a farm near Staunton in Virginia's fertile Shenandoah Valley. An adventurous youth, he set out for the Texas frontier, where he joined the Texas Rangers and served in the Mexican War. He then returned to Staunton, prospered in the livestock trade, and purchased a stagecoach line with his brother Asher that monopolized business in the upper Shenandoah Valley. He also served as a county magistrate and a major in the Virginia militia, and was the father of 13 children, all of which helped prepare him for the task of supplying an army in wartime and keeping it moving.

John A. Harman

In May 1861, he became the first and only quartermaster Jackson ever had. That was remarkable, for Harman and Jackson were strong personalities who often clashed but somehow managed to avoid a permanent rupture. Harman's limited experience as an officer, his inability to keep secrets, and his frequent disputes with Jackson made him a troublesome figure. Yet his management of a 14-mile-long wagon train during Jackson's triumphant Valley Campaign in early 1862 remains one of the singular feats of the war and a tribute to his imposing presence. A fellow staff officer described him as a "big-bodied, big-voiced, untiring, fearless man and devil who would have ordered Jackson himself out of the way if necessary to obey Jackson's orders." Soldiers called him "the old

Major," and gave him a wide berth. Unpolished in manners, short in temper, Harman got things done through boundless energy, intimidation, and profanity that turned the air blue.

In September 1862, as Lee's army was fording the shallow Potomac River into Maryland for the first invasion of the North, Jackson's wagon train became hopelessly snarled. An exasperated Jackson summoned Major Harman. The quartermaster splashed into the water among the wagons, kicked stubborn mules, and unleashed a volume of profanity that, as one witness put it, "would have excited the admiration of the most scientific of mule drivers." His tirade struck teamsters and their mules like a barbed whip, and the traffic jam dissipated in moments.

Harman expected a stern lecture on his language from the onlooking Jackson, whose aversion to profanity was biblical. "The ford's cleared, General!" Harman declared in his own defense. "There's only one language that will make mules understand on a hot day that they must get out of the water!"

Jackson's lips twitched slightly, but he offered no rebuke. "Thank you, Major," he said, and resumed the crossing, shaking his head in resignation.

After the war, Harman returned to Staunton, farmed a bit, and managed a popular resort. Convinced that the South must reconcile with the North, he joined the Republican Party. That brought him sharp criticism from neighbors, who abhorred the party of Lincoln and Grant. President Grant appointed Harman postmaster of Staunton shortly before the old quartermaster died in 1874.

An unfriendly journalist described him as "a man of strong convictions and uncompromising in his beliefs, caring little for the opinion of others." John Harman would have nodded agreement at that—and probably added a few four-letter words for emphasis. ✶

"THE QUARTERMASTER SPLASHED INTO THE WATER AMONG THE WAGONS, KICKED STUBBORN MULES, AND UNLEASHED A VOLUME OF PROFANITY THAT, AS ONE WITNESS PUT IT, 'WOULD HAVE EXCITED THE ADMIRATION OF THE MOST SCIENTIFIC OF MULE DRIVERS.'"

Vital Transport *These drawings by Northern artist Edwin Forbes show a standard army wagon and a supply train fording the Rappahannock River. An army required hundreds of ambulances, supply wagons, and specialty transport, all drawn by teams of mules or horses.*

McClellan's Lost Chances

During the Civil War and ever after, people wondered what might have been had commanders responded differently in crucial situations. For Unionists, some of the most agonizing might-have-beens involved the actions of Gen. George McClellan during the campaign that culminated at Antietam on September 17, 1862.

Early that month, following his victory at Manassas, Robert E. Lee led Confederates into Maryland, hoping that a decisive victory on Union ground would shatter enemy morale and bring foreign recognition to the Southern cause. He paused in his advance at Frederick, Maryland, to take stock. A large Union garrison at Harpers Ferry blocked his lines of supply and communication with the Shenandoah Valley. He sent two-thirds of his army under Stonewall Jackson to seize Harpers Ferry. Lee would cross South Mountain, a ridge west of Frederick, with his remaining forces and anxiously await Jackson's return.

All this was spelled out in Special Orders No. 191. Lee was taking a huge gamble by splitting an army much smaller than his opponent's in enemy territory. Yet as one Confederate officer remarked, Lee's "name might be audacity."

The same could not be said of McClellan, who had recently regained command of the Army of the Potomac. Meticulous and deliberate, he reached Frederick a few days after the Confederates departed. His troops camped in the same fields abandoned by Lee's men. On the morning of September 13, an Indiana soldier spied three cigars in a paper wrapper, partially hidden in weeds. The Hoosier was enjoying his smoke when he noticed that the wrapper bore the heading: "Army of Northern Virginia, Special Orders No. 191."

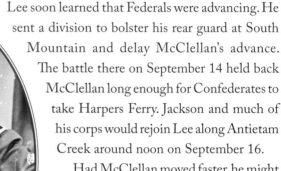

"HERE IS A PIECE OF PAPER WITH WHICH IF I CANNOT WHIP BOBBIE LEE, I WILL BE WILLING TO GO HOME."

GEN. GEORGE B. MCCLELLAN

By noon, those orders had reached McClellan. He now knew that the enemy was divided and could be conquered if he moved quickly through the passes of South Mountain, knifed between Lee's two wings, and polished them off separately. Armed with this intelligence, he exclaimed, he was ready to "whip Bobbie Lee." He issued marching orders that evening.

Lee soon learned that Federals were advancing. He sent a division to bolster his rear guard at South Mountain and delay McClellan's advance. The battle there on September 14 held back McClellan long enough for Confederates to take Harpers Ferry. Jackson and much of his corps would rejoin Lee along Antietam Creek around noon on September 16.

Had McClellan moved faster, he might have broken through at South Mountain before Confederate reinforcements arrived there and achieved the smashing victory he hoped for. As it was, he still had a golden opportunity when he arrived at Antietam late on September 15 and confronted Lee's vastly outnumbered forces. Many people wondered afterward what might have been had McClellan attacked on September 16 instead of taking a full day to prepare for battle. That delay—and McClellan's reluctance to throw all he had into the fight and attack Lee at every point simultaneously—allowed the remainder of Jackson's corps to reach Antietam from Harpers Ferry late on September 17 as the battle reached its climax and avert a potentially disastrous Confederate defeat.

No single day of fighting in American history produced more casualties. Lee withdrew his battered army to Virginia. McClellan gave only perfunctory pursuit and was later sacked by Lincoln, who agonized as much as anyone over what might have been at Antietam. ★

Aftermath of Antietam
Confederate dead (above) lie in rows in front of an abandoned limber near the Dunker Church, the scene of fierce fighting during the opening stages of the Battle of Antietam. In another post-battle photograph (right), Federal soldiers stand beneath a lone tree shading the temporary grave of Pvt. John Marshall of the 28th Pennsylvania Infantry.

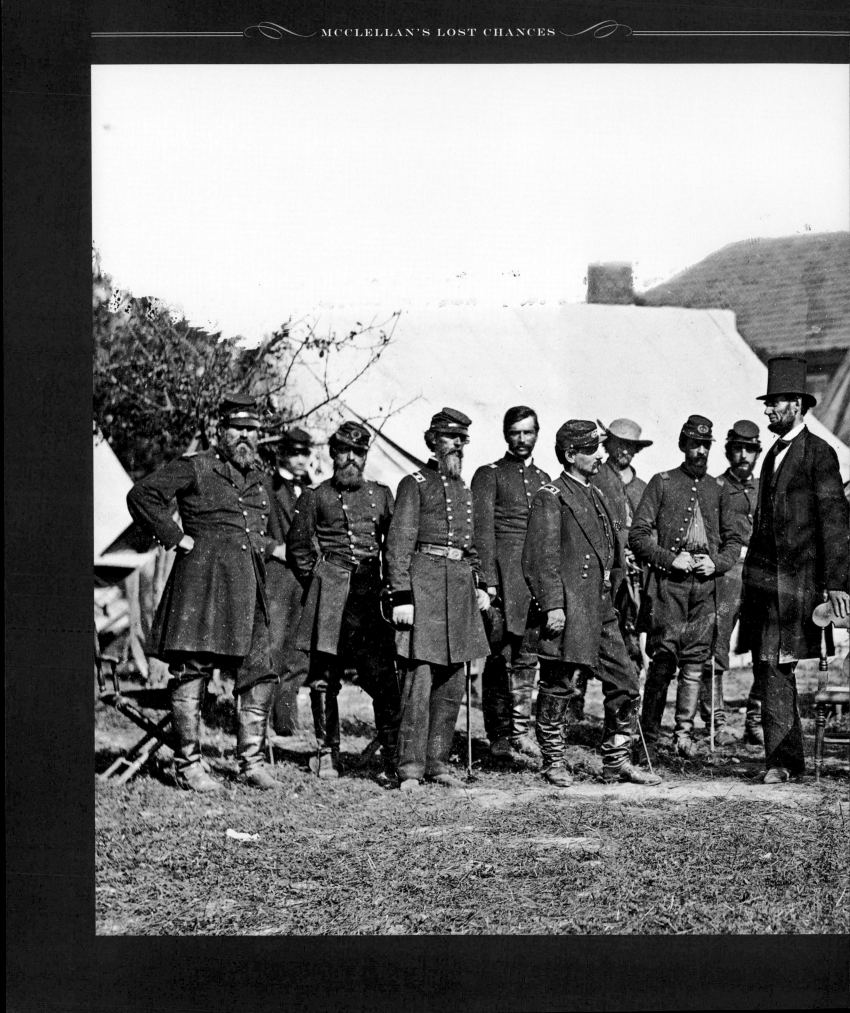

"LEE WITHDREW HIS
BATTERED ARMY TO VIRGINIA.
MCCLELLAN GAVE ONLY
PERFUNCTORY PURSUIT . . .
LINCOLN AGONIZED AS MUCH
AS ANYONE OVER WHAT MIGHT
HAVE BEEN AT ANTIETAM."

Commander-in-Chief *On
October 3, 1862, two weeks
after the Battle of Antietam,
President Lincoln meets with
McClellan, who stands facing
his commander-in-chief at
field headquarters, surrounded
by senior officers.*

The Angel of Marye's Heights

Thousands of Civil War monuments dot our land. At major battlefields, they are so numerous that all tend to look the same to visitors. Yet one of those memorials, in Fredericksburg, Virginia, is unique and poignant. The monument is a testimonial to how close the states of the Union have grown since the conflict ended.

In December 1862, a large and lopsided battle occurred on the frozen fields of Fredericksburg. Wave after wave of Union soldiers assaulted Confederate lines that simply could not be broken. From the Sunken Road at the base of Marye's Heights, massed Southerners unleashed withering volleys that shattered one Federal attack after another.

Richard Kirkland was among those Confederate defenders. A 19-year-old farm boy, Kirkland was a good soldier who had risen to sergeant in the Second South Carolina Infantry Regiment. On the day after the great battle, with hundreds of injured Union soldiers lying helplessly on the field and moaning for water, human sympathy overcame Kirkland's sense of partisanship.

Richard Kirkland

No truce had been arranged to allow for the dead and wounded to be retrieved. Kirkland went to his brigade commander and asked permission to go out on the field and give water to suffering soldiers. "Kirkland," the general exclaimed, "don't you know you would get a bullet through your head the moment you stepped over the wall?"

"Yes, sir," he replied, "I know that. But if you will let me, I am willing to try."

The commander, touched by the request, nodded assent. Yet Kirkland was not permitted to show a white flag, lest the Federals think that the Confederates were asking for an armistice.

Humanity amid Horror *Draped with canteens, Sergeant Kirkland gives water to a wounded Federal soldier in the casualty-strewn field below the Sunken Road at Fredericksburg. Confederate soldiers carried a wide variety of canteens, including the "drum" type at right.*

So Dick Kirkland, loaded with all the canteens he could carry, climbed out of the Sunken Road and onto the battlefield. He stood exposed to every sharpshooter in the Union Army of the Potomac. Not a gun was fired. Kirkland slowly made his way forward to the first line of wounded Federals. He knelt and, lifting the head of a wounded Yankee, gave him a long drink of water.

Then, for an hour and a half that cold Sunday afternoon, Kirkland moved from soldier to soldier. He administered water, and if asked, uttered simple prayers. Several times he went back to his lines to refill canteens. Each time he returned, no gunfire broke the silence. Both sides knew his mission and watched with a mixture of astonishment and admiration. When Kirkland's task was done and he climbed back over the stone wall for the last time, no cheers saluted his act. None were necessary.

The following autumn, Kirkland was one of 4,000 men killed at the Battle of Chickamauga in Georgia, but his act of mercy at Fredericksburg continued to live in memory.

In 1965, as the Civil War centennial reached its climax, commissions in South Carolina, Virginia, and New Jersey worked together to fashion a memorial to Kirkland. They asked sculptor Felix de Weldon, who had produced the famous Iwo Jima memorial for the Marine Corps, to portray Kirkland on a merciful errand that December afternoon in 1862.

The stone-and-bronze monument, dedicated in September 1965, stands today in front of the Sunken Road on the Fredericksburg battlefield—an eternal tribute to a brave soldier, esteemed by troops on both sides and hailed by Northerners and Southerners alike as "The Angel of Marye's Heights." ✴

"KIRKLAND, DON'T YOU KNOW
YOU WOULD GET A BULLET
THROUGH YOUR HEAD
THE MOMENT YOU STEPPED
OVER THE WALL?"

GEN. JOSEPH B. KERSHAW

"YES, SIR, I KNOW THAT.
BUT IF YOU WILL LET ME,
I AM WILLING TO TRY."

RICHARD KIRKLAND

*Confederate
drum canteen*

"The Bread Riot"

Heaven has no rage like love to hatred turned / Nor hell a fury like a woman scorned."

That famous poetic couplet by William Congreve was borne out one April morning in 1863 in Richmond, Virginia. Women of Richmond cared deeply for the troops defending the Confederate capital and did much to support them. But some blamed Confederate officials for food shortages and inflation that brought speculators handsome profits while poor families went hungry. On April 2, angry women began gathering in Capitol Square. "As soon as enough of us get together, we are going to the bakeries and each of us will take a loaf of bread," one emaciated woman told a bystander. "That is little enough for the government to give us after it has taken all our men."

The crowd quickly swelled in number. Complaints became louder and more heated, thanks to the leader of the movement. Mary Jackson was a house painter's wife described by one witness as "a tall, daring, Amazonian-looking woman," with a long white feather standing erect from her hat. Characterizations of her in print ran the gamut from Jezebel to Joan of Arc.

Men lounging in Capitol Square joined the crowd of about 1,000. A journalist later dismissed the throng as "a handful of prostitutes, professional thieves, Irish and Yankee hags, gallows birds from all lands but our own."

They surged down Ninth Street toward food markets on Cary Street, chanting "Bread! Bread!" Some of the women were armed. Shopkeepers shut their doors, but rioters broke in by sheer weight of numbers. Using aprons and baskets, they carried away all the food in sight. Firemen arrived and hosed down the mob. Undeterred, vandals headed a block north to the general stores on Main Street, broke plate glass windows, and made off with clothing and jewelry.

When Governor John Letcher and Mayor Joseph Mayo were unable to restore order, troops moved in, formed two lines across Main Street from sidewalk to sidewalk, and stood ready to fire. One little spark could have set off an explosion. Then Jefferson Davis arrived. Climbing atop an overturned wagon, he shouted down hundreds of angry voices and tried to reason with the mob. What they were doing, he said, would only make the food shortages worse. The guns pointed at them would be better used against the enemy. "You say you are hungry and have no money—here is all I have," he declared, emptying his pockets and flinging coins at the crowd. Then he pulled out his watch and gave them five minutes to disperse before he would order the soldiers to fire.

Slowly the crowd disbanded. About 70 lawbreakers were arrested. Half were convicted of misdemeanors; the rest were acquitted. Richmond's provost marshal asked newspapers to overlook the affair lest "it embarrass our cause and encourage our enemies." Editors waited 24 hours before informing the world.

Thus ended what was labeled "The Bread Riot" or "The Women's Riot." This was not a singular affair. A dozen such outbursts occurred on a smaller scale in Southern towns during the war. Whether the women involved were heroines or culprits remained a matter of debate. But few could deny that they rioted because they were too proud to beg. ★

> "HEAVEN HAS NO RAGE LIKE LOVE TO HATRED TURNED / NOR HELL A FURY LIKE A WOMAN SCORNED."

First Couple *Jefferson and Varina Howell Davis, shown here before the war, remained in Richmond with their children until the city was about to fall to Union forces in 1865.*

Confederate national flag, 1863

Disorder in Richmond *A female ringleader brandishing a revolver stands watch while women loot a Richmond bakery in this engraving from* Frank Leslie's Illustrated Newspaper. *By April 1863, inflation in the Confederacy had raised bread prices 80 percent above normal.*

A Truce Among Masons

In the spring of 1863, Union forces laid siege to Port Hudson, Louisiana. That town and the city of Vicksburg, 150 miles to the north, were the last two Confederate strongholds blocking Union control of the vital Mississippi River. Port Hudson's defenders were in a bind, but they still had hope that food and other supplies could be smuggled downriver from the town of St. Francisville, ten miles away. To neutralize that source, the gunboat U.S.S. *Albatross* was dispatched to bombard the town.

Lt. Cmdr. John Hart was captain of that warship. He was dedicated, efficient, and a loving husband. Hart directed shell fire at St. Francisville, situated on high ground overlooking the river, but the bombardment was not incessant. On June 7, he found time to write his wife in Schenectady, New York. He mentioned the heat and how much he longed for a glass of cold water. A cat aboard the *Albatross* had given birth to kittens. The men occasionally picked blackberries from vines along the riverbank. Mockingbirds overhead screamed at the intruding Yankees. Hart's vessel was performing well. He looked forward after the war to taking his wife on a trip down the Mississippi to see the battlefields.

Four days later, crew members heard a shot from their commander's cabin. They found him lying dead on the floor, a smoking revolver in his hand. Had he taken his life—or had he suffered a fatal accident while cleaning his weapon?

They would never know the answer, but one thing was clear: In the stifling June heat and humidity, Hart had to be buried quickly. Officers of the *Albatross* wanted to inter their friend onshore rather than in the river. Yet using enemy territory for burial seemed impossible.

Then someone remembered that Hart was a Mason. He belonged to one of the oldest continuing fraternities in the world, one whose bonds extended beyond national boundaries and battle lines.

Under a flag of truce, men from the *Albatross* went into St. Francisville—a town they had recently bombarded. A Union officer asked if there were Masons in the area.

It so happened that Feliciana Lodge No. 31 was located in St. Francisville. Its senior warden was Capt. W. W. Leake of the First Louisiana Cavalry, which was busy making life miserable for nearby Union soldiers. When Leake learned of Hart's death, a sense of Masonic duty overcame his reluctance to offer comfort to his enemies. He rode to St. Francisville.

On June 12, for a brief interlude, the Civil War came to a halt at the Louisiana river town. Federals brought Hart's body ashore. Confederates who belonged to the local lodge met the party at the cemetery of Grace Episcopal Church, where the commander's remains were laid to rest with those of other Masons. One group of mourners returned to the *Albatross*. Another galloped back to Confederate duty with Captain Leake. The conflict resumed.

A few months after the war ended in 1865, Mrs. Hart journeyed to St. Francisville to take her husband's body back to New York. When she saw how lovely and peaceful the town was, and how carefully its citizens tended the grave, she decided to leave her husband where he was.

The grave is still there. Two stones mark its place. One is the simple marker for a Union soldier. The other is more ornate—placed there in 1955 by Louisiana Masons in tribute to a fallen member of their brotherhood. ✷

International Order *This Masonic certificate welcomed the recipient into that international brotherhood as a Master Mason in a regular lodge.*

"ON JUNE 12,
FOR A BRIEF INTERLUDE,
THE CIVIL WAR
CAME TO A HALT
AT THE LOUISIANA
RIVER TOWN."

River War *In the spring of 1863,
Adm. David Farragut's Federal
flotilla waged an aggressive campaign
against Port Hudson, Louisiana, on
the Mississippi River (above). Union
Cmdr. John Hart was laid to rest in
nearby St. Francisville, in the Masonic
burial lot of Grace Church (right).*

The Other Gettysburg

For three days in the Civil War's third summer, Confederates made furious charges against stout Union defenses at Gettysburg. The final shots echoed over the rolling hills of southern Pennsylvania on the evening of July 3, 1863. Then the Second Battle of Gettysburg began. In that grim struggle, the living disposed of the dead, and doctors, nurses, and desperately wounded soldiers contended with trauma, terror, and agony. The story of that other Gettysburg needs to be told again and again because it is the truest picture of America's cruelest war.

Nearly 6,000 soldiers died on the battlefield, but many more were gravely injured and perished afterward. They were among tens of thousands of wounded soldiers who inundated the village of Gettysburg, which had a population of barely 2,500. Most were dumped in makeshift field hospitals whose staffs were ill-prepared to treat so many victims. Surgeons performed triage, separating those who had a chance at survival from those deemed likely to die, who were then taken into the woods and laid in rows. There, semiconscious, they moaned and twitched painfully, awaiting an end to their suffering.

Treatment for those who were not given up as dead was torturous and often ended in the loss of life, limb, or both. Luther Hopkins, a Virginia soldier, wrote of the harrowing night of July 3: "The moon and stars came out, and the surgeons with their attendants appeared with their knives and saws, and when the morning came there were stacks of legs and arms standing in the fields like shocks of corn."

A young Quaker who answered the call for nurses was shocked when she got to Gettysburg. The foul stench of infection and death was overwhelming. It was an atmosphere, she said, that "robbed the battlefield of its glory, the survivors of their victory, and the wounded of what little chance of life was left in them."

On July 4, while the two bloodied armies remained in place, a teenage soldier from Alabama sent a note to his mother. "I am here a prisoner of war and mortally wounded," he wrote. "I can live but a few hours more at farthest . . . I am very weak. Do not mourn my loss. I had hoped to have been spared, but a righteous God has ordered it otherwise . . . Farewell to you all."

The following day, Lee's army started back to Virginia. Thousands of mangled Confederate soldiers were piled into wagons lacking springs, mattresses, or other basic comforts. Col. John Imboden was in charge of the ambulance train. For four hours, as he rode past the line of wagons, he heard the groans and screams of men trapped in a living hell. From the ambulances, Imboden heard desperate appeals: "O God! Why can't I die? . . . Will no one have mercy and kill me? . . . For God's sake, stop just for a minute! Leave me to die along the roadside!"

No help could be given, Imboden noted, and he added: "During this one night I realized more of the horrors of war than I had in all the two preceding years." A Union surgeon later observed that Gettysburg was an "occasion of the greatest amount of human suffering known to this nation since its birth."

Such is the true picture of war. Countless monuments exist to the dead, but how do we commemorate the unbearable suffering that made men long for death? ✶

Bloody Craft *Surgeons' kits contained an assortment of saws and knives needed to perform amputations.*

"THE MOON AND STARS CAME OUT, AND THE SURGEONS WITH THEIR ATTENDANTS APPEARED WITH THEIR KNIVES AND SAWS, AND WHEN THE MORNING CAME THERE WERE STACKS OF LEGS AND ARMS STANDING IN THE FIELDS LIKE SHOCKS OF CORN."

LUTHER HOPKINS,
EYEWITNESS TO THE HORROR OF GETTYSBURG

Lost in Battle *The fields and pastures around Gettysburg were covered with the bodies of the slain, as recorded in this version of Timothy O'Sullivan's image, "Harvest of Death." Another photograph (top) documents the grisly result of the surgeon's work.*

A Fatal Loss of Temper

The powerful emotions aroused by war could topple common sense and send people of sound mind over the edge. Such was the case with a physician in Norfolk, Virginia, who spent much of his life saving others but died a condemned murderer in 1863.

David Wright, born in 1809, was one of Norfolk's most esteemed doctors. When a yellow fever epidemic swept the area in 1855, he himself came down with the disease but still did all in his power to bring the scourge under control. He was, said one admirer, a man who never entertained "an unkind thought."

That changed with the Civil War. Wright continued his medical practice after Federals occupied Norfolk in May 1862. He watched helplessly as businesses and schools closed and Union soldiers commandeered private property. Lincoln's Emancipation Proclamation encouraged slaves in Virginia to leave their masters and seek freedom under Union authority in Norfolk. Freed slaves there did not show whites the deference they were accustomed to receiving from blacks and angered Confederate loyalists by burning an effigy of Jefferson Davis.

Wright had two sons in the Confederate army, one of whom was reported missing in action at Gettysburg and presumed dead. On July 11, 1863, a company of brightly uniformed black troops entered Norfolk. They were among nearly 180,000 black recruits who served as Union soldiers during the war, including free men from the North and emancipated slaves from the South. Commanding the company was a white officer, Lt. Anson Sanborn.

Dr. Wright was standing on the sidewalk when the black soldiers marched past.

> "DR. WRIGHT WAS STANDING ON THE SIDEWALK WHEN THE BLACK SOLDIERS MARCHED PAST. THE SIGHT CAUSED SOMETHING IN HIM TO SNAP."

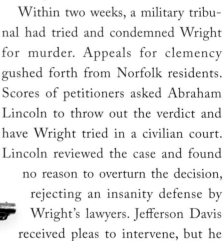

Confederate revolver

The sight caused something in him to snap. He stepped out into the street and, with clenched fists, shouted at Lieutenant Sanborn: "Oh, you coward!" Sanborn halted his men and told Wright he was under arrest. The two exchanged heated words, and Sanborn drew his sword. The physician raised a pistol and fired twice, killing Sanborn.

Within two weeks, a military tribunal had tried and condemned Wright for murder. Appeals for clemency gushed forth from Norfolk residents. Scores of petitioners asked Abraham Lincoln to throw out the verdict and have Wright tried in a civilian court. Lincoln reviewed the case and found no reason to overturn the decision, rejecting an insanity defense by Wright's lawyers. Jefferson Davis received pleas to intervene, but he had no legal authority over the case. The fact remained that a Southern civilian had killed a Union officer in Federal-occupied territory. Wright almost escaped the gallows. His daughter visited him in jail and bravely changed clothing with him. Her disguised father made it out of the building before a guard noticed his odd gait, caused by the leg irons Wright wore. He was soon back behind bars.

On Friday, October 23, 1863, Dr. Wright was hanged at the Norfolk fairgrounds as thousands looked on. A newspaper stated that he went to his death "touched with inner serenity." His body lay in state in Christ Episcopal Church before being buried in a nearby cemetery. The conflicting emotions aroused by his execution and the deed that led to it lingered for decades in Norfolk. Many citizens of long standing viewed Wright as a martyr, while other residents who gained freedom and citizenship only after the Union triumphed here were less inclined to feel that he had been denied justice. ✶

Ruined and Occupied *Parts of Norfolk, including the Navy Yard (right), lay in ruins when black troops like those portrayed here (inset) entered the city as occupiers.*

The Kinston Executions

War can bring out the best and the worst in people. In the case of Gen. George Pickett, celebrated for leading a valiant but futile charge against the Union line at Gettysburg on July 3, 1863, the worst came seven months later, when he presided over the largest mass execution of soldiers during the conflict.

In early February 1864, Pickett led a combined army-navy expedition against a Union force stationed at the North Carolina coastal town of New Bern. Speed and secrecy were necessary for Southern success. Pickett displayed neither. The expedition was a blundering failure. As the campaign unraveled, an angry Pickett was heard to say that every man "who didn't do his duty, or deserted, ought to be shot or hung."

The Confederates managed to capture about 200 Federals. Among them were 22 North Carolinians who had once served the Confederacy. Most of them had belonged to state home guard units before joining the Union army. Suddenly, Pickett had scapegoats for the frustrations and failures he had experienced in the New Bern campaign. He ordered all 22 men court-martialed for desertion.

The culprits were marched 30 miles in harsh winter weather to Kinston, North Carolina, and there incarcerated in a local jail. Pickett allowed the men little food or clothing and minimal contact with local family members. Meanwhile, his opponent, Union Gen. John Peck, learned of the planned courts-martial. Peck sought assurances that the accused men would be treated as prisoners of war. Pickett replied in an angry and sarcastic letter and persisted in treating the men as deserters, subject to the death penalty.

A military tribunal at Kinston heard one case after another, found each man guilty as

> "FOLLOWING EACH EXECUTION, PICKETT ALLOWED HIS MEN TO STRIP CORPSES OF CLOTHING AND SHOES. CONFEDERATES JEERED AND TAUNTED WIDOWS WHO ATTEMPTED TO CLAIM THEIR HUSBANDS' BODIES FOR BURIAL."

charged, and handed down death sentences. John Paris, the Methodist chaplain of the 54th North Carolina, offered baptism to the condemned. He told those who accepted his offer that they "had sinned against the country, and their country would not forgive them, but they had also sinned against God, yet God would forgive them if they approached [death] with penitent hearts."

Executions began the day after the court-martial went into session. On one occasion, thirteen men were hanged side by side from the scaffold as tearful wives, mothers, and children watched. On February 22, the last two condemned men were executed. They were brothers who were baptized together in the river, taken back to jail to change their clothes, and then marched to the gallows.

There were no prayers for those who were hanged, and corn bags were used in place of traditional black hoods. One victim was a 14-year-old drummer boy. Following each execution, Pickett allowed his men to strip corpses of clothing and shoes. Confederates jeered and taunted widows who attempted to claim their husbands' bodies for burial. The unclaimed corpses were buried in a mass grave beneath the gallows.

Pickett's haste in executing the men, and his denial of every plea for clemency, were remarkable considering that deserting a home guard unit was not a crime in North Carolina.

After the conflict ended, the War Department and Congress held inquiries into the executions, but Pickett never faced charges for what some considered a war crime. Not all those in authority felt his misdeeds rose to that level. Gen. in Chief Ulysses Grant, for one, opposed placing him on trial. Yet the best that could be said about George Pickett at Kinston was that the incident revealed him at his worst. ★

Study in Elegance *Maj. Gen. George Pickett preferred carefully tailored uniforms and took pride in his long hair, often heavily scented and reaching to his shoulders.*

The Wit of Abraham Lincoln

Abraham Lincoln was a comic philosopher—a prairie Socrates brimming with wilderness wit and frontier sagacity. Humor was the safety valve that released the dreadful pressures he faced as president and helped preserve his sanity. He was not just a man who liked to laugh; he had to laugh for sheer survival. Few things offered him greater relief amid the endless crises of his presidency than laughing heartily at one of his own jokes. "When he told a particularly good story, and the time came to laugh," one congressman recalled, Lincoln would throw his left foot across his right knee, grasp the foot with both hands, and shake until "his whole frame seemed to be convulsed with laughter." Once when chastised for his habitual joking, Lincoln turned serious and responded wistfully: "I laugh because I must not weep—that's all, that's all."

Some of his jokes were old and a bit lame, but he trotted them out and made fresh use of them. A master of brevity in his own compositions, he once reacted to an overly long report by remarking that it brought to mind the lazy preacher who was asked why he wrote such long sermons. Once he got to writing, the preacher explained, he was "too lazy to stop."

Pompous generals and politicians were the bane of Lincoln's existence, and he aimed some of his sharpest barbs at them. He remarked of one long-winded, dim-witted orator that he could pack more words into fewer ideas than "any man I ever met." The death of a vain, attention-grabbing commander led Lincoln to comment: "If the general had known how big a funeral he would have, he would have died long ago." At times, he let the target of his wit off lightly by altering his tone from scorn to forbearance. Once, when Cabinet members were denouncing the bumbling actions of cross-eyed Gen. Benjamin Butler, Lincoln interrupted the conversation. "Ah, gentlemen," he said gently, "you must remember

Presidential Winner
An 1860 cartoon portrays the lanky figure of Lincoln leaping triumphantly to the presidency.

that General Butler does not see things quite the way we do."

Lincoln sometimes found humor helpful when denying a request, something he often had to do. Late in 1863, in refusing a man who wanted a pass to travel through Union lines into Confederate territory to visit Richmond, Lincoln stated: "I would gladly give you the pass if it would do any good, but in the last two years I have given passes to 250,000 soldiers and not one of them has managed to get there yet."

Some of his best jokes were at his own expense. He liked to tell about the time a stranger accosted him while he was splitting rails in Illinois and aimed a gun at his head. Lincoln asked what the man meant by threatening him so. The stranger replied that he had vowed to shoot the first man he met who was uglier than he was. Lincoln stared at the man for a moment, pondered whether it was worth living with such horrid features, and declared: "If I am uglier than you, then blaze away!"

Many of Lincoln's anecdotes are not that funny when one reads them. But they were not intended to be read. They were meant to be related by a master storyteller with a mobile face, a quick tongue, and a superb sense of timing. A reporter likened the many stories he had at his command to the newly invented Gatling gun, "the next cartridge always ready and always pertinently adapted to some passing event."

His success as a candidate and president owed much to his comic timing and his uncanny ability to use humorous parables to enlighten and persuade people whose origins were as humble as his own. "They say I tell a great many stories," he once remarked. "I reckon I do, but I have found in the course of a long experience that common people—common people—are more easily influenced and informed through the medium of a broad illustration than in any other way." ★

"IF THE GENERAL
HAD KNOWN HOW BIG A
FUNERAL HE WOULD HAVE,
HE WOULD HAVE DIED
LONG AGO."

ABRAHAM LINCOLN

Humorless Reactions *Not everyone
appreciated Lincoln's wit. In an 1864
cartoon (above), the President is accused of
callous disregard for the misery of Union
troops in the field. Another illustration
(right) depicts Columbia asking for the
return of her half million sons while
Lincoln tries to recall a humorous story.*

Massacre at Fort Pillow

Civil wars are like family feuds, turning love that knows no bounds into hatred that has no limits. The bloody feud between North and South intensified following Lincoln's Emancipation Proclamation and the recruitment of black troops. What Unionists saw as "a new birth of freedom," in Lincoln's words, Confederates viewed as an attempt to set slaves against white Southerners. This bitter dispute led to one of the worst atrocities of the war, committed in western Tennessee in the spring of 1864 at Fort Pillow.

Confederates built the fort in 1861 on a high bluff 40 miles up the Mississippi River from Memphis to shield that city. Union forces seized Fort Pillow the following year and made it part of a chain of garrisons protecting communication and supply lines along the river.

By early 1864, the Fort Pillow garrison consisted of newly trained black soldiers, many of them recently emancipated, and white troops of the 13th U.S. Tennessee Cavalry. To Confederates, the defenders at Fort Pillow were runaway slaves and renegade Tennesseans. Gen. Nathan Bedford Forrest of Tennessee, a wealthy planter and slave trader before the war who excelled as a Confederate cavalry commander, set out to attack the isolated post.

He arrived there on the morning of April 12 with some 1,500 cavalrymen, who outnumbered the fort's defenders more than two to one. Confederate sharpshooters opened fire from high ground near the fort. One of the first Union fatalities was the garrison commander, Maj. Lionel Booth, leaving the inexperienced Maj. William Bradford in charge. By early afternoon, Forrest's men had surrounded Fort Pillow and driven through the first line of defense. He sent Bradford a message demanding unconditional surrender. Otherwise, Forrest stated, "I cannot be responsible for the fate of your command."

Bradford refused to yield. Forrest's men swarmed over the parapets and fired point-blank at the outmanned defenders. Some Union men went down fighting. Some fled toward the river. Many tried to surrender, but were shown no mercy.

Forrest later claimed that he was too far from the action to control his men and blamed panic-stricken Federals who continued to fire for prolonging a battle in which those who sought to surrender were not easily distinguished from those still fighting. Union soldiers insisted that when they laid down their arms, many were shot or bayoneted in cold blood. Confederate Sgt. Achilles Clark wrote to his sister afterward that men on both sides shouted "no quarter" (no mercy) but blamed his commander for failing to halt the slaughter once the Federals were overwhelmed. "The fort turned out to be a great slaughter pen," he wrote. "I with others tried to stop the butchery . . . but Gen. Forrest ordered them shot down like dogs and the carnage continued."

Nathan Bedford Forrest

Casualty figures point to a massacre in which black troops were the chief targets. In Civil War battles, the number of men wounded was usually several times the number killed. This was true for the Confederates at Fort Pillow, who had 14 killed and 87 wounded. Of the 262 black soldiers engaged at Fort Pillow, however, only 58 were still alive when the fighting ended. They made up most of the 231 Union men killed and a small portion of those Federals who survived, included 120 wounded and 230 captured.

No Quarter *Enraged Confederate soldiers murder helpless black Federals in this illustration of the storming of Fort Pillow published in the April 30, 1864, issue of Harper's Weekly.*

After this massacre, black units vowed never to yield to their foes and raised the battle cry: "Remember Fort Pillow!" ★

"I WITH OTHERS TRIED TO
STOP THE BUTCHERY . . .
BUT GEN. FORREST ORDERED
THEM SHOT DOWN LIKE DOGS AND
THE CARNAGE CONTINUED."

SGT. ACHILLES V. CLARK
OF FORREST'S COMMAND

Death of a Cavalier

In May 1864, General Grant paused to confer with commanders during his costly campaign against Lee's army in Virginia. Someone mentioned the possibility that Jeb Stuart's Confederate cavalry might pose an unforeseen threat. "Damn Stuart!" Union cavalry chief Philip Sheridan sneered. "I can thrash hell out of him any day!" That night Sheridan received orders to lead his cavalry corps southward, find Stuart, "and clean him out."

Stuart, then 31, was fabled as the embodiment of the Southern cavalier—a shining knight on horseback. High-spirited and aggressive, he led by example and enjoyed the trust and devotion of his men. Stuart had the faults of vanity, boisterousness, and impulsiveness. He had twice ridden completely around the Army of the Potomac—once outside Richmond in 1862, which earned him laurels, and again during the Gettysburg campaign in 1863, depriving Lee of his presence at a critical time. Southerners were quick to overlook his faults because this "illustrious cavalry commander," in the words of one Richmond diarist, was "so full of life, so bright, so gay, so brave."

Sheridan's 10,000 horsemen, superbly mounted and equipped with Spencer repeating carbines, started southward through Virginia with an understandable air of superiority. Blueclad troopers made an impressive sight riding four abreast in a column stretching for miles. "Little Phil" Sheridan made no effort to conceal his location as he burned storehouses and railroad tracks in his path. Sooner or later, he knew, Stuart would meet his challenge.

Confederate numbers had dwindled badly by now. Stuart scraped together a weary force of 5,000 cavalrymen and led them to Yellow Tavern, a strategic crossroads six miles north of Richmond. They dismounted and deployed for battle in

Cavalier's Cap *Confederate cavalry commander Jeb Stuart wore this plumed hat on the campaign trail.*

a V-shaped line. Late on the morning of May 11, Sheridan attacked. For three hours, the outnumbered Confederates managed to repulse one assault after another. Then an eerie lull descended. At 4 p.m., 24-year-old Gen. George Custer led a hammer-like charge by mounted men and dismounted troopers that captured two artillery pieces and threw half of Stuart's command into disorder.

Up galloped Stuart to rally his disintegrating flank. He emptied his revolver at one group of Federals. Union soldiers were falling back under pressure when a Michigan private saw a big, redheaded officer on horseback shouting orders. The Yankee fired a single shot that sliced through Stuart's stomach before exiting his back.

Aides placed the stricken general in a mule-drawn wagon. As he was being borne from the field, he shouted at some retreating Confederates: "Go back! Go back! Do your duty as I have done mine! I had rather die than be whipped!" The rickety wagon carried Stuart slowly and painfully to the home of his brother-in-law in Richmond.

The battle at Yellow Tavern ended at nightfall with the once invincible Confederate cavalry driven from the field. When Sheridan found the defenses of Richmond too strong to penetrate, he led his corps eastward to the protection of river gunboats. It had been a bold raid, one that helped make Sheridan the Union's shining knight.

He also achieved his primary objective. Stuart's internal hemorrhaging was untreatable. Loved ones could only stand by the bedside and watch. He died after 26 hours of often intense pain. To Confederate leaders in Virginia, his passing was a blow second only to Stonewall Jackson's death a year earlier. Robert E. Lee wrote his wife: "A more zealous, brave & devoted soldier, than Stuart, the Confederacy cannot have." ✯

Jeb Stuart

"DAMN STUART!
I CAN THRASH HELL
OUT OF HIM ANY DAY!"
UNION GEN. PHILIP SHERIDAN

"I HAD RATHER DIE
THAN BE WHIPPED."
CAVALRY COMMANDER JEB STUART

Union Cavalry *Chief Maj. Gen. Philip Sheridan stands proudly at center with his division commanders (left to right): Henry Davies, Jr., David Gregg, Wesley Merritt, Alfred Torbert, and James Wilson. By 1864, Northern cavalrymen were on a par with Confederate horsemen.*

Carnage at Cold Harbor

Few place names associated with the Civil War have more chilling overtones than Cold Harbor. A crossroads ten miles northeast of Richmond, it was the site of an old tavern, said to be "cold" because it offered no hot meals to guests harbored there. But what chilled the hearts of Union soldiers who survived the battle here on June 3, 1864, was the memory of a half hour of systematic slaughter, which cut down more men per minute than any other bloodbath in this entire conflict.

For the past month, Grant had been trying to slip around Lee and come between his army and Richmond. Time and again, Lee blocked his way, resulting in heavy losses for both sides, first in the Wilderness and later at Spotsylvania. A determined Grant then made an unusually wide sweep in an effort to seize the Cold Harbor intersection and control roads leading to Richmond. Yet Lee again moved adeptly and beat his opponent to that crossroads.

No general could match Lee when it came to building field fortifications, and his troops labored furiously. In a few days, they constructed a six-mile network of trenches, ramparts, and gun emplacements, as strong as any defensive works produced on the eve of battle during the war.

When Grant reached Cold Harbor and saw Confederates digging in, he mistakenly concluded that Lee's army was losing heart and on the verge of defeat. After two days of sporadic fighting, he ordered a major attack at dawn the next morning against the center of the enemy line.

On the night of June 2, Union soldiers huddled in the rain, awaiting a battle that few thought they could win and many doubted they would survive. One of Grant's aides saw men calmly writing their names and addresses on slips of paper and pinning them to their coats, "so that their dead bodies might

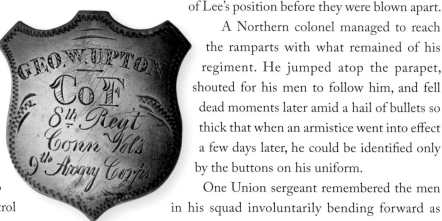

Proof of Identity *This engraved silver badge belonged to Connecticut soldier George W. Upton, who was mortally wounded at Cold Harbor.*

be recognized upon the field, and their fate made known to their families at home."

Their fears were well founded. As Federals swept forward on June 3, Confederate cannon and musketry opened with one unceasing roar. A Union observer described the assaults as "a wild chain of doomed charges, most of which were smashed in five or ten minutes." Few Federal units got to within 50 yards of Lee's position before they were blown apart.

A Northern colonel managed to reach the ramparts with what remained of his regiment. He jumped atop the parapet, shouted for his men to follow him, and fell dead moments later amid a hail of bullets so thick that when an armistice went into effect a few days later, he could be identified only by the buttons on his uniform.

One Union sergeant remembered the men in his squad involuntarily bending forward as they charged, as if they were moving into a driving rainstorm instead of concentrated musketry. Another soldier involved in the attack saw all of his companions suddenly drop to the ground. He thought that an officer had ordered them to lie down, so he did the same, only to discover that all those lying beside him had been killed in one blast of gunfire.

Never before or after in this war were assaults broken up as quickly—or men killed as rapidly—as at Cold Harbor. The Union army suffered some 7,000 casualties, most of them in the space of 30 minutes. Confederate Gen. Evander Law had witnessed many scenes of carnage at Fredericksburg, Manassas, and other battlefields. "But I had seen nothing to exceed this," he wrote. "It was not war; it was murder."

Cold Harbor haunted Grant to his grave. "I regret this assault more than any one I have ever ordered," he wrote that evening. Twenty years later, ailing and near death, he expressed the same remorse in his memoirs. ★

"ONE OF GRANT'S AIDES SAW MEN CALMLY WRITING THEIR NAMES AND ADDRESSES ON SLIPS OF PAPER AND PINNING THEM TO THEIR COATS, 'SO THAT THEIR DEAD BODIES MIGHT BE RECOGNIZED UPON THE FIELD, AND THEIR FATE MADE KNOWN TO THEIR FAMILIES AT HOME.'"

Launching a Bloodbath *Grant, shown here with his staff at his City Point, Virginia, headquarters, ordered the army to break through the Confederate earthworks at Cold Harbor. Federal troops launched a series of desperate attacks, including the assault of the 164th New York depicted in the sketch at top.*

"I REGRET THIS ASSAULT
MORE THAN ANY I HAVE
EVER ORDERED."
ULYSSES S. GRANT

Recovering the Dead
*Grant's six-week campaign
from the Wilderness to
Petersburg brought Union
forces back to the battlefields
of General McClellan's
1862 Peninsular
Campaign. Burial details
including black laborers
were sent to recover bodies
of Federal soldiers who had
been hastily interred
in shallow graves by the
victorious Confederates
two years before.*

Civil War Oddities

Little things often make big impressions on our minds. Robert E. Lee is remembered for a host of achievements. But the fact that he wore a size 4½ C shoe is something that, once learned, is not easily forgotten. Union Gen. Ambrose Burnside may be better known for his sideburns—a term that originated as a play on his name—than for anything he accomplished as a commander during the conflict. Amid the annals of the Civil War are many small but engaging oddities that help make that conflict more personal and memorable.

For example, the mammoth 128-volume Official Records of the Union and Confederate Armies contains thousands of reports, describing battles and troop movements in encyclopedic detail. Hidden in the accounts of Gen. William T. Sherman's Atlanta campaign in 1864 is this unforgettable anecdote. "General," a division commander wrote Sherman, "Col. Brownlow performed one of his characteristic feats today. I had ordered a detachment to cross at Cochran's Ford. It was deep, and Brownlow took his men over naked, they wearing nothing but guns, cartridge-boxes, and hats. They drove the enemy out of their rifle-pits, captured a non-commissioned officer and three men . . . They would have got more, but the rebels had the advantage of running through the bushes with their clothes on."

Near Washington, D.C., around the same time, occurred another unusual confrontation. A Confederate army was threatening the capital. One afternoon, President Lincoln inspected the city's defenses. He climbed atop a parapet and began looking at the enemy in the distance. A Union captain rode down the line and, not recognizing the civilian, shouted: "Get down from there, you damned fool, or you'll get killed!"

General Lee's Boots *Lee wore tall cavalry boots, with protective knee guards, while on campaign. Despite his small feet, he was a competent horseman.*

Lincoln climbed down with a smile. The two men never met again. The Union officer had a long and eventful postwar career, but he never forgot that fleeting moment when he scolded his commander-in-chief. The captain was future Supreme Court Justice Oliver Wendell Holmes, Jr.

Another Union soldier who achieved notoriety after the war was Albert D. J. Cashier of the 95th Illinois, who enlisted in 1862 at the age of 19 and saw much action in the Western theater. Not until long after the conflict ended did a startling revelation come to light: Albert was a woman, born Jennie Hodgers in Ireland before emigrating to America as a stowaway. She was not the only female to conceal her gender and fight in the Civil War, but few kept the secret as long as she did. Her true identity remained hidden until she was hit by a car in 1910 and hospitalized.

If a hard-luck award were offered for those caught up in the war, Wilmer McLean would be a likely candidate. This Virginia farmer owned land near Manassas when war began. On July 1861, his farm became part of the war's first battleground. McLean sought peace, so he packed up his family and moved south to a small, quiet, isolated community in Appomattox County. Four years later, armies marched again onto McLean's property. It was in the front parlor of his home at Appomattox Court House that Grant and Lee signed documents ending the great struggle. Like many Civil War–era figures, McLean was credited with a memorable saying that he may never have spoken but should have: "The war began in my front yard and ended in my front parlor." ✶

Woman Soldier in 95th Ill.

ALBERT D. J. CASHIER
OF
COMPANY G, 95TH ILLINOIS REGIMENT

Photographed November, 1864

ALBERT D. J. CASHIER
OF
COMPANY G, 95TH ILLINOIS REGIMENT

Photographed July, 1913

Woman in Disguise
The soldier known as Albert Cashier successfully concealed her true sex for a half century. This newspaper clipping shows Cashier as a Union recruit and in old age.

Memorable Muttonchops
Gen. Ambrose Burnside's spectacular whiskers inspired the popular term "sideburns."

"ANOTHER UNION SOLDIER WHO ACHIEVED NOTORIETY AFTER THE WAR WAS ALBERT D. J. CASHIER OF THE 95TH ILLINOIS, WHO ENLISTED IN 1862 AT THE AGE OF 19 AND SAW MUCH ACTION IN THE WESTERN THEATER. NOT UNTIL LONG AFTER THE CONFLICT ENDED DID A STARTLING REVELATION COME TO LIGHT: ALBERT WAS A WOMAN, BORN JENNIE HODGERS IN IRELAND BEFORE EMIGRATING TO AMERICA AS A STOWAWAY."

The Little Mascot

One of the Union army's most faithful and devoted comrades did not wear a uniform or carry a musket.

The war had just begun, and a new regiment was training at the fairground in West Chester, Pennsylvania. A civilian came into camp with a wicker basket and presented it to one of the officers. The captain reached inside and, with a smile, withdrew a pug-nosed, black female terrier scarcely four weeks old. When placed on the ground, the puppy toddled about on clumsy legs.

In the weeks that followed, the dog won hundreds of new friends in uniform. Each could be counted on to give her a pat or a morsel of food. The soldiers named her after one of the local beauties in West Chester and made Sallie the official mascot of the 11th Pennsylvania Infantry Regiment.

The little terrier soon developed a distinct personality. Sallie was even tempered and affectionate with members of the regiment but disdained all civilians and strangers, whether male or female. She was clean in her habits and proud in her bearing.

Sallie knew the drumroll announcing reveille. She was first out of quarters to attend roll call. During drills, she latched on to a particular soldier and pranced alongside him throughout the exercise. At dress parade, the dog marched proudly beside the regimental colors. At encampments, she slept by the captain's tent after strolling leisurely through the grounds on her own kind of inspection.

Her first battle came in 1862 at Cedar Mountain. Sallie remained with the colors throughout the engagement. She did the same at Antietam, Fredericksburg, and Chancellorsville.

"SALLIE RECEIVED HIGH TRIBUTE IN THE SPRING OF 1863 WHEN PRESIDENT LINCOLN REVIEWED THE ARMY OF THE POTOMAC AND SAW THE DOG MARCHING ALONGSIDE THE 11TH PENNSYLVANIA. WITH A TWINKLE IN HIS EYE, HE RAISED HIS STOVEPIPE HAT IN SALUTE."

Sallie, Mascot of the 11th Pennsylvania

No one ever thought of sending Sallie to the rear in time of combat. She was the regiment's guardian and inspiration. And she would not willingly have stayed in the rear anyway.

Sallie received high tribute in the spring of 1863 when President Lincoln reviewed the Army of the Potomac and saw the dog marching alongside the 11th Pennsylvania. With a twinkle in his eye, he raised his stovepipe hat in salute. On the first day's fighting at Gettysburg that summer, the regiment was driven back a mile from its original position. Sallie disappeared in the smoke and chaos. Three days later, she was found on the battleground, unharmed, standing guard amid her wounded and dead comrades.

The following May at Spotsylvania, Sallie received her "red badge of courage" in the form of a neck wound. As the war neared its conclusion, she spent a restless night with her regiment at Petersburg, awaiting the battle that began there early on February 5, 1865. The 11th Pennsylvania made a concerted attack that morning at Hatcher's Run. Men in the second wave were advancing under heavy fire when they found Sallie on the battlefield. She had been shot through the head and killed instantly. Weeping soldiers buried the little dog where it lay on the battlefield.

In 1890, surviving veterans of the 11th Pennsylvania dedicated a monument at Gettysburg. From afar, it looks like most other regimental memorials: a bronze statue of a defiant soldier standing atop a tall and ornate marble pedestal. Near the base of the monument, however, on a small ledge, lies the bronze likeness of a dog. Sallie appears to be sleeping. She rests there peacefully, reunited in spirit with men of her beloved regiment who died here defending their state and country. ★

Faithful unto Death *Grace, the mascot of the Confederate Second Maryland Battalion, is shown running ahead of the men of her unit as they attack Federals on Culp's Hill at Gettysburg in this painting by Peter Rothermel. Like Sallie, Grace was killed in battle. Union Gen. Thomas Kane ordered that she be given decent burial "as the only Christian-minded being on either side."*

The Fall of Richmond

Nothing during the war quite matched what happened here that April evening. It was Dante's *Inferno* come to life. Pandemonium, lawlessness, dejection, helplessness—all overwhelmed in one terrible night what were perhaps the proudest people in the Confederacy, the citizens of Richmond, Virginia.

Shortly before noon on April 2, 1865, Robert E. Lee informed President Jefferson Davis that the Petersburg defenses, impenetrable for nine months, had snapped under heavy Union attacks. That meant Richmond was doomed. The Confederacy was about to lose its capital, its cultural center, and its industrial hub, whose railroads, docks, and manufacturing plants constituted an asset unmatched anywhere else in the South. Back in 1861, a Confederate official newly arrived in Richmond had been dazzled by what he called "this glorious old city" and declared that it embodied "the fullest expressions of the highest type of civilization America has ever seen."

Richmond stood valiant and unconquered for four years, resisting all Union efforts to seize it. Now suddenly it lay defenseless. What remained of the Confederate government departed for safety, leaving a once beautiful city to suffer defilement.

Mobs spilled into the streets. Looters broke into stores and made off with everything they could carry. Government commissioners had poured barrels of whiskey into the streets. It flowed for blocks in the gutters, to the delight of rampagers who scooped it up with hands or dippers. Criminal elements feasted on Richmond, one observer noted, "like fierce, ferocious beasts." And the worst was yet to come.

Freedmen in Richmond *The fall of the Confederate capital in April 1865 brought these former slaves freedom and left part of the city in ruins (right).*

Confederate officials had ordered that large warehouses filled with tobacco and other valuable commodities be burned to prevent their capture by the enemy. The fires began in mid-afternoon and were fanned by strong winds. Soon all of downtown Richmond was engulfed in flames.

Young Sallie Putnam lived with her parents in the capital. The fires spread "with fearful rapidity," she wrote. "The roaring, the hissing, and the crackling of the flames were heard above the shouting and confusion of the immense crowd of plunderers who were moving amid the dense smoke like demons…From the lower portion of the city, near the river, dense black clouds of smoke arose as a pall." Beneath that dark shroud, she added, lurked "devouring flames, which lifted their red tongues and leaped from building to building as if possessed of demonic instinct, and intent upon wholesale destruction."

It was a savage, sleepless night in Richmond. Fire converted 20 square blocks into a waste of smoking ruins, blackened walls, and lonely chimneys. The devastation would have been even greater save for one of the most profound paradoxes of the war. On the morning of April 3, the first Federal forces arrived and entered the chaos of Richmond. Homeless women, children, and old men were huddled in Capitol Square. They were too much in shock to react to the presence of Federal soldiers. Similarly, the men in blue were too stunned by gutted avenues and smoldering buildings to give heed to the needy. Officers shouted quick commands, and Northern soldiers became Southern firefighters. Their day-long efforts, under the most hazardous conditions, spared the city from total destruction.

The Union men who saved Richmond—one of the last bastions of the old slaveholding South—were members of the XXIII Corps, a unit composed largely of black soldiers. ✶

"CRIMINAL ELEMENTS
FEASTED ON RICHMOND,
ONE OBSERVER NOTED,
'LIKE FIERCE, FEROCIOUS
BEASTS.' AND THE WORST
WAS YET TO COME."

"The Silent Witness"

On April 9, 1865, Robert E. Lee surrendered to Ulysses S. Grant in the front parlor of Wilmer McLean's home at Appomattox Court House. In addition to Lee and Grant, 18 other officers were in the room, looking on as the Civil War in Virginia came to an end. Another witness to that dramatic scene on Palm Sunday went largely unnoticed—a silent witness, unable to speak, hear, or see.

Wilmer McLean had a seven-year-old daughter named Lucretia. Everyone called the child "Lula." Her most prized possession was a rag doll, roughly a foot tall and dressed like a girl. The doll's hairless head had a painted face, blurred by many tears and kisses from a child experiencing the confusion and dis-location of war.

On that sunny April morning, Lula was playing with her doll in the corner of the front parlor when shouts were heard and hundreds of Union soldiers began gathering in the front yard. An important meeting was about to take place in her home. Her father hastily collected the family and sought ref-uge at a friend's house. All their household furnishings were left behind—including the rag doll on the parlor floor. There it lay through the meeting as the two opposing army commanders negoti-ated an end to their conflict.

Among the Union officers who sat on the steps of the front porch while the talks proceeded was 21-year-old Capt. Robert Todd Lincoln, the President's son and a member of Grant's staff. After the surrender, the officers rushed into the room to obtain souvenirs, making off with a pencil, a table, candlesticks, and other possessions of the McLeans.

Someone saw the doll on the floor. One Federal laughingly tossed it about like a ball.

Witness to History *This rag doll was in the room when Lee surrendered to Grant.*

They dubbed it "The Silent Witness," wishing they could have been as fortunate to observe what the doll had beheld. The fact that this was a child's precious keepsake did not save it from being carried off as a trophy. Eventually, Gen. Philip Sheridan, the Union cavalry chief, gained possession of the doll. Sheridan gave it to an aide, Capt. Thomas W. C. Moore, who returned home to New York after the war with his treasured souvenir. At his death, his son Richard inherited the doll and kept it in a glass case in the library of his Long Island home.

The McLean House was eventually restored. It opened to the public in April 1950. Few of the original furnishings were there. The table at which Lee signed the surrender docu-ment, for example, remained the property of the Chicago Historical Society. Lula McLean's rag doll was not there either. It still belonged to the Moore family. Years after Richard Moore's death in 1952, however, his widow made an unannounced visit to Appomattox Court House National Historical Park. She was impressed by the careful restoration of the village and the park's devoted staff. She decided to bequeath the doll to the house from which it had been taken long ago.

In 1993, National Park Service Ranger Joe Williams brought the doll from New York to Appomattox. Its features were now barely discernible. Yet the unbleached burlap body, head of woven cotton fabric, and floral print bodice were still in remarkably good condition.

Appropriately, "The Silent Witness" first went on display on Memorial Day that year. The old-est and tiniest Confederate prisoner of war had at last come home. ✶

"ON THAT SUNNY
APRIL MORNING, LULA WAS
PLAYING WITH HER DOLL
IN THE CORNER OF THE FRONT
PARLOR WHEN SHOUTS WERE
HEARD AND HUNDREDS OF UNION
SOLDIERS BEGAN GATHERING
IN THE FRONT YARD . . .
HER FATHER HASTILY COLLECTED
THE FAMILY AND SOUGHT
REFUGE AT A FRIEND'S HOUSE.
ALL THEIR HOUSEHOLD
FURNISHINGS WERE LEFT BEHIND—
INCLUDING THE RAG DOLL
ON THE PARLOR FLOOR."

War's End *The meeting between Lee and Grant lasted less than two hours. Several Union officers, including Sheridan, Custer, and Grant's military secretary, Ely Parker, looked on as Lee, accompanied by a single aide, signed the terms of surrender.*

Camp Mess *Union soldiers cluster in front of their mud-daubed log cookhouse in winter quarters near Falls Church, Virginia, in 1863. One soldier stands with an axe in front of empty salt meat barrels.*

THE FIGHTING IRISH

Few Irish immigrants in the North welcomed the Civil War. They had their own battles to fight, toiling at hard jobs that paid so little, some called the Irish and other Northern laborers wage slaves. Freeing slaves in the South, they worried, might result in blacks flooding the North and competing for those low-paying jobs. Yet when war became stern reality, Irishmen flocked to enlist. Nearly 150,000 joined the Union ranks, bringing with them a fighting spirit that was evident in camp as well as on the battlefield.

(See "At Home in the Army," pages 92-93.)

TARHEELS AT WAR

North Carolina service records offer many insights into the life of Civil War soldiers. Lt. Silas Beck died after eating a poisoned apple. Musician Thomas Ballard was mistaken for a bear and shot dead while brushing his teeth in a moonlit creek. Cpl. Thomas Cabe was captured and went insane amid the squalor of Camp Douglas Prison. Artilleryman Edward Cooper deserted after receiving a desperate appeal for help from his wife and was court-martialed. (See "Duty and Desertion," pages 142-3.)

WELL-WORN SHOES

The ankle-high Federal army shoe, or "bootee," introduced in 1859, was relatively light in weight and made of leather with the rough side out. Army shoes were produced by hundreds of Northern contractors in a wide range of quality. Many soldiers received ill-fitting shoes that caused them pain. One Pennsylvanian complained that the shoes he was issued were "much too large in every way . . . They are wide enough to contain both of my feet." (See "The Problem With Shoes," pages 102-103.)

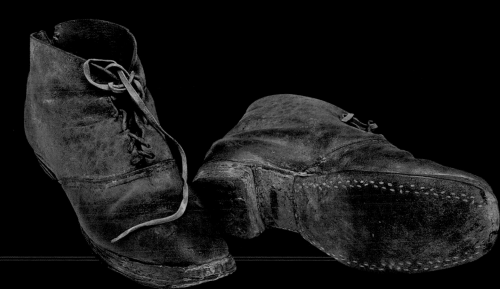

Billy Yank and Johnny Reb

The common soldiers of the Civil War were men of every shape, size, and sort. Many regiments were fairly uniform, consisting largely of farmers, or students, or members of a particular ethnic group, but others were remarkably diverse. The 19th Virginia, for example, from the Piedmont region east of the Blue Ridge, started out with 749 men on its roster, of whom 302 were farmers, 80 were laborers, and 56 were machinists. Among the remainder were 10 attorneys, 14 teachers, 24 students, 3 blacksmiths, 2 artists, a well digger, and 4 self-described "gentlemen."

The average Civil War soldier was five feet, seven inches tall and weighed 135 pounds. He was Protestant, single, and about 20 years old. That was the norm for Billy Yank (the typical Union soldier) and Johnny Reb (his Confederate counterpart), but recruits on both sides covered a broad spectrum. Boys often marched alongside men old enough to be their fathers. Many youngsters served as drummer boys, but David Scanlon of the Fourth Virginia was a drummer at the age of 52.

Charles C. Hay was probably the youngest Confederate. He enlisted in an Alabama regiment at the age of 11. The youngest "blue baby" (as underage Union recruits were termed) was Edward Black of Indianapolis, who was nine when he joined his father in the ranks as a musician. Although 18 was supposedly the minimum age for soldiers on both sides, many boys in their early teens fought and fell. At Shiloh in 1862, 15-year-old John Roberts of Tennessee went down twice after being hit by spent bullets and had his musket blown to pieces in his hands. Roberts's colonel praised the lad for displaying "the coolness and courage of a veteran."

"INDIANA'S DAVID VAN BUSKIRK ROSE TO A WHOPPING 6 FEET 11 INCHES. IN 1862 VAN BUSKIRK WAS CAPTURED AND SENT TO A RICHMOND PRISON. THE 380-POUND CAPTAIN AGREED TO BE DISPLAYED AS 'THE BIGGEST YANKEE IN THE WORLD.'"

Union infantry cap badge

At the far end of the spectrum were a number of men in their 60s and a few who were even older. One elderly Confederate, E. Pollard of the Fifth North Carolina, claimed to be 62 but was probably more than 70 when he died, a month after enlisting. The oldest Civil War soldier was Curtis King, who served briefly with other "graybeards" in an Iowa home guard regiment at the age of 80.

Height also varied greatly in the ranks. Confederate Gen. James Longstreet stood six feet, two inches tall, while Union Gen. Philip "Little Phil" Sheridan was nearly a foot shorter. One soldier in the Tenth Rhode Island was only 4 feet 11. "His first pair of army drawers reached to his chin," a messmate quipped. "This he considers very economical, as it saves the necessity of [wearing] shirts."

The shortest Union soldier on record was an Ohioan who stood 40 inches in his stocking feet.

Two such men standing atop one another would not have matched the tallest known Billy Yank. Indiana's David Van Buskirk rose to a whopping 6 feet 11 inches. In 1862 Van Buskirk was captured and sent to a Richmond prison. The 380-pound captain agreed to be displayed as "the biggest Yankee in the world."

The tallest Confederate was Martin Van Buren Bates of Kentucky. He stood over six feet when he enlisted in September 1861 at the age of 15 and was still growing at a prodigious rate. Bates topped out in his 20s at a phenomenal 7 feet 11½ inches. In 1871, he married Anna Hanen Swan, the so-called Giantess of Nova Scotia, and lived with her in a house built expressly for them, with 14-foot-high ceilings. Just how tall Bates was when he left the army remains unclear, but one thing is certain: He was the tallest Civil War veteran. ✯

Exceptional Soldiers
The tallest Civil War veteran, former Confederate Martin Bates, poses in an 1870s photo with Anna Swan and their agent. Ages of Civil War soldiers ran the spectrum, from nine-year-old drummer Edward Black to men a few generations older (below).

*Edward Black,
21st Indiana*

Unknown elderly soldier

At Home in the Army

"Home" for Civil War troops was their regiment, in which they took great pride. "Every true soldier," a Billy Yank stated, "holds himself in perpetual readiness to demonstrate that no other regiment ever passed in review so handsomely, marched so far, fought so bravely, or suffered so much, as his own."

State regiments were recruited locally, and its members were often "bound by community, ethnic, and family ties," as one soldier remarked. Theoretically, a regiment consisted of ten 100-man companies. Few regiments had 1,000 men when they entered service, however, and sickness, death, and disability discharges quickly reduced many regiments to half strength. By mid-war, a colonel with a 300-man regiment was considered fortunate.

Many Civil War regiments had unique characteristics that set them apart from the mainstream. All-Irish units in the North such as the 69th New York and 90th Illinois had a feisty reputation, whether battling enemies or themselves. In the war's first summer, a sergeant wrote from camp: "The 7th Missouri, or as it is called, the 'Missouri Irish Brigade,' arrived here yesterday . . . It is said that there are 800 men and the first day they came here there were 900 fights."

Most regiments were cohesive, well-behaved units. The few who were not were conspicuous. In 1862, the adjutant of the Tenth Maine stated of a sister unit: "They can steal more sheep and honey in one day than the 10th can do in a week." One of the more notorious regiments was the 39th New York, a hodgepodge of a half dozen nationalities known as the "Garibaldi Guards." One of its companies mutinied after a few weeks in camp, and its colonel later went to jail.

Recruitment Broadsides

These printed appeals tout the virtues of joining regiments organized in New York and Massachusetts, where men were urged to fight the Rebels.

Many regiments acquired nicknames that were not of their choosing. Men of the Third New Jersey Cavalry were known mockingly as "the Flying Butterflies" for their gaudy uniforms. The 14th Iowa Infantry was dubbed the "Temperance Regiment" because all soldiers solemnly pledged at the outset to "touch not, taste not, handle not, spirituous or malt liquor, wine or cider." Later in the war, members of the regiment violated that oath, one veteran admitted, but only for use as a stimulant when "under the overruling power of military necessity." The 23rd Pennsylvania was called the "Boy Regiment" because most of its soldiers were in their teens. Faculty from the Illinois State Normal College dominated the officer corps of the 33rd Illinois. Known as the "Teacher Regiment," it was said to obey only those orders that were correct in grammar and syntax.

The 26th Alabama, made up of poor farmers who had no uniforms and wore patchwork blankets over their shoulders, was dubbed the "Bed Quilt Regiment." That was not as bad as the title foisted on the 21st Indiana Heavy Artillery, which had the misfortune to enter service with mules rather than horses pulling its guns. Despite a sterling war record, those Hoosiers forever bore the label "Jackass Regiment."

Some units became legendary for the terrible losses they suffered. No Civil War regiment fared worse than the First Minnesota, which lost 85 percent of its men to death or injuries in one day at Gettysburg. The First Texas lost 82 percent of its strength at Antietam. Five Virginia regiments composed the celebrated Stonewall Brigade. Some 6,000 men served in those regiments during the course of the war. At Appomattox, only 210 were left—none above the rank of captain. ✮

> "EVERY TRUE SOLDIER
> HOLDS HIMSELF IN
> PERPETUAL READINESS
> TO DEMONSTRATE THAT
> NO OTHER REGIMENT
> EVER PASSED IN REVIEW
> SO HANDSOMELY,
> MARCHED SO FAR,
> FOUGHT SO BRAVELY,
> OR SUFFERED SO MUCH
> AS HIS OWN."
>
> **UNION SOLDIER**

Willing Westerners *Many enlistees came from west of the Mississippi River. Veterans of the Eighth Kansas Infantry strike a belligerent pose near Chattanooga, Tennessee, in 1863.*

With God's Grace *Soldiers of Col. Patrick Kelly's Irish Brigade kneel to receive absolution from their Catholic chaplain before an attack on the second day at Gettysburg. The brigade of Massachusetts, New York, and Pennsylvania volunteers suffered 202 casualties in the ensuing fight.*

Families at War

The Civil War divided some families and devastated others. In many tragic instances, it left irreplaceable vacancies at the dinner table.

Family honor was a powerful force in 19th-century America. For many men, defending family was a higher obligation than defending state or country. Robert E. Lee, in declining command of the Union army, said he could not "raise my hand against my relatives, my children, my home." Strong family ties existed on both sides. The 24th Michigan contained 135 sets of brothers. The 15th Wisconsin, a predominantly Norwegian unit, had dozens of men named Ole Olson. The perplexed colonel finally brought order out of chaos by officially numbering each man.

Southerners helped overcome the numerical superiority of the North by contributing many members of the same family to Confederate forces. Ten sons and five sons-in-law of the Bledsoe family of Mississippi wore the gray. Mrs. Enoch Cook of Alabama watched a husband, ten sons, and two grandsons depart for military service.

The Stonewall Brigade was called the Commonwealth of Virginia's "cousinwealth." Families in the Shenandoah Valley and southwest Virginia sent so many fathers, sons, brothers, cousins, and nephews into the army that the muster rolls resembled genealogical tables. One company of the Fifth Virginia had 18 members of the Bell family. Six were killed in action; five died of disease. David Barton of Winchester gave six sons to Jackson's brigade. Two were killed and two permanently injured. Three Sexton brothers and a cousin served in the Fourth Virginia. All died in battle or in prison. Four Timberlake brothers enlisted together in the Stonewall Brigade. Three were crippled

Siblings in Arms *Brothers Daniel, John, and Pleasant Chitwood served in the 23rd Georgia Infantry. Pleasant died in a Richmond hospital in 1862 and Daniel and John were captured at Chancellorsville.*

for life. Four Carpenter brothers served in an artillery battery led by the oldest brother, Joseph. He fell in 1862. Brother John succeeded to command and lost an arm in 1864. A bullet in the lung left the third sibling permanently impaired. The fourth brother had a leg amputated in the struggle's closing months.

Such family sacrifices were not limited to the Confederate side. In December 1861, 64-year-old David Wescott enlisted in a New York regiment. So did two of his sons, 22-year-old Orlando and 16-year-old Philetus. Orlando died of typhoid fever after six months in service. The heartbroken father was discharged because of "age and sickness," his personnel record states. He barely made it home in time to die. Philetus received a discharge so that he could care for his bereft mother, who died shortly thereafter.

Family ties often snapped in border states like Virginia and Kentucky, where opinion was divided on slavery and the merits of secession. Mary Todd Lincoln had three brothers in Kentucky who served as Confederate officers while her husband led the Union war effort against them. Union Gen. Philip St. George Cooke of Virginia fought against two relatives: his son-in-law, Gen. Jeb Stuart, and his nephew, Lt. John Esten Cooke. Kentucky Senator John Crittenden had two sons who became generals—on opposite sides. A similar fate befell the father of James and William Terrell of Virginia, who became Confederate and Union brigadiers respectively. One died in battle in 1862; the other was killed two years later. Legend has it that the grieving father buried the brothers in a single grave, over which he placed a marker with the epitaph: "Here lie my two sons. Only God knows which one was right." ✯

"A HOUSE DIVIDED AGAINST ITSELF CANNOT STAND."

ABRAHAM LINCOLN

Rebel Kinfolk *Mary Todd Lincoln, shown at right in a photograph taken in the 1840s, lost several relatives during the Civil War. When her half sister's husband, Confederate Gen. Benjamin Hardin Helm, was killed in 1863, she welcomed the bereaved Emily Todd Helm in the White House without reproach for her loyalty to the South.*

Brothers at War *Liberated former slaves gather on the Port Royal, South Carolina, estate of Confederate Gen. Thomas Drayton. Thomas's brother, Union naval commander Percival Drayton, participated in the expedition that seized the estate and freed his brother's slaves.*

"Liberty Hall Volunteers"

In the Lee Chapel at Washington and Lee University, a tarnished plaque pays tribute to college students of another time, many of whom perished before completing their education. They belonged to Company I of the Fourth Virginia Infantry Regiment. Known as the Liberty Hall Volunteers for the Revolutionary War–era academy from which Washington and Lee evolved, they were among the best of the Civil War's "college companies."

The unit formed soon after Virginia seceded. Fifty-seven of the company's original 73 members were students at what was then Washington College. A fourth of them were studying for the ministry. They may well have been, as one authority declared, "the most educated infantry company" in the Confederacy.

Their average age was 20, and many were still boys, with little exposure to the world and its ways. Most were from the Shenandoah Valley and had grown up in a strict Calvinistic environment. Their first captain was James J. White, a 32-year-old Greek professor at the college known to his young recruits as "Old Zeus."

Brimming with enthusiasm and utterly lacking in experience, the little band departed for war. Patriotic ladies in the community outfitted the company completely, down to their undergarments, including red flannel waistbands, to be worn next to the skin to ward off diarrhea—an affliction few soldiers avoided, no matter what precautions they took. The boys also had a flag donated by the local Presbyterian church and inscribed with the Latin motto *Pro Aris et Focis*: "For Altar and Home."

Seven of the lads died in the opening battle at Manassas. For a year thereafter, the company served as headquarters guard for Stonewall Jackson. The boys took their job seriously until

Lost Banner *The battle flag of the Fourth Virginia was captured by Union troops in 1864. Liberty Hall Volunteers like the soldier portrayed at right formed Company I of the Fourth Virginia.*

late one evening, when a sentry started whistling and the rest joined in. Their shrill concert awakened Jackson, who stepped from his tent and "squelched it," as one youngster recalled.

Following Jackson's triumphant Valley Campaign in the spring of 1862, the Liberty Hall Volunteers joined their commander in defending Richmond and went on to fight under Robert E. Lee in some of the war's bloodiest battles.

Their esteemed leader, Capt. Hugh White, brother of James White and son of Jackson's pastor in Lexington, was killed at Second Manassas while leading a charge with the flag of the Fourth Virginia in hand. Also slain in that battle was "Willie" Preston, the 17-year-old son of one of Jackson's closest friends. In a rare show of emotion, Jackson walked away in tears when told of young Preston's death.

At Chancellorsville, 16 members of the company fell wounded. Only 21 remained when the army reached Gettysburg. In the second day of fighting there, the Liberty Hall Volunteers ran out of ammunition while under attack on three sides. Some fell; others surrendered. Only three men escaped. One of them was teenager Theodore Barclay, who wrote home: "I would like to survive the conflict. I would like to see our land free . . . but if I am to fall, God help me to say, 'Thy will be done.'"

Replacements partially replenished the ranks, but by late 1864 the company was again reduced to a precious few—a lieutenant and two privates. That trio surrendered with Lee at Appomattox.

Of 181 members of the company, 26 were killed in action, 58 died of disease or other causes, and many others were wounded or captured. True to their upbringing, no original member of this "college company" was ever punished for misconduct. ✭

"I WOULD LIKE TO
SURVIVE THE CONFLICT,
I WOULD LIKE TO SEE
OUR LAND FREE . . .
BUT IF I AM TO FALL,
GOD HELP ME TO SAY,
'THY WILL BE DONE.'"

**THEODORE BARCLAY,
TEENAGE MEMBER OF THE
LIBERTY HALL VOLUNTEERS**

Un-uniform Uniforms

The Civil War did not begin as a struggle between Blue and Gray. At the start of the conflict, every conceivable type of uniform existed in the Northern and Southern armies.

A dozen or more regiments appeared for duty dressed in gaudy Zouave attire, modeled after uniforms worn in French North Africa. The outfit consisted of a short, dark blue, collarless jacket with red trim, sleeveless vest, baggy red trousers and woolen sash, white canvas leggings, a tasseled red fez, and turban. One reporter observed: "It is a dress which gives the human figure a barbaric picturesqueness." Such garb had disadvantages. It drew ridicule from conventionally attired soldiers, who mocked Zouaves for wearing "bloomers." In the wear-and-tear of army life, their uniforms were the first to look soiled and seedy. Not even thick battle smoke could hide the bright colors from opposing marksmen. Most soldiers during the war advanced in clear view of the enemy, however. Zouaves reckoned that if they were destined to die, they would at least go out in style.

Other units went to war in the heavy, antique garb of ancient militia organizations. In some Northern regiments, each of the ten companies wore different uniforms. Both sides in 1861 had units clothed in blue as well as gray. Every shape and form of hat was initially in evidence, from the snappy French-inspired kepi to towering stovepipe hats.

Most uniforms were made of wool and worn year-round. They were soaked repeatedly with perspiration and covered with nature's elements but were rarely washed because the clothing would shrink and no longer fit.

> "AT THE START OF THE CONFLICT, EVERY CONCEIVABLE TYPE OF UNIFORM EXISTED IN THE NORTHERN AND SOUTHERN ARMIES."

Capt. James A. Holeman,
24th North Carolina, captured in 1865

By the time of the first winter encampment, uniforms were a far cry from their original appearance. Exposure to all kinds of weather without anything akin to a full change of clothing soon reduced most soldiers to some stage of raggedness. "Our uniforms at this time would disgrace a beggar," one Union soldier complained in 1862. An Illinois major confessed to his wife: "If you could see me in my rags and dirt as I am now, you would laugh first and then cry." A South Carolina veteran gave a similar report to his spouse concerning his trousers: "They will soon be gone forever, but I am perfectly satisfied that they will go in peace, for there is no doubt of their hol[e]-iness . . . If you were to see me in them, you might mistake me for a zebra, leopard, or something equally outrageous."

How bad was it by 1863? A Louisiana soldier declared after watching the passage of 400 Texas cavalrymen: "If the Confederacy has no better soldiers than those, we are in a bad row for stumps, for they look more like Baboons mounted on goats than anything else."

Union soldiers were more likely than Confederates to receive new uniforms. Initially, the clothing Northern manufacturers produced was made of a flimsy material called shoddy—a term that came to mean cheap or despicable—but the quality of Federal uniforms improved as the war went on.

Most soldiers bore their lot stoically and put up with dirty, ragged clothing as they did other indignities. A Pennsylvanian spoke for many in uniform, however, when he stated in 1864: "If Congressmen at Washington, or the Rebel Congress in Richmond, were required to endure the hardships of a soldier's life during one campaign, the war would then end." ★

ELLSWORTH'S CAMPAIGN & BARRACK OR DRESS UNIFORMS.

PLATE 1.

Eye-catching Garb *French Zouave regiments, wearing a uniform based on the clothing of native Algerians, gained worldwide fame during the Crimean War. The United States Zouave Cadets, the subject of this 1861 lithograph, were organized by Chicago lawyer Elmer E. Ellsworth and were considered the finest militia unit in the Midwest.*

Zouave George F. Murray
of the 114th Pennsylvania served with
the Army of the Potomac.

Thomas Holman of the 13th Tennessee
wears plumed headgear based on the
army dress hat of the period.

Brandishing a huge bowie knife,
an unidentified Georgia volunteer sports an
extravagantly tasseled fatigue cap.

"Rebel Rags" *Virginia artillerist John Blair Royal's gray shell jacket (below) turned tan, or "butternut," with wear. Blair's jacket, issued by the Richmond depot, was made of a cotton-wool mixture called jean. Royal was wounded in the left arm at Chancellorsville.*

Georgia kepi

Confederate slouch hat

Rebel Finery *Replete with a revolver and borrowed officer's sword, Mississippi soldier Alexander "Long Whiskers" Price strikes a stern pose in this ambrotype made early in the war.*

Confederate shell jacket

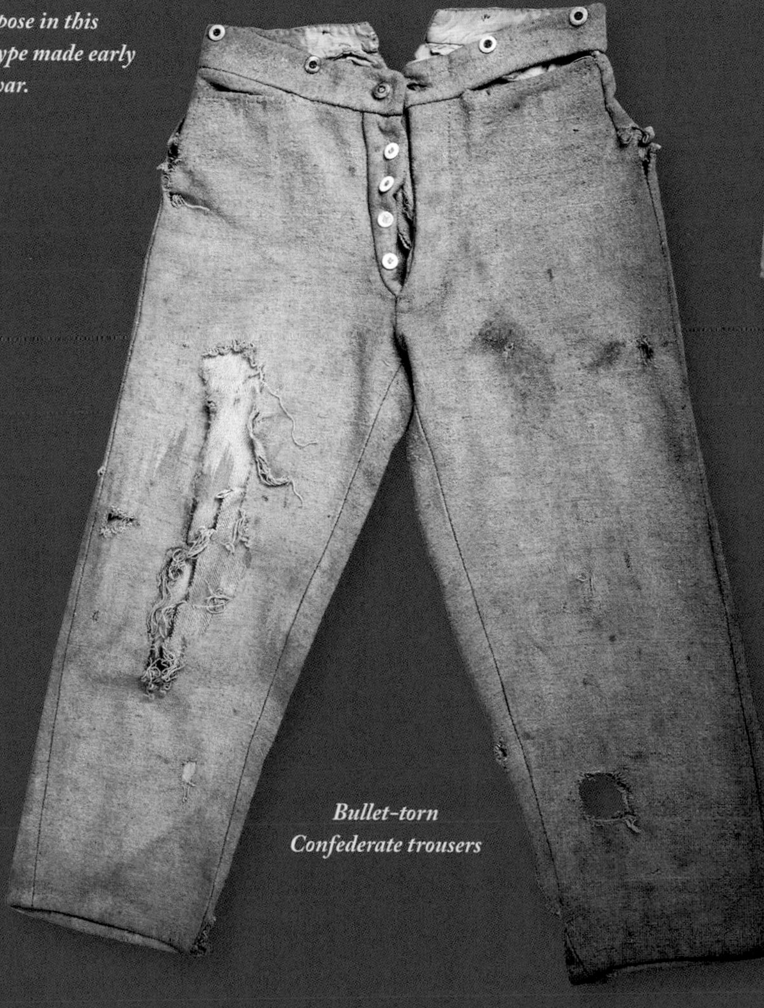

Bullet-torn Confederate trousers

"MOST UNIFORMS WERE MADE OF WOOL AND WORN YEAR-ROUND. THEY WERE SOAKED REPEATEDLY WITH PERSPIRATION AND COVERED WITH NATURE'S ELEMENTS BUT WERE RARELY WASHED BECAUSE THE CLOTHING WOULD SHRINK AND NO LONGER FIT."

Faded Coat of Blue *This young, unidentified Federal wears the Union army's standard four-button fatigue or "sack" coat, probably the most widely issued garment of the war. His hat appears to be a personalized 1858 U.S. Army or "Hardee" hat.*

1858 U.S. Army dress hat

Artillery corporal's sack coat

Forage cap, Union XII Corps

Overcoat of Ezra Carman, 13th New Jersey

Yankee Cloth *By the second year of the war, the output of massive Federal establishments such as the Cincinnati Arsenal and Philadelphia's Schuylkill Arsenal ensured that most Federal soldiers were well clothed.*

Bullet-riddled hat of John Mitchell, 79th Illinois

The Problem With Shoes

Most men who fought for the Union and the Confederacy were foot soldiers, and the most painful deficiency they faced was marching with poor shoes or no shoes. "Posterity will scarcely believe," declared the *Daily Richmond Dispatch* in October 1862, that "terrible marches and desperate battles [were] made by men, one-fourth of whom were entirely barefooted."

The standard army shoe at the outset of hostilities was low-cut and lightweight, with wide soles of cheap leather. Some shoes were shapeless and could be worn on either foot. By one account, their life expectancy was about a month. Not only were many shoes of poor quality; they were often a poor fit. A Louisiana private recalled instances when "No. 6 shoes were gravely provided for No. 10 feet." The reverse was usually the case. A Pennsylvanian found his new shoes "much too large in every way . . . They are wide enough to contain both of my feet." Another Union soldier recalled that "there was always plenty of room to spare in all directions, except in one or two places where they pinched." Soldiers called the clunkers they wore "gunboats" and "pontoons," among other epithets.

Long marches inevitably produced swollen, blistered, and infected feet from ill-fitting shoes. A New Jersey sergeant wrote during the 1862 Fredericksburg campaign that every time his regiment halted and he removed his shoes, he found blood and pus acting as glue between his sock and skin. One of the war's classic quotations came from an unthinking private who, after a long march, wrote his wife: "I am all right except [for] the doggoned blisters on my feet, and I hope these few lines find you enjoying the same blessings."

Even worse than marching in bad shoes was marching without them. Quartermasters were unable to meet the demand. A reporter estimated that 40,000 Confederates lacked shoes when Lee's army invaded Maryland in September 1862. Even allowing for journalistic exaggeration, there can be little doubt that the bare or sore feet of many of Lee's men contributed to their defeat at Antietam. Afterward, a North Carolinian wrote: "One-fifth of Lee's army were barefooted, one-half in rags and the whole of them famished. The marvel of it is that any of us were able [to fight]." Their costly battle at Gettysburg the following summer was triggered when Confederate Gen. Henry Heth heard that shoes were stocked there. "If there is no objection, General," Heth told his commander on June 30, "I will take my division tomorrow and get those shoes."

In Tennessee in late 1864, another Confederate army suffered a crushing defeat at Nashville. It retreated southward through blowing snow. The route was clearly marked by smears of blood in the snow and ice. Things were not a lot better on the Union side. After four weeks of campaigning through Virginia that May, 50,000 soldiers in the Army of the Potomac were in desperate need of shoes.

Some soldiers tried to solve the problem by making crude moccasins from fresh cowhide they obtained from army slaughter pens. Feet wrapped thickly in cowhide "were laughable affairs," one Billy Yank stated, "and put one in mind of the foot of an elephant." A Texan described his wrappings as looking "as big as two 20-pound canvas hams." The ability to laugh at their misfortunes was among the chief assets of the war's foot-sore foot soldiers. ★

"IF THERE IS NO OBJECTION, GENERAL, I WILL TAKE MY DIVISION TOMORROW AND GET THOSE SHOES."

MAJ. GEN. HENRY HETH, BEFORE THE ACTION THAT SPARKED THE BATTLE OF GETTYSBURG

Gift From Home *These half-finished cotton socks were reportedly knitted from unraveled Union tent material. The task was abandoned, with the needles still attached, when news arrived of the war's end.*

Pegged Brogans *Confederate Pvt. M. Page Lapham's shoes feature soles and heels attached with wooden pegs. Less sturdy than stitched footwear, shoes with pegged construction could be more quickly and cheaply produced.*

Edibles and Indigestibles

The army rations doled out during the war did not go down well with soldiers and prompted many complaints. When food was available, it was often poor in quality and monotonous. "Sometimes we had a good meal," a Tennessee soldier recalled, but he and his messmates often "had to buckle up our belts to find whether we possessed stomachs."

Coffee was the soldier's mainstay. Life without it "was misery indeed," an infantryman asserted. Soldiers preferred it black and heavy. As one Billy Yank remarked, coffee should be "strong enough to float an iron wedge and innocent of lacteal adulteration." Prepared in that fashion, it "gave strength to the weary and heavy laden, and courage to the despondent and sick at heart." Soldiers boasted of being able to consume up to four quarts of coffee daily, to the detriment of their kidneys and nervous systems. This "subtle poison," a Maine veteran wrote, was as indispensable to the men as the air they breathed. Confederates could not always obtain coffee and sometimes had to make do with ground peanuts, peas, corn, or other poor substitutes.

Meat rations were skimpy and suspect. Some armies on the march drove cattle along with them, but otherwise beef and pork were in short supply. That may have been for the best, for meat that was not fresh was either subject to spoilage or heavily pickled with salt. Some men consumed their share raw because it tasted the same whether cooked or not. The results were predictable. A Union soldier once declared after an issue of beef: "Every man who had eaten any of the stuff was laid up, and what with the heaving up and the back door trots, we had a sorry time of it."

> "CAMP GOSSIP SAYS THAT THE CRACKERS HAVE BEEN IN STORAGE SINCE THE MEXICAN WAR."
>
> **PENNSYLVANIA SOLDIER**

Hardtack inscribed "Yours Truly"

For their daily bread, Johnny Rebs relied on cornmeal that was coarse, unsifted, and had a consistency when cooked that one soldier likened to rubber. Billy Yanks ate stale, three-inch-square crackers known as hardtack. Some were covered with mold and infested with worms. Others were so dense and dry they resisted rot. "Camp gossip says that the crackers have been in storage since the Mexican War," one Pennsylvania soldier confided to his diary. They were "almost hard as a brick, and undoubtedly would keep for years." A New Yorker finished a meal of hardtack and informed his sweetheart: "Well, I have been to dinner and my teeth have become easier and I will make another stab at writing you." Favorite nicknames for the bread were "sheet-iron crackers," "teeth-dullers," and "worm castles." Many men preferred to eat hardtack in the dark so that they could not see what they were swallowing.

Much of the sickness so prevalent in army camps came from poor rations. Diarrhea, dysentery, and scurvy were attributable to a diet of bad meat, hard bread, and pungent coffee—supplemented on occasion with unripe fruit. Unsanitary practices made things worse. As one Billy Yank confessed, their "mess pans were used to fry our pork in and also as a wash basin. Our soup, coffee and meat were boiled in camp kettles…which were also used for cleaning our clothes."

As poor as their food was, soldiers could not do without it. "Hunger is one thing dreaded more than balls from the enemy guns," an Illinois soldier stated. A Confederate concurred that lack of food was the thing "we suffered from most." Another soldier informed his family: "I am hungry enough to eat a nail." Whatever was placed on their plate, men seized it, swallowed it, and hoped for the best. ★

Taste Test *Federal soldiers crowd around the cook-fire as an officer samples the cooks' offering in this photograph taken early in the war. Some units had assigned cooks while others issued rations to soldiers who organized informal "messes," small groups who cooperated to cook their rations.*

"Old Red Eye"

Before the Civil War was a year old, General McClellan concluded that so many soldiers were rendered unfit by drunkenness that eliminating this "degrading vice" would be worth 50,000 men for the Union army. A few years later, a Massachusetts colonel lamented: "Two-thirds of the troubles which have arisen in our regiment since its formation can be traced to intoxicating liquor alone."

Confederates imbibed to excess as well, but liquor was more abundant in the North, and Union soldiers had more money with which to purchase it. Occasionally, they were issued whiskey in camp. The 22nd Massachusetts bivouacked after a long wintry march and received a whiskey ration that its men did not welcome. "We were temperance to the backbone," one soldier wrote, "yet freezing outwardly, and being dry inwardly, with wet feet and chattering teeth, we hesitated but a brief moment, and then, with a feeling akin to desperation, worried it down."

Soldiers took to liquor for various reasons. Removal of home restraints, the boredom of camp life, fear of the future, loneliness, and the desire to be "one of the boys"—all led soldiers to seek the fleeting euphoria that whiskey offered.

What those men consumed packed a kick that few drinkers ever forgot and some barely survived. Soldiers were known to simmer their liquor over a campfire in hopes of boiling away the fuel oil, turpentine, and other lethal ingredients thought to be lurking there. One authority on the subject has estimated that the bourbon Civil War soldiers consumed was more than 150 proof.

> **"IF CLARENCE HAD BEEN AS FOND OF HIS MOTHER'S MILK AS HE IS OF WHISKEY, HE WOULD HAVE BEEN AWFUL HARD TO WEAN."**
>
> **A LOUISIANA PRIVATE**

The nicknames soldiers applied to their brew testified to its stupefying impact: "Old Red Eye," "Spider Juice," "Pop Skull," "Bust Head," and "Rock Me to Sleep, Mother," to mention just a few. Yet many soldiers could not get enough of that potent and punishing liquor. A Louisiana private said of a messmate: "If Clarence had been as fond of his mother's milk as he is of whiskey, he would have been awful hard to wean." Whiskey had different effects on different nationalities, a Virginia sergeant philosophized. "It induces a Frenchman to talk . . . A German becomes gloomy and morose; an Englishman grows affectionate; four fingers of stone-face whiskey will set an Irishman fighting as surely as St. Patrick was a gentleman." Irishmen had to put up with many such jibes in those days. They were by no means the only ones who took to fighting under the influence of "Pop Skull" or "Bust Head."

Tales of drunkenness among common soldiers were legion. However, officers were just as guilty of overindulgence. In February 1864, Union officers gave a party for their retiring colonel. It ended up "a big drunk," one captain declared. "Such a weaving, spewing, sick set of men I have not seen for many a day . . . Col. Harlan was dead drunk. One Capt., who is a Presbyterian elder at home was not much better." One colonel told of an unnamed Union corps commander who became intoxicated, walked straight into a tree in front of his tent, and then had to be restrained from arresting on charges of felonious assault the officer of the guard who responded alertly to the disturbance he caused.

The drunken behavior of officers, a chaplain sadly concluded, "was the common talk around the campfires, and the men of the rank and file always claimed the privilege of imitating their leaders." ✶

Alabama officer's flask and cup

Drunken soldiers tied up for fighting and other unruly conduct.

Wages of Sin *Unless they were issued whiskey, enlisted men were not allowed to drink liquor in camp and were punished for being drunk and disorderly. Artist Alfred Waud's sketch (top) shows "Drunken soldiers tied up for fighting and other unruly conduct." Officers, however, were permitted judicious use of alcohol, as shown in this photograph of officers of the Third and Fourth Pennsylvania Cavalry, taken at Westover Landing, Virginia, in 1862.*

Picturesque Language

The citizen-soldiers of North and South were not schooled in military terminology like West Point cadets. They came up with their own irreverent figures of speech to describe army life and enshrined that colorful language in letters, diaries, and memoirs.

Many recruits used slang that reflected their rural background. If a soldier fought bravely, for example, he was as "cool as a man hoeing corn." If he grew frightened and began sputtering, he "mumbled like a treed coon." If he panicked, he scampered away "like a bob-tailed dog in high oats."

Both sides used the designations "Yank" and "Reb." (Some Confederates abhorred the term "Rebel," but many wore it proudly, likening themselves to American colonists who rebelled against the British.) Men on both sides were also called "doughboys," which referred originally to a kind of dumpling and entered wider use during World War I.

Almost everything Civil War soldiers came in contact with had at least one nickname. Muskets were "smoke poles" and "pumpkin slingers." Tents were "doghouses," sewing kits were "housewives," and tall hats were "tar buckets." Body lice—the bane of every man in camp—were known variously as "crumbs," "graybacks," or "Bragg's bodyguards" for Confederate Gen. Braxton Bragg, a strict disciplinarian disdained by his men. Few soldiers could spell the dreaded word "diarrhea" correctly, so they referred to it in writing using such evocative terms as "Tennessee trots" and "Virginia quick-steps."

No facet of army life inspired more vivid invective than the wretched food. "It would tax the digestive tract of a salamander," a Union surgeon concluded. Soldiers referred to their victuals as "hellfire stew," "desecrated vegetables," and "embalmed beef." Army cooks were collectively labeled "dog robbers." Even coffee, that indispensable beverage, was derided as the "last grind" and "dirty mud."

Several Civil War generals inspired new figures of speech. The term "Butlerize," meaning to steal, originated with Union Gen. Benjamin Butler, known as "Spoons" for allegedly confiscating the silverware of wealthy residents during his infamous occupation of New Orleans. As Gen. William T. Sherman swept across Georgia in his 1864 March to the Sea, he had his men dismantle railroads, heat the rails, and twist them around trees to form "Sherman's neckties." Sherman's marauding soldiers torched so many buildings that burning meat to a crisp became known as "Shermanizing" it.

Soldiers who witnessed their first battle had "seen the elephant." If a man ran off, he "skedaddled." Other terms devised by Billy Yank and Johnny Reb have meanings that can only be guessed at. One soldier wrote with feeling: "I was squashmolished." Another confessed after unburdening himself publicly somehow: "I flumized right in front of him."

Civil War–era slang provided many permanent additions to the American lexicon. The expression "snug as a bug in a rug" originated then. So did "scarce as hen's teeth." A change in postal regulations during the struggle gave rise to "first class mail." Both sides resorted to conscription as the war dragged on, fostering such enduring terms as "draftees," "draft dodgers," and "bounty jumpers," meaning men who received cash bounties as replacements for those who were drafted, then deserted and collected another bounty elsewhere. Today, we might call such behavior shoddy—yet another term of Civil War vintage that remains as useful now as it was then. ✶

> "SHERMAN'S MARAUDING SOLDIERS TORCHED SO MANY BUILDINGS AND FARMS THAT BURNING MEAT TO A CRISP BECAME KNOWN AS 'SHERMANIZING' IT."

Gen. William T. Sherman

"ALMOST EVERYTHING CIVIL WAR SOLDIERS CAME IN CONTACT WITH HAD AT LEAST ONE NICKNAME. MUSKETS WERE 'SMOKE POLES' AND 'PUMPKIN SLINGERS.' TENTS WERE 'DOGHOUSES,' SEWING KITS WERE 'HOUSEWIVES,' AND TALL HATS WERE 'TAR BUCKETS.'"

"Tar bucket" hat

Confederate "housewife"

Officers' Amenities *During the nine-month siege of Petersburg, Virginia, many Federal officers had the time to establish comfortable quarters. Here officers of the 114th Pennsylvania and their black servants pose in front of a tent, or "doghouse," with a spacious living area behind it.*

Tramp, Tramp, Tramp

A Civil War army on the march was an unforgettable sight. The prospect of 75,000 or more soldiers moving in the same direction down the same roads, accompanied by a seemingly endless procession of wagons, was an awesome thing for soldiers to behold and be part of.

David Thompson of the Ninth New York characterized the Army of the Potomac on the move this way: "The gathering of such a multitude is a swarm, its march a vast migration." The advancing forces cut a broad swath, he added, "with long ammunition and supply trains disposed for safety along the inner roads, infantry and artillery next in order outwardly, feelers of cavalry all along its front and far out on its flank; while behind, trailing along for miles . . . are the rabble of stragglers—laggards through sickness or exhaustion, squads of recruits, convalescents from the hospitals."

The average speed of an army on the move was about two and a half miles an hour. Men marched four abreast, in part because country roads seldom permitted a wider breadth. The manner of march was "route step," which meant "go as you please." "If the march has just begun," Thompson continued, "you hear the sound of voices everywhere, with roars of laughter in spots . . . Later on, when the weight of knapsack and musket begins to tell, these sounds die out; a sense of weariness and labor rises from the toiling masses streaming by, voiced only by the shuffle of a multitude of feet . . . So uniformly does the mass move on that it suggests a great machine." A column of men on the march, Thompson added, was "a monstrous, crawling,

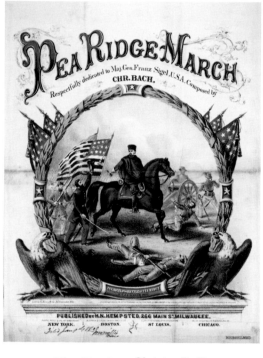

Marching Song *Christian Bach's "Pea Ridge March," composed in 1862, was dedicated to Union Gen. Franz Sigel.*

blue-black snake, miles long, quilted with the silver slant of muskets at a 'shoulder [arms],' its sluggish tail twisting slowly up over the distant ridge."

Frontliners at the head of the column had the roads when they were in best shape. Men at the rear of the line often had to fight heavy layers of dust. For many soldiers, the worst aspect of a march was the stop-and-go as the column contracted like an accordion, bringing men to a halt before things got moving again. This could be maddening on night marches like the one a soldier from Vermont endured on his way to Gettysburg: "It took all night to march about seven miles," he wrote. "Marching by rods is like dying by inches, and it gets an impatient man in misery. Scolding and swearing is dispensed at an awful rate when a regiment is compelled to halt and wait every few rods . . . We rarely halted long enough to sit down, but if we did the column would invariably start just as we were fairly seated. Men fell out, whole companies at a time . . . Our Colonel said that he rode on till his men all left him, and he found himself without a command, when he concluded he would stop too."

Tramping soldiers were often plagued by thirst and scooped a handful of water from any pond or puddle they passed. "How many wiggletails and tadpoles I have drunk will never be known," one Confederate quipped. Yet many soldiers displayed a remarkable cheerfulness through it all. Theodore Barclay of the Fourth Virginia wrote after a long trek: "Well, here I am at the old camp near Winchester, broken down, halt, lame, blind, crippled, and whatever else you can think of—but I am still kicking." ✶

"WELL, HERE I AM AT THE OLD CAMP NEAR WINCHESTER, BROKEN DOWN, HALT, LAME, BLIND, CRIPPLED, AND WHATEVER ELSE YOU CAN THINK OF— BUT I AM STILL KICKING."

THEODORE BARCLAY, FOURTH VIRGINIA, AFTER A LONG TREK

Grueling Trek *A ragged Federal soldier dries his laundry on the march (top) in a scene depicted by artist Edwin Forbes. No Union troops remained dry during the infamous and futile "Mud March" (above), which was conducted near Fredericksburg, Virginia, in early 1863 and shattered morale in the Army of the Potomac.*

Picket Duty

Pickets were small groups of soldiers positioned at the outskirts of an encampment or ahead of an advancing army. They served mainly to detect enemies. A shot or two from the picket line would sound the alarm. Pickets also screened soldiers and civilians entering or exiting camp. Occasionally, they scouted or probed an enemy position. They were the army's watchdogs, guarding friends and sniffing out foes.

Soldiers took turns on picket duty. They served in units with other members of their regiment, often remaining on guard for two or three days. Typically, picket posts were about 100 yards apart, with six men assigned to each station. Soldiers constructed a brush lean-to, or sometimes even a small log hut, to shelter them from the weather.

A soldier's first turn on picket duty was the worst. He was in no-man's-land. Every faint sound or moving object spelled danger. False alarms were commonplace. In the autumn of 1861, a Pennsylvania recruit was on his first duty with others new to the task. Around 11 at night, he heard a sentry in the distance call "Halt!" followed by a gunshot. The nature of the threat was soon revealed to the startled Pennsylvanian by the "squealing of a hog, which had refused to give the countersign and as a consequence got shot through the nose." Stray animals were not the only victims of trigger-happy guards. Tree stumps, clothes hanging out to dry, even leaves rustling in the wind were targeted for failing to answer a frightened sentry's call.

When an army camped in friendly territory, selected soldiers were allowed a few hours' leave. Guards were often toyed with

On Picket.

"WHEN I GO OUT ON GUARD DUTY AT NIGHT, I HAVE TO EAT CLOVES, SPANK MYSELF, AND SIT ON THE POINT OF MY BAYONET (GENTLY OF COURSE) TO KEEP FROM GETTING TO SLEEP."

SOLDIER OF THE
FIRST MAINE INFANTRY

at night by men returning through the picket line in noisy groups that could not be mistaken for hostile parties. Even sentinels new to the task could distinguish friend from foe at such times, but they would still go through the ritual by calling out: "Halt! Who goes there?" The returning men would walk rapidly past the bewildered picket and shout: "Pete," "Dick," "Tiger," "the Devil," "Spoon," or any other name that came to mind.

Picket duty was usually uneventful and tedious. Bull sessions and letter writing were popular antidotes for boredom. A picket who dozed did so at his peril. The military manual described a picket as "the sentinel who holds the lives of his countrymen and the liberty of his countrymen in his hands." An unlucky soldier found asleep at his post could be court-martialed. The maximum penalty for the offense was death by firing squad.

Mindful of the consequences, a soldier of the First Maine wrote: "When I go out on guard duty at night, I have to eat cloves, spank myself, and sit on the point of my bayonet (gently of course) to keep from getting to sleep." Picket duty, he added, "uses a man up for two days and if you don't wish yourself and all mankind to blazes, you must be remarkably good-natured."

Early in the war, soldiers convicted of minor crimes were often sentenced to perform extra guard duty. Commanders soon thought better of entrusting their security to offenders and assigned more dependable soldiers to this vital task. Confederate Gen. Thomas Hindman explained: "Standing guard is the most honorable duty of a soldier, except fighting, and must not be degraded." ✷

Lonely Vigil *A Federal picket in stormy weather finds little shelter behind a tree trunk in this sketch by Edwin Forbes. Standing guard was monotonous, boring, and occasionally dangerous.*

On Picket
A Stormy day

"The Last War Between Gentlemen"

Gilbert Hays of Pennsylvania never forgot the scenes he witnessed while he and other Union troops were laying siege to Petersburg in 1864. Although communication with the enemy was strictly forbidden, Hays wrote, Yanks and Rebels "were on the most friendly terms, amicably conversing and exchanging such commodities as coffee, sugar, tobacco, corn meal and newspapers." Hays even saw men from the two sides "bantering and joking together, exchanging the compliments of the day."

There were many such occasions during the Civil War when animosity between foes gave way to friendship and compassion. Sir Winston Churchill later went so far as to call this "the last war between gentlemen." Why opponents from North and South found common ground is easily explained. They fraternized, or acted like brothers, because they were indeed akin to each other. They spoke the same language, hummed the same tunes, endured the same hardships, and worshipped the same God. Such ties helped bind them when they camped or entrenched within sight or hearing of each other.

Fraternization in such circumstances often took the form of banter. One day in 1864 an entrenched Union soldier put his hat on a stick and raised it above the earthworks to see if it would draw fire. From across the way came a shout: "It won't do, Yank, your neck is too skinny! Place your head under your hat and we'll accommodate you!" In another instance, a Union general climbed atop a parapet and began surveying the enemy lines through a telescope. Soon a rock bounced into the rifle pit. Around the stone was a piece of paper on which was the message: "Tell the fellow with the spy glass to clear out or we shall have to shoot him."

The "smart talk" or "jawing" that went on between opponents often led to barter and other friendly intercourse. Foes who engaged in such give-and-take were reluctant to do to their enemies what they did not want done to themselves. One Union officer reportedly ordered his men not to fire on a Confederate picket line because it was "nothing but murder to kill a poor picket while on duty." There appears to have been an unwritten rule in the Civil War that forbade the capture—or interruption—of any man who was, in the words of one soldier, "attending to the imperative call of nature."

Acts of mercy by soldiers to their foes occurred frequently. At Gettysburg, a Virginian named Patrick McNeil was manning a battery when he saw an injured Union soldier lying in front of the guns. McNeil crawled forward and pulled the Yankee to safety within Confederate lines. As he completed that merciful deed, an incoming cannonball severed both of McNeil's legs.

> "MCNEIL CRAWLED FORWARD AND PULLED THE YANKEE TO SAFETY WITHIN CONFEDERATE LINES. AS HE COMPLETED THAT MERCIFUL DEED, AN INCOMING CANNONBALL SEVERED BOTH OF MCNEIL'S LEGS."

To be sure, compassion and kind words were less common in close combat than brutality and profanity. Rutherford B. Hayes, a Union officer during the war and the nation's commander in chief in later years, wrote after hand-to-hand fighting at Winchester: "The names the Rebels called me reflected disrespect upon my parentage." Hayes himself cast similar aspersions on his foes at the Battle of South Mountain in 1862 when he urged men of his Ohio regiment to "give the sons of bitches hell!"

The instinctive hatred men felt for enemies in battle often faded, however, when the fighting was done. In the aftermath of one bloody encounter, a Confederate major watched soldiers from both sides burying their dead together on the battlefield. "Brave men who fight one another must come to love one another," he declared. If not, he concluded, there would be no end to fighting and war. ★

Friendly Foes *When Confederate Lt. James B. Washington was captured in 1862, he asked to see his old West Point classmate, George A. Custer (far right). A photographer, working for Mathew Brady, placed a black child between them to add interest to the photograph.*

BRADY'S ALBUM GALLERY.

No. 428.

Custer

Washington

Lieut. Washington, a Confederate Prisoner,

5th U.S. Cavalry AND *aid*

CAPT. CUSTIS, U. S. A. *to Gen Lee*

Fun and Games

Civil War soldiers spent far more time in camp than they did campaigning. A member of the 102nd Illinois wrote home in 1863: "The monotony of camp life at times becomes almost intolerable. Our daily duties degenerate into a dull routine. We have long hours to while away . . . the question frequently arises: in what new mode can we relieve the tedious hours?"

The most prevalent pastime was conversation. Topics ran the gantlet from the perils of army life to the pleasures awaiting men on the home front. Memories of the past mingled with fantasies of the future. Truth was often blended with fiction. "This is a great place for telling lies," a New Yorker stated. "There is not one in the Company that you can believe under oath."

Johnny Reb and Billy Yank were fun-loving mischief makers and sought laughs by any means, fair or foul. Spreading rumors provided merriment to many bored soldiers. "Rumor furnishes the morning and evening news," an Iowan commented, "some of it well-founded, much of it baseless and imaginary." Practical jokes occurred wherever gullible or defenseless victims were to be found. Cutting the seat out of the trousers of a man suffering from diarrhea was but one popular prank.

Bible reading and hymn singing were frequent, as were other literary and musical diversions. Songs were heard wherever soldiers gathered. Men sang when they left for war, sang on the march and in the trenches, sang when they charged into battle and when they buried friends who fell. Few soldiers sang well. A Confederate stationed at Baton Rouge told his parents that the singing voice of one Texan was a "cross between the bray of a jackass and the note of a turkey buzzard, and far excels either in melody."

Sports were many and varied, including boxing, wrestling, foot races, and horse races. The new game of baseball was a favorite summer pastime. High scores were the general rule because the base runner had to be hit by a thrown or batted ball before he was out. Snowball fights were common in winter. They sometimes involved entire regiments and got out of hand. When two New Hampshire regiments squared off in a snowball fight, one participant wrote, "tents were wrecked, bones broken, eyes blacked, and teeth knocked out—all in *fun*."

Gambling with cards or dice was a pervasive vice that offended some devout soldiers, as did the profanity that laced much of the griping, joking, and storytelling that went on constantly. "Around me is the gibber of reckless men & I am compelled to listen day and night to their profanity, filthy talk and vulgar songs," one Union recruit complained. "I have some conception how Lot felt in Sodom when he had to listen to and be cursed by the filthy conversation of the wicked."

Others recognized that most of those "reckless men" in camp were still youngsters and reasoned that boys will be boys. One Union officer noted that soldiers in his regiment were addicted to chuck-a-luck, a game of chance involving three dice, and kept at it on Sundays rather than attending services in camp. "I think this unfair," he remarked with dry humor, "as the church runs only once a week but the game goes on daily." Officers were well advised to tolerate the diversions of young men facing deprivation and possible death. Most soldiers who indulged freely in raucous camp activities just as freely relinquished them on returning home at war's end. ✴

Board Games *Soldiers on both sides of the conflict enjoyed board games such as cribbage, checkers, and chess.*

"FEW SOLDIERS SANG WELL. A CONFEDERATE STATIONED AT BATON ROUGE TOLD HIS PARENTS THAT THE SINGING VOICE OF ONE TEXAN THERE WAS A 'CROSS BETWEEN THE BRAY OF A JACKASS AND THE NOTE OF A TURKEY BUZZARD, AND FAR EXCELS EITHER IN MELODY.'"

Fun and Fury
Anything that helped pass the time was a welcome diversion in camp. Making music was always popular, and men like this Union soldier, shown with his guitar, would often entertain their mates. High spirits might lead to a "sword fight" such as the one below, staged by officers of Gen. Joseph Hooker's staff, fighting with wooden weapons.

"SPORTS WERE MANY AND VARIED, INCLUDING BOXING, WRESTLING, FOOT RACES, AND HORSE RACES. THE NEW GAME OF BASEBALL WAS A FAVORITE SUMMER PASTIME."

Contests in Camp *Soldiers engaged in various tests of strength or skill, including boxing matches like the one at right, simulated by Union soldiers, and the horse race below, sketched by Edwin Forbes during festivities of the Army of the Potomac's Irish Brigade on St. Patrick's Day.*

What's in the Cards *Rules against gambling in camp were often broken, and card playing remained a constant, as shown in this photograph of officers of the 114th Pennsylvania Zouaves (below). Northern-made card decks (inset) occasionally featured patriotic motifs in place of the usual suits.*

Keeping in Touch

The Civil War produced the greatest outpouring of letters in the nation's history. Soldiers were seldom granted furloughs, and letters were the only contact men in the army had with loved ones for months or years on end. Any man who could write did so. Tender emotions were deeply implanted in people of all ranks during that romantic age. The emotional impact of their wartime letters was heightened by the knowledge that each one might be the last a soldier ever wrote or received. A Yankee from Maine wrote in reply to a precious letter he received while serving at an isolated coastal garrison in the South: "Sophronia, you cannot think how much good it does a poor soldier out here to get a kind, cheering word from home now and then. It shows him he is not forgotten and gives him courage to stand up against the hardships he has to endure."

The surviving letters soldiers sent home from camp have much in common. When writing a wife or a sweetheart, their salutation was usually simple and straightforward. "Dear Wife" or "Howdy Kate" were typical greetings. The letter might then begin: "I seat myself and take pen in hand to drop you a few lines." There would follow a rambling report of his health, camp life, marches, enemy threats, food, weather, lack of clothing, and personal opinions on the war and his comrades. Interspersed at random would be queries about children, siblings, crops, and other matters at home. When the soldier was running out of paper, he would close with "Your affectionate husband," "Your dear friend," or the like. On occasion, enterprising men might insert a poetic couplet such as this: "When this you see, remember me / Though many miles apart we be."

Some of those letters are models of literary excellence,

Union soldier's writing kit

precise in their prose and penmanship. The great preponderance contain rough grammar, phonetic spelling, and crude handwriting reflective of the low educational standards of the time. "John, I want you to write more plainer than you have bin writing," Alabamian Charles Futch told his brother back home. Charles added that he had shown John's last letter to soldiers in two regiments: "They was not a man that could even read the date of the month." Another soldier wrote his intended: "Last Sunday evening I received a letter from you in your own hand wrighting whitch was the best of all. I could read every word except one. If you will keep trying you will soon get so as to wright first rate. You must learn to spel, to."

Mail delivery was sporadic on both sides because postal service was undependable. Soldiers departing on furloughs or returning from leave, as well as ministers and friends visiting camp, found themselves loaded with mail to distribute. Camp sutlers sold paper, pens, ink, and envelopes, some of them plain and others commemorative. Beginning in 1864, the U.S. Postal Service began free delivery of all mail marked "Soldier's Letter."

Not receiving mail could plunge a man into despair. "I stood by the postmaster when he called out the mail," a Virginia soldier informed his fiancée. "My heart at times was at my throat at the sight of some of the letters with small white envelopes so much like yours . . . I could scarcely hide my disappointment when the last letter was called out, and none from you."

One Billy Yank spoke for all Civil War troops when he wrote that mail from home seems "to lighten their many arduous duties, gives them an elastic step upon the weary march, and nerves the soul for the dreadful shock of battle." ✶

Mail Call *Letter carriers for the Army of the Potomac stand by their II Corps mail wagon at Brandy Station, Virginia, in 1864. The previous year, new army commander Joseph Hooker made marked improvements in postal service. Artist Edwin Forbes, in the sketch at right, captured the total concentration of a soldier who had just received news from home.*

"SOPHRONIA, YOU CANNOT THINK HOW MUCH GOOD IT DOES A POOR SOLDIER OUT HERE TO GET A KIND, CHEERING WORD FROM HOME NOW AND THEN. IT SHOWS HIM HE IS NOT FORGOTTEN AND GIVES HIM COURAGE TO STAND UP AGAINST THE HARDSHIPS HE HAS TO ENDURE."

A SOLDIER'S LETTER HOME

Faithful Companions

The affectionate bond between man and animal was one that not even war could sever. Many Civil War regiments had mascots. They were proud totems like the mascots of many competitive teams today. Many were also beloved pets, with whom men developed strong ties of loyalty and devotion, lending a human touch to the often inhuman business of war.

A wide range of animals became mascots. The most famous was a bald eagle named Old Abe (pages 124-5). There was also a mascot named Jeff Davis, a pig in the Ninth Connecticut that was taught to stand on its hind legs when commanded. The 104th Pennsylvania had both a cat and a raccoon, neither of which lived long in service. Tame bears traveled for short periods with three regiments. Members of a Minnesota unit bragged that their young bear "smelt powder in a dozen engagements before being sent home in good condition."

The 43rd New York had a semi-tame pigeon that came and went at random. A donkey named Jason accompanied one Confederate regiment on a long journey across Texas. The animal, if left alone, had a bad habit of meandering into the colonel's tent. The most unusual Civil War mascot was Old Douglas, a camel with the 43rd Mississippi. The animal faithfully carried heavy loads of supplies but had to be tethered outside camp because horses stampeded at the sight of the camel. A Union skirmisher killed Old Douglas during the 1863 Vicksburg campaign.

As might be expected, dogs were the most prevalent pets in camp, kept individually by soldiers and collectively by companies and regiments. "The dog is not a mercenary," Lt. George Harding of the 21st Indiana declared. "He is a faithful friend until death." Some recruits brought their dogs with them from home. Other canines appeared from nowhere for duty and settled in. Feeding, cleaning, and grooming the animals provided a comforting distraction from the stresses of wartime and helped compensate for the loneliness of army life, which was often intense despite the fact that soldiers were almost never alone. Soldier and pet played, ate, slept, and marched alongside one another.

Among the canine mascots that regularly entered battle with their regiments were Sallie of the 11th Pennsylvania (pages 80-81), Sergeant of the Third Louisiana, Major of the Tenth Maine, and Stonewall of the Richmond Howitzers. When the Second Kentucky surrendered en masse at Fort Donelson in 1862, its mascot, Frank, accompanied the men to a six-month imprisonment at Camp Morton, Indiana.

High commanders were as fond of dogs as were lowly privates. Union Gen. George Custer allowed them to swarm in his tent and sleep with him in bed.

There were many incidents of dogs guarding dead masters. A Wisconsin captain fell early in the fighting at Antietam. His Newfoundland lay beside the captain and was found dead the next morning in the same position.

Most mascots perished during the war, and losing them could hit men hard. But when one pet fell, others stepped forward to fill the gap. The 34th Massachusetts had 40 canines in its ranks. Men camped near that "Barking Dog Regiment" got little sleep at night. ✶

Canine Veteran *This memento features Old Jack, mascot of the 102nd Pennsylvania Volunteer Infantry, and lists the battles in which he appeared.*

"THE DOG IS NOT
A MERCENARY,
HE IS A FAITHFUL FRIEND
UNTIL DEATH."

**LT. GEORGE HARDING,
21ST INDIANA**

Four-legged Followers *In the sketch above by Edwin Forbes, a pet dog follows a picket party returning to their snow-shrouded winter camp.
At top, Union Gens. Henry M. Naglee (seated, third from left) and George Stoneman (seated, far right) pose with their aides—and a canine mascot—
at Harrison's Landing, Virginia, in the aftermath of the 1862 Peninsular Campaign.*

Old Abe

One famous mascot provided inspiration not just to its regiment but to the Union as a whole. Early in 1861, settlers in Wisconsin obtained an eaglet in a swap of goods with Chippewa Indians. Not long after the Civil War began, a company of recruits accepted the bird as a mascot, named it Old Abe, and went off to fight as part of the Eighth Wisconsin Infantry Regiment.

In some ways, Old Abe was a pathetic sight. He was bound by a strong cord to a shield-shaped perch atop a wooden pole, carried by one soldier after another during the war. (He had six bearers in all.) Men clipped the eagle's wings continually to keep him from flying away. Old Abe could never fly far and was unable to soar majestically as free eagles do. Nonetheless, he brought renown to the Eighth Wisconsin, known as "the Eagle Regiment." And Old Abe won fame in his own right as a symbol of the United States—resembling the bald eagle on the nation's Great Seal—and the namesake of its President. He was a great curiosity and conversation piece, known to soldiers on both sides of the conflict throughout the Western theater.

When the army was marching, Old Abe was always with the color guard. In battle, two soldiers were assigned to bear and protect the bird. The eagle found combat stimulating and reacted by flapping its wings and screeching loudly. Southern soldiers tried to belittle Old Abe with shouts of "Wild Goose!" and "Yankee Crow!" Three of his bearers were wounded in action during the war, but their precious mascot came through unscathed. He lost a few feathers but was never pierced by a bullet, despite seeing battle at Corinth, Vicksburg, and Nashville, among other engagements.

By war's end, the bird was a national hero. He even had a popular song dedicated to him—"Old Abe the Battle Eagle." Men of the regiment took the bird home to Wisconsin. He lived thereafter in a cage in the capitol at Madison. He often served as the guest of honor at veterans' reunions and other patriotic gatherings.

Renowned Raptor *Lithographs of the Eighth Wisconsin's famous mascot, Old Abe, were sold to benefit soldiers.*

Legends about Old Abe abounded. In campaigns, it was said, the eagle made aerial reconnaissance missions and passed vital information along to Union commanders—just how was never explained. One oft-told story had Old Abe swoop down on a Confederate council of war and deftly steal the battle map from the table. None of these accounts was true, but they made for lively telling and enhanced the eagle's reputation.

In March 1881, Old Abe died in the arms of his keeper. He was stuffed and put on display in the capitol. A fire 13 years later destroyed his remains. A nation mourned what one official called the "irreparable loss of our most treasured emblem of liberty."

Yet Old Abe lives on in memory through two memorials. One is the Wisconsin state monument on the Vicksburg battlefield, a tall granite column, atop which stands a six-foot bronze statue of Old Abe. The other memorial originated during World War II when the 101st Airborne Division adopted a shield-shaped shoulder patch adorned with the head of a bald eagle. In late 1942, the state of Wisconsin honored Old Abe by giving the "Screaming Eagles" of the 101st Airborne an eagle called Young Abe, which served as their mascot at the division's training ground.

Old Abe would have liked that. ★

"SOUTHERN SOLDIERS TRIED TO BELITTLE OLD ABE WITH SHOUTS OF 'WILD GOOSE!' AND 'YANKEE CROW!'"

War Eagle *The desperate fighting at Vicksburg, shown at left, was but one struggle at which Old Abe, mascot of the Eighth Wisconsin Infantry, was present. The regiment's color guard (below) protected both their colors and their beloved mascot.*

The Biggest Killers

Two years into the war, an Illinois soldier swore that "we are dying faster from the sicknesses of the camp than from the casualties of war." A Virginia volunteer on the other side informed his sister: "I had rather face the Yankees than the sickness." These men were not exaggerating. Diseases were the war's biggest killers. For every soldier who perished in action, two died behind the lines from sickness.

Poor food and sanitary conditions made camps stalking grounds for the most widespread killer, referred to variously as diarrhea or dysentery (an infectious disease marked by severe diarrhea). One million cases were reported among the two million men who served in Union armies. How many tens of thousands of others suffered in silence can never be known. The condition was not necessarily fatal, but in drastic or chronic cases men died of dehydration or wasted away. A Georgia soldier at Chattanooga in late 1863 told his family: "I have had the direar every scence I have bin hear and it have reduce me down rite smarte." Army surgeons groped for a cure and prescribed a wide variety of medicines—the most common being a mixture of opium and castor oil. Few of them did much good.

An Illinois private who barely survived an attack commented: "Inflammation of the bowels was so severe and painful that it seemed as though death would be a welcome relief." The diary of Luther Jackson of the 12th Iowa contains this entry: "June 1, 1862. I am still suffering from diarrhea. I lie still all the time, hoping to be better soon." Jackson died a week later.

Typhoid fever, associated with contaminated water, struck the army camps early and hard. In August 1861, almost 1,300 of 1,800 recruits in a Kentucky brigade fell ill with typhoid.

"IT SCARES [A] MAN TO DEATH TO GET SICK DOWN HERE."

A CONFEDERATE SOLDIER IN 1861

Wartime Medicine *These tins carried by army surgeons contained quinine, used for malaria, and small pills of painkilling opium.*

One soldier who contracted what he called this "break bone fever" was "delirious for days" but managed to survive.

The disease caused more than 17,000 Confederate deaths in an 18-month period. One hard-fighting regiment, the 18th Virginia, suffered more fatalities from typhoid fever than from combat.

Physicians had little idea what caused the disease. A Texas surgeon, after expressing helplessness in stemming a typhoid epidemic in his regiment, closed his letter home with this statement: "We have had an awful time drinking the meanest water not fit for a horse." Many authorities suspected, however, that typhoid fever and other deadly ailments in camp were related to poor sanitation. As the U.S. Sanitary Commission and other organizations worked to improve hygiene in camps, typhoid fever tapered off and practically disappeared in the war's last months.

One of the few debilitating diseases for which army physicians had an effective treatment was malaria, spread by mosquitoes in low-lying, swampy areas where soldiers often camped. Hundreds of thousands of men contracted the disease and suffered fever and chills, but doses of quinine helped keep the wartime death toll down to about 10,000.

Nearly every regiment faced an outbreak of red measles (rubeola) soon after its members began camping together. "It seemed that half or more of the army had the disease the first year of the war," declared a Virginian. Measles could weaken the constitution of those who survived and leave them vulnerable to other fatal illnesses such as pneumonia.

Small wonder that, with the war less than six months old, a Confederate recruit wrote his parents: "It scares [a] man to death to get sick down here." ✶

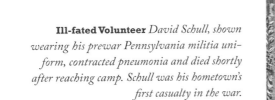

Ill-fated Volunteer *David Schull, shown wearing his prewar Pennsylvania militia uniform, contracted pneumonia and died shortly after reaching camp. Schull was his hometown's first casualty in the war.*

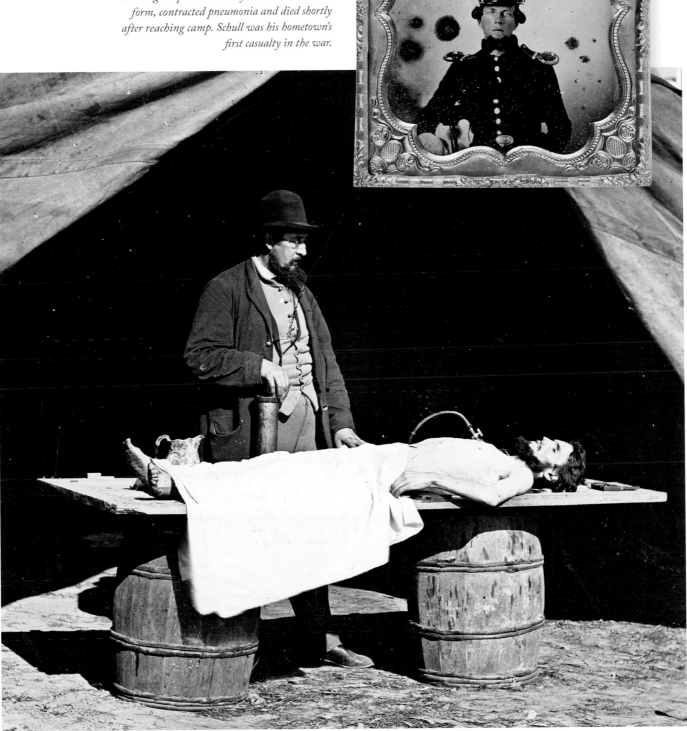

Preserving the Fallen *Arterial injection of embalming fluid came into use on the eve of the Civil War. The photograph above is thought to show William J. Bunnell, a New Jersey embalmer who proclaimed on a large banner that the bodies he treated were "Free from Odor and Infection."*

Camp Itches

Soldiers wore the same, usually unwashed, uniform 12 months a year. Soap, and opportunities for bathing, were scarce. Those musty garments drew flies and mosquitoes and became havens for lice, fleas, and the burrowing mites that caused scabies.

Rare indeed was the Civil War soldier of any rank who was not infested with some sort of vermin. They all had something to say about those pests. Much of it consisted of exasperation mixed with exaggeration. Mosquitoes around one camp, a New Yorker informed his sister, were "as thick as the hair of a dog . . . If you was to stay here for one Knight, you would want the patience of Job to stand it." A Union officer confessed while writing a letter: "I have to stop after every sentence to scratch myself & drive off the bugs." A Confederate complained that mosquitoes "seemed resolved to take me dead or alive." Since soldiers scratched with dirty hands, mosquito bites often became infected.

Flies were no less exasperating. In 1862, a North Carolina soldier told a lady friend: "I get vexed at them and commence killing them, but as I believe forty comes to every one's funeral, I have given it up as a bad job."

An all-too-familiar sight in camp was that of soldiers, their shirts in their laps, attentively going through each square inch of cloth in search of lice. Others learned how to take a stick, hold their shirt near a fire, and incinerate the lice, which made a popping sound like corn. Lice had no respect for rank or station. Gen. Rutherford B. Hayes was once observed hiding behind a tree in a state of partial undress, feverishly extracting lice from his clothing. They were "the

> "RARE INDEED WAS THE CIVIL WAR SOLDIER OF ANY RANK WHO WAS NOT INFESTED WITH SOME SORT OF VERMIN."

A Welcome Dip *During a pause in Grant's grueling 1864 campaign in Virginia, Union soldiers swim and bathe in the South Anna River, washing away pests in the process.*

most cunning and most impudent" of wartime insects, one veteran observed. One Pennsylvanian concluded that lice were using his body as a training ground: "I woke up the other night and found a regiment of them going through the manual of arms on my back."

The maddening skin disease called scabies, or "camp itch," was readily communicated by mites from one soldier to another in crowded camps. The tiny mite, a Union surgeon declared, "squats upon a new recruit with every prospect of a long life and large family, and burrows away, undisturbed by soap, until the poor soldier's skin is like a New York tenement house—full inside and out." Treatment of scabies was varied and largely unsuccessful. An ointment made from the bark of an elder tree, mixed with lard and sulfur, was considered worth trying. Patients using this salve were advised to wear the same underclothing for a week so that it would soak up the ointment, eliminating the need for reapplication.

When mosquitoes, lice, and scabies were not driving men to distraction, fleas did the job. At an 1862 battle in Virginia, Union soldiers saw their flea-ridden colonel waving them into action with a sword in one hand while earnestly scratching himself with the other. Some soldiers had long experience with the pests, having spent many an hour before the war picking fleas off their own bodies and those of friends and loved ones. Writing to his wife, Joel Puckett of Alabama estimated that he had at least 50 of those vermin crawling on him and grew nostalgic: "May, I have thought of you often while mashing fleas; if you were here you could have your own sport." ★

Family Affair *A Pennsylvania soldier is joined by his wife and children at a camp in northern Virginia. Early regulations permitted Northern regiments to carry up to four laundresses on their rolls to improve sanitation.*

Battling a Toothache

For some soldiers, having a tooth extracted could be nearly as harrowing as going to war. In the 1860s, teeth went largely uncared for until they fell out or were pulled out, an operation usually performed without anesthesia. Lt. Ziba Graham of the 16th Michigan underwent that ordeal shortly after fighting in the Battle of Gettysburg. The surgeon he consulted, "who had been hard at work all night on the amputation table, made but short work and little ado about one tooth," Graham recalled. "He laid me on the ground, straddled me, and with a formidable pair of nippers pulled and yanked me around until either the tooth had to come out, or my head off . . . I then made up my mind never to go to a surgeon for a tooth-pulling matinee the day after a fight."

The dental profession was in its infancy when the Civil War began. The first American school devoted to that practice, the Baltimore College of Dentistry, had opened in 1840 with five students. Twenty years later, some 400 graduates from three dental schools were practicing across the nation. They were greatly outnumbered by itinerant dentists who had little training but easily obtained state licenses and traveled from town to town, treating patients who had no way of knowing whether they were competent or quacks, as most were. Gum disease was treated with cauterization, or burning. The transplantation of teeth was attempted repeatedly—and failed just as often.

Efforts in the 1850s to establish a dental corps in the U.S. Army faltered for lack of funding from Congress. That left Union soldiers at the mercy of surgeons with no training in dentistry. Extractions were often slipshod and broke the tooth from its roots, which remained in the jaw to cause the soldier fits.

The Confederate army, although it lacked many things, had a small corps of competent dentists. They were not present in camps but could be found at every major military hospital. All soldiers admitted to those hospitals had dental exams. The workload for Confederate dentists could be prodigious, amounting to 20 extractions and 25 fillings daily. Materials used for fillings at that time included lead, gold, and thorium, a radioactive substance resembling tin. One tooth found in a Confederate grave had a filling of shotgun pellets. Dentures, which had long been ill-fitting contraptions, were now more affordable and comfortable, thanks to a recent invention: Charles Goodyear devised a hard rubber called vulcanite that could be molded to fit the jaw and served as a base for false teeth.

Because the Union army had no dentists, Northern soldiers requiring services other than extractions had to await opportunities to consult civilian dentists. When General Sherman's army completed its March to the Sea in 1864 by occupying Savannah, Georgia, soldiers flooded dental offices in the city. One practitioner there estimated that the emergency cases alone "would have required 100 dentists to work six months on these soldiers."

The loss of teeth could render men unfit for service. By 1863, Union physicians were required to disqualify enlistees if they lacked the four front incisors, because soldiers had to tear open paper powder cartridges with their teeth to load muskets. Those gap-toothed prospects may have been the first men classified "4F," which came to mean exemption from military service for any physical disability. ✶

> "CHARLES GOODYEAR DEVISED A HARD RUBBER CALLED VULCANITE THAT COULD BE MOLDED TO FIT THE JAW AND SERVED AS A BASE FOR FALSE TEETH."

Charles Goodyear

DENTAL.

EXTRACTION OF TEETH.

Tooth Forceps.

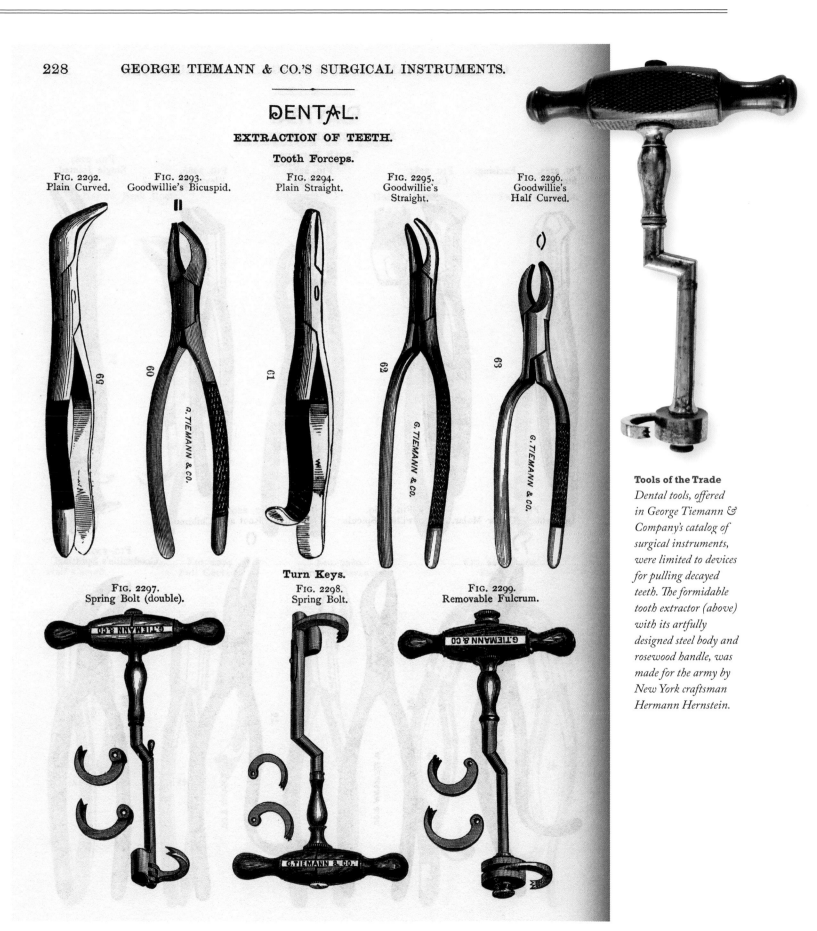

FIG. 2292.
Plain Curved.

FIG. 2293.
Goodwillie's Bicuspid.

FIG. 2294.
Plain Straight.

FIG. 2295.
Goodwillie's
Straight.

FIG. 2296.
Goodwillie's
Half Curved.

Turn Keys.

FIG. 2297.
Spring Bolt (double).

FIG. 2298.
Spring Bolt.

FIG. 2299.
Removable Fulcrum.

Tools of the Trade
Dental tools, offered in George Tiemann & Company's catalog of surgical instruments, were limited to devices for pulling decayed teeth. The formidable tooth extractor (above) with its artfully designed steel body and rosewood handle, was made for the army by New York craftsman Hermann Hernstein.

"Home, Sweet Home"

One sickness that prevailed in Civil War armies was not listed in any medical directory. Surgeons had no treatment for it. It was as common among Johnny Rebs as among Billy Yanks. It was known simply as homesickness.

A New York hospital steward told his wife shortly after reaching the front lines in Virginia: "My health is good with the exception of 'homesickness,' a disease, I am thinking will never be cured, though in my case, I hope it will not assume that malignant type that will unfit me for duty." Valerius Giles of the Fourth Texas recalled: "I honestly believe that genuine homesickness killed more soldiers in the army than died from measles."

Many soldiers of the 1860s had youth's terrible capacity for loneliness. And they lived in a highly sentimental age, one in which absence made the heart ache deeply. A Tennessee private confessed: "When I think of my native home, in a moment I seem to be there. But, alas! recollection soon hurries me back to despair. Oh! tell me I yet have a home."

Most of those soldiers were away from home for the first time. Life in camp left them with too much idle time for reminiscence and regret. The longer soldiers remained inactive, the worse homesickness became. Nostalgia was a hidden enemy, eating away at the morale of youngsters in their teens and older married men. A Union captain told his wife of meeting a homesick private in camp. "I found one crying this morning. I tried to comfort him but had hard work to keep from joining him."

During the war's last autumn, a lonely Confederate told his sweetheart that only a letter from her would heal his aching heart. "If I was where I could not hear from you," he added, "it don't seem to me like I could stand it, for you are my daily study." J. B. Crawford of the 38th Mississippi informed his wife: "I wood give the Confedracy to the yankeys if it was mine to see you and the little ones." An Illinois volunteer expressed similar sentiments. "One does not know how sweet home is till he goes through the roughs of a soldiers life," he wrote his wife. "You must not think I am despondent for I aint, but I would take a discharge if one was given to me."

Loneliness became deeper and more painful during the Christmas season. Near Yuletide in 1862, Lt. Jonathan Evans of the Fourth Virginia stated to his cousin: "I anticipate you will have a nice time at your proposed dinner. I would like to be one of the pertisipants but alas I am doomed to wear away the time in dull camp." A man in his position, he added, could not help thinking of "friends far away with the faint hope that one day he may be spared to see them again." Evans was killed in action the following year.

Lonely letters from loved ones made things harder for the homesick soldier. Joel Angle of Virginia was sorely moved by these lines from his wife, Mary Ann: "I sit and study ten thousand things to make me miserable and unhappy and when I sleep I sometimes see you coming home and wake myself jumping up to meet you but when I wake you are gone and I lay down and cry myself to sleep again."

Alabama soldier John Cotton voiced the feelings of many dedicated recruits on both sides when he wrote: "I never knew what pleasure home afforded to a man before. If it were not for the love of my country and family and the patriotism that burns in my bosom for them, I would be glad to come home and stay there. But I know I have as much to fight for as any body else."

Cotton went home in the autumn of 1865 after long confinement as a prisoner of war. Love of home and family had made him a soldier. Dreams of home and family sustained him in the field. Returning home safely was his ultimate reward. ✶

> "MY HEALTH IS GOOD WITH THE EXCEPTION OF 'HOMESICKNESS,' A DISEASE, I AM THINKING WILL NEVER BE CURED, THOUGH IN MY CASE, I HOPE IT WILL NOT ASSUME THAT MALIGNANT TYPE THAT WILL UNFIT ME FOR DUTY."
>
> **A UNION HOSPITAL STEWARD**

Letters from loved ones

Soldier and child

Sergeant and sweetheart

Christmas Apart *This Christmas scene of a soldier and his distant family by cartoonist Thomas Nast appeared in a January 1863 issue of* Harper's Weekly. *Nast contrasts festive views of Santa Claus bringing gifts at top with the sobering image of a military burial ground at bottom.*

Romance in War

Leaving home could be heartbreaking, but steadfast love was a great consolation for Civil War soldiers and helped them through many trials. In those days, when sweethearts said: "I love you with all my heart," they truly meant it. That assurance gave men in peril cause for hope. After one hard battle, an Arkansas surgeon wrote his fiancée: "During the fight, when cannon balls were "all the go," I several times became so absorbed in thinking of you that I actually forgot where I was . . . If it were not for you, I would have nothing—no object in the world worth living for."

When an Illinois veteran returned to camp after getting married in March 1864, he wrote his bride: "Never allow yourself to be down hearted. Always remember that there is one who will ever think of you while he is living. Always while there are thoughts, the last one will be of you." A North Carolina soldier declared to his sweetheart: "Nancy, I am many a mile from you but my heart and love and affection—is and will be with you as long as I live. That you may depend on."

Many men expressed similar sentiments—sometimes using grammar that left a good deal to be desired. Edwin Goolsby of the Tenth Georgia Battalion informed his wife in mid-November 1863: "I uster think you rather be with som body else if you had your rathers but I hop I was mistaken fer I no I lov you beter than any thing else in this world and all ways did." Georgia surgeon George Peddy was more precise in spelling out his devotion to his wife. "This crewl war may keep us separated a long while yet," he stated in February 1864, "but there is one thing that nothing can accomplish, that is to sever the cord of true love which binds my heart and affections to you with a firmness that no power can sever."

Little correspondence from the home front exists, but what survives indicates that strong sentimentality was a two-way

Gift From the Heart *Mrs. Retta Coleman made this lovingly decorated tobacco pouch as a gift for her husband, Confederate Col. John P. Coleman.*

street. In the war's first autumn, a civilian wrote a Georgia soldier: "I saw your sweetheart last Sunday, and she looked just like a pealed apple ready for eating. Tell Fate I saw his sweetheart and she was looking at his ambrotype and the tears rolling down her cheeks as big as turnips. Since you have been gone the gals are so downharted."

Many young recruits remained single and carefree, of course. Charles Mosher of the 85th New York told his sister: "You tell some of those pretty girls, that when the war is over, that I am going to lay aside the military and take up the matrimonial." He was in no great hurry to tie the knot: "I shall be in the market for 8 or ten years." Mississippi cavalryman Harry St. John Dixon was a prolific pursuer of "the fairer sex." His wartime journal is little more than a tabulation of his romantic escapades. "I wish I was not such a fool about women," he confessed. "It is so easy for them to gain the mastery over me." Other soldiers longed in vain for romantic attachments. A young man of the 18th Virginia wrote in reply to a note from his sister: "You never Sed iny thing About the girls. I want to no wether they all is ded or not. I aint hear nothing from thim."

Men who faced death in battle had a hunger—an almost desperate yearning—to be with their loved ones. Some soldiers of literary inclination imagined in writing a hoped-for reunion that they could not be sure of experiencing while the fighting continued. Confederate William Stillwell wrote in verse to his sweetheart following the bloody Battle of Chancellorsville in 1863: "I watch for thee when eve's first star / Shines dimly in the heavens afar, . . . When not a breeze or sound is heard / To startle evening's lonely bird, / But hushed is even the humming bee. / It is then, dearest, that I watch for thee." ★

"SARAH MY LOVE FOR YOU IS DEATHLESS,
IT SEEMS TO BIND ME WITH MIGHTY CABLES
THAT NOTHING BUT OMNIPOTENCE COULD
BREAK; AND YET MY LOVE OF COUNTRY
COMES OVER ME LIKE A STRONG WIND
AND BEARS ME UNRESISTABLY ON WITH
ALL THESE CHAINS TO THE BATTLE FIELD . . .
NEVER FORGET HOW MUCH I LOVE YOU,
AND WHEN MY LAST BREATH ESCAPES ME ON THE
BATTLE FIELD, IT WILL WHISPER YOUR NAME."

MAJ. SULLIVAN BALLOU, KILLED AT BULL RUN

Camp Wedding *Artist Alfred Waud sketched the wedding of New Jersey Capt. Uriah De Hart and Nellie Lammond at a service held in the camp of the Seventh New Jersey Volunteers on March 18, 1863.*

The Post of Honor

The first realistic novel of the Civil War to gain international fame was Stephen Crane's 1895 work, *The Red Badge of Courage*. The central character, an Ohio soldier named Henry Fleming, loses his nerve in battle and bolts from the field. Overcome by shame, young Fleming soon returns to action. Seizing the battle flag from a fallen comrade, he leads his regiment to victory, with no thought for his own safety.

Crane's novel was not meant to glorify war, but many such acts of bravery were performed during the conflict by soldiers who carried regimental and national flags. Those standards were the most visible signs of patriotism. They signaled the devotion of men to their unit, state, country, and cause. The most consistent record of heroism during the war came from the men who bore the flag. It was the symbol around which soldiers rallied in the heat of battle. To keep the flag flying was their all-consuming objective.

Enemy soldiers delivered their deadliest fire at those holding aloft the colors. Capturing a battle flag was one of the war's outstanding feats. Losing one's banner to the enemy was a shame second only to cowardice in action. Troops took to heart a saying often repeated: "The post of danger is the post of honor." No shortage of volunteers existed for the dangerous duties of color-bearers or color guards—typically a unit of a dozen men or fewer who shielded the flag and took it up one after another when bearers fell in battle. Few honors were greater than being selected to lead an attack with flag in hand.

Official battle reports are filled with citations of courageous conduct by a private, corporal, or sergeant carrying the flag. A New York colonel wrote of his regiment at Gettysburg: "The color-bearer, Sergeant Michael Cuddy . . . on this occasion displayed the most heroic bravery. When he fell, mortally wounded, he rose by convulsive efforts and triumphantly waved in the face of the rebels, not 10 yards distant, that flag he loved so dearly of which he was so proud and for which his valuable life, without a murmur, was freely given up."

One of the prouder moments for Iowans during the war came in February 1862, at Fort Donelson, Tennessee. The Second Iowa was in the front line of the Union assault. Every member of the color guard save one was killed. The survivor, Voltaire Twombly, bore the flag to the end and later received the Medal of Honor for his brave conduct.

There were similar sacrifices on the Confederate side. At the Battle of Seven Pines, a South Carolina battalion lost 10 of 11 color-bearers. The First Texas at Antietam had eight flag-bearers killed in quick succession. At Gettysburg, the 26th North Carolina reportedly lost 14 men who bore a single flag in battle, one after another. Members of a Mississippi regiment, in the thick of fighting at Corinth, saw their flag reduced by bullets to a ragged remnant. One soldier wrote that the color-bearer was last glimpsed going over the breastworks, waving the flag "and shouting for the Southern Confederacy."

Color-bearers and their beloved standards are an honored legacy of the Civil War. American soldiers still sing one of the conflict's most popular songs: "Yes, we'll rally 'round the flag, boys, we'll rally once again, shouting the Battle Cry of Freedom." ★

> "AT GETTYSBURG, THE 26TH NORTH CAROLINA REPORTEDLY LOST 14 MEN WHO BORE A SINGLE FLAG IN BATTLE, ONE AFTER ANOTHER."

The 46th Pennsylvania's tattered national flag, retired after Gettysburg

Holding Up the Colors *William C. Montgomery, color-bearer of the Seventh Ohio Infantry, was 23 years old when he carried this flag in heavy fighting at Ringgold, Georgia, in November 1863. The banner was shot to pieces and Montgomery lost an arm.*

*Regimental colors of the 18th Ohio Infantry,
bearing the battle honor, Stones River*

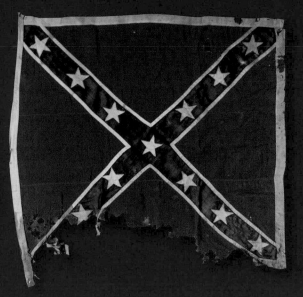

*Remnant of a blood-soaked Confederate cavalry flag,
captured in March 1865*

Colors of a Federal heavy artillery regiment

*Swallowtail guidon of the 12th New York
Artillery Battery, emblazoned with names of
battles in which it took part*

Capturing the Flag *Cpl. Harry Davis of the 46th Ohio Infantry
seizes the battle flag of the 30th Tennessee at the Battle of Ezra
Church, Georgia, in July 1864. Many Union soldiers received the
Medal of Honor for capturing an enemy flag.*

Headquarters flag of Union Gen. John F. Reynolds's
I Corps, carried at Gettysburg

Flag of the Sixth Kentucky (Confederate) Infantry,
based on the Confederacy's first national flag
and carried at Shiloh

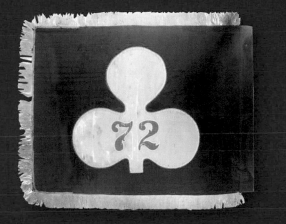

Regimental marker used to indicate the flank of the
72nd Pennsylvania Infantry in line of battle

Headquarters guidon for the Cavalry Corps,
Army of the Potomac

Silk flag presented by the ladies of the London Bridge
Baptist Church to a company of the 14th Virginia
Cavalry Battalion

Homemade battle flag, Ninth Virginia Cavalry

The Real Picture of War

Only soldiers know the real hell of combat. Battlefields of the 1860s were ferocious, grotesque places, with agony and death present in all their ghastly forms. Even the most disturbing pictures cannot convey what it was like to take part in such slaughter or witness its aftermath—the stench of decaying flesh, the maddening buzzing of flies, the uncanny silence of the dead.

When a Michigan private came upon his first corpse-strewn battlefield on the Virginia Peninsula in 1862, his attention was glued to a sight he would never forget—a dead Confederate, his face "the very picture of despair and fright . . . his right hand pointing up, ready, as it were, to grasp at something." Every man in the private's regiment turned "his head with loathing at the horrid sight."

Chancellorsville would be remembered as the place where in 1863 Robert E. Lee won his most spectacular victory and lost Stonewall Jackson, the officer he called his "right arm." Jackson died a week later and spoke in his last moments of crossing a river and resting on the far side. But few of the more than 20,000 men killed or wounded at Chancellorsville found any rest or respite there. A New York soldier went down with gunshot wounds in the jaw and hip. Stretcher-bearers took him about 50 yards to a small creek whose banks offered some protection from the gunfire. "When I reached the stream," he stated, "I found it already lined with many dead and wounded men. Some had been carried there, others had dragged themselves to the place . . . some of the wounded were slowly and needlessly bleeding to death."

A church on the battlefield became a temporary hospital. "The floor, the benches, even the chancel and pulpit, were all packed almost to suffocation" with living and dying men, a Georgia colonel reported. "Amputated limbs were piled up in every corner almost as high as a man could reach; blood flowed in streams along the aisle . . . screams and groans were heard on all sides."

While the fighting still raged, gunfire set trees and underbrush on fire. A Confederate who later helped bury the dead wrote that the woods "burnt rapidly and roasted the wounded alive . . . we could see where they had tried to keep the fire from them by scratching the leaves away as far as they could reach. But it availed not; they were burnt to a crisp."

A few days after the battle, Virginia's Theodore Barclay described the scene: "Our own dead had been buried and wounded removed, but the Yankee dead and wounded lay thickly over the field. Many had not yet had their wounds dressed and lay groaning on the wet ground, praying every passerby to change their position or give them a drink of water . . . The dead lay thick over the ground. Some had died without a struggle. Others could hardly be recognized . . . And the poor horses were not spared. Here laid some literally torn to pieces, others with feet shot off endeavoring in vain to get up. Our men humanely shot them."

Today, millions of tourists annually visit battlegrounds where the nation's cruelest and costliest war was fought. The fields are poignant and peaceful. One Civil War veteran hoped those sacred grounds would stand forever as silent reminders "of the price that was paid to insure the peace we now enjoy." Those woods and fields, so tranquil now, honor men who braved the unimaginable horrors of war because they loved their home and country more than they loved life itself. ★

> "WHEN A MICHIGAN PRIVATE CAME UPON HIS FIRST CORPSE-STREWN BATTLEFIELD ON THE VIRGINIA PENINSULA IN 1862, HIS ATTENTION WAS GLUED TO A SIGHT HE WOULD NEVER FORGET—A DEAD CONFEDERATE, HIS FACE 'THE VERY PICTURE OF DESPAIR AND FRIGHT . . . HIS RIGHT HAND POINTING UP, READY, AS IT WERE, TO GRASP AT SOMETHING.'"

THE LAST MEASURE: *A young Confederate soldier lies dead in the earthworks of Fort Mahone after Federal troops stormed the fort and broke through at Petersburg on April 2, 1865. This young soldier died with only a week remaining in the war.*

Duty and Desertion

The most common capital crime in Civil War armies was desertion. Many deserters were conscripts who never wanted army life. Some were good men who found the war too much to bear. Others abandoned the ranks from a sense of higher duty to those they loved. One such case stands out.

In the winter of 1862-63, a Confederate court-martial went into session near Fredericksburg, Virginia. A murmur went through the audience when the bailiff announced: "*The Confederate States v. Edward Cooper. The charge: desertion.*"

Cooper had enlisted in August 1861 in the Third North Carolina Artillery. The Beaufort County farmer had served faithfully for more than a year before fleeing his regiment just before the Battle of Fredericksburg. He pleaded "not guilty" to each of the specifications in the charge. Cooper had no attorney to represent him. Asked to introduce his witnesses, Cooper replied that he had none.

His colonel, the president of the court, asked in disbelief: "Have you no defense? Is it possible that you abandoned your comrades and deserted your colors in the presence of the enemy without any reason? You are charged with the highest crime known to military law, and it is your duty to make known the causes that influenced your actions."

Cooper's eyes swelled with tears. He stepped forward and handed a sheet of paper to the chief justice. "This is why I did it," he said.

It was a letter from Cooper's wife, Mary. The judge's voice broke as he read it aloud:

"Dear Edward: I have always been proud of you, and since your connection with the Confederate army I have been prouder of you than ever before. I would not have you do anything wrong for the world, but before God, Edward, unless you come home we must die! Last night I was aroused by little Eddie's crying. I called and said, 'What's the matter, Eddie?' and he said, 'Oh Mama, I am so hungry.' And Lucy, Edward, your darling Lucy, she never complains, but she is growing thinner and thinner every day. And before God, Edward, unless you come home we must die. Your Mary."

Three times Cooper had applied for a leave of absence; three times he was rejected. The husband and father in Cooper overcame the dutiful soldier in him. He fled the army to see his family. On his arrival, his wife hugged him joyfully. But when she learned he had come home without a furlough, she urged him to go back. Neither her life nor that of their children, she told him, was worth disgracing the family's name.

So Cooper went back and was court-martialed. He told the judges: "Here I am, gentlemen, in obedience to the command of my wife, to abide the sentence of the court."

Under military law, the court had no choice but to find Cooper guilty. Yet it recommended leniency rather than the death penalty. General Lee concurred. He pardoned Cooper and ordered him to return to duty as an artillerist.

Cooper was mortally injured in the next engagement. As he lay wounded beside his cannon, he asked his commander: "Colonel, have I saved the honor of Mary and Lucy?" The officer raised his hat in salute.

What became of Mary, Lucy, and Eddie is unknown. Perhaps the Civil War consumed them too. ★

Military Justice *The armies used two types of execution: firing squad and hanging. The latter was usually reserved for heinous crimes. Pictured above is a Union soldier hanged near Petersburg, Virginia, for rape.*

"LAST NIGHT I WAS
AROUSED BY LITTLE
EDDIE'S CRYING. I CALLED
AND SAID, 'WHAT'S THE
MATTER. EDDIE?' AND HE
SAID, 'OH MAMA,
I AM SO HUNGRY.' AND
LUCY, EDWARD, YOUR
DARLING LUCY, SHE NEVER
COMPLAINS, BUT SHE IS
GROWING THINNER AND
THINNER EVERY DAY.
AND BEFORE GOD,
EDWARD, UNLESS YOU
COME HOME WE MUST DIE.
YOUR MARY."

**MARY COOPER
TO EDWARD COOPER**

Public Event *At top, a Union chaplain offers a final prayer for a condemned man
while members of his division watch from afar. Moments later, the dead man lies beside his coffin.
The body was buried in an unmarked grave.*

"Hell Holes"

Recruits in 1861 went off to war with many expectations. Being captured was never one of them. Yet 409,000 soldiers became prisoners of war, and some 56,000 of them died largely from neglect in makeshift compounds in both North and South. Civil War prisons were aptly called "hell holes" and sparked more violent passions and bitter accusations than any other aspect of the war.

The sordidness and suffering that occurred in Civil War compounds stemmed not so much from malice and intent as from inexperience, indifference, and incompetence. Some 150 soldier-prisons existed during the war. Only about 20—10 on each side—were large enough to become notorious. Prisoners in those major compounds suffered from overcrowding, vermin, malnutrition, unsanitary practices, and inadequate medical care, resulting in appalling death rates.

Confederate-run Camp Sumter, better known as Andersonville, was an open, treeless plain, miles from nowhere in south-central Georgia. The 27-acre plot had no barracks for prisoners, who slept in tents or lean-tos. Its walls were still being erected when the first 5,000 Federal prisoners were transferred there in early 1864. By August 1864, 33,000 emaciated soldiers were jammed into a space that offered each man roughly enough room to lie down. Had Andersonville been a city, it would have been the fifth largest in the Confederacy.

One small stream meandered through Andersonville. It served simultaneously as a garbage dump for the cookhouse, a latrine for thousands of prisoners, and their only source of drinking water. Inmates in desperate need of medical

Penned Up *Robert Knox Sneden produced this watercolor map of Andersonville from wartime sketches made while a prisoner there. At right, an August 1864 photograph shows Andersonville prisoners gathered to receive their meager rations.*

treatment languished in what inmate Robert Knox Sneden called "the pest house known as the hospital." Food was scarce in the South at this point in the war, and the rations at Andersonville were abominable. "All the meat had turned blue, green, yellow, and black," Sneden noted, and kept inmates who consumed it "running to the sinks all night." Of 45,000 prisoners confined at Andersonville, 12,900 perished during its one year of existence.

Conditions were little better at the Union-run "hell hole" called Fort Delaware, situated on a 178-acre island downriver from Wilmington. Captured Southerners began flowing into that prison in March 1862. In all, more than 40,000 men were confined there during the war, living in hastily constructed shanties and barracks that began sinking into the mud soon after construction. Summers were muggy, with pests in abundance. Winters were even worse for the undernourished, ill-clad prisoners, some of whom froze to death where they lay.

At Fort Delaware as at Andersonville, prisoners drank contaminated water and suffered ill effects. Only a few men at a time were allowed to go to the latrines. One inmate later recalled: "I have seen as many as 500 men in a row waiting their turn. The consequence was that they were obliged to use places where they were." Diarrhea, typhoid fever, scurvy, pneumonia, and smallpox all struck Fort Delaware. Thousands of prisoners died, but the exact toll is uncertain. Survival meant making do with whatever was at hand. "The prisoners scrambled for the rats like school boys for apples," recalled one man held here. "Of course but few were lucky enough to get a rat." Life for men in such "hell holes" was a greater struggle than anything they had faced in battle. ✶

"BY AUGUST 1864, 33,000 EMACIATED
SOLDIERS WERE JAMMED INTO A SPACE
THAT OFFERED EACH MAN ROUGHLY
ENOUGH ROOM TO LIE DOWN."

"ONE SMALL STREAM MEANDERED THROUGH ANDERSONVILLE.
IT SERVED SIMULTANEOUSLY AS
A GARBAGE DUMP FOR THE COOKHOUSE,
A LATRINE FOR THOUSANDS OF PRISONERS,
AND THEIR ONLY SOURCE OF DRINKING WATER."

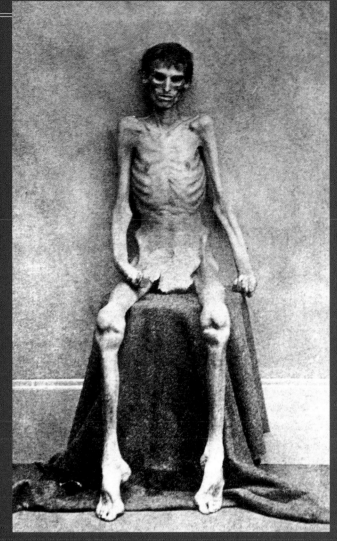

Victims of Neglect
This shocking photo–graph records a Union soldier ravaged by long imprisonment and chronic dysentery. Held at Richmond's Belle Isle Prison, he somehow survived to become part of a medical exchange. At left, tents and makeshift shelters fill the interior of the Andersonville stockade. The open wooden latrine in the foreground is located along the stream from which prisoners drew water.

Burial Duty *Union prisoners bury fellow inmates who died of disease, malnutrition, or other causes at Andersonville. In mid–1864, the brutal conditions there claimed more than 100 lives per day.*

Going Home

When Sgt. James Whitehorne of the 12th Virginia was paroled at Appomattox in April 1865, he wondered what he and his comrades would do now that the war was over: "How can we get interested in farming or working in a store or warehouse when we have been interested day and night for years in keeping alive, whipping the invaders, and preparing for another fight?"

A Union sergeant felt the same way. Rice Bull of the 123rd New York observed when he was mustered out: "There was a sadness deep in our hearts in this parting hour. We boys had been together for three years; we had formed close friendships; … we had borne danger, hardship, and privation alike … So it was hard to separate and say goodbye, one with the other; but we shook hands all around, and laughed and seemed to make merry, while our hearts were heavy and our eyes ready to shed tears."

Some veterans were understandably bitter. Union soldier Austin Stearns concluded that he had been treated worse than an animal. The army, he wrote, thought it better "to save the life of a mule for they cost money, but let the soldier be killed, for he costs nothing."

Defeat was painful to many Southern soldiers. Virginia artillerist Hampden Chamberlayne closed his diary by lamenting: "Ah! What hardships, what sufferings, what trials, what deaths, what sorrows, what tears, what great losses of men and property have I seen." He felt that "this deep well of sorrow, suffering and affliction must contain some pure and clear waters of comfort, of resignation, and of hope," but his greatest hope was that he and others would "never see another war."

"JOHNNY, IF A BOY DIES FOR HIS COUNTRY, THE GLORY IS HIS FOREVER, ISN'T IT?"

WILLIAM POPE'S LAST WORDS

The U.S. flag lowered at Fort Sumter on April 14, 1861, and raised again on April 14, 1865

Fateful Day *Recently paroled Southern soldiers mingle with Federal troops and local civilians beneath the equestrian statue of George Washington in Capitol Square, Richmond. The odd tranquillity hovering over the ex-Confederate capital on this day—April 14, 1865—faded when word arrived that President Lincoln had been assassinated that evening.*

Friends lost in the war lingered in the memory of the living for many years thereafter. The dead never knew the sweet taste of victory or the bitter taste of defeat. John Green of Kentucky's Confederate Orphan Brigade—so called because they felt they had lost their home when Kentucky came under Federal control—would not soon forget his messmate William Pope, who underwent two amputations after the Battle of Shiloh and contracted gangrene. Pope "met death with a patriot's heart," Green wrote. Yet he had no answer for Pope's last words: "Johnny, if a boy dies for his country, the glory is his forever, isn't it?"

Many Confederate veterans felt that defeat had not deprived them or those who died beside them of honor. Texas soldier John Stevens put it simply: "Let us be true to the memory of our slain, and be faithful to our country." The country Confederates fought for was not the country many later rejoined as Americans, but Stevens and others felt that those who had died for the South should be honored no less than those who had perished for the North.

Most men who fought under either flag were volunteers. Military service was not easy for those citizen-soldiers. They had to learn to accept the stern necessity of discipline and unquestioning obedience. Once they did so, however, they became first-class fighting men. Many returned home to become physicians, teachers, or to enter other professions. Yet at life's end, many Johnny Rebs and Billy Yanks had etched on their gravestones the meanest and lowest-paying job they ever had—that of a soldier.

Call it patriotism; call it determination; call it the foundation of American greatness. ★

Union Labor *Black laborers employed by the U.S. Military Railroad Construction Corps assemble at the railway docks in Alexandria, Virginia. By mid-1862, thousands of blacks, many of them fugitive slaves, contributed to the Federal war effort as craftsmen, laborers, spies, hospital workers, and teamsters.*

RESOURCES, RESOLVE, & INGENUITY

The disparity between Union and Confederacy in manpower and matériel was overwhelming. The North had as many factories—110,000—as the South had factory workers. Twenty-seven Northern cities built streetcar systems during the war years. Towns in the Confederacy could not maintain their dirt roads. Fifteen new colleges came into being in the North, while fewer than a half dozen managed to remain open in the South. The future Union commander William T. Sherman, who lived for a while in Louisiana, foresaw the outcome in a letter to a Southerner in 1860: "In all history no nation of mere agriculturists ever made successful war against a nation of mechanics . . . You are bound to fail." Yet the Confederacy lasted four years, because the war had as much to do with resolve and ingenuity as it did with resources.

FIGHT FOR FREEDOM

To some critics, Lincoln's Emancipation Proclamation seemed pointless. It granted freedom only to those slaves who were beyond his authority in Confederate territory. It did not apply to slaves held in states like Missouri that were under his authority. Secretary of State William Seward grumbled: "Where he could, he didn't. Where he did, he couldn't." Yet the proclamation, together with the enlistment of black troops like the soldier pictured here, transformed the Union war effort. (See "First Step to Freedom," pages 180-83.)

MUD AND MISERY

Civil War soldiers spent far more time fighting mud and other natural enemies than they did battling opposing armies. Union troops advancing on the Confederate capital in 1862 had to contend with heat, high humidity, and swarms of mosquitoes while building corduroy roads like this one to lift their wagons out of the muck. Soldiers dubbed their filthy bivouacs "Camp Muddy" and "Camp Misery," and tens of thousands fell ill before the campaign ended. (See "The Other Enemy," pages 178-9.)

"SHRIEKING DEMONS"

The shrill war cry was first heard in July 1861 at Manassas when Stonewall Jackson sent his men forward in a counterattack. "When you charge," Jackson told the soldiers, "yell like furies!" The strange "Rebel Yell" rang high above the din of battle and tormented Union soldiers for the remainder of the conflict. At Chancellorsville, a New York captain recalled, "the heavens seemed filled with hot-breathed, shrieking demons." (See "The Rebel Yell," pages 168-9.)

The Geography of War

A war can never be fully fathomed without an understanding of the terrain involved. The sheer size of the Southern nation was one of its major assets. The Confederacy encompassed 750,000 square miles, making it twice as large as the original 13 Colonies. To conquer so vast a country proved to be a herculean task for the Union.

The South was surrounded by water. It was like a vast island, bounded by the Potomac and Ohio Rivers to the north, the Mississippi River to the west, the Gulf of Mexico to the south, and the Atlantic Ocean to the east. In the long run, that favored the Union, which used its superior navy to blockade, invade, and eventually divide the Confederacy by seizing control of the Mississippi, separating Texas, Arkansas, and Louisiana from the rest of the rebellious states.

When invading Union forces moved by land rather than by water, however, they often encountered rough terrain that favored their opponents. The Appalachian Mountains divided the huge arena in which the war was fought into two distinct theaters of operations. In the Western theater, Northern armies made great strides, thanks in part to their command of the Ohio, Mississippi, and Tennessee Rivers. Yet the Appalachians, with few passes, prevented them from advancing eastward into the populous coastal states of the Confederacy until General Sherman captured Atlanta in late 1864 and marched to the sea.

In the Eastern theater, Southerners repelled Northern advances for much of the war by holding fast in Virginia, the apex of the Confederacy, where the terrain offered good defenses. The Shenandoah Valley of Virginia was a natural avenue of invasion for both sides but was more useful for the Confederacy. The valley ascended toward the southwest, away from Richmond and the main battleground. For Southern armies, on the other hand, the Shenandoah pointed northeastward like a spear toward the heart of the Union.

The two opposing capitals, Richmond and Washington, were only about 100 miles apart, but they were separated by six rivers, all running from west to east and blocking Federal advances southward once bridges were destroyed. Rivers such as the Rappahannock and the Rapidan were too deep for soldiers to wade across in all but a few places. Crossing at those fords, or on pontoon bridges constructed by Federal engineers, was treacherous. Every component of an advancing army—long columns of marching men, scores of cannon and caissons, and hundreds of supply wagons—had to cross the river or men ran the risk of being caught short of food, ammunition, and other basic needs.

With the Blue Ridge looming to the west, an advancing Federal army in Virginia had little room to maneuver and little chance of outflanking watchful Confederate defenders. The Union battle cry "Forward to Richmond!" became a siren's song, enticing Federals into killing grounds like the tangled Wilderness below the Rappahannock. "I was not prepared to find it an almost impenetrable thicket," remarked Gen. Joseph Hooker, whose army came to grief there in the Battle of Chancellorsville.

The South's poor roads also became an asset for Confederates by miring invaders. Most were dirt tracks that became impassable in foul weather. Wagons and artillery could easily sink to their axles, especially in Virginia. Some roads there were almost as old as the Old Dominion itself, and the red-clay soil formed a mud not unlike quicksand. A Union officer campaigning on the Virginia Peninsula in 1862 swore that he saw an army mule sink out of sight except for its ears—although the officer did admit that "it was a small mule." ✷

> "THE SOUTH WAS SURROUNDED BY WATER. IT WAS LIKE A VAST ISLAND, BOUNDED BY THE POTOMAC AND OHIO RIVERS TO THE NORTH, THE MISSISSIPPI RIVER TO THE WEST, THE GULF OF MEXICO TO THE SOUTH, AND THE ATLANTIC OCEAN TO THE EAST."

Western Yankees *The young soldiers pictured here were among many Midwestern recruits who swelled the Union army. As shown on the map below, much of the Union (green) lay west of the Appalachians. Federal regiments from that region were concentrated in the Western theater, whose rivers facilitated their movements.*

BACON'S
MILITARY MAP OF THE
UNITED STATES
Shewing the
FORTS & FORTIFICATIONS.

Published by BACON & C⁰ 48 Paternoster Row

LONDON 1862

EXPLANATION.

Free or Non-Slaveholding States.
Population 19,000,000, Area 1,228,697 Square Miles
Border Slave States
Pop.ⁿ 5,000,000, 500,000 are Slaves Area 761,423 d⁰
Seceded or Confederate States
Pop.ⁿ 10,000,000, 3,500,000 are Slaves Area 853,144 d⁰

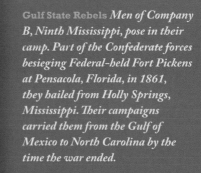

Gulf State Rebels *Men of Company B, Ninth Mississippi, pose in their camp. Part of the Confederate forces besieging Federal-held Fort Pickens at Pensacola, Florida, in 1861, they hailed from Holly Springs, Mississippi. Their campaigns carried them from the Gulf of Mexico to North Carolina by the time the war ended.*

CHESAPEAKE BAY

ATLANTIC OCEAN

"THE TWO OPPOSING
CAPITALS, RICHMOND
AND WASHINGTON,
WERE ONLY ABOUT
100 MILES APART, BUT
THEY WERE SEPARATED
BY SIX RIVERS,
ALL RUNNING FROM
WEST TO EAST AND
BLOCKING FEDERAL
ADVANCES SOUTHWARD
ONCE BRIDGES WERE
DESTROYED."

Seat of War *Lithographer John Bachmann produced this 1861 bird's-eye view of the heavily contested Tidewater and Piedmont region of Virginia, as viewed from Chesapeake Bay. The popularity of ballooning during the mid-19th century inspired such aerial perspectives.*

A Tale of Two Capitals

When Richmond, Virginia, became the Confederate capital in May 1861, it was in many respects equal if not superior to Washington, D.C. Founded in the 1730s, when most of what is now the District of Columbia was an uninhabited swamp, Richmond was the third largest city in the South. Its population of nearly 40,000 swelled to three times that number during the Civil War and rivaled that of Washington, which had more than 60,000 residents when the war began.

The imposing Virginia State capitol in Richmond, designed by Thomas Jefferson, became the seat of the Confederate government, overlooking Capitol Square and an equestrian statue of George Washington. Secessionists called that revered Virginian the Father of the Confederacy and felt he belonged to their capital, not to Washington, D.C. Stately public buildings and gracious residences—including the Confederate White House, near Capitol Square—gave Richmond an elegance few other American cities possessed.

Richmond was the South's leading manufacturing center. Five railroads converged there. It was also a thriving port, linked to the sea by the James River—navigable below Richmond—and to western Virginia by a canal that carried more freight than the five railroads combined. Richmond had 13 carriage manufacturers, eight flour mills, four gunsmiths, and the prodigious Tredegar Iron Works, the largest such foundry in America. After Virginia seceded, its owner, Joseph Reid Anderson, offered its services to the Confederacy: "Will make anything you want—work day and night if necessary, and ship by rail." Before the war was over, Tredegar would turn out more than a thousand cannon.

The city had to be defended to the last. As one newspaper editor stated: "To lose Richmond is to lose Virginia, and to lose Virginia is to lose the keys to the Southern Confederacy."

By contrast, Washington, D.C., in 1861 was still more a dream than a reality. Established in the 1790s, it had to begin anew in 1814 after British troops burned the U.S. Capitol, the presidential mansion, and other public buildings. At the start of the Civil War, the city remained unfinished. A half dozen federal buildings were sprinkled here and there. The Capitol lacked a dome. Fine residences along Pennsylvania Avenue lay near slums occupied largely by free blacks. Washington was a Southern town, hemmed in by Confederates in Virginia and secessionists in Maryland, who threatened to take over that state before President Lincoln cracked down on them.

Like Richmond, wartime Washington swelled with wounded men as well as able-bodied soldiers. It also swarmed with lobbyists, contractors, crooks, and cranks. Much of the city was unpaved and overwhelmed by the traffic and turmoil. A Pennsylvania cavalryman wrote in January 1862: "Of all the Mud Holes that I have been in I think Washington will take the Premium. The Store Keeper and People in general are nothing but a set of Thieves." A New England soldier found little in Washington to admire except its public buildings, which loomed "like diamonds on a dung hill."

The Civil War reversed the fortunes of the two capitals. Richmond was devastated by fire at war's end. Washington survived the conflict intact. The Capitol had its dome by 1865, and the increasing power of the Federal government thereafter accelerated the growth and vitality of the city on the Potomac, which had three times the population of Richmond by 1880. In 1885 the long-delayed Washington Monument was finally completed. No one could deny now that this was truly the city of Washington, the nation's founder. ✯

> "TO LOSE RICHMOND IS TO LOSE VIRGINIA, AND TO LOSE VIRGINIA IS TO LOSE THE KEYS TO THE SOUTHERN CONFEDERACY."
>
> **A NEWSPAPER EDITOR IN RICHMOND**

> "OF ALL THE MUD HOLES THAT I HAVE BEEN IN I THINK WASHINGTON WILL TAKE THE PREMIUM."
>
> **A UNION SOLDIER IN WASHINGTON, D.C.**

White House Sentinels
Fully armed but garbed in civilian frock coats and top hats, men of the "Frontier Guard" parade in front of the White House in April 1861. Raised in Washington by Kansas Senator James H. Lane, the company protected the executive mansion while awaiting reinforcements from the North.

City on Seven Hills *Flanked by the spire of St. Paul's Episcopal Church, the Virginia state capitol—which served as the Confederate capitol during the war—dominates the Richmond skyline in this photograph taken from Church Hill in April 1865.*

Guru of the Generals

T he art of war is simple enough," Ulysses Grant once remarked. "Find out where your enemy is. Get at him as soon as you can. Strike at him as hard as you can and as often as you can. And keep moving on." Grant was less interested in military theory than in military practice, but much of what he and other officers in his day knew about the art of war was instilled in them by one professor. More than 500 Civil War commanders were West Point graduates. All but a few of them studied under a legendary teacher, Dennis Hart Mahan.

Born in 1802 to Irish immigrants, the frail Mahan sought admission to West Point because drawing was part of the curriculum and he wanted to become an artist. So outstanding was his performance as a cadet that at the end of his sophomore year Superintendent Sylvanus Thayer made him assistant professor of mathematics.

Mahan graduated at the head of his class in 1824. He would remain on the faculty at West Point for the next 47 years. Sent in 1826 to Europe to study civil and military engineering, Mahan absorbed the lessons of Napoleon's campaigns. The young professor then created a new course called Engineering and the Science of War that became the keystone to a West Point education. Embracing both tactics and strategy, it made Mahan the father of American military theory.

Thin, goateed, and equipped with piercing eyes and a penetrating voice, Mahan never witnessed a battle and refused to wear a uniform. Irritable and erudite, he was relentlessly demanding in the classroom.

CONFEDERATE	UNION
Robert E. Lee	Ulysses S. Grant
Jefferson Davis	William T. Sherman
Stonewall Jackson	George G. Meade
James Longstreet	George B. McClellan
Albert S. Johnston	Henry W. Halleck
Pierre G. T. Beauregard	George H. Thomas
John B. Hood	John Sedgwick
Richard S. Ewell	Ambrose E. Burnside
James E. B. Stuart	Joseph Hooker
William J. Hardee	Philip H. Sheridan

He detested sloppy posture as much as he did sloppy thinking. When a man's body is at attention, he maintained, so is the mind. He had an uncanny talent for spotting the most unprepared student in class, barraging him with questions, and leaving him in shreds. Yet his only aim in life, he insisted, was to "make soldiers worthy of the Republic."

Few military textbooks then existed in English. Mahan solved the problem by producing his own, including an 1847 manual known in short as *Outposts* that served as a bible for every cadet in America. War was a science derived from military history, Mahan taught. He stressed the Napoleonic principle of rapid maneuver to concentrate one's forces at a critical point of enemy weakness. The fundamentals for military success, he emphasized, were celerity (a word he much preferred to quickness) and boldness, tempered by common sense.

Many Civil War commanders applied his tactical lessons, but relatively few possessed that rare combination of celerity, audacity, and sound judgment that he extolled. Among them were Robert E. Lee, Stonewall Jackson, William Sherman, and Ulysses Grant. A poor student at West Point, Grant later lived up to Mahan's standards with his swift and daring encirclement of Vicksburg and earned high praise from the professor: "European warfare can produce nothing equal to it since the 1st Napoleon."

West Point officials forced Mahan's retirement in 1871 because of his age. A few days later, he fell from a boat and drowned in the Hudson River within sight of the academy. ✫

Professor of War *In his years at West Point, Dennis Hart Mahan (right) instructed most of the prominent military leaders of both North and South, including these notable figures (above).*

"MORE THAN 500 CIVIL WAR COMMANDERS WERE WEST POINT GRADUATES. ALL BUT A FEW OF THEM STUDIED UNDER A LEGENDARY TEACHER, DENNIS HART MAHAN."

"Old Fuss and Feathers"

He had long been Washington's most imposing monument. Standing six feet, four inches tall, General-in-Chief Winfield Scott by 1861 was beset with age, infirmity, and an epicurean appetite that had ballooned his massive frame to somewhere beyond 300 pounds. He could not mount a horse to inspect soldiers, much less lead them into battle. Only his vanity, swollen with age like his girth, was equal to his reputation as the nation's foremost military hero since the sainted Washington. Yet "Old Fuss and Feathers" had one more contribution to make in this, his third war.

Born in 1786 on a farm near Petersburg, Virginia, Scott entered the U.S. Army by appointment of President Thomas Jefferson. He was the hero of the Canadian campaigns in the War of 1812 and the architect of American victory in the Mexican War. In 1852, Scott ran as Whig candidate for President.

When Fort Sumter fell and Virginia seceded, he was asked to cast his lot with the Old Dominion. "I have served my country, under the flag of the Union, for more than fifty years," he shot back, "and so long as God permits me to live, I will defend that flag with my sword, even if my native State assails it."

Although his body was crumbling with age, Scott still had a clear eye for war. He quickly developed a plan for Northern victory. The Confederacy, he insisted, could not be defeated quickly by an army advancing on Richmond, as many Unionists

Constricting the Rebellion *General in Chief Winfield Scott, pictured at right late in life, devised the Anaconda Plan, lampooned above in a cartoon published in Cincinnati in 1861, showing a snake coiled around the rebellious Confederacy.*

hoped. He proposed a broader offensive that would take time to implement. Lincoln had imposed a naval blockade on the South just days after the war began. In conjunction with that blockade, Scott proposed sending some 80,000 troops down the Mississippi River in a fleet shielded by gunboats. They would take control of the Mississippi down to the Gulf of Mexico, while other Union forces would mass along the Confederacy's northern border. The South would be caught in a stranglehold and would have to surrender or die of suffocation.

When Scott's plan leaked out, the public heaped contempt on the general. Newspapers labeled it the "Anaconda Plan." The image of a huge snake slowly constricting the enemy to death struck many Northerners as ridiculous. There was no dash in it, nothing to stir the national pulse. Besides, such a plan would take too long in a war that one big battle would surely decide—or so people thought.

Scott's plan was shelved, and the old soldier retired in late 1861. It soon became clear, however, that the defiant South would indeed have to be squeezed systematically until it yielded. Taking control of the Mississippi River became a major strategic objective for the Union. That goal was achieved by Grant in July 1863 with the surrender of Vicksburg and Port Hudson, the last Confederate bastions on the Mississippi.

When Winfield Scott died in May 1866, the Union was victorious—thanks in no small part to a plan hatched by Old Fuss and Feathers before he stepped down. ★

"SCOTT'S PLAN WAS SHELVED, AND THE OLD SOLDIER RETIRED IN LATE 1861. IT SOON BECAME CLEAR, HOWEVER, THAT THE DEFIANT SOUTH WOULD INDEED HAVE TO BE SQUEEZED SYSTEMATICALLY UNTIL IT YIELDED."

Those Damn Torpedoes

The term "torpedo" was used broadly during the Civil War to refer to any kind of mine, on land or in water. Most naval torpedoes were stationary or drifted with the tide. Such weapons were not new. During the American Revolution, an attempt was made to sink a British warship with a small barrel filled with gunpowder. Torpedoes were deployed out of necessity by Confederates, who lacked the ships and heavy artillery to wage traditional naval warfare. They were placed at the entrance to ports such as Richmond, Wilmington, Charleston, and Mobile to shield them from Union warships.

The mastermind of such Confederate defenses was Matthew Fontaine Maury. When the war began, the 51-year-old Maury was superintendent of the U.S. Naval Observatory, responsible for the navy's charts and instruments. Disabled by a carriage accident as a young officer, he had devoted himself to the science of navigation and was known as the Father of Oceanography. A native of Virginia, he resigned his post in 1861 and became a Confederate naval commander. He developed a torpedo that could be detonated electronically from land using insulated telegraph wire. Unlike torpedoes that blew up on contact and could harm friendly vessels, Maury's device could be used discriminately against hostile ships.

After a demonstration in which he detonated a torpedo in the James River, sending water bursting into the air, he was placed in command of the South's coastal, harbor, and river defenses. He later clashed with Confederate Secretary of the Navy Stephen Mallory, who sent Maury off to England, where he procured ships for the South as well as wire and batteries for electric torpedoes.

Both electric and contact mines were deployed by the Confederate Torpedo Service, led by Gen. Gabriel Rains. Mines of any sort were considered unsporting, if not diabolical, because they gave the enemy no warning. Federals dubbed them "infernal machines." Maury had no qualms about using torpedoes at a time when the Union naval blockade was preventing medicine as well as weapons from reaching the South. Rains remarked that warfare was "legalized murder of our fellow men." Torpedoes, he concluded, were no worse than other weapons that were considered barbarous until their "efficacy in human slaughter" made them widely acceptable.

Torpedoes served the Confederacy well. During the course of the war, they sank 7 Union ironclads and 22 wooden gunboats and damaged 14 other vessels. Not a single enemy vessel reached Richmond until it fell in April 1865. A Union naval veteran later declared: "We dreaded torpedoes more than anything else." They would have been even more effective had not some torpedoes been corroded by long exposure to salt water and malfunctioned. When Adm. David Farragut led a Federal fleet into Mobile Bay in August 1864, he shouted famously: "Damn the torpedoes! Full speed ahead!" He gained victory and glory because many of those damn torpedoes failed to detonate. ✷

Rebel Scientist *Matthew Fontaine Maury, portrayed here in 1855, developed and deployed underwater mines for the Confederacy— including some of the first successful electrically fired torpedoes.*

Rains keg torpedo

Tin-sheathed torpedo

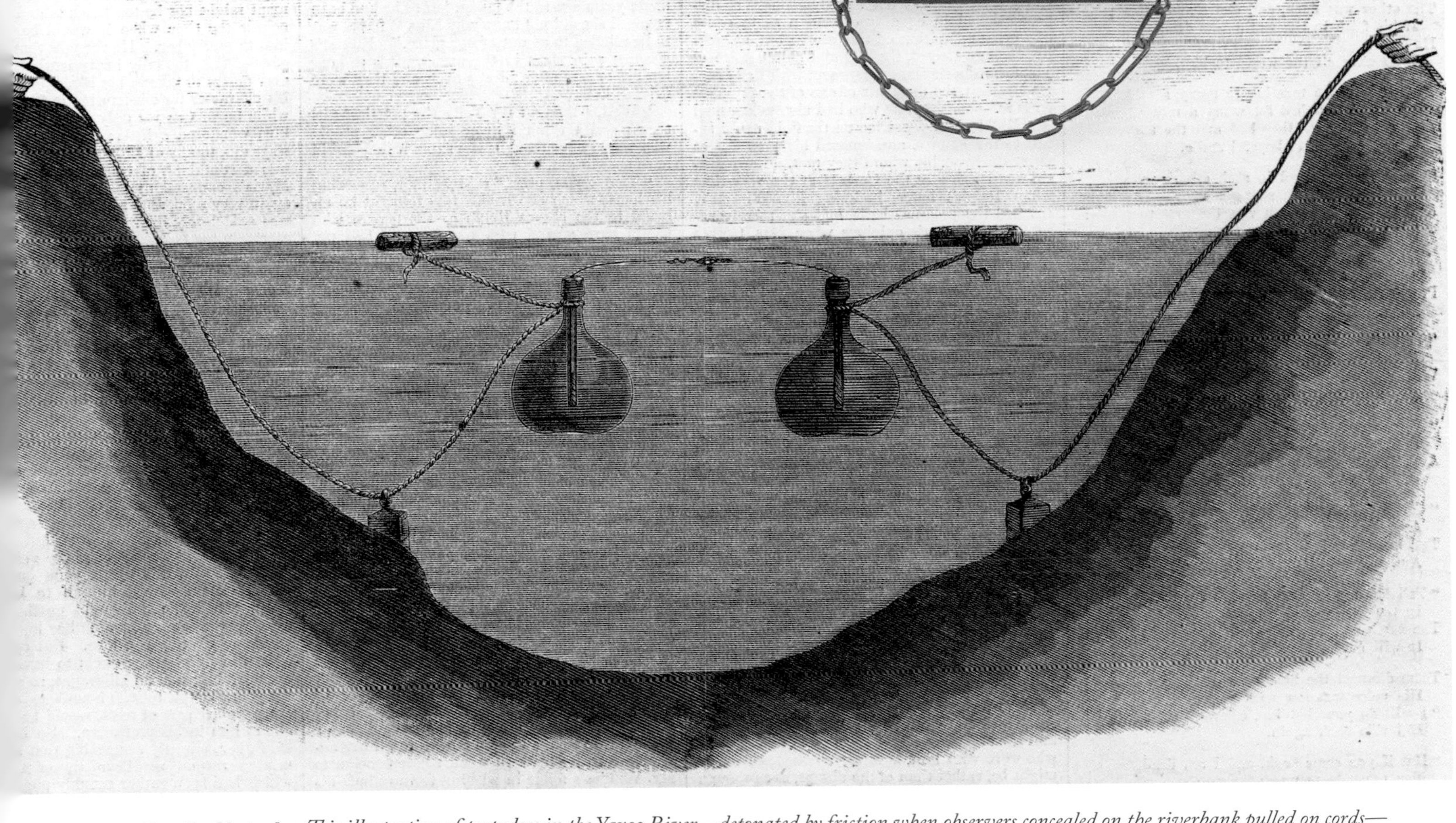

"MINES OF ANY SORT WERE CONSIDERED UNSPORTING, IF NOT DIABOLICAL . . . MAURY HAD NO QUALMS ABOUT USING TORPEDOES WHILE THE UNION NAVAL BLOCKADE WAS PREVENTING MEDICINE AS WELL AS WEAPONS FROM REACHING THE SOUTH."

Deadly Obstacles *This illustration of torpedoes in the Yazoo River—detonated by friction when observers concealed on the riverbank pulled on cords— appeared in a February 1863 issue of* Harper's Weekly. *The contributor, a Federal naval officer, observed that "the business of seeking for torpedoes and fishing them up is one of the most exciting and perilous duties of our Western sailors."*

Gunsmith Par Excellence

If the Confederacy had a real "miracle worker," it was Gen. Josiah Gorgas. What he accomplished for the always hard-pressed South during the war almost defied belief.

Gorgas was a Pennsylvanian, who had graduated near the top of his class at West Point and devoted his career in the U.S. Army to ordnance, or munitions. While commanding arsenals in the South, Gorgas met and married Amelia Gayle, whose father was governor of Alabama. In February 1861, while in charge of the Philadelphia arsenal, Gorgas was offered the post of Confederate chief of ordnance. He agonized over the decision but eventually accepted the commission at a cost of severing ties with his brothers, sisters, and friends in the North.

Gorgas organized a massive ordnance production program in the largely agricultural South. Starting almost from scratch, he improvised and he industrialized. Because the region's overburdened rail system could not be counted on to deliver munitions from manufacturing centers like Richmond throughout the South, he developed factories in many places. Experienced workers trained new employees at those plants to get them started.

Gorgas knew that it would take time to bring those plants up to speed and sought other sources of weapons and war matériel. He purchased munitions in Europe and swift ships designed to run the Federal blockade and deliver those goods.

> "ONCE A TEMPERAMENTAL OFFICER WHO QUARRELED OFTEN WITH SUPERIORS, GORGAS THRIVED WHEN HE HAD HIS OWN BUREAU TO RUN. THE RURAL SOUTH BECAME MOBILIZED FOR WAR TO AN EXTENT NO ONE ENVISIONED . . . CONFEDERATE SOLDIERS OFTEN LACKED FOOD AND CLOTHING, BUT NEVER, UNTIL THE END, DID THEY LACK FOR MUNITIONS."

He increased production from mineral and ore deposits such as the lead works at Wytheville, Virginia. Ordnance officers roamed the South, buying or confiscating whiskey stills to provide copper for rifle percussion caps. They melted down bells from churches, schools, and plantations for the bronze needed to build cannon. Gorgas encouraged soldiers to scavenge battlefields for weapons and amassed 100,000 discarded Union firearms in one year alone. The South lacked saltpeter for the manufacture of gunpowder, so he used a composting method that combined uric acid from urine with other organic waste to produce saltpeter.

Once a temperamental officer who quarreled often with superiors, Gorgas thrived when he had his own bureau to run. The rural South became mobilized for war to an extent no one envisioned. Gorgas himself wrote that the results were "beyond my utmost expectations." Confederate soldiers often lacked food and clothing, but never, until the end, did they lack for munitions. One authority later commented that the world had probably never seen "such a miraculous transformation of ploughshares into swords."

That miracle was not enough to alter the war's outcome. Following the twin Confederate defeats at Gettysburg and Vicksburg in July 1863, Gorgas wrote in his diary: "Today absolute ruin seems to be our portion. The Confederacy totters to its destruction." And so it did, despite his amazing feats. ✶

Confederate Munitions *Southern armaments ranged from this Fayetteville rifle to the projectiles that littered the ruins of the Richmond Arsenal (right).*

Gen. Josiah Gorgas

The Rebel Yell

In July 1861 at Manassas, as the war's first major battle hung in the balance, Stonewall Jackson sent his Virginia brigade forward in a counterattack. "When you charge," Jackson told the soldiers, "yell like furies!" They did just that, issuing a fierce, wild cry that rang high above the storm of battle. During the course of the war, Union soldiers would come to dread that so-called Rebel Yell. The Confederate battle cry became famous and remains so today, although no one alive knows precisely what it sounded like.

The shout was intended as much to relieve the attacker as to frighten the defender. Soldiers employed every means to gain courage in battle. Yelling or howling was an ancient way for warriors to translate fear into fury. "I always said that if I ever went into a charge, I wouldn't holler," one Confederate remarked. "But the very first time I fired off my gun, I hollered as loud as I could, and I hollered every breath until we stopped."

One authority on the subject, historian Bell Irvin Wiley, has described the Rebel Yell as "an unpremeditated, unrestricted and utterly informal hollering" that possessed "a mixture of fright, pent-up nervousness, exultation, hatred, and a pinch of pure deviltry." In reality, there was no one Rebel Yell. There were several, which varied depending on the origins of the men raising the cheer. Three versions are described by Wiley. One was "a blood-curdling, full-throated caterwaul." Another—the type most imitated—consisted of "a quick succession of high-pitched yelps, like a foxhunter's call." The third kind was "a peculiar, apelike grunt that rose gradually into a piercing howl."

True to the Colors
William Smith, color-bearer of the 12th Virginia, exudes the proud defiance that made Confederate attackers daunting to their foes.

The Rebel Yell evidently varied by state. At the Battle of Chickamauga, one commander told his men to attack "with a regular Mississippi yell." In the same contest, a Tennessee colonel reported, "I ordered three times three of Old Tennessee and a charge, both of which were responded with alacrity."

Some described the Rebel Yell as resembling an Indian war whoop. That may in fact have been one inspiration for the Confederate battle cry, which could help make attackers seem more numerous or better armed than they really were. In 1864, profane Gen. Jubal Early directed his Confederates to make a charge near Richmond. Officers replied that the soldiers were out of ammunition, whereupon Early bellowed: "Damn it, holler them across!" His men made the attack with bayonets fixed, yelling like banshees.

Southerners attacking in full cry appeared to their enemies to be demons. One Billy Yank recalled with dismay "that terrible scream and barbarous howling." Another Union soldier confessed that hearing the Rebel Yell in the hear of battle "made the hair stand up on my head."

Union soldiers had nothing that could match the shrill holler of their opponents. Yanks often shouted "Hooray!" or "Huzzah!" in unison as they entered combat, but they could not drown out the high-pitched keening of the Confederates. Those unearthly screams, declared one Federal, were "the ugliest any mortal ever heard." ★

"SOUTHERNERS ATTACKING IN FULL CRY APPEARED TO THEIR ENEMIES
TO BE DEMONS. ONE BILLY YANK RECALLED WITH DISMAY
'THAT TERRIBLE SCREAM AND BARBAROUS HOWLING.'
ANOTHER UNION SOLDIER CONFESSED THAT HEARING THE REBEL YELL
IN THE HEAT OF BATTLE 'MADE THE HAIR STAND UP ON MY HEAD.'"

Into the Pit *The Rebel Yell often accompanied Confederate assaults like this one, carried out by the 12th Virginia and other regiments of William Mahone's brigade during the Battle of the Crater at Petersburg on July 30, 1864.*

"Make Me a Map"

Few good maps existed in 1861 because few were needed. Americans as a rule rarely traveled far from their homes. When war swept the land, military commanders scurried to find reliable charts for troop movements. Many units became lost in the early months of the conflict. That Stonewall Jackson never made that error in the Shenandoah Valley with its uneven terrain was the result of having the foremost mapmaker of the war, Jedediah Hotchkiss.

The New York–born Hotchkiss left home at the age of 17 to seek a career. He eventually settled in Staunton, Virginia, where he became principal of a boys' academy. Mapmaking was his hobby. Formal training in that craft was available only at military schools, but Hotchkiss pored over atlases, taught himself the basics of surveying, and proved to be a skilled draftsman, with a keen eye for the varied topography of the valley.

He closed his school when the war began and volunteered as a Confederate topographical engineer. The following March, following a long bout with typhoid fever, he joined Jackson's staff. Hotchkiss, who was then 33, bore little resemblance to a professional soldier. Almost six feet in height, he had sleepy eyes and a scraggly beard. Like his commander, he shunned both whiskey and tobacco. He tended to be long-winded in conversation, but the taciturn Jackson soon cured him of that.

The general's first order to Major Hotchkiss was sweeping: "Make me a map of the Valley, from Harpers Ferry to Lexington." That was an area of more than 2,000 square miles, but he took up the daunting task with energy and enthusiasm. Hotchkiss was equipped with compasses, an altimeter, and other surveying instruments. He had a wagon and driver but often went off on horseback to sketch remote terrain. Using colored pencils to distinguish features, he pinpointed woods for campfires, fields for forage, and water for drinking. He soon translated his sketches and measurements into a comprehensive map of the area. Meticulous yet clear, it proved vital to Jackson's fast-moving Valley Campaign that spring, enabling him to outmarch and outmaneuver numerically superior opponents who lacked his detailed knowledge of the terrain, highways, and back roads. Thanks to Hotchkiss, Jackson was able to apply his formula for victory: "Always mystify, mislead and surprise the enemy, if possible."

After mapping the valley, Hotchkiss remained with Jackson and served as cartographer for Lee's Army of Northern Virginia. He gave that army and its commander a new set of eyes and charted the way for advances. He was with Jackson when he was critically wounded at Chancellorsville in May 1863. Hotchkiss was completing a map of the battlefield when word arrived of Jackson's death. "Our revered and adored Commander is gone," wrote Hotchkiss, who shared Jackson's belief that all misfortunes were ordained by God and must be accepted: "The singular but good and great man that directed everything is no longer at his post and everything wears an altered and lonely look, but such is earth and such are earthly things." ✷

Stonewall's Cartographer
Maj. Jedediah Hotchkiss, a talented, self-taught topographer, produced reconnaissance maps for use during campaigns as well as more artistic charts to accompany official after-battle reports.

Charting the Valley *Jedediah Hotchkiss's map of the lower Shenandoah Valley, created for Stonewall Jackson in the spring of 1862, was drawn in waterproof India ink on fine drafting linen. The enlargement at far right shows carefully surveyed detail, including roads and other man-made features, along with watercourses, forest cover, and elevation, shown using contour lines.*

This volume is my field sketch book that I used during the war. Most of the sketches were made on horseback just as they now appear. The colored pencils used were kept in the places fixed on the outside of the other cover.

These topographical sketches were often used in conferences with Generals Jackson, Ewell and Early.

The cover of this book is a blank Federal Commission found in Gen. Milroy's quarters at Winchester.

Jed. Hotchkiss

Record of Battle *The map at right, rendered in ink and watercolor, was created by Hotchkiss to accompany his report on the positions of General Richard Ewell's II Corps of the Army of Northern Virginia during the Battle of Spotsylvania in May 1864. All officers, down to the regimental level, were required to submit accounts of their actions in battles.*

Tools of the Trade *Jedediah Hotchkiss used basic surveying tools, including the vernier compass and portable altimeter below, to sketch field surveys in colored pencil in his pocket notebook (above). Hotchkiss inscribed and signed the book's cover.*

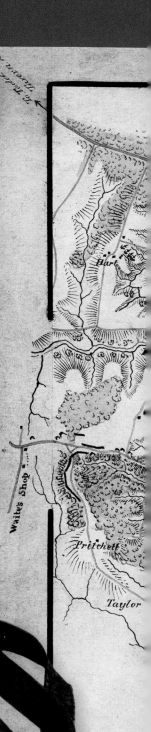

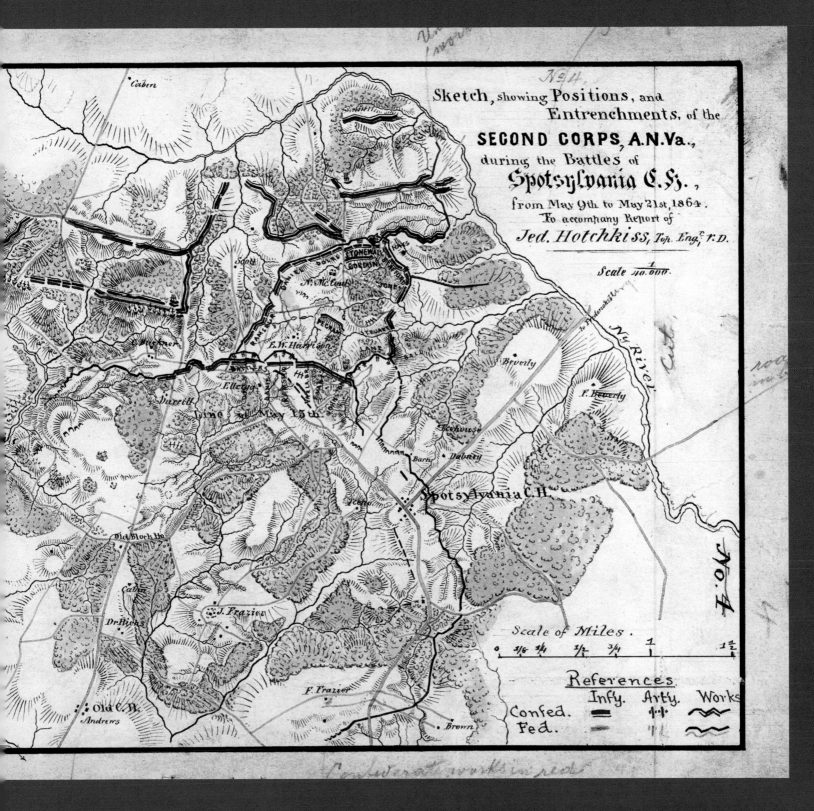

"Silent Battle"

In early April of 1862, Confederate Gen. Albert Sidney Johnston left his base at Corinth, Mississippi, and marched northward with 44,000 recruits into Tennessee. His plan was to mount a surprise attack on the army of Ulysses Grant, encamped around a Methodist meetinghouse called Shiloh.

Johnston's Confederate force was not yet an army. It was a collection of rowdy civilians in snappy uniforms. They called themselves soldiers but had little idea of what the word meant.

Pelting rain slowed their advance to a crawl. They cheered or yelled as officers passed, aimlessly fired muskets to see if the powder was dry, or shot at deer bounding through the woods.

Johnston halted his horde within a half mile of the enemy on the night of April 5. Officers pleaded with him to postpone the attack. The Rebels had raised such a racket that surprise was seemingly out of the question. Johnston held firm. "We shall attack at daylight tomorrow," he declared.

At dawn, Confederates slammed into the exposed division of Gen. William Sherman and caught him completely off guard. Grant's army was nearly shattered before he managed to avert defeat at great cost. "At Shiloh, we were not surprised," Sherman remarked afterward. "We were astonished!"

This was one of many strange instances during the Civil War when musketry or cannon fire that should have been heard nearby went undetected. Sometimes, the fault lay with listeners who were distracted and failed to notice sounds that should have alarmed them. But in most cases, thunderous noises that would otherwise have been audible many miles

"AS PICKETT AND FITZHUGH LEE FEASTED ON SHAD ROE, THEY COULD NOT HEAR THE FURIOUS BATTLE THAT ERUPTED AT FIVE FORKS, JUST A MILE AND A HALF AWAY."

Fitzhugh Lee

away were muffled by a phenomenon called acoustic shadow, or "silent battle," caused by atmospheric conditions and terrain features. Among the factors responsible were wind and rain, dense woods with wet foliage, broken terrain with hills and hollows, and differences in temperature or air pressure between the site of battle and listeners at another elevation nearby. At the Battle of Gaines's Mill near Richmond in 1862, wrote author and Civil War veteran Ambrose Bierce, civilians less than two miles away observed "one of the fiercest conflicts of the Civil War, with a hundred guns in play." Smoke billowed from those cannon, but the baffled spectators "heard nothing of what they clearly saw. "

Other battles at which acoustic shadows were reported included Seven Pines, Perryville, and Chancellorsville. The most famous instance took place at Five Forks in Virginia as the war drew to a close. Robert E. Lee had entrusted defense of that vital road junction on his right flank at Petersburg to Gen. George Pickett. On April 1, 1865, Pickett and Gen. Fitzhugh Lee, the army commander's nephew, received an irresistible invitation. They went off to a fish bake. As Pickett and Fitzhugh Lee feasted on shad roe, they could not hear the furious battle that erupted at Five Forks, just a mile and a half away. By the time they learned of the attack and responded, Union forces were well on their way to seizing Five Forks and a nearby railroad. Lee's army withdrew toward Appomattox soon after.

"All's quiet along the front" was a common report during the war. As Pickett and others learned through bitter experience, however, silence could sometimes be deadly. ★

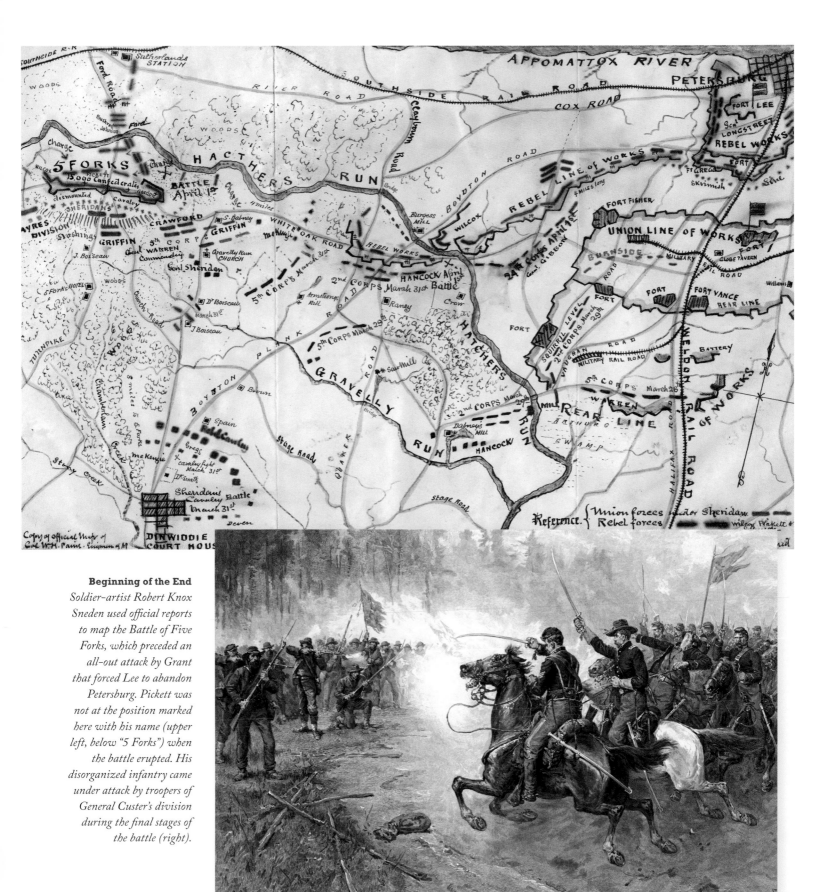

Beginning of the End

Soldier-artist Robert Knox Sneden used official reports to map the Battle of Five Forks, which preceded an all-out attack by Grant that forced Lee to abandon Petersburg. Pickett was not at the position marked here with his name (upper left, below "5 Forks") when the battle erupted. His disorganized infantry came under attack by troopers of General Custer's division during the final stages of the battle (right).

Unsung Heroes

The enormous human cost of the Civil War—more than 620,000 fatalities among soldiers in four years—cannot be forgotten. Often over-looked, however, is the fact that more than three times as many deaths occurred among creatures on whom both sides in the conflict depended: horses and mules.

In 1860, the horse population in America was about six million. Sixty percent were heavy draft animals that hauled plows, wagons, and carriages. The remainder were smaller, sleeker horses bred to serve as mounts. Civil War armies had great need of both types of horses as well as mules. Mules sometimes hauled artillery but were more likely than horses to bolt under fire. Confederate Gen. John Imboden recalled a battle in which the mules pulling his big guns grew frantic: "They kicked, plunged and squealed . . . Several of them lay down and tried to wallow their loads off." Mules proved their mettle not in the heat of battle like warhorses but when harnessed to heavy, lumbering wagons in trains that moved continually through the day and sometimes into the night, regardless of weather conditions.

Mules and horses did more to keep armies moving and supplied than did either railroads or riverboats. To bear heavy bur-dens, war departments on both sides sought horses that were four to six years old and about 16 hands high on the shoulder blades, and that weighed up to 2,000 pounds. On a good road, a horse could more than pull its own weight.

Horses and mules never had an easy time in the Civil War. They were prime targets in battle. Killing them could send charging cavalrymen sprawling and immobilize artillery. "When the enemy's infantry gets within musket range," one Union artilleryman remarked, "they can kill horses faster than we can change them."

Commanders whose campaigns covered hundreds of miles relied as much on their horses and mules as they did on their men. General Sherman issued an order urging that "extra-ordinary care be taken of the horses upon which everything depends." Unfortunately, the care animals received while in service was often inadequate. Cavalrymen and team-sters alike abused horses and mules out of necessity or indifference. Many animals died of hunger or exposure. In October 1862, a Massachusetts soldier wrote home: "Two horses froze to death last night . . . and you ought to see the poor horses and mules tremble and shake in the morning. They suffer everything."

Diseases such as glanders and colic, and injuries caused by poorly fitting bits or other faulty equipment, took a steep toll as well. The life expectancy of a horse or mule in the Civil War was seven months. For every mount killed in battle, three animals died of disease or mistreatment.

A unique monument to the suffering many animals endured during the conflict stands on the lawn of the Virginia Historical Society. The bronze statue depicts a starved and worn-out horse, head bowed, looking as if it might soon collapse. The statue serves as a reminder that nearly two million of God's creatures were sacrificed in this pitiless war, never to be put out peacefully to pasture as they deserved. ✵

Prime Movers *A woodcut of a dashing stallion ornaments a poster offering "good prices" for army horses. The dead artillery mule at right, photographed in the aftermath of Gettysburg, graphically illustrates the fate of so many army draft animals and saddle horses.*

"HORSES AND MULES NEVER
HAD AN EASY TIME IN THE CIVIL WAR.
THEY WERE PRIME TARGETS IN BATTLE.
KILLING THEM COULD SEND CAVALRYMEN
SPRAWLING AND IMMOBILIZE ARTILLERY.
'WHEN THE ENEMY'S INFANTRY
GETS WITHIN MUSKET RANGE,'
ONE UNION ARTILLERYMAN REMARKED,
'THEY CAN KILL HORSES FASTER THAN
WE CAN CHANGE THEM.'"

The Other Enemy

The Peninsular Campaign of 1862 was the first major Union effort to seize the Confederate capital. By early May, Gen. George McClellan had shipped 120,000 Union soldiers from the outskirts of Washington to the tip of the peninsula formed by the York and James Rivers. That brought him 30 miles or so closer to Richmond and gave him what looked to be an easier path to his goal.

McClellan's plan was to sweep up the peninsula with his massive army—which outnumbered the opposing forces nearly three to one—while Union gunboats guarded his flanks. He had seemingly accounted for everything, but he overlooked two factors that would work against him: his own caution and indecisiveness and an unpredictable force that would cause him nearly as much trouble as the Confederates—weather.

McClellan spent May plodding westward toward Richmond. That month was extraordinary because it rained every one of 31 days. Sometimes it was a fine mist, at other times a driving thunderstorm or an all-day downpour. The Union offensive became a floundering advance along unspeakable roads and soaked fields.

When precipitation was not coming down, humidity was going up. It was oppressive to Northerners unaccustomed to such weather. Uniforms faded, brass tarnished, plumed hats sagged and dripped. The muddy ground would not hold tent poles. Exhausted men would awaken in the morning to find themselves lying in mud puddles with clammy canvas collapsed on top of them. Roads had to be laboriously corduroyed, or covered with wooden planks, before they could bear the weight of wagons.

Things were no better for Confederates retreating in the face of the Union advance. "The weather has been unusually wet," a Georgia soldier wrote home. "We have had no shelter save what we could lug on our shoulders . . . When standing we were in a bog of mud; when lying down to refresh ourselves in sleep, we were in a pool of water." The conditions did more to handicap the Federals, however, by slowing their advance and giving their foes time to fortify the capital and summon reinforcements.

> "THE RAIN AND BURDENSOME HEAT WERE BAD ENOUGH. EVEN WORSE WERE THE SWARMS OF MOSQUITOES AND FLIES, THE STENCH OF GARBAGE AND OVERFLOWING LATRINES, AND THE FILTHY DRINKING WATER."

The rain and burdensome heat were bad enough. Even worse were the swarms of mosquitoes and flies, the stench of garbage and overflowing latrines, and the filthy drinking water. Soldiers sent letters home from bivouacs nicknamed "Camp Muddy" and "Camp Misery." In such conditions, diseases thrived—diarrhea, dysentery, typhoid fever, and the mysterious "Chickahominy fever," which may have been malaria. Even slight lacerations could become infected.

Officers as well as enlisted men suffered during this punishing campaign. Malaria struck General McClellan. Nine other Union generals fell seriously ill, one of whom, William Keim of Pennsylvania, died. Six Confederate generals were incapacitated by various illnesses.

By the time McClellan's men slogged their way to the outskirts of Richmond in June, Robert E. Lee had replaced the wounded Joseph Johnston as Confederate commander and Stonewall Jackson was on his way from the Shenandoah Valley to bolster Lee. In the fierce battles that followed, the two sides together suffered 35,000 casualties—10,000 fewer than the number of Union soldiers listed as too sick for duty.

History would record that McClellan was defeated by Lee and had to withdraw from Richmond. But the Union commander had another foe that took a heavy toll on his forces—Mother Nature. ★

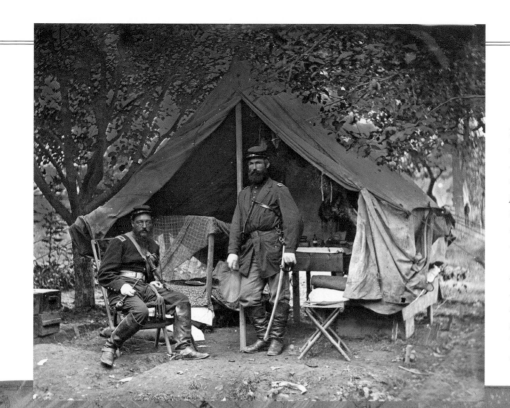

Nature's Toll *Exhaustion shows in the sunburned faces of Lts. Alexander M. Wright and John W. Ford of the Third Pennsylvania Cavalry, photographed by Alexander Gardner in their sweltering encampment on the Virginia Peninsula in August 1862.* Harper's Weekly *artist Alfred Waud entitled the February 1862 sketch below "Why the Army of the Potomac Doesn't Move," and labeled the details: "The Relief" and "Going to Camp" (top frame), "Difficulties of Teaming" (middle), and "King Mud in Camp" (bottom).*

First Step to Freedom

From the beginning of the war, free blacks sought to volunteer for the Union army. Yet Lincoln and his advisers were reluctant to put them into uniform. "To arm the Negroes," Lincoln stated in the spring of 1862, "would turn 50,000 bayonets from the loyal Border States against us that were for us."

The issue of black enlistment went hand in hand with the question of emancipation. Was Lincoln prepared to wage war against slavery? Pressure increased from abolitionists like William Lloyd Garrison, who called him "nothing but a wet rag." At the same time, Lincoln faced protests from white Northerners who did not want blacks to have rights and opportunities. He could not satisfy both sides, but he hoped to energize those citizens who might support emancipation and black enlistment if they thought that would help bring the Union victory. Lincoln also had to take action that would block recognition of the Confederacy by Great Britain, which had abolished slavery.

He waited months for an opportunity. It came with the marginal Union victory at Antietam. On September 22, Lincoln issued a preliminary Emancipation Proclamation. It stated that as of January 1, 1863, all slaves in areas still in rebellion against the United States were "henceforth and forever free" and that the federal government would "recognize and maintain the freedom of such persons." Lincoln defended the proclamation by stressing that emancipation was "a military necessity, absolutely essential to the preservation of the Union." He added: "We must free the slaves or be ourselves subdued." As commander in chief, he claimed constitutional authority to take this measure, which was intended to encourage slaves to leave their masters and deprive the Confederacy of their services.

> "WE MUST FREE
> THE SLAVES OR BE
> OURSELVES SUBDUED."
> **ABRAHAM LINCOLN**

Path to Freedom *Liberated slaves follow Sherman's army in Georgia in this 1864 sketch by Edwin Forbes. The Emancipation Proclamation promised freedom under federal authority to slaves who fled servitude in Confederate territory.*

Reaction was mixed. Abolitionists praised Lincoln's move, but many other Northerners were opposed or ambivalent. Skeptics pointed out that Lincoln's decree did not free any slaves because it applied only to those in Confederate-held territory and did not apply to those in areas the Union controlled. Secretary of State William Seward grumbled: "Where he could, he didn't. Where he did, he couldn't."

Ultimately, the proclamation proved even more effective than Lincoln hoped. White Southerners recognized that it threatened their war effort and their way of life and were outraged. One Confederate general called in retaliation for the execution of Union prisoners beginning on the first day of 1863. Both Britain and France backed away from recognizing the Confederacy.

Most Northerners eventually accepted emancipation and black enlistment as contributions to victory. More and more slaves fled bondage and sought refuge in Federal-occupied territory, where their labors furthered the Union war effort. Some enlisted as Union soldiers, as many Northern blacks did, and demonstrated by fighting for freedom that they were more than worthy of it. For many, the Emancipation Proclamation was simply the first step on a long and hard road to true liberty and equality. As a black preacher said to his congregation in prayer: "Lord, we ain't what we oughta be. We ain't what we wanna be. We ain't what we gonna be. But, thank God, we ain't what we was." ✴

Mementos of Liberty *This illuminated broadside of the Emancipation Proclamation was published in Chicago. A footnote states: "It will be a powerful incentive to the slave to fight for the Union instead of his rebel master." Photographs of former slaves, such as this image of a freedman in tattered clothing (below), were widely distributed in the North to promote the Union war effort as a crusade against slavery.*

Out of Slavery
The Virginia teamsters at right and the women and infants at left, on St. Helena Island, South Carolina, were among those who found freedom in Union-occupied territory during the war.

Union Man
A Maryland soldier wears the uniform of the U.S. Colored Troops in this family portrait. As of May 1863, all black soldiers except those in a few state regiments were designated U.S. Colored Troops, a branch of the U.S. Army.

"LORD, WE AIN'T WHAT WE OUGHTA BE.
WE AIN'T WHAT WE WANNA BE. WE AIN'T WHAT WE GONNA BE.
BUT, THANK GOD, WE AIN'T WHAT WE WAS."

A BLACK PREACHER TO HIS CONGREGATION,
AFTER THE EMANCIPATION PROCLAMATION

Slavery and the Confederacy

The Southern experiment in nationhood would have collapsed by 1863 without the labor of slaves, who formed the bedrock of its workforce. They constituted most of the farm labor in the war years. Large numbers of blacks helped maintain and repair Southern railroads, strained by the heavy demands of war. Others labored in coal and lead mines or toiled at saltworks.

Thousands of slaves were directly involved in military activity such as constructing earthworks, river obstructions, or other defenses. Thanks to black labor, the fortifications of Richmond were among the strongest in the world. Slaves served in the army as cooks, teamsters, ambulance drivers, and hospital attendants. An untold number accompanied their masters as servants. (Officers on both sides had personal attendants, and some free blacks served Union officers in that capacity.)

On the home front, most slaves remained outwardly loyal to their owners, either from habits of obedience or from fear of the consequences of disobedience. Some masters used threats to keep slaves in line. One Arkansas planter warned his slaves that if they attempted to flee to Union-held territory, he would take aim and "free you with my shotgun!" Nonetheless, many slaves deserted their owners when Union armies drew near. Booker T. Washington, born in bondage in Virginia in 1856, observed that his fellow slaves kept "pretty good track of the movements of different armies" during the war. When they learned of Union progress, Washington added, "there was more singing than usual. It was bolder, had more ring, and lasted later into the night." When Confederates lost control of territory, they began losing control of their slaves.

As the South began to crumble and suffered ruinous casualties that depleted its forces, officials debated using slaves as soldiers. Robert E. Lee proposed granting freedom to slaves who enlisted to fight for the Confederacy, but objections were raised. Some opponents feared uprisings if slaves were armed. Others argued that doing so would imply that whites were not truly superior to blacks and not entitled to hold them in bondage. Enlisting slaves as Confederate troops would be "the beginning of the end of the revolution," declared Howell Cobb of Georgia. "If slaves make good soldiers, our whole theory of slavery is wrong." And if the South was not fighting for a distinct way of life based on slavery, Cobb and others reasoned, its painful struggle for independence made little sense.

No blacks were officially accepted into Confederate military service. Had any black units been formed, some mention of it would have made its way into the voluminous official military reports. No such mention appeared. In the last months of the war, however, the desperate shortage of soldiers induced the Confederate Congress to adopt a measure that would have been soundly defeated earlier in the conflict. Late in February 1865, by a margin of one vote, the Congress authorized recruitment of black soldiers.

Fewer than three dozen men answered the Confederate call. The only action they saw was to parade around Capitol Square in Richmond as a curious crowd watched. They had no weapons in hand. ★

Servant and Master *Dressed in uniform as a kind of livery, a slave stands with his Confederate owner in a photograph taken in Richmond.*

"ENLISTING SLAVES AS CONFEDERATE TROOPS WOULD BE 'THE BEGINNING OF THE END OF THE REVOLUTION,' DECLARED HOWELL COBB OF GEORGIA. 'IF SLAVES MAKE GOOD SOLDIERS, OUR WHOLE THEORY OF SLAVERY IS WRONG.'"

Slaves for the Army *In an 1861 sketch by William Waud, slaves impressed into state service mount a cannon under the direction of South Carolina engineers before the attack on Fort Sumter. Reports of slaves in arms inspired a sketch entitled "Rebel Negro Pickets" (top), illustrating a January 1863* Harper's Weekly *editorial on the recruitment of black soldiers.*

The Aura of Invincibility

Generations of critics have questioned the fateful decisions by Robert E. Lee that led the Confederacy's finest army to defeat at Gettysburg—a setback so costly that the combative Lee had to remain on the defensive for the remainder of the war. Second-guessing by those who had the benefit of hindsight began soon after that battle ended and did not go unnoticed by Lee. "After it is all over," he told a friend in 1867, "as stupid a fellow as I am can see the mistakes that were made. I notice, however, my mistakes are never told me until it is too late."

Lee had many reasons for risking an invasion of the North in 1863. The mere containment of the enemy in central Virginia was at best a stalemate, and one the South with its limited resources could not sustain indefinitely. Lee's costly victory at Chancellorsville in May convinced him of that. "Our loss was severe," he wrote afterward, "and again we had gained not an inch of ground." Invading the North would give battle-torn Virginia a respite because the Union army would have to give pursuit. Lee's forces could gather supplies from areas that had not felt the hand of war. Should Confederates win a major victory on Northern soil, it might pressure Lincoln into offering the South peace or result in the election in 1864 of a presidential opponent who favored such an outcome.

One other significant, if not dominant, element influenced Lee's decision to take the offensive. Often short on supplies, his troops were nevertheless as tough as leather. Over the past year, since Lee took command of the Army of Northern

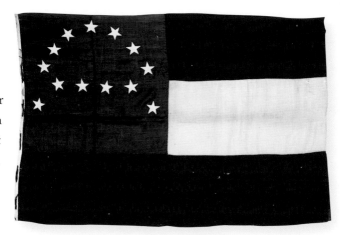

Stars and Bars *This Confederate flag may have flown early in the war at the headquarters of Robert E. Lee, pictured at right in 1863. His army's invincible reputation was shattered at Gettysburg when Union troops beat back Pickett's Charge, portrayed here.*

Virginia outside Richmond and repulsed McClellan, a tight bond had formed between soldiers and their leader. Lee had given his men the habit of victory. They concluded that he could do no wrong. "Such is the unbounded confidence in our Chieftain," wrote Sgt. Daniel Lyon of Virginia, that wherever he led them, "we know it is the best place to go. Genl. Lee I believe has more brains than all the balance of our big men put together." A Texas soldier who joined Lee's force two months before Gettysburg commented: "One day's observation has led me to believe that no army on earth can whip these men. They may be cut to pieces and killed, but routed and whipped, never!"

Soldiers felt a reverence for Lee, and he returned that adoration. He considered his army invincible, and said so. "There never were such men in an army before," he told one of his generals. "They will go anywhere and do anything if properly led."

That feeling was strengthened by the first day's successes at Gettysburg, then tested in the setbacks of the second day's fighting. Still convinced that his army was insuperable, Lee launched a head-on assault on the third day. It was doomed from the start by the forbidding Union concentration of men and artillery on Cemetery Hill. Lee met the survivors of Pickett's Charge as they fell back and confessed: "You men have done all that men could do. The fault is entirely mine." In less than an hour, the aura of invincibility surrounding Lee and his men had vanished.

The Army of Northern Virginia would never be quite the same again. ✶

"ONE DAY'S OBSERVATION HAS
LED ME TO BELIEVE THAT NO ARMY
ON EARTH CAN WHIP THESE MEN.
THEY MAY BE CUT TO PIECES AND KILLED,
BUT ROUTED AND WHIPPED, NEVER!"

**A TEXAS SOLDIER
TWO MONTHS BEFORE GETTYSBURG**

"THERE NEVER WERE SUCH MEN IN AN ARMY
BEFORE. THEY WILL GO ANYWHERE
AND DO ANYTHING IF PROPERLY LED."

ROBERT E. LEE

Could the South Have Won?

One of the neverending arguments about the Civil War is whether the Confederate States could have won. The debate is complex and involves much speculation, but the question can in fact be answered.

There was no inevitability to the war's outcome. Neither North nor South had a clear, inside track to victory. The war was a classic case of two strong wills at odds. Both countries were proud republics with nearly identical constitutions. Yankees and Rebels alike could lay claim to the old Revolutionary War motto, "Liberty or Death!"

Despite the North's enormous superiority in manpower and matériel, the South remained equal if not superior to its adversary in fighting spirit. Furthermore, it had two ways of winning the war, while the Union had only one. The North's fundamental objective in the Civil War was to force the South back into the Union. To do this, Federals had to invade the Confederacy, defeat its armies, seize and occupy its strategic points, and cause enough destruction and suffering among the populace to shatter the Southern will to resist.

The South could not wage war in similar fashion. It lacked the resources to overrun and smash the Union, but it could still hope to defeat the North by taking the offensive and winning a decisive battle or campaign. That was not a far-fetched idea in the first few years of the war. It would take time for the Northern war machine to get into full gear.

> "AS LONG AS ONE
> CONFEDERATE FLAG FLEW
> DEFIANTLY SOMEWHERE,
> AS LONG AS THE WORD
> 'CONFEDERATE' HAD
> GENUINE MEANING,
> THE SOUTH WOULD NOT
> BE DEFEATED."

Change of Flags *This Confederate battle flag of the 42nd Virginia was captured late in the war. Bringing the entire South back under the U.S. flag, displayed at right by a patriotic young Unionist, required concerted effort by the more populous and productive North.*

The South put more troops in the field in 1861 than did the North. Southern generals in the early stages were abler and more audacious than their Union counterparts. Not until Lee withdrew from Gettysburg in 1863 did Southern hopes of achieving a decisive victory in battle fade.

The other way for the South to win was more passive, and perhaps more realistic. The Confederacy might achieve its freedom simply by frustrating Northern efforts and avoiding a decisive defeat. If the South defended itself well enough and long enough, then the North might conclude that the cost of continuing the war was too high. A negotiated peace would follow, in which the Union would recognize Southern independence while seeking something in return, such as recognition of its claims to U.S. territories in the West, to soothe the Northern populace.

Unlike the Confederacy, the Union could win only by waging total war—as Grant and Sherman did against the South in 1864— and by achieving total victory. As long as one Confederate flag flew defiantly somewhere, as long as the word "Confederate" had genuine meaning, the South would not be defeated. The North needed all its advantages in numbers, wealth, arms, and supplies to achieve such an absolute victory. And it needed something else—an unbreakable devotion to the Union on the part of its military and political leaders and the millions of soldiers and civilians who stuck with them. It was a triumph of patriotism and persistence. ✶

Big Gun *Henry J. Hunt (front right), chief of artillery of the Army of the Potomac, stands with binoculars in hand beside officers and men of the First Connecticut Heavy Artillery on a rail car conveying a giant mortar called Dictator at Petersburg, Virginia, in 1864.*

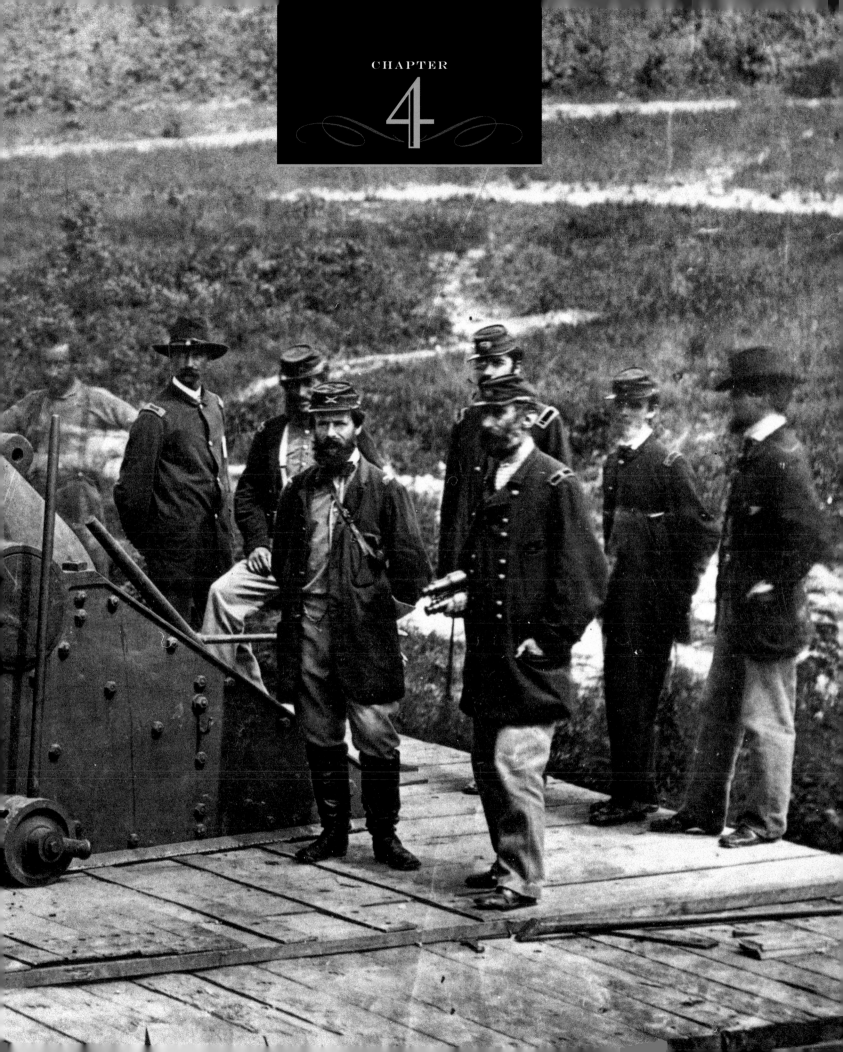

A WAR OF FIRSTS

Traditional American optimism collapsed with the breakup of the Union. "It's a sick nation," New York attorney George Templeton Strong noted on the eve of war, "and I fear it must be worse before it's better." What followed was history's first modern war. It was an upheaval of "terrible significance," historian Bruce Catton wrote. Americans knew from the start that nothing was "ever going to be the same again." What General Sherman termed "the hard hand of war" would eventually touch and transform every aspect of national life. For all its destructive fury, the Civil War fostered remarkable innovations that gave rise to a dynamic new society. In the words of historian William Hesseltine, this struggle was "the fiery crucible in which the old nation was melted down, and out of which modern America was poured."

THE SEWING MACHINE

The Civil War spurred the mass production of clothing and other goods, using recent inventions such as the sewing machine, perfected in the mid-1800s. That device turned out wool uniforms ten times faster than could be stitched by hand and was widely used in Northern factories, keeping Union soldiers from going threadbare and freezing in their winter camps. The McKay boot-stitching machine could turn out 50 pairs of shoes in the time it took to hand-sew a single pair. New machines and production techniques also turned weapons at a fast clip at the massive Colt factory in Hartford, Connecticut, and other armories. (See "Rapid-fire Weapons," pages 200-201.)

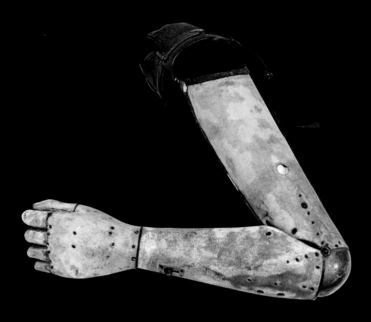

ARTIFICIAL LIMBS

In June 1861 at Philippi, Virginia, an 18-year-old Confederate cavalryman named James Edward Hanger received a serious leg wound in battle. A Union surgeon removed Hanger's mangled leg in one of the first of many amputations performed during the Civil War. The enterprising Hanger whittled barrel staves and fashioned them into an artificial limb. After a short imprisonment, he set up shop in Richmond and began making artificial legs and arms for other crippled soldiers. After the war, Hanger expanded his business and became the world's largest manufacturer of artificial limbs. He was one of many medical innovators during the war, including Union surgeon Jonathan Letterman, who organized the first ambulance corps. (See "The Union's Lifesaver," pages 216-17.)

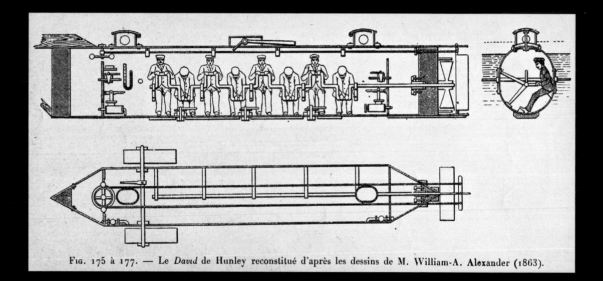

FIG. 175 à 177. — Le *David* de Hunley reconstitué d'après les dessins de M. William-A. Alexander (1863).

SUBMARINE WARFARE

The first submarine to sink an enemy ship was not the result of an elaborate government-sponsored development program. It was the work of Horace L. Hunley, a New Orleans lawyer and businessman who had no training in naval engineering. Hunley teamed up with two machinists, Baxter Watson and James McClintock, and financed production of a submarine to help break the Union blockade of Southern ports. By 1863, their experimental craft, *H. L. Hunley*—barely 30 feet long and driven by crewmen turning a crank propeller—was being tried out at great risk in Charleston Harbor. Hunley was among those who died testing the sub, which had an explosive device attached to its bow. On the night of February 17, 1864, it went into battle for the first and last time. (See "Underwater Warfare," pages 208-209.)

Victory Rode the Rails

The Civil War was the first conflict involving railroads on a large scale. Some troops and supplies had been carried by rail during the Crimean War in the mid-1850s, but the American rail network was by far the world's biggest. Between 1850 and 1860, it grew from 8,500 miles of track to 31,000 miles.

Two-thirds of that network lay in the North, knitting together its fast-growing cities and industries. A trip that took ten days by wagon a decade earlier could now be made in a single day by rail. Shipping costs were cut in half because of the time saved. Railroads brought benefits to the South as well, but much of that region still relied more on the saddle horse than the iron horse.

Neither side was prepared for the surge in wartime rail traffic. Chicago had 11 railroad stations and 11 unconnected rail lines. A standard rail gauge did not exist. Tracks in North Carolina and Virginia were of different width, and goods had to be unloaded and transferred to other cars. Gaps in the Southern rail system added to the delays. When Jefferson Davis left Jackson, Mississippi, in early 1861 for his inauguration in Montgomery, Alabama, the first Confederate capital, he had to travel 750 miles by rail to reach a destination just 250 miles away.

Rail travel was hazardous. Wood-burning engines belched clouds of smoke, much of which flew into the open windows of the cars along with cinders. Trains moving at a mere 30 miles an hour swayed precariously. Heavily used tracks and equipment fell into disrepair, resulting in many accidents and fatalities. A New York newspaper editor wrote sarcastically late in the war that there were "half a dozen railroads upon which a man has less chance for life and limb in a fifty-mile trip than our soldiers had in the battles of the Wilderness."

For all their deficiencies, railroads had much to do with how the war was waged and how it ended. Entire campaigns were fought for control of a single rail line. The Baltimore & Ohio Railroad, a vital link between Washington, D.C., and the Midwest, passed through northwest Virginia. Keeping that line intact was a big reason the North worked to pry that part of Virginia away from the Confederacy and create a new Union state—West Virginia. Confederate raiders struck the B & O 143 times during the course of the war but could not put it out of commission.

Railroads proved decisive in several campaigns. In late 1863, Joseph Hooker moved his 20,000-man army 1,200 miles by rail from Virginia to Tennessee in just five days and helped Ulysses Grant break the Confederate siege at Chattanooga. Railroads in Virginia opened and closed the war. Confederates won the first big battle in July 1861 by rushing troops in boxcars to Manassas Junction. When Lee abandoned Petersburg in April 1865, he retreated along railroad tracks, hoping they might serve as his lifeline, until Grant surrounded his forces at Appomattox Station.

Railroads helped the Union achieve victory and helped bring a divided nation back together afterward. Veterans from North and South worked together on the transcontinental railroad. Competing companies set aside their differences and adopted a standard rail gauge. Eventually, railways in many cities converged at a common depot, known for that reason as Union Station. ✶

"RAILROADS IN VIRGINIA OPENED AND CLOSED THE WAR. CONFEDERATES WON THE FIRST BIG BATTLE IN JULY 1861 BY RUSHING TROOPS IN BOXCARS TO MANASSAS JUNCTION. WHEN LEE ABANDONED PETERSBURG IN APRIL 1865, HE RETREATED ALONGSIDE RAILROAD TRACKS, HOPING THEY MIGHT SERVE AS HIS LIFELINE, UNTIL GRANT SURROUNDED HIS FORCES AT APPOMATTOX STATION."

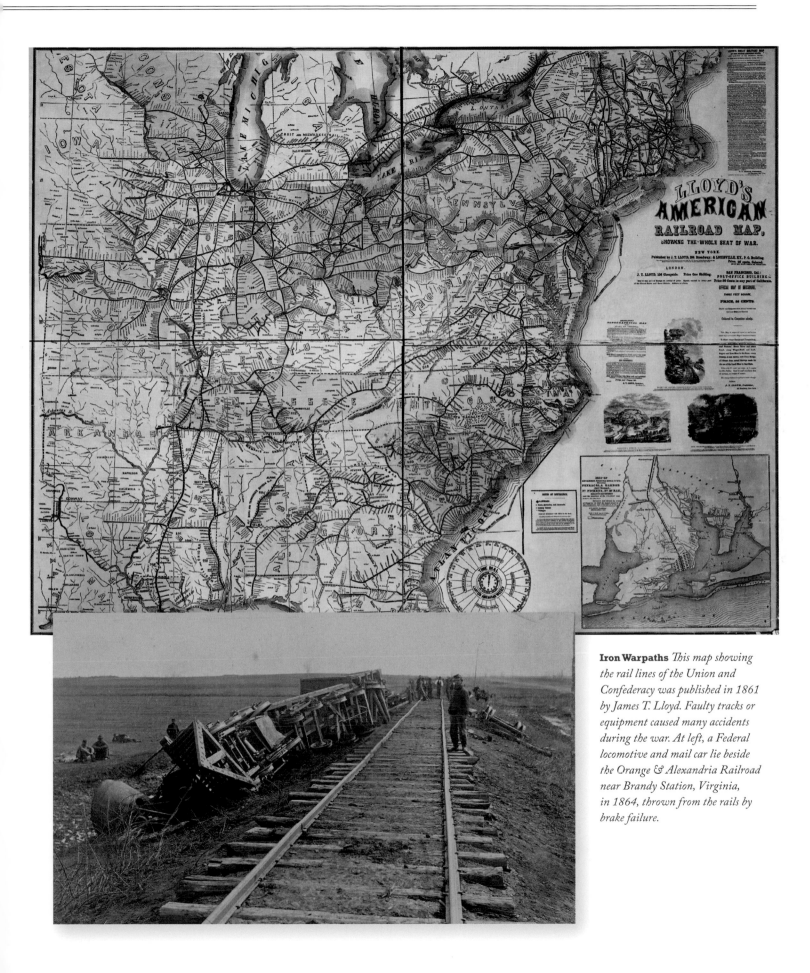

Iron Warpaths *This map showing the rail lines of the Union and Confederacy was published in 1861 by James T. Lloyd. Faulty tracks or equipment caused many accidents during the war. At left, a Federal locomotive and mail car lie beside the Orange & Alexandria Railroad near Brandy Station, Virginia, in 1864, thrown from the rails by brake failure.*

Strong Hand on the Throttle

Herman Haupt was an abrasive, pigheaded genius. Although he served the Union for only 18 months, he did as much as anyone to set the North on track to victory.

The Philadelphia-born Haupt entered West Point at the age of 14, the youngest cadet ever to enter the military academy. Soon after he graduated, he resigned from the army to pursue his fascination with a new mode of transportation—railroads. He built much of what became the Pennsylvania Railroad and earned a reputation as the nation's foremost engineer of railways and bridges. Early in 1862, Secretary of War Edwin Stanton summoned the 45-year-old Haupt to Washington to superintend all Federal military lines. He found a logistical mess. Transportation bottlenecks were everywhere. In one glaring instance, horses in Gen. John Pope's army perished for lack of forage while 78 railroad cars loaded with grain stood idly on tracks a day's march away.

In accepting command, Haupt refused the rank of colonel and took no compensation except expenses. That left him free to speak his mind to high-ranking officers. A grudging admirer called him "pugnaciously efficient." Others thought him blatantly arrogant. When government bureaucrats or army generals irritated him, he never failed to tell them so.

One superior who did not mind his brusque, business-like manner was President Lincoln, who recognized that Haupt was a superb organizer with absolute integrity and a rare talent for stating "in the fewest words the information most sought for." Lincoln went out of his way to witness one of Haupt's greatest wartime feats—rebuilding an enormous railroad bridge over Potomac Creek in 1862 to keep trains moving on the vital line between Alexandria and Fredericksburg. Using untrained men and cheap materials, he completed the span in nine days. Lincoln marveled that Haupt had erected a structure "400 feet long and nearly 100 feet high, over which loaded trains are running every hour, and upon my word, gentlemen, there is nothing in the bridge but beanpoles and cornstalks."

Engineer of Genius *Herman Haupt, director of the U.S. Military Railroad Construction Corps, applied innovative engineering and organizational skills to supply the Federal armies by rail.*

A constant concern for Haupt was securing his system against Confederate raids. He placed stockades at machine shops around Washington and armed and drilled repair crews to repel surprise attacks. After studying the methods Confederate raiders used, he wrote a manual in 1863 advising Federals how to wreck tracks more efficiently than their foes, using a steel hook he helped devise that could dislodge rails and bend them out of shape at the same time.

Rail lines to Gettysburg were in disrepair when battle loomed there in the summer of 1863. Haupt ordered up rolling stock from the Washington yards, used teams of workers to lay more rails, and built water tanks and wood-fueling stations. His railway transported 1,500 tons of supplies daily to the embattled Union army in Pennsylvania and brought back 15,400 sick and wounded soldiers afterward to hospitals around the capital.

Three months later, Haupt stepped down to return to civil engineering. By then, he was known as General Haupt, although he had declined a commission as a brigadier. He later quipped that he was the only man "ever guilty of the crime of refusing to be made a general." After the war, he helped revitalize Southern railroads. Haupt died of a heart attack at the age of 88. Appropriately, he was riding a train at the time. ★

"LINCOLN MARVELED THAT
HAUPT HAD ERECTED A STRUCTURE
'400 FEET LONG AND NEARLY 100 FEET
HIGH, OVER WHICH LOADED TRAINS ARE
RUNNING EVERY HOUR, AND UPON MY
WORD, GENTLEMEN, THERE IS NOTHING
IN THE BRIDGE BUT BEANPOLES
AND CORNSTALKS.'"

Improvised Span *A locomotive crosses the Potomac Creek Bridge linking Aquia Landing on the Potomac River with Fredericksburg. The original bridge was destroyed by retreating Confederates in the spring of 1862, and the replacement was completed by Haupt in nine days using an estimated two million feet of locally cut timber.*

Waging War by Wire

When Samuel F. B. Morse invented the telegraph in 1837, he launched a revolution in communications that transformed warfare. Orders and reports that might take hours, days, or weeks to deliver by military courier could now be reduced to Morse code and sent by wire at the speed of light.

America in 1861 was the first embattled country thoroughly equipped for electronic communications. By then, more than 50,000 miles of telegraph lines crisscrossed the nation. The U.S. Military Telegraph Corps, staffed by civilians, strung another 15,000 miles of wire during the war years. Both the Union and Confederacy had a Signal Corps, responsible for military communications by telegraph and other means.

Union officers and officials sent 6.5 million telegrams during the Civil War, an average of 4,500 messages per day. Abraham Lincoln spent hours in the telegraph office of the War Department awaiting news from his commanders. He had access to all messages sent to Secretary of War Edwin Stanton, but some of those dispatches were censored—among them an incendiary telegram from General McClellan that could have led to his dismissal had Stanton and Lincoln read the message in full. "I owe no thanks to you or any person in Washington," McClellan wired Stanton during his ill-fated advance on Richmond in June 1862. "You have done your best to sacrifice this army." By speeding communications, the telegraph encouraged this hasty outburst by the prickly McClellan.

Most officers benefited greatly when the slow process of sending messages by courier was replaced by the quick, conversational give-and-take of telegraphy. It extended the

Federal Lineman *Equipped with spiked climbing boots, a U.S. Military Telegraph corpsman splices wire onto an insulator atop a telegraph pole.*

vision of commanders far beyond what they could personally observe. In July 1864, for example, while Union General-in-Chief Grant was besieging Lee's army at Petersburg, he was communicating by wire with another Federal army down the James River, with the War Department and President Lincoln in Washington, with General Sheridan in the Shenandoah Valley, and with General Sherman as he advanced on Atlanta—all at the same time. Nothing remotely akin to this had occurred heretofore in warfare.

Telegraphy posed problems. Lines could easily be cut unless soldiers were detached to protect them. Each side became adept at wiretapping, which necessitated the use of cipher systems that were far more complicated than Morse code and sometimes took hours to decipher. Telegraph wires made it easier for reporters to keep the public informed but harder for commanders to keep secrets. Reporters had to submit telegraphic dispatches to military authorities, who frequently suppressed reports they considered damaging. At times, correspondents were excluded from camps by secretive generals like Sherman, who loathed reporters. He once remarked after hearing that several correspondents had been lost in a steamboat accident: "We'll have dispatches now from hell before breakfast."

Some 2,000 civilian "key pounders" worked during the war, among them Louisa Volker, the first woman employed as a military telegrapher. Operating close to battle arenas, they often faced danger and received little recognition for their services.

The Civil War ushered in the modern age of electronic warfare. For good or ill, the world has not been the same since. ★

"UNION OFFICERS AND OFFICIALS SENT 6.5 MILLION TELEGRAMS DURING THE CIVIL WAR, AN AVERAGE OF 4,500 MESSAGES PER DAY. ABRAHAM LINCOLN SPENT HOURS IN THE TELEGRAPH OFFICE OF THE WAR DEPARTMENT AWAITING NEWS FROM HIS COMMANDERS."

Quick Messaging *At top, a telegraph form records a message to President Lincoln from Gen. William T. Sherman dispatched on December 25, 1864, announcing his "Christmas gift" of the captured city of Savannah, Georgia. Above, a sketch by Alfred Waud shows Union telegraphers running wire on the banks of the Rappahannock River during the Battle of Fredericksburg in December 1862.*

Rapid-fire Weapons

Samuel Colt died in 1862 when the Civil War was less than a year old. Yet he had a powerful impact on this conflict, which was among the first waged with mass-produced, rapid-fire weapons, many of them of his making.

Born in Hartford, Connecticut, in 1814, Colt displayed early talent as a gunsmith and perfected his famous revolver—the first pistol of its kind—when he was in his 20s. After initial setbacks, he built a factory in Hartford and prospered using such innovative techniques as interchangeable parts and assembly lines. By 1861, he was operating the largest privately owned armory in the world. As war loomed, he told his superintendent: "Run the armory night and day with double sets of hands."

The most widely used Colt weapons during the war were the Army .44-caliber and Navy .36-caliber revolvers, which were of similar design and were not in fact associated with any one branch of service. Both were six-shooters and could be loaded with prepackaged paper cartridges or with loose powder and lead bullets. The Union purchased nearly 130,000 Colt revolvers during the war. Individual soldiers purchased around 70,000.

Colt was not the only company turning out rapid-fire weapons at a fast clip when the war began. Other manufacturers produced rifles that were easier to handle and quicker to load and fire than the long-barreled muzzle-loaders most infantrymen carried. The Sharps .54-caliber rifle, designed by gunsmith Christian Sharps, was a single-shot breech-loader developed around 1850. Abolitionist bands used

Gunsmith *Samuel Colt, shown here with a Colt pistol, had rivals like Griswold & Gunnison in Georgia, who made the Confederate revolver above.*

them against pro-slavery forces in "Bloody Kansas" in the mid-1850s. They could fire eight to ten rounds per minute, three times faster than the typical muzzle-loader of the time. Breech-loading Sharps carbines—shorter and lighter than standard rifles—were used by some Union and Confederate cavalrymen, who carried pistols but also needed a long-range weapon that was compact and quick.

The leader in that category was the .52-caliber, seven-shot Spencer repeating rifle, a carbine designed by Christopher Spencer, who served his apprenticeship in the Colt armory before starting his own company in 1860. His gun featured a self-priming metallic cartridge that did not require a separate percussion cap. A loading tube containing seven bullets, end to end, was inserted into the stock. It could fire 14 rounds, or two full loads, per minute. One of the first units to carry this Spencer was the Lightning Brigade, organized by Union Col. John Wilder of Illinois, who equipped his mounted infantrymen with the carbines at his own expense. "With our Spencer rifles, we felt ourselves to be well-nigh invincible," recalled one of Wilder's soldiers. Union Gen. George H. Thomas considered the Spencer "the most effective weapon in the war."

The fastest firing gun produced during the conflict was the .44-caliber Henry rifle. Designed by Benjamin Henry for the Oliver Winchester Company in Connecticut, this was a lever-action weapon like the Spencer but had a magazine that could hold 15 bullets. Not enough of these carbines were produced to rival the Spencer in use, but they gained a formidable reputation. Confederates claimed that the Yankees "loaded the Henry on Sunday and fired it all week." ✶

"WITH OUR SPENCER RIFLES,
WE FELT OURSELVES TO BE
WELL-NIGH INVINCIBLE."

SOLDIER FROM JOHN WILDER'S
LIGHTNING BRIGADE

Spencer repeating rifle

Armed for Battle *Pvt. John Munson of Col. John Wilder's
Lightning Brigade, a mounted infantry unit in the Army of the
Cumberland, holds a .52-caliber Spencer repeating rifle like the
one at left. Wilder's men received their Spencer carbines while
campaigning in Tennessee in the summer of 1863 and used them
to devastating effect while fighting dismounted at the Battle of
Chickamauga in Georgia that September.*

New Age for Navies

The first ironclads to wage war were designed and constructed for the Union in late 1861 by naval engineer James B. Eads of St. Louis. Steam-powered gunboats sheathed in armor, each weighed 600 tons but drew only six feet of water. In riverboat parlance, they could "run on a heavy dew," or enter shallows on the Western rivers where they were built to operate. Known as "Mud Turtles," they proved highly effective in campaigns against Fort Henry in 1862 and at Vicksburg a year later. One crewman noted that they "struck terror into every guilty soul as they floated down the river."

The first battle between ironclads occurred in March 1862 in Hampton Roads, where the James River enters the Atlantic. The Union navy was blockading Hampton Roads to seal off the port of Norfolk and prevent Richmond from communicating by sea with the outside world.

The opposing ironclads that dueled there bore little resemblance to anything ever seen afloat. After Federals abandoned the Norfolk Navy Yard in 1861, Confederates had salvaged a scuttled frigate, the U.S.S. *Merrimack*. Shipbuilders spent months refashioning it into a nautical monster. Its thick wooden superstructure was covered by four inches of iron plating. The vessel was 275 feet long and sported ten guns and a four-foot-long iron ram. From a distance, it looked like a floating barn—or, as one observer remarked, a "huge half-submerged crocodile." Confederates christened it C.S.S. *Virginia*.

On March 8, 1862, the fearsome black ironclad steamed out of Norfolk harbor into Hampton Roads. Five wooden warships were enforcing the Union blockade. The *Virginia* sank one with its ram, blasted apart a second with its guns,

Master Builder *James Buchanan Eads, an expert at salvaging wrecks in the Mississippi before the war, designed shallow-draft, ironclad warships for Union operations on western rivers, the first such vessels to see combat.*

and ran a third Federal vessel aground. The ironclad proved its superiority in battle to unarmored ships but did not come through unscathed. Two of its guns were disabled by enemy fire and about 20 crewmen were injured, a few of them fatally. That evening, another ironclad entered Hampton Roads— U.S.S. *Monitor*, built to challenge the *Virginia* but utterly unlike its foe in design. Sailors likened it to a "tin can on a shingle." Protruding from its deck, which lay barely a foot above the waterline, was a revolving turret with two 11-inch guns. Although smaller and slower than the *Virginia*, the *Monitor* was far more maneuverable.

On March 9, the two bizarre ironclads met in Hampton Roads for their historic duel. They circled each other like prizefighters and closed in, exchanging blow after blow with little effect. Shots glanced off their iron plating "like so many pebbles thrown by a child," one observer remarked. But some salvos did damage by striking chinks in the armor. One shot from the *Virginia* hit the peephole of the *Monitor*'s pilothouse, temporarily blinding its commander, Lt. John Worden. After dueling furiously for four hours, the antagonists backed off, battered but intact, and settled for a draw.

The battles in Hampton Roads were heralded as the end of the era of wooden ships and the dawn of the iron age in naval combat. They also revealed that ironclads were vulnerable, however, and that no amount of armor would render warships unsinkable. Neither of the ironclads involved in the famous duel survived the year. Confederates had to abandon Norfolk and blew up the *Virginia* to prevent its capture. The *Monitor* was ordered to blockade duty at Charleston, South Carolina. Unseaworthy because of its low deck and low draft, it was being towed south when it sank in a storm on New Year's Eve off the Outer Banks of North Carolina. ✫

"KNOWN MOCKINGLY AS 'MUD TURTLES,' THE IRONCLADS PROVED HIGHLY EFFECTIVE IN UNION CAMPAIGNS . . . ONE CREWMAN NOTED THAT THEY 'STRUCK TERROR INTO EVERY GUILTY SOUL AS THEY FLOATED DOWN THE RIVER.'"

Mud Turtle Fleet *At top, Union ironclads of the Western Gunboat Flotilla bombard Fort Henry on the Tennessee River in February 1862. The ironclad* Cairo *(above), built by James B. Eads and Company at Mound City, Illinois, was sunk by a torpedo in the Yazoo River, near Vicksburg, in December 1862.*

Battered Monitor *Federal sailors relax on the deck of U.S.S. Monitor in the James River on July 9, 1862, after taking part in an unsuccessful attack on Confederate batteries guarding Richmond. The Monitor's revolving turret bears marks from shells fired during that engagement and its celebrated showdown in March with the C.S.S. Virginia.*

Dueling Ironclads
The Monitor *and* Virginia *exchange fire at point-blank range during their battle in Hampton Roads on March 8, 1862. The* Monitor's *commander, Lt. John L. Worden, recovered his sight after being blinded in the battle and rose to the rank of rear admiral, as shown here in 1872.*

War in the Sky

The first American to conduct aerial reconnaissance in wartime was a showman and scientist named Thaddeus S. C. Lowe, who dreamed of flying in a balloon to Europe but ended up as an aeronautical observer for the Union army. Lowe's interest in flight began as a boy in New Hampshire in the 1830s. He often sent the family cat aloft in a basket connected to a kite. Often called "Professor," Thaddeus Lowe was a self-educated man who never went beyond grammar school and earned that title on the stage, performing scientific tricks.

During the 1850s, Lowe began performing outdoors as an aeronaut and become one of the country's best. In April 1861, with war clouds gathering, he embarked on a balloon flight from Cincinnati, hoping to reach the Atlantic coast. He climbed into a two-foot-high wicker basket suspended from the gas-filled balloon and soared skyward. Unexpected air currents swept the craft southeast to Confederate South Carolina. After covering a phenomenal 900 miles in nine hours, he ended up in jail as a suspected spy. Officials concluded that his exploit was too bizarre to be espionage and set him free.

The 29-year-old Lowe then used his knack for self-promotion to secure a commission in Washington. In June, he staged an ascent 500 feet above the capital. His craft remained tethered to the ground and connected to telegraph lines, allowing him to send a cable to President Lincoln at the White House. "I take great pleasure in sending you this first dispatch ever telegraphed from an aerial station," he announced, adding that he welcomed the opportunity to pursue "the science of aeronautics

in the military service of this country." With Lincoln's backing, he was soon conducting aerial reconnaissance for Federal forces in Virginia.

Lowe monitored Confederate troop movements after the opening battle at Manassas. In November 1861, he and his crew converted an abandoned coal barge into a platform from which he launched his balloon, which remained moored to the vessel with ropes. The barge drifted 13 miles down the Potomac River as Lowe surveyed enemy territory on the Virginia side. Thus was born America's first aircraft carrier.

In 1862, Lowe accompanied McClellan's army as it advanced up the Virginia Peninsula toward the Confederate capital. His equipment included four wagons, two deflated balloons, and an apparatus for generating hydrogen gas. Lowe made ascents from Yorktown to the gates of Richmond. His flights were normally at dawn, when he would soar as high as 1,000 feet. Forested terrain hampered his observations, but campfires helped him pinpoint enemy positions. Confederate cannon fired often at the balloon with no effect because the guns could not be angled high enough. Fortunately for Lowe, there were as yet no antiaircraft weapons.

Lowe made his last observations at Chancellorsville in May 1863. By then, his operation had been subsumed with the Corps of Engineers. After arguing with his superiors over a reduction in pay and other matters, he resigned. He went on to a successful postwar career as a businessman and inventor. Lowe was hard at work on an aircraft design when he died in 1913, not long before pilots began reconnaissance flights in World War I. ★

"OFTEN CALLED 'PROFESSOR,' THADDEUS LOWE WAS A SELF-EDUCATED MAN WHO NEVER WENT BEYOND GRAMMAR SCHOOL."

Dangerous Ascent *In a scene witnessed and portrayed by Union soldier-artist Robert Knox Sneden, Confederates fire on one of Lowe's balloons ascending over Yorktown, Virginia, on April 17, 1862. A telegraph operator went along on this flight and sent observations by wire to a listener on the ground. Below, crewmen of Lowe's corps inflate the balloon* Intrepid *with hydrogen from portable gas generators at Fair Oaks, Virginia, in May 1862.*

Underwater Warfare

Horace L. Hunley of Louisiana gave his money and ultimately his life to produce the first submarine ever to sink an enemy ship. It was one of the war's most dramatic ventures, and one of its riskiest.

A New Orleans lawyer and businessman, Hunley had no training as a naval engineer but set out to build a submarine to combat the Union blockade that threatened the livelihood of his city and other Southern ports. He teamed up with two Southern machine shop operators, Baxter Watson and James McClintock. Together, they built a three-man submarine called *Pioneer*, which had to be scuttled in 1862 when Union forces seized New Orleans. The team moved to Mobile and constructed a second, larger underwater craft, which sank in rough water while being towed out for a trial.

Hunley continued to devote his fortune and energy to the project and financed construction of a third vessel, christened *H. L. Hunley*. Its frame was a cylindrical metal boiler, 30 feet long, 4 feet wide, and 5 feet high. It carried a crew of nine. Eight of the men, seated side by side, turned a crank propeller. The ninth member steered the submarine and controlled its depth by filling ballast tanks with water or pumping water out.

The *Hunley*'s single weapon was a large powder charge at the end of a 22-foot pine boom attached to the submarine's bow. After ramming the torpedo into its target's hull, the submarine would back away. The charge would be detonated from a safe distance, using a line attached to the trigger.

> "HUNLEY HIMSELF WAS AT THE HELM IN LATE 1863 WHEN HIS SUBMARINE AGAIN PLUMMETED TO THE BOTTOM OF THE HARBOR."

Submersible Pioneer *Horace Lawson Hunley, a successful New Orleans attorney and entrepreneur, partnered with two talented machinists to develop a submarine capable of sinking enemy ships—an effort that cost his life.*

After being tested at Mobile, the *Hunley* was transported by rail to Charleston, South Carolina. A trial run there in August 1863 ended disastrously when the vessel flooded and sank, killing several of the crew. The submarine was raised and repaired. Hunley himself was at the helm in late 1863 when his submarine again plummeted to the bottom of the harbor, with the loss of all those aboard.

Sailors in Charleston remarked that the ill-fated *Hunley* would sink at a moment's notice—and sometimes without notice. Undeterred, another brave crew stepped forward to man the submarine after it was salvaged. No more trials were permitted. On its next outing, it would do battle.

Shortly after 8 p.m. on February 17, 1864, the *Hunley* slipped from its berth and headed toward the Union blockading fleet. Its target was U.S.S. *Housatonic*, a 23-gun sloop-of-war. Union sailors aboard that ship saw something strange approaching their vessel underwater and thought it might be a porpoise. A short time later, a tremendous explosion tore a gaping hole in the *Housatonic*. The wooden vessel sank quickly. The *Hunley* went down as well that night, along with its crew.

In May 1995, divers found the wreckage of the pioneering submarine lodged in sediment near the harbor entrance. It was far from where the *Housatonic* sank, and there was no evidence that it was damaged when its torpedo exploded. One theory was that since the *Hunley* had no source of fresh air when submerged, its crew might have died of asphyxiation on the return journey. Their remains were buried with full military honors. ✶

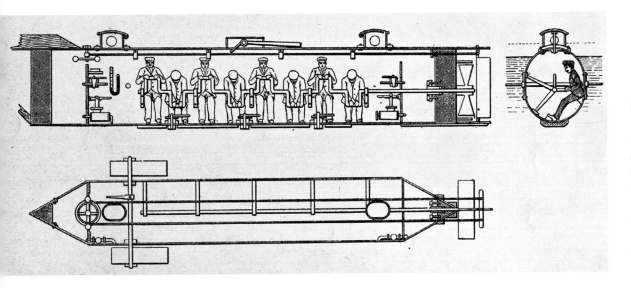

Desperate Innovation
The plan at left, based on a sketch by mechanic W. A. Alexander, who helped build the H. L. Hunley, *shows its cramped interior. The crewmen went without heat or toilet facilities and had to breathe the same stale air for as long as the vessel was underwater.*

Fish out of Water *Confederate artist Conrad Wise Chapman portrayed the Hunley, which some called a "fish boat," docked on an island in Charleston harbor.*

Weapons of the Future

The idea of chemical warfare did not originate in World War I. Killing troops with poison gas was proposed 50 years earlier during the American Civil War. Another fearsome weapon that would slaughter men in droves in the 20th century—the machine gun—was conceived and designed during the Civil War.

The Union had to take the offensive to defeat the Confederacy and faced the forbidding prospect of attacking entrenched enemies. One estimate was that attackers would lose three men for every such defender they killed. Many suggestions were made to help Federals alter those odds in their favor. Some ideas were absurd but offered a grim preview of future wars in which no weapon, however terrible, would be ruled out.

In 1861, a Hartford, Connecticut, resident named Joseph Lott proposed sending fire engines close to enemy lines to spray chloroform on Confederates, rendering them unconscious. Union forces could then seize enemy positions unscathed—assuming that some way could be found to keep them from being chloroformed as well. (As yet, there were no gas masks.)

A few months later came a more ominous scheme. John Daughty, a New York schoolteacher, suggested to Secretary of War Edwin Stanton that poison gas be used against the enemy. Daughty proposed a weapon containing liquid chlorine, which, he wrote, "is so irritating in its effects upon the respiratory organs, that a small quantity diffused into the atmosphere, produces incessant & uncontrollably violent coughing." Daughty recommended that liquid chlorine could be loaded into artillery shells and exploded over an entrenched enemy, producing clouds of chlorine gas. The choking gas would render defenders as helpless "as though both legs were broken." Stanton made no reply to Daughty's letter. Neither did President Lincoln when he received the same proposal. Eventually, an underling in the War Department informed Daughty by letter that the government was too busy to test the concept.

Fifty-three years later, German troops fired chlorine shells for the first time. Greenish yellow clouds enveloped Allied soldiers. According to a British observer, men abandoned their positions, "reeking and retching, eyes bloodshot and weeping, some with blistered flesh."

Confederate soldiers escaped such a fate. They also narrowly avoided being victims of a new and lethal weapon that made rapid-firing guns like the Spencer carbine look like dueling pistols by comparison. An Indiana physician grew weary of seeing eager young men leave for war and never return home. "It occurred to me," Dr. Richard Gatling later wrote, that "if I could invent a machine—a gun—which would by its rapidity of fire enable one man to do as much battle as a hundred, then the number of men exposed to danger would be greatly diminished."

In 1864, Gatling created a hand-cranked weapon featuring six barrels designed to rotate about a central axis. When one barrel fired, the barrels not in use had time to cool. The weapon was capable of delivering a staggering 175 rounds per minute.

Design and production problems kept the Gatling gun out of the Civil War. In 1866, the army officially adopted an improved model for use in campaigns against Indians in the West. Later types of machine guns would cause horrendous casualties in World War I—a murderous prospect that could be glimpsed during the Civil War as ever more destructive weapons loomed. ★

> "DAUGHTY RECOMMENDED THAT LIQUID CHLORINE COULD BE LOADED INTO ARTILLERY SHELLS AND EXPLODED OVER AN ENTRENCHED ENEMY, PRODUCING CLOUDS OF CHLORINE GAS. THE CHOKING GAS WOULD RENDER DEFENDERS AS HELPLESS 'AS THOUGH BOTH LEGS WERE BROKEN.'"

Burst of Fire *Gatling's deadly-quick weapon, shown in his 1865 patent drawing, was cranked by hand and loaded by feeding loose rounds into a hopper.*

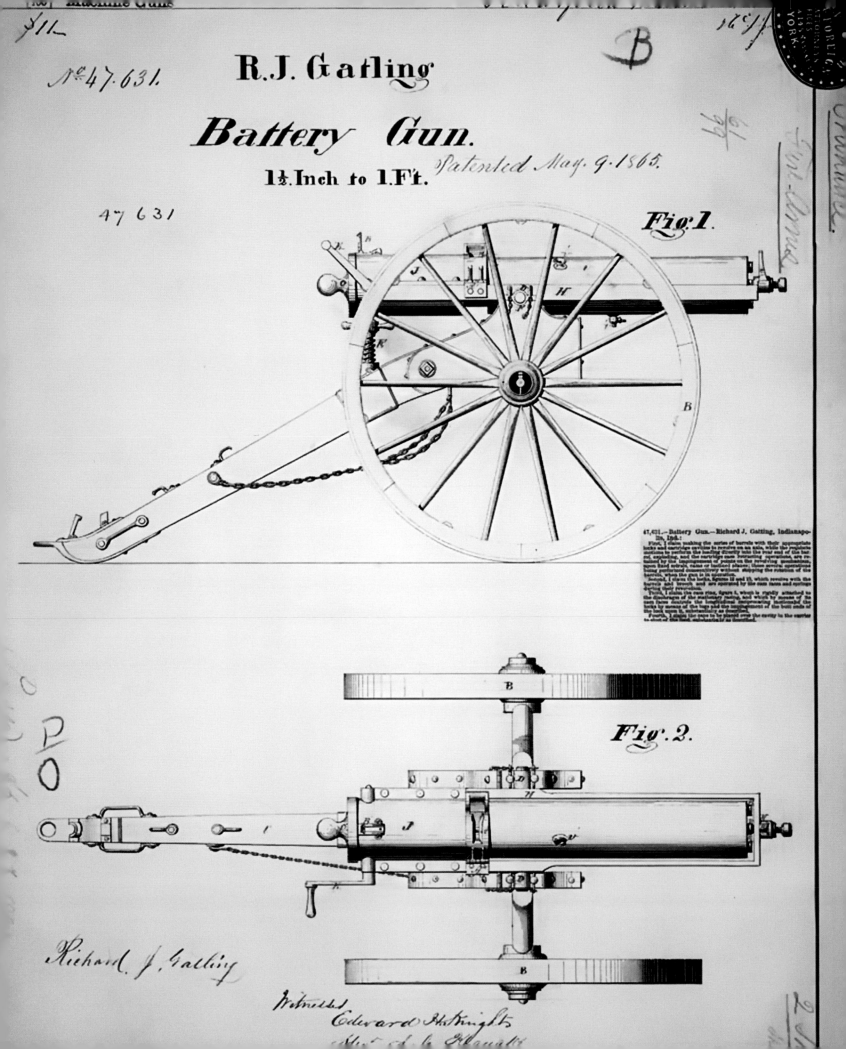

An Illustrated War

War means news, and the public hunger for news of the Civil War was a boon to daily and weekly newspapers on both sides. The *New York Herald* put 30 correspondents in the field by 1862 and had 63 reporters filing dispatches on site by the end of the conflict. Some 500 reporters from North, South, and Europe traveled throughout military theaters in quest of stories. No war up to that time had received nearly this much journalistic exposure.

The wartime press coverage was highlighted by portraits, political cartoons, and other illustrations, which took time to prepare and were featured prominently in weeklies. The most popular was *Harper's Weekly*, founded by Fletcher Harper in 1857 and modeled after the pioneering *Illustrated London News*. Harper devoted much of his "Journal of Civilization" to news and editorials, accompanied by some of the finest woodcut illustrations of that era. Those vivid pictures made it a precursor of 20th-century newsmagazines and the leading interpreter of the Civil War for the Northern public.

Editorially, the weekly started out Democratic and conservative. As war threatened, it urged compromise with Southerners on the volatile slavery question. Following the bombardment of Fort Sumter, the newspaper echoed Northerners of both parties in calling for military action. Not until 1863, however, did *Harper's Weekly* become a strong supporter of

> "THE WARTIME PRESS COVERAGE WAS HIGHLIGHTED BY. . . ILLUSTRATIONS, WHICH TOOK TIME TO PREPARE AND WERE FEATURED PROMINENTLY IN WEEKLIES. THE MOST POPULAR WAS *HARPER'S WEEKLY*, FOUNDED BY FLETCHER HARPER IN 1857 AND MODELED AFTER THE PIONEERING *ILLUSTRATED LONDON NEWS*."

Lincoln. Two additions to the staff prompted that change in tone. One was a new chief editor, George William Curtis, who gave the journal a more partisan and patriotic flavor. The other was artist Thomas Nast, a passionate young Republican whose drawings stirred readers more than any written words could.

Harper's Weekly also sent artists to accompany Union armies. Sketches drawn in the field by Alfred Waud and Theodore Davis offered vivid insights into the war and its impact on soldiers and civilians. The technology required to reproduce photographs in print did not yet exist, but Curtis ran woodcut facsimiles of scenes by Civil War photographers. Those images, together with contributions by Nast—who helped raise the political cartoon to an art form—brought the Civil War home to Northerners with clarity and urgency. Some considered the weekly not just patriotic but propagandistic. One competitor snorted: "Those who draw their conception of the rebel soldiery from *Harper's Weekly* would hardly recognize one on sight." But President Lincoln praised Nast as the North's "best recruiting sergeant."

The paper's wartime circulation was around 120,000, which made it America's leading weekly. Afterward, it gradually declined in sales until it finally folded in 1916. *Harper's Weekly* remains an invaluable historical record of how the Civil War was portrayed by the press and viewed by the public. ✱

Pictorial Journals Harper's Weekly *and two wartime competitors,* Frank Leslie's Illustrated Newspaper *and the Confederate* Southern Illustrated News, *all featured huge woodcut illustrations.*

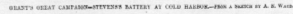

[JUNE 25, 1864.

GRANT'S GREAT CAMPAIGN—STEVENS'S BATTERY AT COLD HARBOR.—FROM A SKETCH BY A. R. WAUD.
[SEE PAGE 410.]

Capt Stevens battery on the 6th Corps skirmish line . . . A R Waud

Combat Artist *Alfred Waud, photographed at work on the Gettysburg battlefield in July 1863 (upper right), sent his editors annotated pencil drawings such as the sketch above, showing Capt. Greenleaf T. Stevens's Fifth Maine Battery at Cold Harbor. Waud's sketch was then translated into a wood-block print and published in the June 25, 1864, issue of* Harper's Weekly *(right).*

Embedded Reporters **New York Herald** *reporters, accompanying the Army of the Potomac, enjoy a drink by their wagon near Bealeton, Virginia, in 1863. In 1861, publisher James Gordon Bennett's* Herald *was the North's most popular daily newspaper with a circulation of 84,000. By the war's end, the* Herald *had 63 newsmen in the field.*

Man Overboard *This cartoon, issued soon after Lincoln became the Republican nominee for President in 1860, shows fickle Republicans tossing overboard their earlier favorite, New York Senator William Seward.*

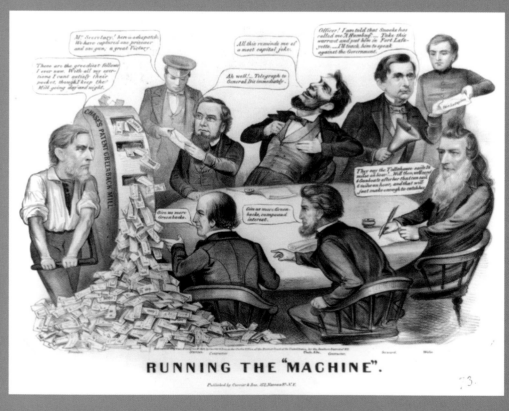

Mocking the Cabinet *A political cartoon published in 1864 by the highly successful lithographers Currier & Ives portrays Lincoln idly telling a joke while members of his Cabinet wastefully expend greenbacks.*

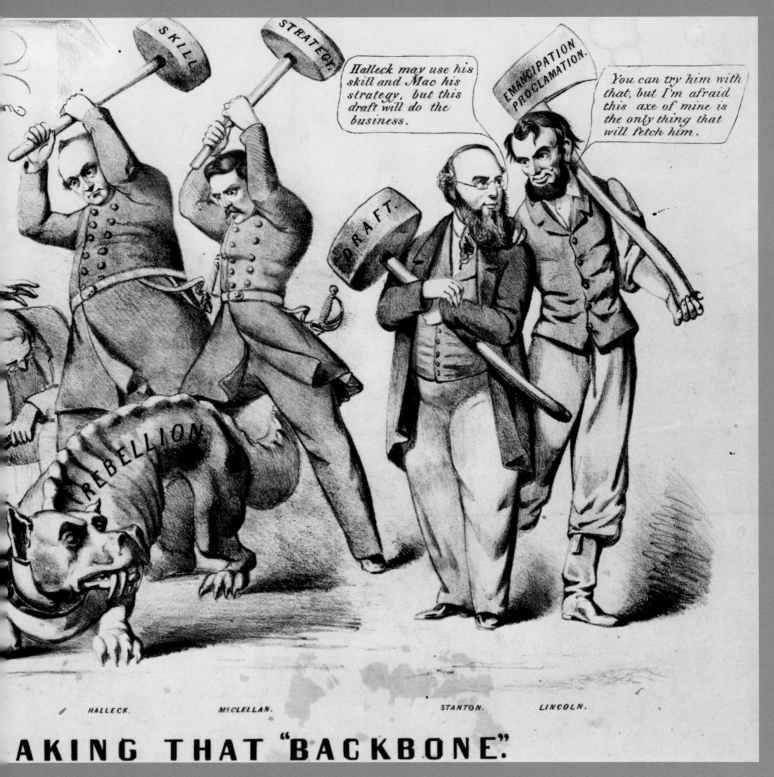

AKING THAT "BACKBONE".

A Backbreaking Task *Another Currier & Ives print published in late 1862 or early 1863 portrays Union generals swinging hammers marked Skill and Strategy at a monstrous canine labeled Rebellion, held by Jefferson Davis. At right, Lincoln and Secretary of War Stanton prepare to use the draft and the Emancipation Proclamation as weapons against the Confederacy.*

The Union's Lifesaver

One of the greatest lifesaving advances in American medicine occurred during America's deadliest war. It was the work of Union surgeon Jonathan Letterman, the father of emergency medical care.

Letterman's own father was a surgeon who acted as his mentor until he entered Jefferson Medical College in Philadelphia. Following graduation, he joined the U.S. Army Medical Corps and served in campaigns against the Seminole, Apache, and other tribes until 1861, when he became a surgeon with the Army of the Potomac. In mid-1862, General McClellan found his forces depleted by diseases and battle wounds suffered during his unsuccessful campaign to take Richmond. The medical treatment they and other Union soldiers received was so primitive and inefficient that it was becoming a public scandal. McClellan left much to be desired as a commander, but he spared no effort to care for his men. He named the 38-year-old Major Letterman the army's medical director and gave him the authority and resources he needed to reorganize its medical services.

Like McClellan, Letterman was a master of logistics, which in his case meant making sure that medical care and supplies were readily available at the front and that soldiers in need of treatment quickly received care. When he assumed his duties, there was no system for carrying wounded men from the battlefield. Some limped off with the help of comrades or were carried off on stretchers, but many remained on the field for hours or days, suffering and often dying for lack of care. Letterman's great achievement was to form an independent ambulance corps to take wounded men from the battlefield to medical stations, using stretchers and fully equipped

Field Medicine *This dripper was used to administer ether or chloroform during amputations like the one pictured at right, conducted at a field hospital called Camp Letterman near Gettysburg in 1863. Wounded men were delivered to such hospitals by ambulance crews (inset).*

hospital wagons. The corpsmen wore special uniforms and were trained to give first aid. They often risked their lives to reach the wounded in the midst of battle and evacuate them as quickly as possible. Patients were taken first to field stations, where wounds were dressed and tourniquets applied, and then to field hospitals, where amputations and other operations were performed. Those requiring further treatment were transported to army hospitals far from the battlefield.

Letterman's new ambulance corps was barely in place when the Army of the Potomac fought at Antietam, but it worked wonders. Nearly 10,000 Federals fell wounded there in one day, and all of them were carried from the field and cared for within 24 hours. The corps was tested again at Gettysburg, where it dealt with nearly 20,000 Union casualties and helped keep the death toll down to about 3,000. By instituting a system of triage—or classifying casualties at field stations as lightly wounded, severely wounded, or fatally wounded—Letterman kept field hospitals at Gettysburg and other battle sites from being completely overwhelmed with minor cases or hopeless cases. As terrible as the toll was, it would have been considerably worse without his tireless ambulance corps.

Letterman could not stop the spread of infections that claimed the lives of so many wounded soldiers, but he improved sanitation in army hospitals before he stepped down in early 1864. The emergency care system he instituted became standard procedure for the U.S. Army and a model for other military and civilian medical corps around the world. In the late 1940s, the former surgeon-general for Allied forces in Europe declared: "There was not a day during World War II that I did not thank God for Jonathan Letterman." ★

Jonathan Letterman

"AND MANY A TIME
DID I SEE THE STRETCHER-
CARRIERS FIRED UPON
AND WOUNDED WHILE
BEARING AWAY THE
WOUNDED. BUT THEY DID
NOT DESIST FROM THEIR
HUMANE WORK."

LT. JOHN S. SULLIVAN,
14TH INDIANA, AT GETTYSBURG

A Commanding Surgeon General

In a country short on resources, isolated by the Union blockade, and besieged by Federal armies, Samuel Preston Moore somehow managed to keep the Confederate States Medical Department alive and well and affording legions of sick and wounded troops better treatment than many hospitals offered before the war.

A 48-year-old South Carolina–born physician with huge, bushy sideburns, Moore had spent a quarter century at U.S. Army outposts before reluctantly accepting the position of surgeon general of the Confederate army in the summer of 1861. He enjoyed the confidence of President Davis but started out with only about four dozen physicians in his department. Bright, brusque, and demanding, Moore refused to accept incompetent doctors simply because the Confederacy had need of medical help. Few physicians of that day were skilled in surgery or hospital management. Moore established examining boards to weed out unqualified physicians and set high standards for hospitals as well. In an age ignorant of bacteriology, he insisted that patients and wards be scrupulously clean. Moore was among the first in his day to establish diets for soldier-patients.

To combat shortages in medicine, he established four pharmaceutical laboratories to produce medicinal substitutes from ingredients native to the South. Cottonseed tea was used in place of quinine; hemlock became a substitute for opium; dandelions seemed to work as effectively as calomel.

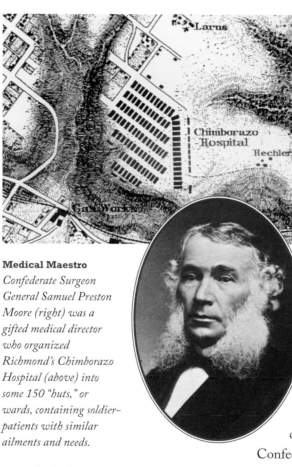

Medical Maestro
Confederate Surgeon General Samuel Preston Moore (right) was a gifted medical director who organized Richmond's Chimborazo Hospital (above) into some 150 "huts," or wards, containing soldier-patients with similar ailments and needs.

The surgeon-general prescribed cucumbers for burns and persimmons for diarrhea. A catchall potion nicknamed "old indigenous" was prepared from dogwood bark, poplar bark, willow bark, and whiskey.

Moore introduced the concept of the hospital "hut" by organizing the sick and wounded in groups with the same ailment, each in its own small building, rather than lumping all patients together in a large hospital. Typical of this new arrangement—the forerunner of the modern ward system—was Chimborazo Hospital. Located on hills east of downtown Richmond, Chimborazo could handle 3,500 patients at a time in orderly fashion.

Moore also found time to supervise an expanding medical corps that at the height of the war contained about 3,000 physicians, serving with armies and at military hospitals throughout the South. In all, his department treated more than three million cases of wounds and disease among Confederate soldiers, and more than 200,000 cases of sickness among Union prisoners of war.

Moore was an unbending and difficult boss. Few in his department knew that the stern surgeon general often wrote comforting letters to mothers of hospitalized soldiers. He later downplayed his wartime efforts. "The duties were arduous and exacting," he stated, "the routine was killing, the emergencies to be met were legion, the responsibilities were overwhelming, all decidedly too much for one man." Yet one man handled all of that responsibility remarkably well. ✶

Surgeons' Guides *Samuel Preston Moore's* Manual of Military Surgery *(below), including instructional diagrams for amputations, was one of only two illustrated surgical manuals printed in the Confederacy. Francis P. Porcher's* Resources of the Southern Fields and Forests *(right) was a guide to herbal medicines, on which Southern physicians relied increasingly as the Federal blockade took hold.*

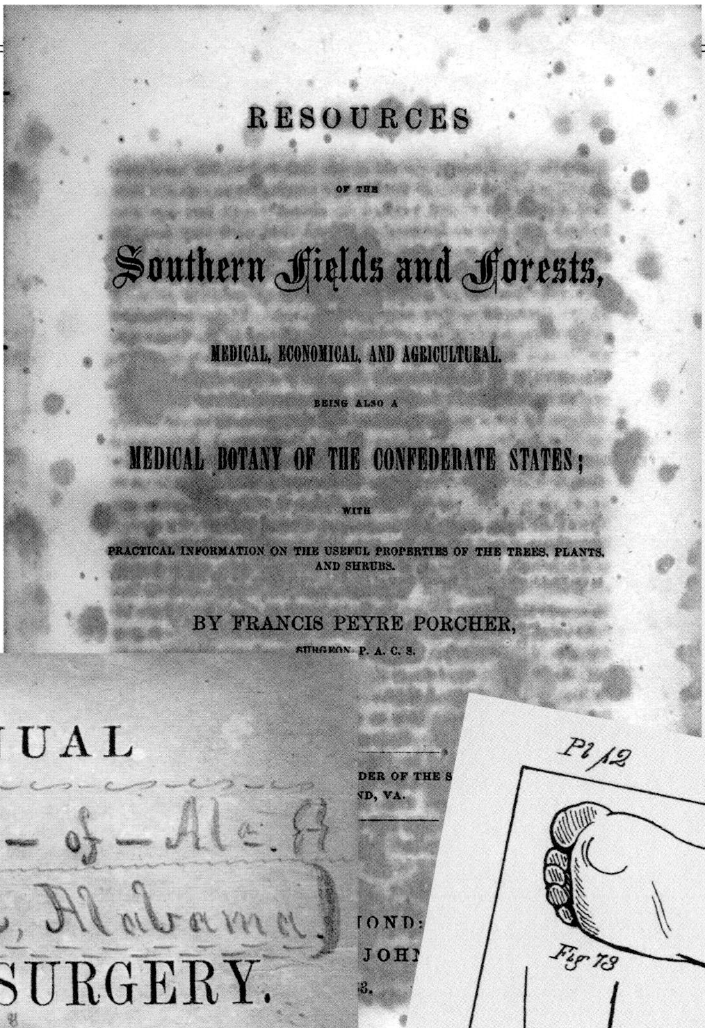
RESOURCES
OF THE
Southern Fields and Forests,
MEDICAL, ECONOMICAL, AND AGRICULTURAL.
BEING ALSO A
MEDICAL BOTANY OF THE CONFEDERATE STATES;
WITH
PRACTICAL INFORMATION ON THE USEFUL PROPERTIES OF THE TREES, PLANTS, AND SHRUBS.
BY FRANCIS PEYRE PORCHER,
SURGEON P. A. C. S.

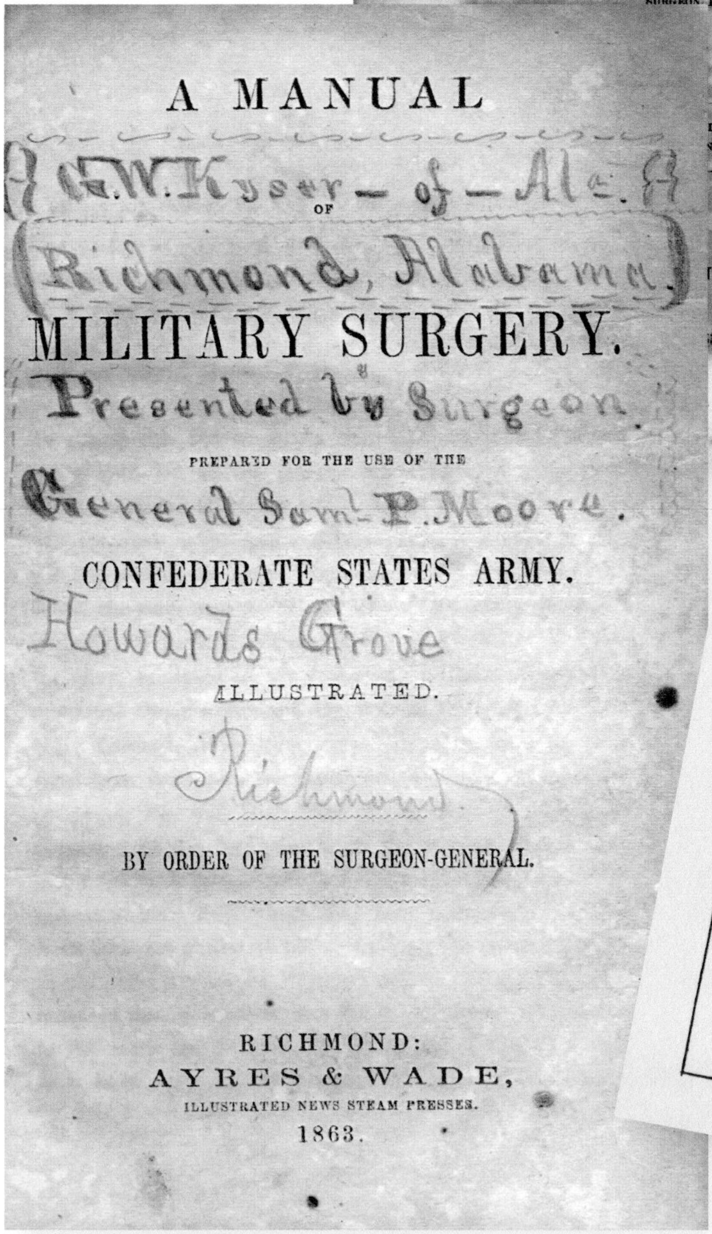
A MANUAL
OF
MILITARY SURGERY.
PREPARED FOR THE USE OF THE
CONFEDERATE STATES ARMY.
ILLUSTRATED.
BY ORDER OF THE SURGEON-GENERAL.
RICHMOND:
AYRES & WADE,
ILLUSTRATED NEWS STEAM PRESSES.
1863.

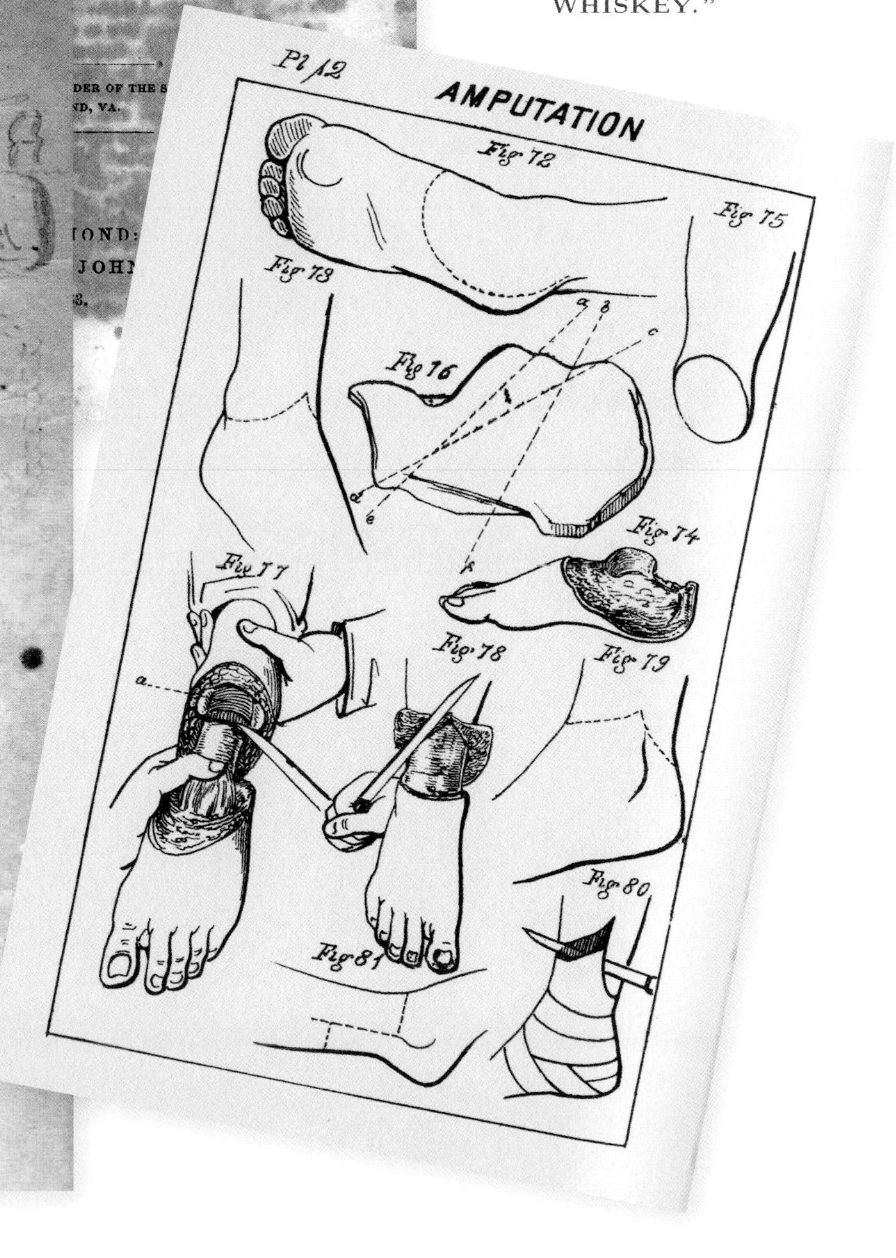
Pl 12
AMPUTATION
Fig 72
Fig 75
Fig 73
Fig 76
Fig 74
Fig 77
Fig 78
Fig 79
Fig 80
Fig 81

"THE SURGEON GENERAL PRESCRIBED CUCUMBERS FOR BURNS AND PERSIMMONS FOR DIARRHEA. A CATCHALL POTION NICKNAMED 'OLD INDIGENOUS' WAS PREPARED FROM DOGWOOD BARK, POPLAR BARK, WILLOW BARK, AND WHISKEY."

Emergence of Southern Women

The long, slow journey of American women toward equal rights got an unprecedented boost during the Civil War. Women in that era were supposed to concern themselves with housekeeping and child rearing. Any woman who did more—especially in public—was viewed with distrust if not disgust. That changed in 1861, especially for Southern women. Wartime demands and manpower shortages on the home front opened doors, allowing them to enter what had been three exclusively male domains in the South.

For the first time, they went to work in factories. While not as muscular as men, women proved better at minutely detailed work such as assembling small arms for soldiers. Many of their labors bordered on the sacrificial. Their pay was a pittance amid galloping inflation in the wartime South. Women could not be assured of making even the standard wage for workers then, which was a mere seven dollars a day—at a time when a pound of butter cost four dollars and a dozen eggs went for twenty dollars.

Another field to which women gained access was teaching. Before the Civil War, teachers at all levels in the South were overwhelmingly male. As the demand for men in Confederate armies grew larger, the supply of schoolmasters dwindled. Women stepped forward as classroom volunteers. Some eventually earned salaries as regular schoolmistresses by demonstrating skills they had developed at home instructing their children or siblings.

The greatest contribution of all by Southern women during the war was in the field of nursing. For most women in those days, the practice of medicine was confined to the home, where they received visits from physicians and cared for sick relatives. Before 1861, no respectable lady went to a hospital with all its stench, bloodshed, and filth if she could possibly avoid it. Male nurses were customary throughout America—and remained common in military hospitals on both sides during the war. Yet the ravages of combat created a critical need for nurses and a shortage of men to fill the void. Southern women assisted surgeons on their daily rounds, fed the sick, changed bandages, bathed the brows of the feverish, and comforted the dying. Some did so officially as nurses, while many others served as volunteers in hospitals or as caretakers in homes where sick and wounded soldiers found shelter. Alabama's Kate Cumming wrote after her first experience as a volunteer nurse in one such home: "Nothing that I had ever heard or read had given me the faintest idea of the horrors witnessed . . . The men are lying all over the house . . . just as they were brought from the battlefield." When she tended the wounded, she found herself kneeling in blood.

Most Southern women in the antebellum period were neither helpless creatures dependent on their husbands nor privileged, pampered Scarlett O'Haras, intent on having things their way. Many Southern women were poor when the war began, and most were struggling to support themselves and their families by the time it ended. At home and at work, they did what needed to be done—and showed what women could accomplish in the process. ✲

> **"NOTHING THAT I HAD EVER HEARD OR READ HAD GIVEN ME THE FAINTEST IDEA OF THE HORRORS WITNESSED."**
>
> **ALABAMA'S KATE CUMMING**

Hope and Prayers *Southern women were urged to pray for the Confederacy in a popular wartime song (right), but they did much more than that for their country.*

PRAY Maiden, PRAY!

A Ballad for the Times To The Patriotic Women of the South.

RESPECTFULLY DEDICATED

POETRY BY
A. W. KERCHEVAL ESQ.R

MUSIC BY
A. J. TURNER.

Entered according to Act of Congress in the year 1864 by Geo. Dunn in the Clerk's Office of the
District Court of the Confederate States of America, for the Eastern District of Virginia.

RICHMOND, VA. LITHOGRAPHED AND PUBLISHED BY **GEO. DUNN & COMP**Y

The First Relief Agency

A number of local ladies' aid societies came into being in the North soon after the war began. The mission of these groups was to improve the health and living conditions of Federal soldiers, whose camps were notoriously unsanitary. The fear of epidemics, which had occurred during the Crimean War and other recent conflicts, was a major concern. Feeling was strong, declared one aid worker, that "a wise, thorough and persistent effort should be made, guided by the Crimean experience, to forestall the insidious march of those diseases, which, if unchecked, would inevitably overwhelm our army and with it [leave] our country in ruin."

Dr. Elizabeth Blackwell, the first woman to receive a medical degree in the United States, proposed consolidating the various aid societies into a national organization. She won support from prominent men in New York, who journeyed to Washington to seek government approval for the idea. The U.S. Army Medical Bureau did not look kindly upon civilians interfering in its business.

President Lincoln was inclined to agree. Creating another organization to attend to the health of soldiers would be like adding a "fifth wheel to the coach," he remarked. After several weeks of effort, however, the War Department approved the new agency, known as the U.S. Sanitary Commission. America's first national relief agency, it had authority not just to provide aid but to investigate soldiers' diet, clothing, housing, camp sites, and medical care. The commission's alarming reports on the filthy conditions in army camps and poor treatment of the sick and wounded antagonized some officials.

One army medical director dismissed the Sanitary Commission as made up of "sensation preachers, village doctors, and strong-minded women." The commission's findings, however, led to congressional hearings and the removal of the Union's inept surgeon-general. The U.S. Army Medical Bureau was reorganized and began conducting its own inspections of camps and field hospitals.

The leaders of the Sanitary Commission were men, but it depended largely on the efforts of women who volunteered their services as nurses, administrators, and fund-raisers. Lotteries and donations at so-called Sanitary Fairs held throughout the North brought in millions of dollars to purchase medicines, bandages, and other necessities for the troops. Vast amounts of food and clothing poured into Sanitary Commission offices for distribution to camps. One woman donated a quilt with a tender note attached: "My son is in the army. Whoever is made warm by this quilt, let him remember his own mother's love."

In 1862, the Sanitary Commission transported sick and wounded soldiers from McClellan's hard-pressed army near Richmond to hospitals in Washington. The agency pressured authorities to put long-overdue pay into the hands of troops. To help families keep track of loved ones, it published a hospital directory containing the names of more than 600,000 soldier-patients.

The overburdened Confederacy never developed an equivalent agency. "We had no Sanitary Commission," one Southerner recalled with regret; "we were poor." The North was wealthier, but its government was too cumbersome and busy waging war to bring relief from the home front to soldiers in need. "Uncle Sam is very rich, but very slow," a Union nurse remarked in 1863; "if it were not for the Sanitary Commission, much suffering would endure." ★

> "ONE ARMY MEDICAL DIRECTOR DISMISSED THE SANITARY COMMISSION AS MADE UP OF 'SENSATION PREACHERS, VILLAGE DOCTORS, AND STRONG-MINDED WOMEN.' THE COMMISSION'S FINDINGS, HOWEVER, LED TO CONGRESSIONAL HEARINGS AND THE REMOVAL OF THE UNION'S INEPT SURGEON-GENERAL."

Supporting the Troops

U.S. Sanitary Commission workers gather in Washington, D.C., at one of the 30 lodges the agency operated in major cities to serve traveling and convalescent Federal soldiers. Funds for the Sanitary Commission were raised at fairs like that portrayed below, held in Philadelphia's Logan Square in June 1864.

A Pioneer at Chimborazo

Phoebe Pember was one of the South's unsung heroes. Her wartime service might have gone unnoticed had she not later composed a memorable account, *A Southern Woman's Story*, relating her experiences as a matron at Chimborazo, the Confederacy's largest hospital. The task she assumed presented many challenges, not the least of which was her pioneering role as a woman working in a man's world.

Born Phoebe Yates Levy in Charleston, South Carolina, in 1823, she was the daughter of a prominent Jewish merchant and a popular actress. In 1856, she married Thomas Pember of Boston, who contracted tuberculosis. Like many women who offered medical care during the Civil War, Phoebe Pember received training at home, nursing a loved one. Her husband died soon after the conflict began, and she returned to live with relatives. In late 1862, she accepted the appointment at Chimborazo and began work at the huge Richmond hospital, spread over 40 acres and containing nearly 150 wards. Before the war ended, physicians there would treat some 75,000 sick and wounded soldiers.

Phoebe Pember was the first woman appointed to the staff. Her principal duty as matron was overseeing food service for a division of more than 30 wards. "Nature may not have intended me for a Florence Nightingale," she wrote, "but a kitchen proved my worth." Although her status when she started out did not "rise above that of chief cook," her presence on the staff drew resentment from surgeons, hospital stewards, and male nurses. Even some of the patients she met as she visited wards to make sure that they were being properly fed and cared for made her feel less than welcome. "You will wear them little feet away running around so much," she was told by one Kentuckian, who added that her feet were "not much to boast of anyway."

"HOW LONG CAN I LIVE?"

INJURED CONFEDERATE SOLDIER AT CHIMBORAZO

"ONLY AS LONG AS I KEEP MY FINGERS UPON THIS ARTERY."

PHOEBE PEMBER

Not easily discouraged, Pember ignored brusque soldiers and rude staff members and focused on her responsibilities. She proved to be an exceptional administrator and eventually won the respect of most of her male colleagues and the affection of many patients. She found enlisted men more courteous than officers, and officers more cultured than physicians.

Pember was sometimes called on to nurse patients in distress as she made her rounds. One haunting incident involved a popular young soldier named Fisher, who patiently endured his long convalescence from a jagged hip wound. On the night following his first success at walking from one end of the ward to the other, Fisher screamed in pain. She dashed to his bedside and found blood spurting from the wound. A splintered bone deep in his thigh had severed an artery. She stopped the blood flow by applying pressure with her fingers above the wound and shouted for a surgeon. He arrived, examined the wound, and shook his head. There was nothing he could do to treat the mortal injury.

When informed of the hopelessness of his situation, Fisher looked up at Pember and asked: "How long can I live?"

"Only as long as I keep my fingers upon this artery," she answered.

Silence followed. Then the soldier told her: "You can let go."

"But I could not," she later wrote, "not if my life had trembled in the balance. Hot tears rushed to my eyes, a surging sound in my ears, and deathly coldness to my lips." For the only time in her years of hospital service, she fainted. By the time she regained consciousness, Fisher's ordeal was over.

Phoebe Pember lived to be 89 and left her memoir as a legacy. But nothing in her long life matched the three years of devoted service she gave to victims of the war and the gratitude they gave her in return. ✶

Southern Matron *As a matron at Richmond's Chimborazo Hospital, Phoebe Pember was one of a small number of Southern women to hold an official position of responsibility.*

"Angel of the Battlefield"

She was born on Christmas Day, 1821, in Oxford, Massachusetts. Much younger than her four siblings, she was a shy, anxious child. She spent two years nursing an invalid brother before going to work as a teacher at the age of 15. Teaching gave her confidence, but she left the classroom after 18 years, resigning in anger when a principal's position she expected went instead to a man. Single and intent on supporting herself, she took a job as a clerk in the Patent Office in Washington, where she was the lone woman in her office. No one saw anything extraordinary in Clara Barton. Then war came.

After the opening battle at Manassas in July 1861, wounded Union soldiers were brought to several makeshift Washington "hospitals." The Patent Office was one. Patients were placed on tables, "knocked together from pieces of scaffolding," Barton wrote, "and surrounded by cabinets holding models of invention." Shocked by how ill prepared the Union was to care for the wounded, Barton became not just a nurse but also a one-woman soldiers' aid society. Gathering medicine and other supplies, she visited battle sites and field hospitals, not only to comfort the wounded but also to prod army surgeons she considered careless into attending to their duties.

Barton's friendship with influential politicians helped her bring political pressure to bear for reforms in army medicine, but she sought no appointment herself. Unlike Dorothea Dix, who organized a corps of female nurses within the U.S. Army Medical Bureau, Barton preferred working independently. She was reluctant to join any agency where she might have to sit at a desk or defer to others. She continued to assemble medical supplies and transport them to battlefields, where she joined other volunteer nurses in caring for the wounded. How badly their services were needed was painfully clear after the Second Battle of Manassas in 1862, where she and others spread straw on the ground as bedding for wounded soldiers. "By midnight there must have been three thousand helpless men lying in that hay," she recalled. "All night we bound up and wet wounds, when we could get water, fed what we could, travelled miles in the dark over those poor helpless wretches, in terror lest someone's candle fall into the hay and consume them all."

In 1864, this five-foot-tall dynamo who did things her way reluctantly accepted the post of superintendent of nurses for the Army of the James. Barton had the uncanny ability to appear in emergencies and make a small amount of supplies work wonders. Time and again, she performed a medical version of the miracle of the loaves and fishes. Before the war was over, she was known to Union soldiers as the "Angel of the Battlefield."

Gift From the Czar *Clara Barton was awarded this Imperial Russian Red Cross Order in 1902 for her work coordinating Red Cross donations and relief supplies during the Russian famine of 1892.*

Her errands of mercy continued after the conflict ended. She visited Andersonville Prison in Georgia and recorded the names on 13,000 soldier graves. For four years, she compiled records on deceased Union troops. Many grief-stricken wives and parents gained information on a loved one's death and burial place through her efforts.

She later volunteered in Europe with the International Red Cross and won decorations from two emperors for her services to wounded men. Her lasting legacy was as founder and first president of the American Red Cross. Clara Barton's spirit endures wherever a red cross waves to signal help for those in need. ★

"BY MIDNIGHT THERE MUST HAVE BEEN THREE THOUSAND HELPLESS MEN LYING IN THAT HAY . . . ALL NIGHT WE BOUND UP AND WET WOUNDS, WHEN WE COULD GET WATER, FED WHAT WE COULD, TRAVELLED MILES IN THE DARK OVER THOSE POOR HELPLESS WRETCHES, IN TERROR LEST SOMEONE'S CANDLE FALL INTO THE HAY AND CONSUME THEM ALL."

**CLARA BARTON,
AT THE SECOND BATTLE OF MANASSAS, 1862**

Mayhem and Mercy *On April 19, 1861, secessionist rioters in Baltimore attack men of the Sixth Massachusetts Infantry, caught in the mayhem while on their way to Washington. When soldiers wounded in Baltimore reached the U.S. capital, Clara Barton took patients into her home, launching her nursing career.*

"Captain Sally"

Sally Louisa Tompkins has been called "the Florence Nightingale of the South," and for good reason.

Born into the Virginia Tidewater aristocracy, she was five when her father died and the family moved to Richmond, where she received a solid education grounded in the Episcopal faith. Her charitable efforts in her parish included nursing slaves and others who fell ill. She was 27 and unmarried when the war began.

In late July 1861, some 1,500 wounded Confederates began pouring into Richmond from the Manassas battlefield. President Jefferson Davis appealed to local citizens to convert their homes into medical aid stations. Tompkins acted swiftly. A friend, Judge John Robertson, was moving to the country and offered her his home at Third and Main Streets. Tompkins had it operating as a hospital only ten days after the battle. Dr. John Spottswood Wellford volunteered to be the hospital's first surgeon.

All went well until September, when President Davis ordered all private facilities disbanded and patients transferred to military installations. Having established one of the best private hospitals of its kind in the capital, Tompkins campaigned to keep it open. With the help of influential Richmond figures and grateful soldiers, she appealed to the president for an exception.

Davis found a unique way of granting her request without breaking the law. He appointed Sally Tompkins a captain of cavalry, which meant that her hospital was now a military facility. Tompkins was the only woman knowingly commissioned an officer in Confederate service. "Aunt Sally," as she was affectionately known, accepted the title of captain but never accepted any military pay. The 25-bed hospital remained open until three months after the surrender at Appomattox.

> "WITH HER MEDICINE CHEST STRAPPED TO HER SIDE AND HER BIBLE IN HER HAND, SHE FLITTED FROM DUTY TO DUTY, EVER READY TO EASE PAIN OR TO RELIEVE A DISTRESSED SOUL."
>
> AN ASSOCIATE OF SALLY TOMPKINS, THE ONLY WOMAN COMMISSIONED AN OFFICER IN CONFEDERATE SERVICE

Tompkins, who possessed a sizable inheritance, personally bore all of the facility's expenses, including feeding patients much better fare than most convalescing soldiers received. She hardly looked like a hospital administrator. A friend described her as barely five feet tall, "with a splendid face" and dark eyes glittering under "smooth hair parted squarely in the middle."

Yet when dealing with her staff, which consisted of Richmond women from fashionable homes and four slaves, she was a serious, tight-lipped matron who expected her volunteers to serve as obediently as army privates. Her regimen included religious and moral instruction as well as medical care. One associate stated: "With her medicine chest strapped to her side and her Bible in her hand, she flitted from duty to duty, ever ready to ease pain or to relieve a distressed soul." Soldier-patients endured her temperance lectures and genuflected dutifully at daily evening prayer services, regardless of their religious inclinations.

During the four years of war, a total of 1,733 ailing soldiers passed through her hospital. Only 73 died while under the care of "Captain Sally"—the lowest mortality rate of any Confederate medical facility.

After the war, Tompkins received more than a few marriage proposals from former patients. "Poor fellows," she would say, "they are not yet well of their fevers."

Tompkins spent a half century living in semi-seclusion while quietly continuing charitable work in Richmond. She died penniless at the age of 82 and was buried as a captain with full military honors in her native Mathews County, Virginia. "To those who knew her history," one obituary declared, she passed away "all armored and panoplied in bravery and beauty. So might a Joan of Arc have passed." ✶

Good Samaritan *Sally Louisa Tompkins, shown below wearing a belted medical bag she carried on her rounds, died at the Confederate Women's Home in Richmond in 1916. She was later honored there at St. James Episcopal Church with a memorial stained glass window based on the artist's drawing (left).*

Eye of the Camera

The Civil War was the first great media event in American history and the first war to be thoroughly documented using the emerging medium of photography. The daguerreotype—an image made on silver-plated copper—had been introduced in 1839. That technique required a long exposure time and was used largely to produce portraits in studios. Twenty years later, a new development called the wet-plate process reduced exposure time and allowed multiple prints to be made from a single glass-plate negative. Photography still involved cumbersome and expensive equipment, but that did not stop enterprising cameramen from loading their gear on wagons and documenting events as they unfolded.

The leading photographer in America in 1861 was Mathew Brady. His New York City studio dominated the field. People of influence had their portraits taken by Brady. Abraham Lincoln sat for him several times.

Brady quickly saw the value of capturing on camera the drama of the Civil War. The wet-plate process did not have a short enough exposure time to picture soldiers in combat, but it was well suited for portraying scenes before and after battles as well as life in camp. Brady asked the War Department to underwrite his ventures into the field to document the conflict. The request was denied, so he set out in a wagon with equipment at his own expense. As he later stated: "A spirit in my feet said 'Go,' and I went." The bespectacled Brady followed Federal troops to Manassas in July 1861 and began recording the campaign. He hoped to portray a triumphant advance on Richmond, but he and his assistants were soon caught up in the hectic retreat to

"THE CAMERA IS THE EYE OF HISTORY"

MATHEW BRADY

Classic Camera *Civil War–era cameras consisted of a fixed lens with a movable frame to focus the image on the glass negative.*

Washington. "Our apparatus was a good deal damaged on the way back," he noted.

Brady made occasional forays into the field thereafter but spent much of his time managing the gifted corps of photographers who worked for him. One employee, Alexander Gardner, took many of the photographs attributed to Brady and gained recognition only after resigning to become his own boss. Others who did fine camera work for Brady on the front lines included Timothy O'Sullivan, George N. Barnard, and James F. Gibson.

They were by no means alone. Some 300 photographers received passes from Union authorities to take photographs. Counting unauthorized photojournalists as well as those who were taking pictures on the Confederate side, about 750 photographers took still shots during the war. A hundred thousand or more exposures were made of corpse-strewn battlefields, shattered buildings, camp scenes, and the like. Yet more than 90 percent of the photographs were group or individual portraits.

Some photographs taken during the war were staged for dramatic effect, but others captured the conflict and its carnage with an authenticity no other medium could match. Following the Battle of Antietam in September 1862, Brady produced an exhibition of photographs taken there by Gardner and Gibson. Entitled "The Dead at Antietam," it caused a sensation. Suddenly, the Civil War was not some heroic event far away. As one reporter wrote, the grim pictures brought "home to us the terrible reality and earnestness of the war." The advent of photography meant that the public could never again close its eyes to the horrible consequences of war. ✶

Candid Shot *A member of the U.S. Military Railroad Photographic Department captured this compelling image of Federal troops waiting anxiously along the Rappahannock River near Fredericksburg, Virginia, before they stormed Marye's Heights on May 3, 1863, during the Battle of Chancellorsville. The blurred features of some men in this candid shot indicate that they were not posing and moved during the exposure.*

Cameraman at Work *A wartime photographer poses with his camera, set on a tripod.*

Helpless Victim *The eerily lifelike horse of a Confederate officer lies dead on the Antietam battlefield in this haunting reminder that men were not the war's only victims.*

Free From Bondage *Photographer Timothy O'Sullivan took this historic portrait of five generations of a slave family, set free when Federal forces occupied their plantation on Beaufort Island, South Carolina. The image was subsequently exhibited at Alexander Gardner's Washington, D.C., gallery in September 1863.*

Siegeworks *Photographer Thomas C. Roche produced a revealing image of the interior of Fort Sedgwick (left), excavated by Union troops during the laborious siege of Petersburg. Below, in a scene captured by photographers Philip Haas and Washington Peale during the siege of Charleston, men of the Third Rhode Island Heavy Artillery prepare their 100-pounder Parrott rifles for action in Battery Rosecrans on Morris Island, South Carolina.*

Experimenting With Espionage

Espionage is a two-stage process. It first entails gathering intelligence on the enemy, often using spies or informants. Once intelligence is collected, it must then be analyzed and interpreted. The second step is often quite difficult. It proved especially so during the Civil War because the nation had no intelligence agency beforehand. That left wartime espionage to soldiers, amateurs, or private investigators like Allan Pinkerton, a Scottish immigrant who founded the country's first detective agency. As the Union's intelligence chief early in the war, he was the first American to hold such a position. Pinkerton succeeded at counterespionage by nabbing Confederate agents but failed at the crucial task of analyzing the intelligence his own spies gathered on enemy troop strength.

Pinkerton came to the notice of Abraham Lincoln in early 1861 when he uncovered a plot to assassinate the President-elect in Baltimore as he made his way to Washington. Pinkerton learned of the scheme by infiltrating a band of Maryland secessionists, one of whom told him: "In a week from today, Lincoln will be a corpse." Pinkerton's role in foiling that plot and his friendship with Gen. George McClellan, a former railroad executive for whom he had worked before, led to his employment as the Union's spymaster. Pinkerton later claimed that he was chief of the U.S. Secret Service, but there was no such agency then. His duties included tracking down Confederate agents or sympathizers in Washington and spying on Confederate forces for McClellan and his Army of the Potomac.

Short, bearded, and inconspicuous, Pinkerton operated in Washington under the pseudonym Major E. J. Allen. His experience in surveillance helped him capture several Confederate spies in the capital, notably socialite Rose O'Neal Greenhow, an indiscreet Southern sympathizer (pages 236-7). As McClellan's intelligence chief, however, Pinkerton was out of his element. He established a small corps of spies and couriers who fanned out behind enemy lines. Some of their informants were Southern soldiers or civilians who pretended to be turncoats but deliberately misled Pinkerton's agents by exaggerating Confederate strength. Pinkerton then padded his figures to make sure that he would not be blamed for underestimating the enemy. He knew that his cautious boss always wanted to be prepared for the worst and reinforced McClellan's natural tendency to ask for more troops and more time before he attacked. In October 1861, for example, based on Pinkerton's initial reports, McClellan claimed that Confederate Gen. Joseph Johnston's army encamped around Manassas was "not less than 150,000 strong." In March 1862, Pinkerton lowered his estimate a bit to 119,000 Confederates. The true number was no more than 50,000.

Pinkerton knew how to gather data, some of which was quite accurate, but he never learned how to verify reports by scouting or other means. When McClellan was ousted in November 1862, Pinkerton lost his job as well. He resumed private detective work and later published a memoir touting his exploits as a wartime spymaster. The intelligence gathered by his "shrewd and daring operatives," he insisted, was so thorough and complete "that there could be no serious mistake in the estimates which I then made to General McClellan." ✷

> "PINKERTON CAME TO THE NOTICE OF ABRAHAM LINCOLN IN EARLY 1861 WHEN HE UNCOVERED A PLOT TO ASSASSINATE THE PRESIDENT-ELECT . . . PINKERTON LEARNED OF THE SCHEME BY INFILTRATING A BAND OF MARYLAND SECESSIONISTS, ONE OF WHOM TOLD HIM: 'IN A WEEK FROM TODAY, LINCOLN WILL BE A CORPSE.'"

Lincoln's Spymaster *President Lincoln stands with spy chief Allan Pinkerton (left) and Gen. John A. McClernand in camp near the Antietam battlefield in October 1862. Pinkerton greatly overestimated Confederate strength during the Antietam Campaign.*

Rose O'Neal Greenhow

On August 23, 1862, Allan Pinkerton and several of his agents went to a fashionable home on 16th Street in Washington and placed the owner under house arrest on charges of espionage. The news sent shock waves through the capital, for the suspect was one of the city's prominent hostesses, Rose O'Neal Greenhow, a woman on close terms with leading men in Congress and the Cabinet.

Born in Maryland, Rose O'Neal was the aunt of powerful U.S. Senator Stephen A. Douglas. She married Robert Greenhow, a Virginia-born physician and State Department linguist. Following his death in 1854, the 40-year-old widow was left with four children and her fine home, where she entertained friends in high places. Politicians, soldiers, and diplomats mingled regularly in her parlors. Massachusetts Senator Henry Wilson, chairman of the Military Affairs Committee, was her frequent guest and ardent admirer. She was formidably intelligent, well informed, and adept at intrigue.

As war loomed, Greenhow openly voiced secessionist sentiments. Northern acquaintances dismissed that as mere talk, but she was in earnest. Greenhow would stop at nothing to advance the Confederate cause. "To this end," she later asserted, "I employed every capacity with which God has endowed me, and the result was far more successful than my hopes could have flattered me to expect." One Union officer called her "the most persuasive woman" in Washington. She had ways of making men talk, and some talked too much.

> **"I EMPLOYED EVERY CAPACITY WITH WHICH GOD HAS ENDOWED ME."**
>
> **ROSE O'NEAL GREENHOW**

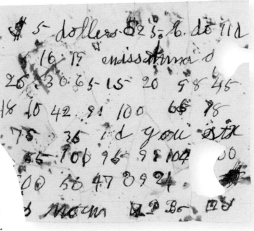

Unbroken Code *Rose Greenhow, shown at right with her daughter in Washington's Old Capitol Prison, used a code that Federal agents were unable to break to encipher messages like the one above, found among other secret papers in her stove when she was arrested on August 23, 1861.*

In mid-July of 1861, Greenhow sent by secret courier to Gen. P. G. T. Beauregard at Manassas cipher messages telling him when to expect Union forces there in what strength. That helped Confederates consolidate their forces along Bull Run and win the battle. Greenhow received tribute in writing from Beauregard and Jefferson Davis: "Our President and our General direct me to thank you," the note read. "The Confederacy owes you a debt."

The Union defeat altered the mood in Washington and focused suspicion on Greenhow. When Pinkerton placed her under house arrest in August, he found incriminating evidence in her home. Other women suspected of spying were detained there with her. In January 1862, they were transferred to Old Capitol Prison, a former boardinghouse where she had lived as a girl. Greenhow became a veritable sideshow for tourists, who flocked there hoping to get a look at her. Greenhow wrote bitterly: "I fear now that my capacity of hate will over-shadow every other feeling."

Exiled to the South in June 1862, she was sent abroad to Britain and France to exert her charms on behalf of the Confederacy. She was returning home on a blockade runner in 1864 when a Union ship ran the vessel aground and the passengers were evacuated. Greenhow had a considerable amount of gold coin on her person. The lifeboat overturned and the weight of the coins dragged her down. The following day, her body washed ashore. She was buried in Wilmington, North Carolina, as she would have wished—wrapped in a Confederate flag. ✶

FROM THE ORIGINAL NEGATIVE   BY BRADY
IN THE COLLECTION OF L C HANDY
WASHINGTON, D.C.

"Siren of the Shenandoah"

Belle Boyd defied belief. Her astounding career as a Confederate spy, fugitive, prisoner of war, actress, and celebrity intertwined fact and fiction so tightly that historians have found it difficult to unravel the truth. One authority considered her among "the most active and reliable of the many secret woman agents of the Confederacy." Another writer thought her exploits were mythical.

In an age when women were supposed to be obedient homebodies and social ornaments, Belle Boyd was overly bold, outspoken, and flashy. Everything from her age to her chastity became a matter of dispute. Boosters touted her as "The Siren of the Shenandoah" and "The Secesh Cleopatra."

She was born in the Shenandoah Valley in 1844 to a well-to-do family and received a good education. Her father enlisted as a Confederate when the war began. When Federal troops occupied her hometown of Martinsburg in the summer of 1861, she shot and killed a Union soldier who insulted her and her mother. "We ladies were obliged to go armed in order to protect ourselves as best we might from insult and outrage," Boyd related. The commanding officer "inquired into all the circumstances with strict impartiality," she added, "and finally said I had 'done perfectly right.'"

Soon after that incident, Boyd began serving as a Confederate courier, carrying messages on Federal troop movements furtively through Union lines. Her most famous escapade came the following May while she was living in Union-occupied Front Royal. When Gen. Stonewall Jackson approached that town with his forces, she made her way to his encampment and informed him of Union strength. A few months later, she was

> "IN AN AGE WHEN WOMEN WERE SUPPOSED TO BE OBEDIENT HOMEBODIES AND SOCIAL ORNAMENTS, BELLE BOYD WAS OVERLY BOLD, OUTSPOKEN, AND FLASHY . . . BOOSTERS TOUTED HER AS 'THE SIREN OF THE SHENANDOAH' AND 'THE SECESH CLEOPATRA.'"

arrested in Washington, D.C., and held in Old Capitol Prison, not long after Rose Greenhow was released from that jail. Like Greenhow, Boyd was let go by the Federals and continued to scheme against them.

Boyd used charm rather than beauty to beguile men who should have been wary of her. Tall, supple, with blue eyes and light hair, she had features that were too sharp to make her classically attractive. Yet in 1864, while carrying Confederate dispatches to England, she caught the eye of a Union naval officer who intercepted her ship—and married her a short time later.

The end of the Civil War was a second beginning for Belle Boyd. In 1865, she published her memoirs, which contain all the drama, manufactured conversation, and flamboyance that readers expected. Her marriage ended abruptly when her husband either died or disappeared, and she took to the London stage, where one critic likened her to Joan of Arc.

Returning to America, she continued to perform on the stage, went through two more husbands, and bore three children. Her shows were even more fanciful than her memoirs. She was introduced in full Confederate uniform as "captain and honorary aide-de-camp of General Stonewall Jackson." Her first two husbands, she stated tearfully, had perished defending the Southern cause.

Boyd was still appearing in public when she died in 1900 of a heart attack in Kilbourn, Wisconsin. The local women's auxiliary of the Grand Army of the Republic—a vast fraternity of Union veterans—collected money for the funeral. Four old Union men bore her coffin to its resting place. It was a strange ending for that notorious Confederate siren. ✷

Confederate Star *Belle Boyd, portrayed here by Mathew Brady after the war, claimed that she became a celebrity "by force of circumstances" but actively promoted her wartime exploits.*

"Crazy Betsy"

If Northerners had set out before the war to plant a spy in the heart of the Old South, they could not have come up with a better one than Elizabeth Van Lew. Born in Richmond in 1818, she was the daughter of a transplanted New York hardware merchant who prospered in Virginia. She attended a Quaker school in Philadelphia, her mother's hometown, and returned a dedicated abolitionist to a slave-owning family. Following her father's death in 1843, she freed the slaves.

Elizabeth Van Lew had little in common with her Richmond neighbors and never married. "I was a silent and sorrowing spectator of the rise and spread of the secession mania," she wrote. When the Civil War began and the Confederate government proclaimed "fast days" to conserve food, she and her mother openly dined in lavish fashion.

The woman who became one of the war's most successful spies hardly looked the part. Small in stature, with piercing blue eyes and dark hair in ringlets about her face, she hid her keen intelligence behind a shy, nervous disposition. Van Lew affected eccentric behavior to make Confederates who knew she sympathized with the Union think she was misguided but harmless. By flattering local officials, she obtained permission to visit captured Federal officers in Libby Prison. She brought in food and brought out secrets that prisoners gleaned from their careless Confederate overseers and shared with her. Prison guards labeled her "Crazy Betsy" and left her alone on her visits.

Federal prisoners were not Van Lew's only informants. She also acquired intelligence from others in Richmond who

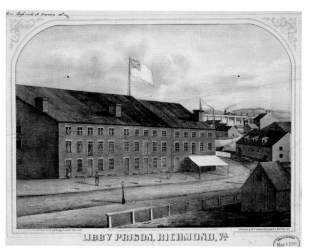

LIBBY PRISON, RICHMOND, VA

A Prison Penetrated *Elizabeth Van Lew gathered intelligence for the Union by visiting Federal officers held in Richmond's Libby Prison, depicted in this lithograph made from a sketch by a former inmate.*

favored the Union, including black slaves or servants working in the households of prominent Confederates. A postwar claim was that Mary Bowser, one of the slaves freed by Van Lew following her father's death, worked for the family of President Davis at the Confederate White House. Varina Davis denied hiring her, but Mary Bowser may well have served as an agent in some capacity for Van Lew, who sent coded messages through Confederate lines to Union officers in parcels carried by black servants.

Suspicious Confederate officials could never pin anything on Van Lew. They thought she might be harboring escaped Federal prisoners and searched her home but found nothing incriminating. They may not have looked hard enough. She was said to have converted the old mansion on Church Hill into a veritable castle, with secret passageways and hidden rooms on every floor. Tunnels supposedly led to the James River.

When Union forces occupied Richmond in April 1865, U. S. Grant placed a strong guard around her home. Van Lew hosted a number of receptions for Union dignitaries. Only then were the suspicions about her confirmed. Grant praised her for providing "the most valuable information received from Richmond during the war." Later as President, he riled those who had backed the Confederacy by appointing her the city's postmaster.

When Van Lew died in 1900, few people attended the funeral service in Richmond's Shockoe Cemetery. Yet an elaborate gravestone soon adorned the site. Some thought the marker a sign that Richmond residents had forgiven and forgotten. They had not. The stone was a gift from appreciative citizens in Massachusetts. ★

"VAN LEW ADOPTED IN PUBLIC A DRESS AND MANNER TO GIVE THE IMPRESSION OF BEING AT THE LEAST DEMENTED AND AT THE MOST INSANE. RICHMOND INHABITANTS SHIED AWAY FROM 'CRAZY BETSY.' SCARED LITTLE BOYS, AT A DISTANCE, CALLED HER A WITCH."

Spy Ring *Elizabeth Van Lew (top) gathered intelligence in Richmond and conveyed it to officers in Federal-occupied territory with the help of numerous informants and couriers, including Mary Bowser (left), a former slave freed by Van Lew. Van Lew encoded messages using the key above, in which numbers and letters within boxes were represented by numerical coordinates at the margins. The letter "m," for example, was encoded as 13.*

Black Billy Yanks

The treatment of black Federal troops by their fellow Unionists and opposing Confederates will forever be an American disgrace. When the war began, Northerners largely opposed enlisting blacks as soldiers. The conflict was seen by many as "a white man's war," intended to restore the Union as it existed before secession rather than to free slaves or promote racial equality.

It was only on the basis of military necessity that Abraham Lincoln was able to implement the Emancipation Proclamation in January 1863 and enroll black troops. Many whites denounced both measures and doubted that freeing blacks or enlisting them would further the Union cause. No proclamation or legislation was going to win blacks their rightful place in the nation as soldiers and citizens. They had to win that themselves, by doing battle and showing that they were indeed an asset and a necessity for the Union.

Confederate authorities threatened to execute any blacks captured in Federal uniforms. That threat was not carried out, but Confederate troops sometimes killed defenseless black troops rather than capture them. One of the worst such massacres occurred at Fort Pillow, Tennessee, in April 1864 (pages 70-71), but similar incidents took place at Poison Spring, Arkansas, and Petersburg, Virginia, among other battle sites.

Federal authorities protested those barbarous attacks but tolerated Union policies and practices that degraded black troops. For the first year of their enlistment, black Billy Yanks received only half the pay of white soldiers. They served in separate regiments (U.S. Colored Troops) led by white officers. Some of these officers were dedicated men

Call to Arms *The text of this 1863 recruiting broadside was drawn from abolitionist Frederick Douglass's editorial, "Men of Color to Arms."*

like Col. Robert Gould Shaw of the 54th Massachusetts, who was buried by Confederates with black men of his regiment after their heroic but futile assault on Fort Wagner, South Carolina, in July 1863. In many instances, however, the white officers were inept castoffs from other units. Blacks in uniform had to endure racial slurs and worse from their so-called comrades-in-arms. Some deaths and injuries among black troops resulted when white units failed to support them—or subjected them in a few instances to "friendly fire."

Black units were routinely assigned to the worst outposts and the worst duties, such as cleaning latrines. Even their food rations were reduced—as indicated by the fact that 60 percent of the predominantly black XXV Corps suffered from scurvy. Their medical treatment was well below the poor standards of the day and administered by some of the army's worst physicians. In one instance, a dead body remained in a hospital ward of sick men for 48 hours. In another case, surgeons refused to give aid to a black soldier with a half-severed foot because, said one doctor, "the man is not in much pain."

Black troops served the Union far better than the Union served them. They participated in 41 major battles and 410 minor engagements. There were nearly 180,000 black soldiers and 20,000 black sailors in uniform, constituting about 12 percent of Union forces. One-third died in service. Of the fatalities, about 3,000 were killed in action. At least 65,000 perished from wounds and disease. Abraham Lincoln understood that the sacrifices they made were necessary to bring about a new birth of freedom. He praised those black men who "with silent tongue and clenched teeth and steady eye and well-poised bayonet ... helped mankind to this great consummation." ✶

Mementos of Service *Like many other volunteers during the Civil War, the two unidentified black soldiers at right had their portraits taken in uniform and framed as family keepsakes. Among the mementos of Pvt. George R. Rome of the all-black 55th Massachusetts Volunteers were the pocket Bible and tintype portrait below.*

"BLACKS IN UNIFORM HAD TO ENDURE RACIAL SLURS AND WORSE FROM THEIR SO-CALLED COMRADES-IN-ARMS. SOME DEATHS AND INJURIES AMONG BLACK TROOPS RESULTED WHEN WHITE UNITS FAILED TO SUPPORT THEM— OR SUBJECTED THEM IN A FEW INSTANCES TO 'FRIENDLY FIRE.'"

Tough Veterans *Company E of the Fourth U.S. Colored Infantry Regiment, seen here at Fort Lincoln in the District of Columbia, served for nearly two years, during which the soldiers built fortifications, guarded Confederate prisoners, and fought in battles at Petersburg, Bermuda Hundred, and Forts Harrison and Fisher.*

"THERE WERE NEARLY 180,000 BLACK
SOLDIERS AND 20,000 BLACK SAILORS
IN UNIFORM, CONSTITUTING ABOUT
12 PERCENT OF UNION FORCES.
ONE-THIRD OF THEM DIED IN SERVICE."

An Integrated Navy *Unlike the prewar U.S. Army, the
U.S. Navy was traditionally open to black recruits and enlisted more
during the Civil War, including the young sailor from Cincinnati
above and members of the racially mixed crew at right, manning the
gunboat* Mendota *on the James River in March 1865.*

The Medal of Honor

Today our nation recognizes the gallantry of those in armed service with a variety of awards such as the Distinguished Service Medal and the Navy Cross. No such honors existed at the time of the Civil War. The Purple Heart, or Badge of Military Merit, had been instituted by George Washington in 1782, but few were awarded and it was not revived until the 20th century. The War Department traditionally regarded titles, decorations, and medals as undemocratic because they were associated with European aristocracy.

That changed during the Civil War, when for the first time vast numbers of Americans from all walks of life entered combat. The U.S. Congress established the highest award this nation can bestow on a member of the military—the Medal of Honor—for acts of "conspicuous gallantry" performed in service to the Union. By 1863, all those in the army or navy were eligible for the award except naval officers, who became eligible in World War I.

During the Civil War, the medal was meant primarily to reward surviving heroes, who wore it as a badge for all to see. Of the 1,527 Medals of Honor bestowed on those engaged in the conflict, only about 30 were awarded posthumously. The first medals were given in March 1863 to the six surviving soldiers who hijacked a train in Georgia a year earlier in a daring attempt to destroy tracks and telegraph lines between Atlanta and Chattanooga (pages 40–41). The first navy medals went to sailors involved in attacks on Confederate forts at the mouth of the Mississippi River that led to the Federal occupation of New Orleans in 1862.

Delayed Award *This Medal of Honor was awarded in 1893 to Charles H. Tompkins of the Second U.S. Cavalry for an act of valor performed in Virginia in 1861.*

The act establishing the Medal of Honor made it retroactive to the start of the war. The first act deemed worthy of the award was performed by Cpl. Francis Brownell, who accompanied Col. Elmer Ellsworth on May 24, 1861, when he pulled down a Confederate flag waving over the Marshall House in Alexandria, Virginia. Ellsworth was then shot dead by hotel owner James Jackson, who was killed just moments later by Brownell.

Many Medals of Honor were given to soldiers who seized Confederate flags or defended the Stars and Stripes. William Carney of the 54th Massachusetts was honored for saving the national colors when his black regiment was pinned down and forced back at Fort Wagner in 1863. Carney was wounded several times during the battle and promoted to sergeant for his bravery, but he did not receive the Medal of Honor until 1900. "I only did my duty," he said. "The old flag never touched the ground!"

The only woman so honored for her Civil War service was Dr. Mary Walker, an assistant surgeon in General Sherman's army. She sometimes crossed enemy lines to care for Southern civilians and was captured by Confederates in 1864. Walker received the Medal of Honor in late 1865, but it was rescinded in 1917 along with many other medals given to those who had not been involved in combat with the enemy. Her award was reinstated in 1977 in recognition of her "distinguished gallantry."

The board that revoked Dr. Walker's medal may have erred in a few instances, but it helped reform a haphazard system that honored many men who took no great risk while leaving some truly gallant soldiers unrewarded. Now the Medal of Honor is so esteemed that the lowliest private who wears it is saluted by those of all ranks. ★

"THE U.S. CONGRESS ESTABLISHED THE HIGHEST AWARD THIS NATION CAN BESTOW ON A MEMBER OF THE MILITARY— THE MEDAL OF HONOR—FOR ACTS OF 'CONSPICUOUS GALLANTRY' PERFORMED IN SERVICE TO THE UNION."

Heroic Firsts
Military surgeon Mary E. Walker (above, left) became the first woman awarded the Medal of Honor in November 1865. Sgt. William Carney of the 54th Massachusetts (above), shown with the flag he saved at Fort Wagner in July 1863, performed the first deed by a black serviceman judged worthy of the Medal of Honor. The first U.S. Navy men to receive the award were honored in April 1863 for their role in a crucial battle on the Mississippi River (left) that led to the capture of New Orleans.

"Taps"

One of the most lasting contributions of the Civil War to American life is the simple melody that remains our most famous bugle call.

The time was July 1862. The place: the Virginia Peninsula in the aftermath of George McClellan's failed offensive against Richmond. Two Union soldiers of different rank were the only actors in the drama.

The first was Gen. Daniel Butterfield, a 30-year-old brigade commander with a heavy, drooping mustache. Butterfield was a New York attorney and an executive with the American Express Company when the war began. Despite a lack of military training, he entered service as colonel of a militia regiment and was promoted to brigadier in late 1861. Gallant action on the Peninsula brought Butterfield a wound, elevation to major general, and eventually the Medal of Honor.

The other participant was Butterfield's brigade bugler. Pvt. Oliver Norton was from northwestern Pennsylvania. He too was a valiant soldier who had been wounded in the recently concluded campaign. Ultimately, Norton would gain an officer's commission.

At that time, two bugle calls ended the day's activities. The first, "Tattoo," summoned the men for roll call. A half hour or so later came the second call, signaling soldiers to extinguish lights in camp and cease all loud conversations and other noises.

Butterfield, a man with a good ear for music, disliked that second melody. "It did not seem to be as smooth, melodious, and musical as it should be," he stated. A better tune, he felt, would instill in men a sense of peace at the end of the day and put them at rest.

Gifted Amateur *Gen. Daniel Butterfield, a New York businessman before the war, demonstrated both military and musical talent as a Union officer.*

One afternoon in the war's second summer, the recuperating general summoned the recuperating bugler. Butterfield whistled a tune and asked Norton to play it. Neither man was pleased with the initial effort, but after repeated trials and refinements general and bugler completed the composition to their mutual satisfaction.

Butterfield ordered the new tune substituted at once in his camp for the original melody used to signal lights-out. That night the haunting strains of the bugle call drifted across the land for the first time.

The following morning, buglers from nearby brigades came to inquire about the new song. They copied the music, returned to their camps, and used it at day's end. Soon the tune was standard throughout the Army of the Potomac. When two corps from that army went west the following year, they took the melody with them. The bugle call known as "Taps" was readily adopted by the postwar U.S. Army and was played at camps as far away as Hawaii and the Philippines by the time the 19th century ended.

The tune is short and simple. It still sounds the end of the day. Yet it serves another purpose as well. Whenever someone is buried with military honors, the bugle notes of "Taps" form the climax of the service. Occasionally some sing the words: "Day is done, gone the sun / From the lakes, from the hills, from the sky / All is well, safely rest / God is nigh."

Bugler Oliver Norton wrote late in his life: "There is something singularly beautiful and appropriate in the music of this wonderful call. Its strains are melancholy, yet full of rest and peace. Its echoes linger in the heart long after its notes have ceased to float through the air."

"Taps" is as immortal as the memory of those it honors. ★

Slowly

mf

Clarion Call *"Taps," shown in musical notation at left, was so memorable that buglers like the soldier portrayed below by artist Alfred Waud could readily play it by ear.*

"BUTTERFIELD ORDERED THE NEW TUNE SUBSTITUTED AT ONCE IN HIS CAMP FOR THE ORIGINAL MELODY USED TO SIGNAL LIGHTS-OUT. THAT NIGHT THE HAUNTING STRAINS OF THE BUGLE CALL DRIFTED ACROSS THE LAND FOR THE FIRST TIME."

Army musician's jacket and bugle

Arlington National Cemetery

The land was once a beautiful estate. It ended as a burial ground. What was intended to be a gracious home for the living became a somber haven for the dead. Few historic places in America underwent a more drastic conversion than Arlington National Cemetery.

George Washington Parke Custis, the stepson and namesake of the first President, inherited the property in 1802. Custis began building a mansion and shrine to the father he adored. He wanted to call the place "Mount Washington," but he eventually named it "Arlington" after the family's first home in Virginia.

Custis and his wife had one child, a daughter, Mary. In 1831, she married a promising young army officer named Robert E. Lee. Arlington, which remained the property of Mary Custis Lee, became the only real home her husband was to have for 30 years. There six of their seven children were born. It was also there, in April 1861, that Lee made the decision to fight for his native state.

The Lee family moved south, and Federals took possession of the Arlington estate. By 1864, it had become the site of fortifications overlooking the Potomac River as well as a settlement called Freedman's Village, inhabited by more than a thousand former slaves.

The transformation of the former Custis-Lee estate into a burial ground was the work of a former friend and longtime colleague of Lee's before the war. Montgomery Meigs, born in Georgia but raised in Pennsylvania, was quartermaster general of the Union army. He was an able officer and a brilliant administrator but was also highly vindictive. He considered all Confederates—including a brother who fought for the South

Wartime Refugee *Mary Custis Lee, portrayed here in 1838 by artist William E. West, fled when her family's Arlington estate was occupied by Federal troops in May 1861.*

—to be nothing but traitors. The death of his son, a Union soldier, in action in 1864 increased his animosity toward the Rebels.

To punish Lee for siding with Virginia in the Civil War, Meigs turned the area surrounding the Custis-Lee Mansion, known as Arlington House, into a cemetery. He began unauthorized burials there in May 1864. When the secretary of war later endorsed the idea, Meigs had more bodies of soldiers who were unidentified or had not been claimed for burial by family members transported to Arlington. He insisted that they be interred as close as possible to the house to ensure that it remained uninhabited. He wrote of his "grim satisfaction" in burying 26 bodies from a military morgue in the middle of the mansion's rose garden. He later had 2,111 unknown Federals buried in a mass grave nearby. In its early years, Arlington National Cemetery served as a burial place only for such unidentified soldiers or those whose families could not afford the cost of funerals.

In 1882, the U.S. Supreme Court found the government guilty of illegally seizing the Arlington estate and returned the property to the couple's eldest son. He had little choice but to sell it to the government, for $150,000. A decade later, Montgomery Meigs was buried there with military honors—a stone's throw from Arlington House.

In 1900, President William McKinley gave permission for a section of the cemetery to be set aside for Confederate dead. In 1955, Arlington House was dedicated as a memorial to Robert E. Lee.

Today, more than 240,000 dead lie in the 600-acre tract at Arlington National Cemetery. An average of 18 funerals occur there daily. It stands as a monument to the great human cost of repairing, protecting, and preserving the United States. ★

"TO PUNISH LEE FOR SIDING WITH VIRGINIA
IN THE CIVIL WAR, MEIGS DETERMINED TO TURN
THE AREA SURROUNDING THE CUSTIS-LEE MANSION,
KNOWN AS ARLINGTON HOUSE, INTO A CEMETERY."

Occupied Ground *Federal troops stand guard
in June 1864 in front of Arlington House on the
Custis-Lee estate, which Quartermaster General
Montgomery Meigs (left) transformed into a Union
cemetery. In October 1864, his son was killed in a
skirmish with Confederates and was buried here.*

Thanksgiving Day

Religious observances of thanksgiving for autumn harvests and other blessings began in colonial times. Before the Civil War, governors sometimes issued state proclamations setting aside certain days for thanksgiving. During the conflict, Confederate President Jefferson Davis ordered occasional days of prayer and thanksgiving to commemorate military successes or seek divine aid in times of crisis. Northern author and editor Sarah Josepha Hale had long been trying in vain to get governors to agree on a uniform date for a national thanksgiving observance. In September 1863, she concluded that a proclamation from President Lincoln "would be the best, surest, and most fitting method of National appointment." So she sent him a letter.

Lincoln made no reply to Hale, but he saw merit in the idea. What gave him pause was the fact that many people in the Union were grieving over the loss of loved ones in uniform. Could he ask those in mourning to give thanks for what they had received? Lincoln possessed a strong belief in what he called "the controlling power of Almighty God" and trusted that God would not subject the nation to such an ordeal without good purpose. Lincoln also believed in his own power to shape the Union's political destiny and recognized that a fervent appeal for national unity might help his embattled Republican Party as crucial state elections approached.

On October 3, 1863, he issued a Thanksgiving Proclamation in which he stressed the gains made by the Union without ignoring the steep price paid by soldiers and their families. "In the midst of a civil war of unequalled magnitude and severity," he declared, "order has been maintained, the laws have been respected and obeyed, and harmony has prevailed everywhere except in the theatre of military conflict," which had been "greatly contracted by the advancing armies and navies of the Union." Lincoln then invited his fellow citizens "to set apart, and observe the last Thursday of November next, as a day of Thanksgiving and Praise to our beneficent Father who dwelleth in the Heavens." Finally, he asked citizens not just to give thanks but to pray to God for "all those who have become widows, orphans, mourners or sufferers in the lamentable civil strife in which we are unavoidably engaged, and fervently implore the interposition of the Almighty Hand to heal the wounds of the nation and to restore it . . . to the full enjoyment of peace, harmony, tranquillity and Union."

Lincoln had much to be thankful for in the weeks following this proclamation. In mid-October, Republican candidates in state elections trounced so-called Copperheads, or Peace Democrats who favored compromise with the Confederacy. Then on Thursday, November 26, the first national day of Thanksgiving, Lincoln received news of the smashing Union victory at Chattanooga. He was sick in bed with a mild form of smallpox, but he felt good enough to joke about it. He was forever besieged by office seekers and told an aide: "I now have something I can give everybody."

Lincoln's 1863 proclamation did not make Thanksgiving a recurring observance. In October 1864, with his reelection all but assured and the Union on the way to victory, he proclaimed a second national day of thanksgiving. He did not live long enough to proclaim a third Thanksgiving Day, but the custom was now firmly established. It was a fitting legacy of the Civil War. From that calamity came nationhood, a gift worthy of thanks and remembrance. ✶

> "LINCOLN THEN INVITED HIS FELLOW CITIZENS 'TO SET APART, AND OBSERVE THE LAST THURSDAY OF NOVEMBER NEXT, AS A DAY OF THANKSGIVING AND PRAISE TO OUR BENEFICENT FATHER . . . AND FERVENTLY IMPLORE THE INTERPOSITION OF THE ALMIGHTY HAND TO HEAL THE WOUNDS OF THE NATION.'"
>
> ABRAHAM LINCOLN,
> OCTOBER 3, 1863

Persuasive Advocate
*Sarah Josepha Hale, editor
of the influential* Godey's
Lady's Book *and a
proponent of a national
day of thanksgiving,
penned this 1863 letter
that helped persuade
Abraham Lincoln
to proclaim the first
such occasion.*

Thanksgiving in Camp *Union soldiers enjoy a thanksgiving dinner in camp in this scene sketched by Alfred Waud on November 28, 1861.
Holding such feasts in late autumn, after the harvest was brought in, was a long-standing American tradition, which Lincoln adhered to
by choosing the last Thursday in November as Thanksgiving Day.*

"The Man Who Made Santa Claus"

He was the pioneer of American political cartooning as well as its greatest practitioner. For 30 years his drawings reduced infamous politicians to clownish characters. His work, one journalist wrote, was "savage and bitter" and stung like a whip: "He tells in ten strokes of his pencil what it would take volumes to express." So vicious could Thomas Nast be in expression that many Americans considered him the basis for the adjective "nasty." Yet he gave shape to one of the most beloved figures in American mythology—Santa Claus.

Born in Germany in 1840, Nast came to America with his family as a boy at a time when many Germans with democratic or revolutionary beliefs were fleeing political repression in their homeland. A precocious talent, he studied briefly in an art school in New York City before going to work at 15 for *Frank Leslie's Illustrated Newspaper*. In 1862, he joined the staff of the more prestigious *Harper's Weekly*. For the next 24 years, Nast would solidify his reputation as a national cartoonist with a social conscience. Graft, corruption, and other social ills plaguing many cities were frequent targets for Nast's pen.

From the mind and hand of Nast came a host of symbols that remain part of the modern cartoonist's repertoire. The Democratic donkey, the Republican elephant, the Tammany Hall tiger (representing corruption), John Bull (the personification of England), and his American counterpart, Uncle Sam—all were created by Nast or given a distinct and unforgettable pictorial treatment by him.

Nast was an avid Unionist and Republican and made no effort to disguise his convictions. He could be fiercely partisan

Father Christmas *Thomas Nast's jolly old Santa Claus was a familiar figure by the time this illustration appeared in* Harper's Weekly *in 1865 to herald a merry and peaceful Christmas.*

in his work, but his wartime drawings also had a broad emotional appeal that crossed party lines. Pictorial centerfolds of homesick soldiers and lonely families helped unite in sentiment Northerners who were champions of Lincoln's war effort and others who were less enthusiastic but supported the troops and hoped victory would come soon. His drawings helped boost spirits when Federal armies failed in the field. General U. S. Grant later declared that Nast had done "as much as any one man to preserve the Union and bring the war to an end."

America's yuletide season fascinated the German immigrant. In late 1862, with a dreary Christmas looming for the war-weary public, Nast made a lasting gift to the nation that was now his home. That gift was his impression of Santa Claus, whom he first depicted as dressed in a suit of stars and stripes while distributing presents in the field to joyful Union soldiers.

Nast was inspired by Clement Moore's then little-known poem, "A Visit from St. Nicholas," also called "The Night Before Christmas." Nast was familiar with European depictions of St. Nicholas (for whom Santa Claus is named) and Kris Kringle but created his own version of the fabled Christmas gift giver: round-bellied, white-bearded, fur-clad, jolly, and bright-eyed, with a sprig of holly in his cap. Nast's Santa Claus was the embodiment of good cheer, produced miraculously during one of the saddest times Americans ever endured.

Public reaction to Nast's creation was enthusiastic and infectious. Subsequent artists made few changes in the figure Nast brought to life. For all of his fine work lambasting politicians and their misdeeds, he is best remembered as "the man who made Santa Claus." ✫

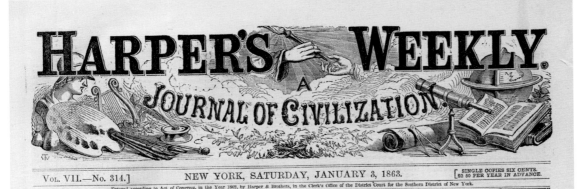

HARPER'S WEEKLY.

A JOURNAL OF CIVILIZATION

VOL. VII.—No. 314.]   NEW YORK, SATURDAY, JANUARY 3, 1863.   [SINGLE COPIES SIX CENTS.
[$2 50 PER YEAR IN ADVANCE.

Entered according to Act of Congress, in the Year 1862, by Harper & Brothers, in the Clerk's Office of the District Court for the Southern District of New York.

SANTA CLAUS IN CAMP.—[SEE PAGE 6.]

"NAST'S SANTA CLAUS WAS THE EMBODIMENT OF GOOD CHEER, PRODUCED MIRACULOUSLY DURING ONE OF THE SADDEST TIMES AMERICANS EVER ENDURED."

The Cartoonist's Gift
Thomas Nast, who portrayed himself in caricature looking rather like a young Santa Claus (below), drew his earliest published image of that beloved figure for the January 3, 1863, issue of Harper's Weekly. *The illustration shows Santa Claus passing out gifts to children and soldiers in camp under a ceremonial arch welcoming him.*

Limbering Up *A Federal horse artillery battery parades on Morris Island, South Carolina, in the summer of 1863, during the prolonged Union siege of Charleston. The war began here in 1861 when ardent secessionist Edmund Ruffin and other Confederates bombarded Fort Sumter.*

WARRIORS, POETS, & SCOUNDRELS

One of the most oft-quoted untruths is Thomas Carlyle's assertion that "the history of the world is but the biography of great men." The Civil War encompassed far more than the political or military feats of a few celebrated figures. It was history made by the American people as a whole. Some who achieved greatness during the war were leaders of common origin like Abraham Lincoln who inspired Americans to perform uncommon acts of heroism and self-sacrifice. Such inspiration came not just from statesmen or generals but also from men and women on the home front whose pens were as mighty as swords. On the battlefronts, warriors often achieved distinction or notoriety not because they were great but because they were good, dutiful, dedicated officers—or in some cases because they were vain, vicious, or reckless men, whose deeds would live in infamy.

STORMING THE HEIGHTS

Son of a Milwaukee judge, Arthur MacArthur went to war as a lieutenant at the age of 16 and earned the Medal of Honor for valor at Missionary Ridge in 1863 when he seized the colors and led men of his regiment up the slope with the cry "On, Wisconsin!" He was only 19 when he was promoted to colonel and later became a distinguished general in the postwar U.S. Army and the father of an even greater commander, Douglas MacArthur. Many precocious young warriors attained high rank during the Civil War, including John Bell Hood, who became a Confederate army commander in his early 30s but proved unequal to that task. (See "The Perils of Promotion," pages 276-7.)

Ridiculed on "Tinklepots"

In the 1860s, indoor plumbing was all but nonexistent. Bedrooms contained what were variously called chamber pots or "tinklepots." On one occasion, they provided a unique opportunity for ridicule. Gruff Gen. Benjamin Butler commanded Union forces occupying New Orleans. At one point, he ordered that any woman showing public disrespect to Federal soldiers could be treated as a prostitute. The notorious decree earned him the title "Beast Butler" and made him the most hated man in the South. Prostitutes in New Orleans demonstrated their contempt for Butler privately by using tinklepots bearing his image. (See "Butler's Beastly Order," pages 302-303.)

"O Captain! My Captain!"

To Walt Whitman, Abraham Lincoln was America's savior, and his assassination on Good Friday in 1865 left the poet deeply in mourning. He composed four dirges for the slain President. One of them, "O Captain! My Captain!," was in rhymed verse uncharacteristic of Whitman, who wrote this poem in traditional form to speak to and for the entire nation in its hour of loss. The popularity of this work—which likens Lincoln to the master of a ship who falls dead after a hard-won victory at sea—exceeded even *Leaves of Grass*, Whitman's masterpiece. "O Captain! My Captain!" was repeatedly republished, sometimes clumsily. In this 1888 rendition, Whitman himself corrected what he called "bad perversions" in the printing. (See "The Poetic Nurse," pages 286-7.)

The "Old Man"

Among the seasoned, high-ranking officers on duty when the war began, a small number gained lasting prominence. Charles F. Smith, who might have become Union general in chief, was regrettably not among them.

Born in Philadelphia in 1807, Smith graduated from West Point and spent 13 years as an academy administrator. One cadet, young Ulysses Grant, regarded Smith and Winfield Scott as the two greatest soldiers in the world. Distinguished service in Mexico and the Far West followed. By 1861, Smith looked the part of a professional soldier: tall, heavyset, with a parade-ground stiffness, blue eyes, ruddy complexion, and an enormous white mustache. Union recruits called him the "Old Man."

Brig. Gen. Smith was a strict disciplinarian with a penchant for profanity. Volunteers did not mind his curses because he taught them to behave like soldiers. Smith was ordered to serve under a former pupil, General Grant. Fifteen years Smith's junior, Grant remarked that "it does not seem quite right for me to give General Smith orders."

Regular Army officers considered Smith a better soldier than Grant, who owed his stars to political pull, they said, while Smith had spent a lifetime gaining rank based on ability. None of that bothered the dutiful Smith.

In February 1862, Smith commanded one of Grant's three divisions in the attack on Fort Donelson in Tennessee. At a critical point in the battle, Grant rode to Smith's position. "General," Grant shouted, "all has failed on our right! You must take Fort Donelson!" Smith replied briskly, "I will do it." Grant noted with admiration that "the general was off in an incredibly short time."

"IT DOES NOT SEEM QUITE RIGHT FOR ME TO GIVE GENERAL SMITH ORDERS."

U. S. GRANT

Smith led a charge against the Confederate flank. When his raw troops hesitated under fire, the "Old Man" exploded in anger and shouted above the roar of battle: "Damn you, gentlemen! I see skulkers! I'll have none here! You volunteered to be killed for love of country, and now you can be! Follow me!" Smith led his men up a wooded slope and straight into the Confederate works. One of his "damn" volunteers wrote afterward: "I was nearly scared to death, but I saw the old man's mustache over his right shoulder, and I went on."

That assault doomed Fort Donelson. When the Confederate commander asked for terms, Smith urged Grant: "No terms with traitors, by God!" Grant demanded unconditional surrender, whereupon Smith exclaimed: "By God, it couldn't be better!"

Although touted as a hero, Grant fell out with his superior, Gen. Henry Halleck, who promoted Smith to major general and gave him command of Union forces advancing up the Tennessee River. Grant, who remained behind, said he would serve "as faithfully under Smith as he had done under me." Yet he was soon back in charge of the army and had to carry on without Smith. The "Old Man" scraped his leg on a piece of rusty metal while leaping from a rowboat. Tetanus resulted. Smith was gravely ill when Confederates surprised Grant at Shiloh and nearly defeated him. A few weeks later, on April 25, 1862, Charles Smith died at Savannah, Tennessee, in the home Grant was using as headquarters.

Gen. William T. Sherman, who succeeded Smith as Grant's most trusted commander, later paid the "Old Man" high tribute. Had it not been for Smith's untimely death, Sherman declared, neither he nor Grant would ever have been well known. ✴

"DAMN YOU, GENTLEMEN!
I SEE SKULKERS!
I'LL HAVE NONE HERE!
YOU VOLUNTEERED
TO BE KILLED FOR
LOVE OF COUNTRY,
AND NOW YOU CAN BE!
FOLLOW ME!"

**CHARLES F. SMITH
DURING THE 1862 ATTACK ON
FORT DONELSON**

Soldier's Soldier
*Gen. Charles F. Smith,
wearing the uniform
of a colonel in the
prewar photograph
at left, took command
in 1862 of rough-
hewn Westerners such
as the men above,
who fought for the
Union in the 21st
Missouri Infantry.*

A Rude Awakening

John Singleton Mosby was a small wisp of a man, always restless and absolutely fearless. Raised on a farm near Charlottesville, Virginia, he entered Confederate service in 1861 as a private in Col. Jeb Stuart's cavalry regiment. Mosby proved such a daring horseman that in January 1863 Stuart detached him to conduct raids in Union-held northern Virginia. As a partisan ranger, he was free to choose his targets.

The 29-year-old Mosby gathered two dozen dedicated horsemen and crossed enemy lines. Employing hit-and-run tactics, they struck Federal outposts, stole horses and supplies, captured soldiers, and destroyed equipment. Then, one dark, rainy night, Mosby made his biggest catch of the war.

Edwin Stoughton was a Vermont native and an 1859 West Point graduate. He led a Union cavalry regiment with such distinction that in November 1862, at 24, he became the youngest brigadier general in the Union army. He took command of forward units defending Washington on the south side of the

Col. John S. Mosby's shell jacket

Potomac River. There Stoughton acquired a reputation as a drinker and womanizer. His base was the strongly garrisoned town of Fairfax Court House, near Manassas.

On March 7, a late winter downpour pelted the countryside. Champagne flowed freely at a brigade headquarters party. Near midnight, an unsteady Stoughton donned his nightshirt and collapsed in bed.

Around 2 a.m., someone lifted Stoughton's bedcovers, raised his nightshirt, and whacked him soundly on the behind. The outraged general sat up in bed. In the dim light he saw a slightly built, sandy-haired figure attired in a wet slicker. "What is the meaning of this?" Stoughton roared. "Do you know who I am, sir?"

The intruder answered calmly: "I reckon I do, General. Did you ever hear of Mosby?" Stoughton's anger gave way to relief. "You've caught him!" he shouted with delight.

"No," the man said, "but he has caught you."

Mosby and his rangers withdrew into the night and made their way to Confederate headquarters at Culpeper. They had bagged a Union general, 2 captains, 30 enlisted men, and 58 horses without losing a man or firing a shot. Northern newspapers issued howls of indignation. The *Washington Star* declared: "There is a screw loose somewhere. It is about time that our brigadier-generals at exposed points brightened up their spectacles a bit." Lincoln said he did not mind losing a general. "I can make a much better brigadier in five minutes," he remarked, "but the horses cost a hundred and twenty-five dollars apiece."

Mosby's deeds with his 43rd Battalion Virginia Cavalry became legendary. So complete was his control over the land lying between the Blue Ridge and the Bull Run Mountains that the region was known to friend and foe alike as "Mosby's Confederacy." The Confederate government disbanded most partisan companies in 1864 because they were growing increasingly lawless and unmanageable, but Mosby and his rangers continued to operate with ruthless abandon.

After the war, Mosby angered former comrades by joining the Republican Party. He held a number of federal posts, including consul to Hong Kong, before he died in 1916 in Washington, D.C., a city where he was once abhorred.

As for the hapless Stoughton, he was released from Libby Prison in May 1863 but received no new assignment. He left the army in disgrace and practiced law in New York City. He would never talk about what happened at Fairfax Court House. ★

Gray Ghost *Col. John Mosby, commander of the 43rd Battalion Virginia Cavalry, poses beside a memento of his clandestine raids—a Federal officer's overcoat.*

Brig. Gen. Edwin H. Stoughton

"AROUND 2 A.M., SOMEONE LIFTED STOUGHTON'S BEDCOVERS, RAISED HIS NIGHTSHIRT, AND WHACKED HIM SOUNDLY ON THE BEHIND . . . 'WHAT IS THE MEANING OF THIS?' STOUGHTON ROARED. 'DO YOU KNOW WHO I AM, SIR?' THE INTRUDER ANSWERED CALMLY: 'I RECKON I DO, GENERAL. DID YOU EVER HEAR OF MOSBY?'"

The Union's Short-lived Hero

John Buford was a highly promising but little publicized officer who died before his full potential was realized. He would be remembered largely for one heroic action as the Battle of Gettysburg unfolded.

Like Abraham Lincoln, Buford was born in Kentucky and came of age in Illinois. An 1848 graduate of West Point, he fought against the Sioux and saw action in "Bleeding Kansas" before the nation split apart, along with his family. A half brother became a Union general, while a cousin held the same rank on the opposing side. Buford himself refused a Confederate commission. "I'll live and die under the Union," he declared.

After serving as assistant inspector of Washington's defenses, Buford jumped at an offer from Gen. John Pope to command cavalry. He quickly whipped Pope's disorganized horsemen into shape. At Second Manassas, Brigadier General Buford was so badly wounded that he was reported killed. He was soon back in the saddle and served as a cavalry commander with the Army of the Potomac under Generals McClellan, Burnside, Hooker, and Meade.

Buford's conduct was more impressive than his appearance. A staff officer described him as "a compactly built man of middle height, with tawny mustache and little, triangular gray eye, whose expression is determined, not to say sinister. His ancient corduroys are tucked into a pair of ordinary cowhide boots and his blue blouse is ornamented with holes." Despite his untidy look, he was a strict disciplinarian and "not to be trifled with." He once captured a Confederate spy and ordered the man hanged from a nearby tree, with a sign overhead that warned: "This man is to hang three days; he who cuts him down before shall hang the remaining time."

Few officers were more admired by their men. One trooper asserted that Buford was

> "ONE TROOPER ASSERTED THAT BUFORD WAS 'THE BEST CAVALRY OFFICER PRODUCED ON THIS CONTINENT.' WHETHER HE WAS THAT IN FACT WAS LESS IMPORTANT THAN THAT HIS SOLDIERS BELIEVED HIM TO BE SO."

"the best cavalry officer produced on this continent." Whether he was that in fact was less important than that his soldiers believed him to be so.

The high point of Buford's career came at the midpoint of 1863. The first Union commander to reach Gettysburg, he arrived there with his cavalry division on June 30 and warned his officers that Confederates would soon descend on the town in deadly earnest. "You will have to fight like the devil to hold your own until supports arrive," he said. Early the next day, as Lee's vanguard approached from the west, Buford deployed his three brigades to meet the enemy. The troopers went into battle position dismounted, each man three feet away from the next. Buford's thin line of 2,750 men confronted an oncoming division of 7,500 Confederates.

As the battle erupted, Union Gen. John Reynolds rode in from the south ahead of his infantry and asked Buford if he could hold out until those reinforcements arrived. "I reckon I can," replied the cavalry commander. His stubborn defenders staved off the surging Confederates for two hours until the first of Reynolds's troops arrived. Gettysburg and the high ground to its south on which Federal hopes rested—remained in Union hands until Lee's army withdrew from the blood-soaked battlefield.

Afterward, Buford seemed destined for higher command. Yet in late autumn, he contracted typhoid fever. On December 16, 1863, the 37-year-old Buford received promotion to major general—and died that same day. "The army and the country have met with a great loss," a fellow officer stated. Buford was "the best cavalry general we had . . . rough in the exterior, never looking after his own comfort, untiring on the march." The Union was fortunate that in its greatest hour of need, it had its toughest trooper on hand. ★

Horse Soldiers *Gen. John Buford sits amid his staff officers in August 1863. Capt. Myles Keogh (left) was killed at the Battle of the Little Bighorn in 1876.*

Armistead and Hancock

Two officers who parted ways when their nation divided in 1861 went on to win renown not just as warriors but also as true and lasting friends. Lewis Armistead was a native of coastal North Carolina. Winfield Scott Hancock, seven years younger, grew up near Philadelphia. Both men attended West Point. Armistead was dismissed in 1836 for breaking a mess plate over the head of cadet Jubal Early. He then enlisted in the U.S. Army. Hancock graduated from the academy in 1844.

Armistead and Hancock met during the Mexican War as officers in the Sixth U.S. Infantry. They served together afterward in a campaign against Seminole Indians in Florida and on a long, toilsome march across the West to Benicia Barracks in California. Shared duty and compatibility made them the closest of friends.

As the Civil War loomed, Southerners began resigning their commissions to join Confederate forces. Hancock's wife gave a farewell party for departing officers of the old Sixth Infantry. The evening was heavy with sadness. As midnight drew near, the wife of Albert Sidney Johnston, who was about to cast his lot with the South, sang "Auld Lang Syne." Armistead and Hancock, two old acquaintances who would never forget each other, embraced tearfully.

Armistead took charge of George Pickett's Virginia brigade when Pickett was promoted to division commander. The Carolinian was a soldier's soldier, beloved by superiors and enlisted men alike. Hancock rose steadily in rank and esteem

> "COME ON, BOYS.
> GIVE THEM THE COLD STEEL!"
>
> **LEWIS ARMISTEAD AT GETTYSBURG**

Parted by War *When Lewis A. Armistead (left) and Winfield Scott Hancock (right) parted company in 1861, Armistead entrusted his prayer book to Hancock's wife. At right, Armistead leads his men at Gettysburg with hat on sword.*

in the Union army. Known as "Hancock the Superb," he was a corps commander in the Army of the Potomac when the paths of the two old friends converged one last time.

At Gettysburg, on July 3, 1863, General Armistead's brigade took part in a desperate Confederate assault known as Pickett's Charge. The attackers advanced for nearly a mile across a wheat field, in full view of Union artillery and infantry massed on Cemetery Ridge. Some 7,000 of 12,000 Confederates went down in the hour-long contest.

Armistead and 150 of his men were the only ones who broke through the Federal line. They fought their way over a stone wall, stumbled forward, then fell amid a blaze of gunfire. Armistead clutched a Federal cannon as he sank mortally wounded to the ground. He asked Union soldiers to give his personal effects to his friend, General Hancock.

It was Hancock's corps that repulsed Pickett's Charge. The Union commander accepted Armistead's valuables with tears in his eyes as he himself was borne to the rear with wounds from which he would eventually recover.

Hancock and Armistead did not meet again, but they would remain linked in memory. A marker placed at Gettysburg in 2000 commemorates the bond between those old "friends and fellow officers in the United States Army" and shows where the leader of the last Confederate thrust at Gettysburg spent his final hours: "Here at the Union Army 11th Corps Field Hospital, George Spangler Farm, Armistead died of his wounds on July 5, 1863." ✶

"Stonewall of the West"

Late on the afternoon of November 30, 1864, Confederates made an ill-considered assault at Franklin, Tennessee. The result was a massacre. Among the 6,000 attackers who fell there in four hours of fighting was the highest ranking Confederate officer of foreign birth, Maj. Gen. Patrick Cleburne.

Son of an Irish physician, Cleburne served a few uneventful years in the British army before migrating to America. On Christmas Day, 1849, he arrived in New Orleans. Cleburne eventually became an attorney in Helena, Arkansas. When his state seceded, he put his army experience to good use as a Confederate officer.

At Shiloh, his brigade fought conspicuously and suffered the steepest losses of any Confederate unit there. Cleburne later introduced new tactics to bolster his infantry, including using sharpshooters during attacks and deploying artillery up front.

A fellow officer described Cleburne as "a blunt, impassive, rather heavy man ... who only needed flames of battle to kindle his dull features." He braved those flames repeatedly, in situations when many other men would have held back. In late August 1862 at Richmond, Kentucky, a bullet pierced his cheek and exited through his mouth. He was speechless for a while but returned to action less than six weeks later at Perryville, where he was wounded in the leg by a shell that killed his horse.

Cool and calculating when exposed to danger, Cleburne became the most dependable division commander under the Confederacy's most unpopular army chief, Braxton Bragg (pages 308-309). Twice in the battles around Chattanooga in

"LEE CALLED PATRICK CLEBURNE 'A METEOR SHINING FROM A CLOUDED SKY,' WHILE PRESIDENT DAVIS DUBBED HIM THE 'STONEWALL OF THE WEST.'"

Battle flag of Confederate First Arkansas Infantry, division of Patrick Cleburne (right)

late 1863, Cleburne saved Bragg's Army of Tennessee from ruin. He should have advanced up the chain of command afterward when Bragg resigned, but he antagonized superiors with a proposal that the Confederacy abolish slavery and recruit blacks as soldiers. Few Southern authorities would contemplate freeing or arming slaves until the war was all but lost. No further promotion came Cleburne's way.

He earned accolades for his gallant performance in defense of Atlanta under Bragg's successor, Joseph Johnston. Lee called Patrick Cleburne "a meteor shining from a clouded sky," while President Davis dubbed him the "Stonewall of the West." Yet when Davis removed Johnston for being too cautious, he replaced him with Gen. John Bell Hood (pages 276-7), an officer younger than the 36-year-old Cleburne and ill qualified for top command. Hood lost Atlanta at great cost, then advanced northward into Union-occupied Tennessee at great peril.

Cleburne knew the risks when Hood ordered the attack on heavily fortified Union forces at Franklin. "If we are to die," he told one officer, "let us die like men." Two horses were shot from under Cleburne, but he proceeded on foot with saber in hand, urging his men forward. Fifty yards from the Union breastworks, he took a bullet in the chest and fell. He was one of six Confederate generals killed in that senseless attack.

Corps commander William Hardee wrote of Cleburne afterward with a heavy heart. "When his division defended, no odds broke its line," Hardy remarked. When it attacked, he added, it was stopped only once, at Franklin, "and there is the grave of Cleburne." ★

"Old Beeswax"

Raphael Semmes earned his place in history as the Civil War's most notorious naval figure, hailed by Southerners as a patriot and reviled by Northerners as a pirate. Often overlooked is the curious fact that this swashbuckler who rose to the rank of rear admiral ended the war as a brigadier general.

Born in Maryland in 1809, Semmes went to sea as a midshipman at 16. He rose through the ranks and commanded the U.S.S. *Somers* in the Mexican War before settling in Mobile, Alabama, where he practiced law when not on duty. Semmes resigned from the U.S. Navy in 1861 to serve the South as a commerce raider. His objective was to prey on Northern merchant ships and draw pursuing U.S. warships away from blockade duty. Some ship captains conducted such raids as privateers, but Semmes did so as a Confederate officer. His first raider, C.S.S. *Sumter*, was small and slow, but he managed to seize 18 prizes before Union warships trapped his vessel at Gibraltar in January 1862.

Semmes escaped to England, where he took command of a swift, new commerce raider, C.S.S. *Alabama*. In mid-1862, he embarked on a two-year odyssey, during which he laid claim to 65 merchant vessels and sank a Union warship. He alone was responsible for a third of all Confederate naval seizures during the war.

Semmes looked the part of a seagoing rascal, with an erect bearing, long hair framing a high forehead, piercing black eyes, and a waxed mustache turned upward. His sailors called him "Old Beeswax," but in the North his name became an

> "HIS SAILORS CALLED HIM 'OLD BEESWAX,' BUT IN THE NORTH HIS NAME BECAME AN OBJECT OF LOATHING AND TERROR."

Commerce Raider *Above, the C.S.S.* Alabama *sets a Union merchant ship aflame in 1862. At right, Capt. Raphael Semmes stands on the* Alabama *in 1863.*

object of loathing and terror. His forays were not too costly in lives, because he spared those who surrendered to him. But the toll of his raids in shipping and goods was steep, exceeding four million dollars in value. He seemed to appear and vanish at will. In one account, he likened a vessel he ran down to a "panting breathless fawn" and his own ship to an "inexorable staghound."

His luck ran out in June 1864 at Cherbourg, France. The *Alabama* was awaiting repairs there in port when the U.S.S. *Kearsarge* appeared offshore. Semmes rose to the challenge and dueled with the more powerful *Kearsarge* for an hour before his ship went down.

A passing British vessel rescued Semmes, who returned in early 1865 to Richmond. He was promoted to rear admiral and took command of the James River Squadron, consisting of ten vessels, all of which had to be destroyed when Richmond fell in early April. Semmes then accompanied President Davis to the temporary Confederate capital at Danville, Virginia. The only high-ranking officer at hand, he was appointed brigadier general in charge of the town's defenses. Although he served in that capacity only briefly before the war ended, he gave his rank as general rather than admiral when he surrendered to the Federals.

Semmes was soon paroled, but he was later jailed for piracy until the charges were dropped. He was in fact no more a pirate than Union commanders who enforced the blockade. Those who knew Semmes well were inclined to agree, however, that "Old Beeswax" had a corsair's heart. ★

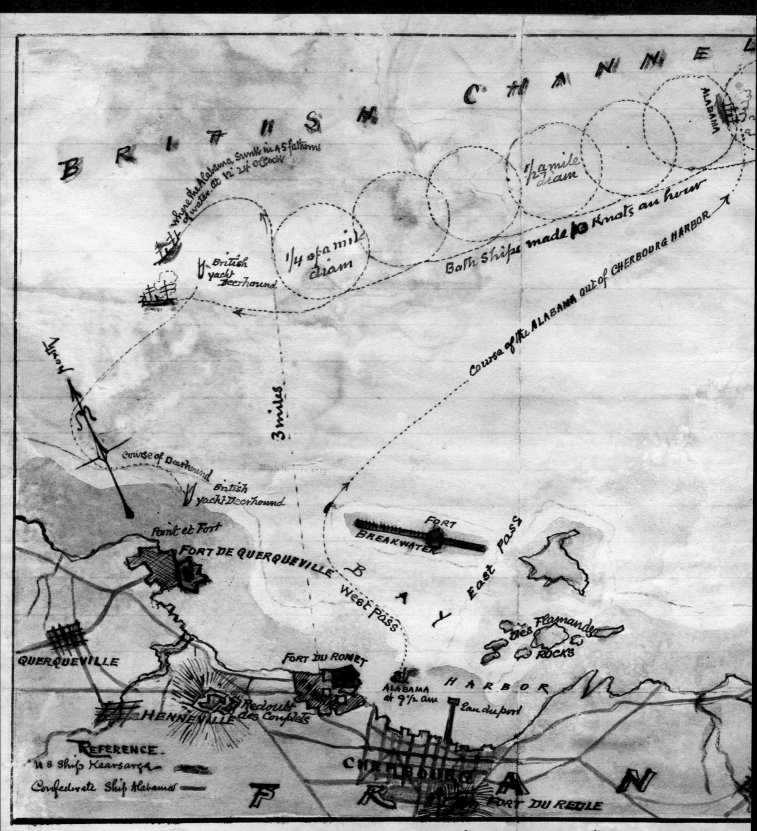

PLAN OF THE CIRCLE BATTLE between the U.S. SHIP "KEARSARGE" Capt Winslow. and "ALABAMA" Capt Raphael Semmes. off the harbor of CHERBURG. France. forenoon of

Raider's End *The map at left, drawn by Robert Knox Sneden, shows the looping course taken by the* C.S.S. Alabama *and* U.S.S. Kearsarge *during their duel off Cherbourg on June 19, 1864. The Currier &* Ives *print above shows the* Kearsarge *blasting the doomed* Alabama *(foreground) shortly before it sank.*

Armed to Kill *Capt. John A. Winslow (third from left) and his officers stand at the bow of the* Kearsarge *in 1864. Carefully aimed and spaced shots from the ship's eight guns, including the massive, pivoting 11-inch Dahlgren in the foreground at left, reduced the* Alabama *to a burning wreck.*

"Every Inch a Soldier"

William Mahone belongs in the same class with James Longstreet and John Mosby as Confederate officers who went from being praised as saviors in wartime to being scorned as Judases in peacetime.

Born to a tavernkeeper in Southampton County, Virginia, Mahone was a small, scrappy youth given to drinking and gambling. The Virginia Military Institute set him straight, and he went into railroad construction after graduating. By 1860, he was president, superintendent, and chief engineer of the Norfolk & Petersburg Railroad.

Soon after his state seceded, Mahone became colonel of the Sixth Virginia. He was made a brigadier general in late 1861. Longstreet called him "one of our best brigadiers" and urged Mahone's promotion, but he retained the same rank even after taking command of a division in Lee's army in May 1864.

On July 30, 1864, Federals used explosives to blast a huge hole in Lee's defenses at Petersburg. The ensuing Battle of the Crater was one of the war's most chaotic struggles. Mahone received orders to send two brigades to block Union troops who were pouring through the breach of the Crater. He would not send those brigades, Mahone replied; he would lead them. His counterattack turned the tide and culminated in the massacre of Union men in the Crater, many of them black soldiers. Some men later blamed Mahone for that massacre. Others said he interceded to halt the slaughter. To Confederates, he was the undisputed hero of the Crater, and Lee promoted him to major general. For the remainder of the war, he was among Lee's top division commanders.

Mahone hardly looked the part of a fighting general. Five feet, one inch tall, he

> "MAHONE RECEIVED ORDERS TO SEND TWO BRIGADES TO BLOCK UNION TROOPS WHO WERE POURING THROUGH THE BREACH OF THE CRATER. HE WOULD NOT SEND THOSE BRIGADES, MAHONE REPLIED; HE WOULD LEAD THEM."

weighed no more than 120 pounds. He was so thin that when his wife heard that he had received a flesh wound in battle, she remarked: "Now I know it is serious, for William has no flesh whatsoever." Haunting eyes peered out from heavy brows. A drooping mustache and long beard concealed much of his face. His voice was that of a falsetto tenor. An aide thought the general "altogether the oddest and daintiest little specimen of humanity I had ever seen." Plagued by dyspepsia that only eggs and milk seemed to ease, Mahone always kept a half dozen chickens and a milk cow at headquarters. Wherever he went, they went.

After the war, Mahone returned to his old profession and built the Norfolk & Western Railroad. He and his wife named the depots along the route. Unable to resolve their dispute over what to call one station, they named the place "Disputanta." It still goes by that name.

Meanwhile, Mahone had become one of the most controversial political leaders in the postwar South. Disdaining the "Lost Cause" movement that rationalized Confederate defeat while embracing Democratic Party principles such as white supremacy, Mahone forged an alliance that included black and white Republicans and some white Democrats. He twice lost bids for the Virginia governorship, but in 1880 his "Readjusters" triumphed and sent Mahone to a stormy term in the U.S. Senate. By the time he died in 1895, Virginia and the South had turned firmly against him.

In politics as in warfare, Mahone was persistent and pugnacious. "Whenever Mahone moves out," soldier who served under him observed, "somebody is apt to get hurt." Another comrade of "Little Billy" summed him up memorably: "He was every inch a soldier, though there were not many inches of him." ★

Defiant One *After the war, former Confederate Gen. William Mahone rebelled against the political views of most of his old comrades.*

The Perils of Promotion

John Bell Hood demonstrated the Peter Principle by rising from ranks at which he excelled to the level of his incompetence. The son of a Kentucky physician, he struggled at West Point with mathematics, the core of the curriculum. Hood stood near the bottom of his 1849 class and received so many demerits he barely avoided being dismissed.

Twelve years of uneventful soldier life followed in the West. In 1861, Hood sided with the South and became colonel of the Fourth Texas Infantry. He molded it into a first-class regiment and demonstrated a newfound discipline and dedication.

His appearance was certainly an asset. Magnificently built, the handsome Hood stood six feet two inches tall. His flowing hair and full beard were auburn in color, and his long, lean face and deep-set blue eyes appeared somber until battle made them glow. He possessed "a melodious and powerful voice," one observer wrote, and "the look of a dashing soldier."

Hood made his reputation with Lee's Army of Northern Virginia. In early 1862, he took command of the Texas Brigade, which proved so valiant that Lee often employed Hood's men as shock troops in battle. On the Peninsula, at Second Manassas, Antietam, and Fredericksburg, Hood was in the thick of the fighting. Stonewall Jackson paid him a rare compliment when he exclaimed: "Oh! He is a soldier!"

Hood's daring attacks won him promotion to major general at the age of 31 but also brought him crippling wounds. At Gettysburg, he was shot in the left arm and never regained

> "EVEN HOOD'S END WAS TRAGIC. IN AUGUST 1879, HE, HIS WIFE, AND A DAUGHTER DIED IN NEW ORLEANS OF YELLOW FEVER. LEFT BEHIND WERE HEAVY DEBTS AND TEN ORPHANED CHILDREN."

Hood family orphans

use of that limb. Three months later, with the Army of Tennessee at Chickamauga, he suffered a horrible wound that cost him his right leg. He hobbled painfully on crutches with one arm dangling uselessly at his side. To ride a horse, Hood had to be strapped to the saddle. His aggressive posture and gritty determination to return to action impressed Jefferson Davis, who placed him in charge of the Army of Tennessee as it was falling back toward Atlanta in July 1864. The appointment surprised Hood's former commander, Lee, who acknowledged that Hood was a "bold fighter" but doubted that he had "the other qualities necessary" to lead an army.

Hood quickly launched a series of ill-conceived attacks that cost him dearly and left his forces stretched thin around Atlanta, which fell to Sherman in September. Hood then led his battered troops into Tennessee, where he was first outmaneuvered and then outfought. His reckless attack at Franklin bordered on the suicidal. In mid-December, Federals routed what remained of his army at Nashville and inflicted on Hood one of the war's most devastating defeats.

Before reaching the top, Hood led some of the Confederacy's best combat units in blistering attacks. At the highest level, however, this brilliant fighter faltered. He was too impulsive, too aggressive, too blind to the big picture to succeed. His performance showed that courage and competence do not always go hand in hand.

Even Hood's end was tragic. In August 1879, he, his wife, and a daughter died in New Orleans of yellow fever. Left behind were heavy debts and ten orphaned children. ★

Uncle Tom's Creator

In 1850, a New England woman of Puritan ancestry and literary inclinations pondered the evils of slavery and the plight of the runaways who fled bondage. Others who shared her concerns produced pamphlets or speeches, but Harriet Beecher Stowe created something far more powerful—a novel that touched the hearts of millions and became the most influential book in America: *Uncle Tom's Cabin.*

Born in 1811, she was the daughter of one famous minister, Lyman Beecher, and the sister of another, Henry Ward Beecher, an ardent abolitionist. In her early 20s, she lived for a time in Cincinnati and got a brief, firsthand knowledge of slavery in neighboring Kentucky. She began writing short stories in the mid-1830s and wed Rev. Calvin Stowe, with whom she had seven children.

Passage of the 1850 Fugitive Slave Act (pages 26-29) sent the Beechers into a frenzy. The men denounced the law from the pulpit, and a sister-in-law urged Harriet Stowe to write something that would make the nation "feel what an accursed" thing slavery was. She soon went to work.

Her inspiration was threefold: a deep commitment to Christian principles, an unwavering belief in the immorality of slavery, and an intense patriotism. Stowe believed that human bondage prevented America from fulfilling its great promise and corrupted both South and North. It weakened the South by promoting idleness and indulgence; it retarded the North by encouraging moral detachment.

By June 1851, Stowe had completed *Uncle Tom's Cabin,* her first novel. She sold it for $300 to an abolitionist journal, and it was first published as a book in 1852. Within a year, 300,000 copies had been sold (the modern-day equivalent of over three million copies).

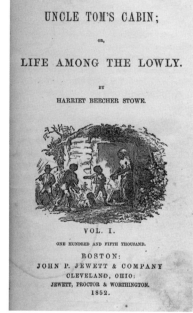

Instant Classic *The two-volume first edition of Harriet Beecher Stowe's* Uncle Tom's Cabin *was a best seller in 1852 and regained popularity during the Civil War.*

From a literary standpoint, the story left something to be desired. The author's style was frequently melodramatic, and she often interrupted the narrative to preach. Nevertheless, *Uncle Tom's Cabin* presented many Northern readers with their first intimate view of slavery. Stowe portrayed slaves as people possessed of the same mental and emotional qualities as whites.

Her audience was moved by the sufferings of the slave mother, Lucy, who drowned herself after her child was taken from her and sold. Readers came away from the book with one picture imprinted on their minds—the death of the kindly, humble slave Uncle Tom at the hands of the demonic Simon Legree. Stowe brought slavery home to Northerners and made real the abstract idea of Southern "slave power." Legree personified that power and gave Unionists what every people must have before they can fight a war with fervor: an image of the enemy.

The book left white Southerners seething. What they found most offensive was the human face Stowe put on slavery and the way she used Christianity—through biblical quotations and allusions—to undermine the system. Some 30 "anti-*Uncle Tom*" novels appeared, nearly half of them published within two years of Stowe's book. One of the first was *Aunt Phillis's Cabin; or, Southern Life as It Is,* by Mary Henderson Eastman, the Virginia-born wife of a U.S. Army officer.

When Harriet Stowe met Abraham Lincoln in late 1862, the President reportedly took her hand and said: "So you're the little woman who wrote the book that made this great war." Stowe lived to see slavery abolished, but its grim legacy still haunted the nation when she died in 1896. Her novel remains, as one authority has proclaimed, "the most influential indictment of slavery of all time." ✶

Author's Models *Among the figures who inspired Harriet Beecher Stowe to write her famous antislavery novel was her brother, abolitionist Henry Ward Beecher, pictured here with the author. She may have modeled the character of Uncle Tom in part on Josiah Henson (above), a devout slave who fled north and eventually settled as a minister in Canada.*

"WHEN HARRIET STOWE MET ABRAHAM LINCOLN IN LATE 1862, THE PRESIDENT REPORTEDLY TOOK HER HAND AND SAID: 'SO YOU'RE THE LITTLE WOMAN WHO WROTE THE BOOK THAT MADE THIS GREAT WAR.'"

A.S. Seer's Print. N.Y. (Copyrighted)

UNCLE TOM'S CABIN.

Slavery Melodramas *Stowe never authorized a dramatization of* Uncle Tom's Cabin, *but her work inspired hundreds of unauthorized productions, ranging from melodramas to racially stereotyped minstrel shows. The poster at left, showing the villainous slave owner Simon Legree with whip in hand, advertises an 1879 production. Another theatrical poster at top shows the slave Eliza crossing the frozen Ohio River with her child, pursued by dogs (top). Above, the saintly Little Eva and the slave child Topsy embrace on the cover of sheet music inspired by Stowe's novel.*

Spokesman for Freedom

Many pioneers helped pave the way for Lincoln's Emancipation Proclamation. Standing head and shoulders above them all was Frederick Douglass, a man who did not just preach abolitionism but also embodied it by rising from bondage to become the heart and soul of the antislavery movement.

Born in Maryland in 1818 to a slave mother and a white father whose identity was unknown to him, he was given the name Frederick Bailey. He learned to read and write from his master's wife and from white children for whom he did favors in exchange for instruction. In 1838, he fled northward and changed his surname to Douglass in an effort to avoid detection.

With what he called "luck, pluck, and remarkable skills," Douglass came to the attention of abolitionist William Lloyd Garrison and emerged as one of the leading orators in Garrison's antislavery network. Possessed of extraordinary eloquence, he told of his slave experiences and his quest for freedom in lectures throughout the North and in England. Douglass was awesome in appearance: a huge man with hair slung back to his shoulders, full beard, and blazing eyes. His deep voice resonated like thunder, and his passionate rhetoric electrified audiences. Suffragist Elizabeth Cady Stanton once exclaimed: "He stood there like an African prince, majestic in his wrath."

Douglass settled with his family in Rochester, New York, and published a newspaper called *North Star* that rivaled Garrison's journal, *The Liberator,* as a voice for the abolitionist cause. Douglass's autobiography, first published in 1845 and later expanded, was so fluent and persuasive that some critics doubted that a former slave could have written it.

As the specter of civil war loomed, Douglass firmly opposed any last-minute compromises with the South. "If the Union can only be maintained by new concessions to the slaveholders [and] a new drain on the negro's blood," he asserted, then "let the Union perish."

From the start of the conflict, Douglass urged "war for the destruction of slavery." When Lincoln issued the Emancipation Proclamation in 1862, Douglass wrote: "We shout for joy that we live to record this righteous decree." Yet he was not satisfied, and pressed for the enlistment of black soldiers. "Once let the black man get upon his person the brass letters U.S.," he declared, "let him get an eagle on his button, and a musket on his shoulder . . . and there is no power on earth which can deny that he has earned his right to citizenship." In early 1863, Douglass helped organize two black regiments in Massachusetts. His two oldest sons were among the first to enlist.

Douglass met Lincoln in July 1863 at the White House and urged him to support equal pay and fair treatment for black troops. During a later meeting between the two men, the governor of Connecticut arrived at the White House to see the President. Lincoln asked him to wait while he finished his talk with his "good friend, Frederick Douglass."

Until his death in 1895, Douglass continued to advocate equality for blacks and women as well. As much as anyone, he led the fight for freedom that ultimately transformed a nation where most people were denied equal rights into a land with liberty and justice for all. ✶

> "IT IS NOT LIGHT THAT WE NEED, BUT FIRE; IT IS NOT THE GENTLE SHOWER, BUT THUNDER. WE NEED THE STORM, THE WHIRLWIND, AND THE EARTHQUAKE."
>
> "NO MAN CAN PUT A CHAIN ABOUT THE ANKLE OF HIS FELLOW MAN WITHOUT AT LAST FINDING THE OTHER END FASTENED ABOUT HIS OWN NECK."
>
> "THE SOUL THAT IS WITHIN ME NO MAN CAN DEGRADE."
>
> **FREDERICK DOUGLASS**

Liberator *Frederick Douglass, photographed in 1866, campaigned tirelessly for an end to slavery and equal rights for all Americans.*

Conceiving the Battle Hymn

The Civil War made her famous, but 42-year-old Julia Ward Howe was already a woman of distinction when the conflict began. High-spirited and highly intelligent, she had six children by her husband, Dr. Samuel Gridley Howe—an abolitionist who helped finance John Brown's insurrection at Harpers Ferry—while pursuing a busy and varied career. She too was an outspoken abolitionist, as well as a suffragist, poet, playwright, editor, and friend of such notables as Ralph Waldo Emerson and Henry David Thoreau. All her previous accomplishments were overshadowed, however, by some verses she composed one morning while visiting Washington, D.C., in November 1861.

The Union capital was a raucous beehive of activity when Julia Ward Howe arrived there. One afternoon she and several friends rode across the Potomac to watch an army review. As they returned to Washington, they passed through groups of soldiers singing a favorite camp song. It was a fine tune, timed to the cadence of marching feet. The lyrics, on the other hand, proclaimed morbidly that "John Brown's body lies a-mouldering in the grave."

A companion suggested to Howe that she use her poetic gift to write "some good words for that stirring tune." She promised to give it some thought.

Fatigued by the day's activities, she had an early dinner, retired to her room in Willard's Hotel, and fell fast asleep. Howe was awakened before sunrise by the tramp of soldiers marching beneath her window. "As I lay waiting for the dawn," she later recalled, "the long lines of the desired poem began to twine themselves in my mind."

Howe bounded from bed, grabbed a pen and a sheet of paper, and began pouring out lyrics: "Mine eyes have seen the glory of the coming of the Lord / He is trampling out the vintage where the grapes of wrath are stored / He hath loosed the fateful lightning of His terrible swift sword / His truth is marching on." By sunrise, she had finished the poem's five remaining stanzas—none of which proved as memorable as the first—and returned to bed. She slept peacefully for several hours.

For the next few weeks, Howe polished the phrases to her liking. She sold the work to the *Atlantic Monthly* for five dollars. The poem appeared in print two months later. When President Lincoln first heard the words sung, he supposedly shouted: "Sing it again!"

The new version was slow to gain acceptance by Billy Yanks, who continued to sing of John Brown. Then Howe's "Battle Hymn of the Republic" suddenly took hold and became the most popular song in the Union ranks. It was not so much a marching melody as it was an uplifting patriotic anthem.

Nothing Julia Ward Howe did before or after brought her anything like the attention and adulation she received for her "Battle Hymn." Without that to her credit, she might not have been the first woman elected to the American Academy of Arts and Sciences. Wherever she lectured, it was to cheering audiences. When she died in 1910 at the age of 91, bands and vocalists gathered throughout the nation on the day of her funeral to perform the song she had immortalized almost 50 years earlier.

All but forgotten was the man who wrote the thrilling melody her lyrics accompanied—William Steffe, a Sunday school teacher in Charleston, South Carolina, who composed the tune for worshippers at camp meetings. As with so many legacies of the Civil War, Ward's hymn was at first purely partisan in nature but belongs now to all Americans. ✶

> "AS THEY RETURNED TO WASHINGTON, THEY PASSED THROUGH GROUPS OF SOLDIERS SINGING A FAVORITE CAMP SONG. IT WAS A FINE TUNE, TIMED TO THE CADENCE OF MARCHING FEET. THE LYRICS, ON THE OTHER HAND, PROCLAIMED MORBIDLY THAT 'JOHN BROWN'S BODY LIES A-MOULDERING IN THE GRAVE.'"

THE
ATLANTIC MONTHLY.

A MAGAZINE OF LITERATURE, ART, AND POLITICS.

VOL. IX.—FEBRUARY, 1862.—NO. LII.

BATTLE HYMN OF THE REPUBLIC.

MINE eyes have seen the glory of the coming of the Lord:
He is trampling out the vintage where the grapes of wrath are stored;
He hath loosed the fateful lightning of His terrible swift sword:
His truth is marching on.

I have seen Him in the watch-fires of a hundred circling camps,
They have builded Him an altar in the evening dews and damps;
I can read His righteous sentence by the dim and flaring lamps:
His day is marching on.

I have read a fiery gospel writ in burnished rows of steel:
"As ye deal with my contemners, so with you my grace shall deal;
Let the Hero, born of woman, crush the serpent with his heel,
Since God is marching on."

He has sounded forth the trumpet that shall never call retreat;
He is sifting out the hearts of men before His judgment-seat:
Oh, be swift, my soul, to answer Him! be jubilant, my feet!
Our God is marching on.

In the beauty of the lilies Christ was born across the sea,
With a glory in his bosom that transfigures you and me:
As he died to make men holy, let us die to make men free,
While God is marching on.

Julia Ward Howe

Union's Anthem
*"The Battle Hymn
of the Republic" first
appeared on the cover of
the February 1, 1862,
issue of the* Atlantic
Monthly, *a leading
American literary
magazine. The poem
was set to music adapted
from a Methodist camp
meeting song, "Say,
Brothers, Will You Meet
Us?," that appeared in
several music collections
published in the 1850s.*

The Poetic Nurse

Someone walking the streets of Washington in the latter years of the Civil War might have encountered an odd man with a scarlet face, bushy beard, and wide-brimmed sombrero that gave him the look of a Southern planter. Stout, slow-moving, with heavy-lidded eyes, he seemed much older than his early 40s. His garments were coarse but carefully selected. He never wore a tie. Few in the Army Paymaster's Office where he worked as a clerk, or the military hospitals where he served as a volunteer nurse, recognized Walt Whitman for who he was—a man of literary genius.

Born on Long Island to parents of modest means with nine children, Whitman left school early and worked for various newspapers. He also developed a remarkable flair for poetry. Whitman led a bohemian life until December 1862, when he hastened to Washington after learning that his brother George had been wounded at the Battle of Fredericksburg. Once assured that his brother was safe, Whitman found fulfillment in comforting sick and wounded soldiers in Washington's wards.

While nursing men in pain and reassuring those in despair, Whitman wrote letters to friends, family members, and newspaper editors, informing them of the many needs of the military hospitals and their patients. Donations poured forth, and Whitman purchased gifts and necessities for the men he so admired. "Love for them lives as long as I draw breath," he declared.

His nursing efforts brought him some recognition, but his literary work led to greater fame. A passive spectator he was not. Whitman had a reporter's eye for detail and a poet's emotional involvement with all that he witnessed. He expanded during the war on his epic poem, *Leaves of Grass,* an innovative work that dispensed with rhyme and meter and incorporated the natural rhythms of American speech—heard in all its variety in the crowded wards Whitman visited. In addition to poetry, he wrote vivid journalism and prose documenting his wartime experiences, including a memoir entitled *The Wound-Dresser.*

Brotherhood and compassion were Whitman's main themes, which is why he found so much to admire in Lincoln. Whitman saw in the President a rare combination of the "purest, heartiest tenderness" and a toughness that allowed Lincoln to persist and prevail. "He conceals an enormous tenacity under his mild gawky western manner," Whitman wrote in 1863. "That he has conserved the government so far is a miracle." Lincoln's assassination moved Whitman to compose two of his most famous poems: "When Lilacs Last in the Dooryard Bloom'd" and "O Captain! My Captain!," which concludes with a mournful tribute to a leader who did not live to share in the triumph he made possible: "The ship is anchor'd safe and sound, its voyage closed and done; / From fearful trip the victor ship comes in with object won; / Exult, O shores, and ring, O bells! / But I with mournful tread, / Walk the deck my Captain lies, / Fallen cold and dead."

Nothing thereafter ever inspired Whitman as much as had the Civil War. He regarded postwar America as hopelessly selfish and corrupt and looked back on the heroic conflict as the nation's defining moment. Whitman would never forget those Yanks and Rebels he nursed. He once claimed that there was no way to convey in writing the "actual soldier of 1862–65, North and South, with all his ways, his incredible dauntlessness, habits, practices, tastes, languages, his fierce friendship, his appetite, rankness, his superb strength and animality." Such men were in fact captured in writing—by Whitman himself, who as poet laureate and inspired journalist of the Civil War left an eloquent record of that era. ★

> "EXULT, O SHORES, AND RING, O BELLS! / BUT I WITH MOURNFUL TREAD, / WALK THE DECK MY CAPTAIN LIES, / FALLEN COLD AND DEAD."
>
> FROM "O CAPTAIN! MY CAPTAIN!"

America's Bard *Walt Whitman was around 50 when he sat for this photograph in 1870. His job then was to interview former Confederate prisoners of war to determine their eligibility for pardons.*

The Music Maker

America was developing its own, distinctive popular music tradition when the Civil War began. Many of the popular tunes of the 1850s, however, were minstrel songs that romanticized the South and slavery like Stephen Foster's "Old Folks at Home" or "Dixie," which later became a Confederate anthem. When the nation broke apart in 1861, Northerners needed stirring songs that celebrated the Union. No composer did more to fill that need than George F. Root. The Civil War would generate some 2,000 songs, more than any other event in the nation's history. Root's compositions were among the best of the lot.

Born on a farm in Massachusetts in 1820, George Root was a precocious talent who played a dozen or more instruments as a child. He studied in Europe and later taught music in Boston and New York. In the 1850s, he began composing popular songs and became involved with his brother Ebenezer in a Chicago music-publishing house.

The Civil War gave George Root an opportunity to display his thorough knowledge of instrumental music, his improvisational skills, and his absolute devotion to the Union. The tunes and lyrics he wrote tapped into the varied emotions of soldiers as well as their families, ranging from hope and inspiration to loneliness and grief. No one matched Root at capturing the fervor of the Union cause or creating rousing martial music that men could sing as they sat in camp or marched into battle.

His 1861 war song, "God Bless Our Brave Young Volunteers," offered the challenge: "Stand up for Uncle Sam, my boys / For he

> "AT WAR'S END, A CONFEDERATE OFFICER TOLD HIS FORMER ENEMIES: 'GENTLEMEN, IF WE'D HAD YOUR SONGS, WE'D HAVE WHIPPED YOU OUT OF YOUR BOOTS!' "

George F. Root

Family Business *This sheet music for "The Battle Cry of Freedom" was published by Root & Cady, a firm managed by George F. Root's older brother Ebenezer.*

has stood by you." His most popular anthem, "The Battle Cry of Freedom," appeared in 1862. A phenomenal 350,000 copies of the sheet music were sold in a year. Northern soldiers and civilians alike sang the chorus: "While we rally 'round the flag, boys, boys, rally once again / Shouting the battle cry of freedom!" One Billy Yank asserted that this melody put "as much spirit and cheer into the army as a splendid victory."

Root also composed heartbreaking ballads like his classic "Just Before the Battle, Mother," written from the standpoint of a Union soldier longing for home and family. In "The Prisoner's Hope," Root opened with these somber lines: "In the prison cell I sit / Thinking, Mother, dear, of you / And our bright and happy home so far away …" Another popular air was "The Vacant Chair," which told of the empty place left at the family table for a soldier lost on some distant battlefield. Thousands knew the opening lines: "We shall meet but we shall miss him / There will be one vacant chair / We shall linger to caress him / While we breathe our evening prayer."

Root had gifted competitors, including composer Henry Clay Work. But Work's biggest hit, "Marching Through Georgia," celebrating Sherman's campaign, did not appear until 1865 when the war was ending. When Root died in 1895, he had the satisfaction of knowing that he had not just caught the spirit of the conflict but also contributed to its outcome with songs that boosted Northern morale. At war's end, a Confederate officer told his former enemies: "Gentlemen, if we'd had your songs, we'd have whipped you out of your boots!" ★

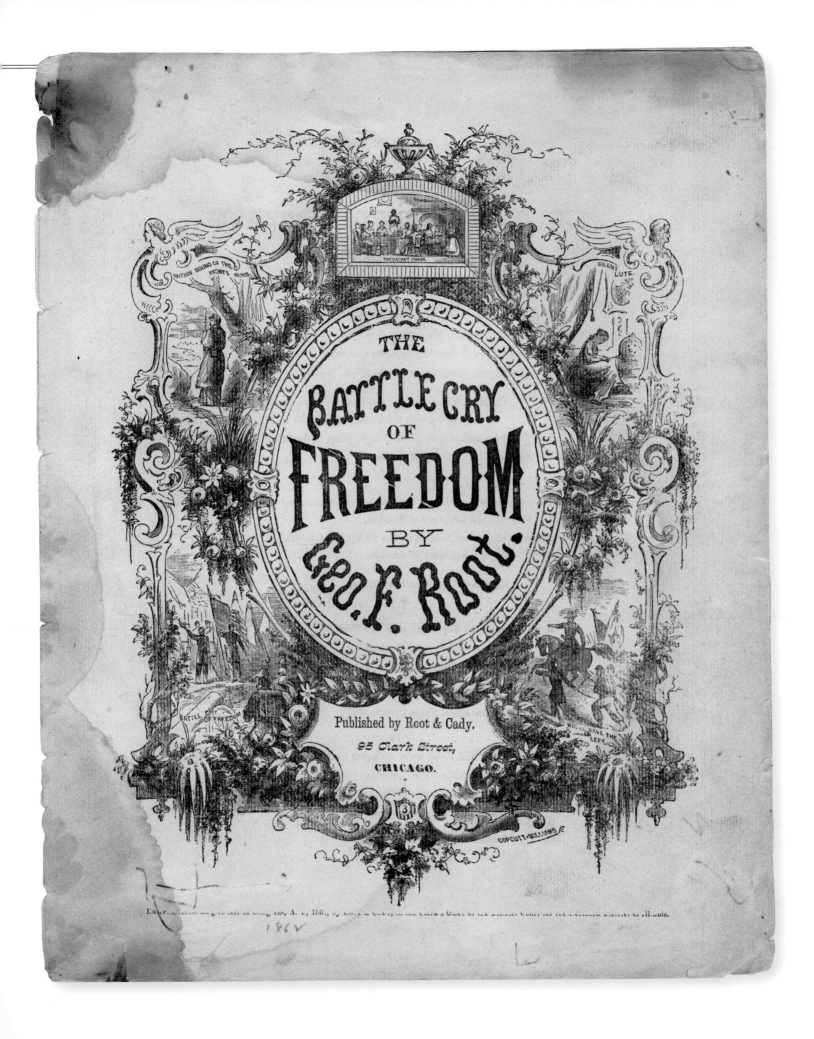

THE
BATTLE CRY
OF
FREEDOM
BY
Geo. F. Root.

Published by Root & Cady.
95 Clark Street,
CHICAGO.

A Literary Heroine

In 1861, Louisa May Alcott was approaching 30 and unmarried, which made her a spinster in those days when women wed early. She was not one to sit at home spinning or weaving, however. She threw herself into the Union war effort on the home front and won renown as a nurse and author well before the appearance of the novel for which she is now remembered, *Little Women*.

Raised in Concord, Massachusetts, she was educated at home by her father, an eccentric philosopher whose friends Emerson and Thoreau also provided her with instruction and inspiration. By the time she was 20, Alcott was publishing essays in women's magazines and writing mysteries and romances that were published under a pseudonym. Her upbringing by reform-minded New Englanders made her an outspoken abolitionist. She fully supported John Brown's 1859 insurrection and referred to him after his conviction and execution as "Saint John the Just."

When war came, Alcott aided Union troops by sewing uniforms and performing in theatricals to raise money for the U.S. Sanitary Commission. Late in 1862, she sought another way to let out her "pent-up energy" by volunteering as a nurse.

Alcott was assigned to Union Hotel Hospital in the Georgetown section of Washington. Her first days there were a severe challenge. Caring for wounded soldiers who were ragged, filthy, and swathed in bandages that had not been changed for days, she experienced "the vilest odors that ever assaulted the human nose."

Alcott worked 12-hour shifts that were physically and mentally exhausting. Once, when a patient lay dying, a surgeon told her: "There's not the slightest hope for him, and

> "ALCOTT WORKED 12-HOUR SHIFTS THAT WERE PHYSICALLY AND MENTALLY EXHAUSTING. ONCE, WHEN A PATIENT LAY DYING, A SURGEON TOLD HER: 'THERE'S NOT THE SLIGHTEST HOPE FOR HIM, AND YOU'D BETTER TELL HIM BEFORE LONG. WOMEN HAVE A WAY OF DOING SUCH THINGS COMFORTABLY, SO I LEAVE IT TO YOU.'"

you'd better tell him before long. Women have a way of doing such things comfortably, so I leave it to you."

After six weeks of nursing duties, Alcott contracted typhoid fever. Surgeons plied her with the catchall drug of that day: calomel. This resulted in mercury poisoning that caused the loss of teeth and hair and also affected the nervous system. She survived only through the constant care of the well-known physician Josiah Bartlett. Alcott was a semi-invalid thereafter.

In the first stages of recuperation, she edited letters she had written home as a nurse. Those appeared in print in 1863 under the title *Hospital Sketches*. Her haunting, firsthand observations of sick and wounded soldiers in that book came as a revelation for readers and served as a model for Walt Whitman's nursing memoirs. Alcott's account encouraged other women to step forward as volunteer nurses in spite of family objections to the difficult and demeaning nature of the work.

The success of *Hospital Sketches* made Alcott a literary celebrity several years before she completed *Little Women*, which appeared in 1868. The novel's heroine, Jo March—one of four sisters in a New England family disrupted when the father departs to fight in the Civil War—is an aspiring author in her 20s, much like young Louisa May Alcott (pictured at right in the 1850s). "An old maid, that's what I'm to be," Jo remarks at one point. "A literary spinster, with a pen for a spouse, a family of stories for children, and twenty years hence a morsel of fame, perhaps."

Alcott achieved more than a morsel of fame before she died in 1888—just days after the passing of her father, to whom she was devoted. As a nurse and author, she too was a heroine in stormy times. ✷

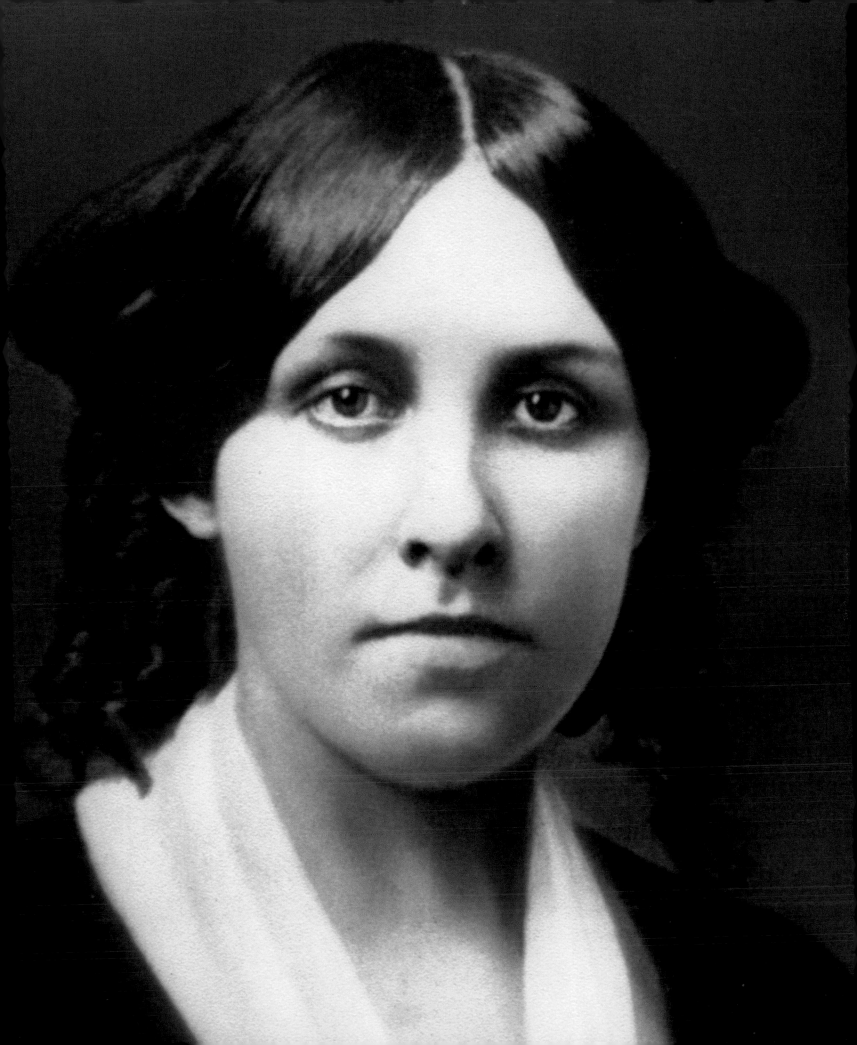

A Professor at War

Joshua Chamberlain was impatient to prove himself in the struggle between North and South. "War is for the participants a test of character," he said. "It makes bad men worse and good men better." By 1862, teaching courses in religion and modern languages at Bowdoin College in Maine was no longer rewarding for him. He was an introvert and a poor instructor—much like another professor named Jackson at the Virginia Military Institute. Chamberlain's training in literature and rhetoric, however, made him both a fine chronicler of the war and an officer who, when put to the ultimate test, lived up to classical ideals of heroism.

Chamberlain obtained a two-year leave of absence from Bowdoin, supposedly to study in Europe. He then joined the army, at a time when the initial rush of enthusiasm for war had faded. "The regiments passing to the front marched not between festoons of ladies' smiles and waving handkerchiefs," he recalled. "They were looked upon sadly and in a certain awe, as those who had taken upon themselves a doom. The muster rolls on which the name and oath were written were pledges of honor—redeemable at the gates of death."

Chamberlain saw action at Antietam, Fredericksburg, and Chancellorsville before becoming colonel of his regiment, the 20th Maine. A lanky man in his mid-30s with a high forehead, drooping mustache, and pensive eyes, he was a gentleman-soldier and a genteel, humane commander.

In the second day's fighting at Gettysburg, the 350 men of the 20th Maine anchored the Union left flank. Chamberlain was told by his brigade commander to hold his exposed position on the south face of Little Round Top at all costs. In two hours of vicious fighting, half of his men fell dead or wounded.

Joshua Chamberlain's gauntlets and major general's shoulder straps

He later recalled the sounds of that chaotic struggle: "All around, strange, mingled roar—shouts of defiance, rally, and desperation; and underneath, murmured entreaty and stifled moans; gasping prayers, snatches of Sabbath song, whispers of loved names."

Chamberlain's men had spent their ammunition and could not hold out any longer. He ordered them to fix bayonets and charge the enemy with a yell. This sudden, desperate action caught the battle-weary Confederates by surprise, and they fled the hillside. Chamberlain saved the Union flank—and later received a Medal of Honor for doing so.

By war's end, he had participated in 26 engagements, received six wounds, and been promoted to major general. Grant gave the former professor the honor of receiving the formal surrender of Lee's army at Appomattox.

His postwar career included four terms as Maine's governor and 13 years as president of Bowdoin College. Chamberlain's most enduring legacy was his memoir, *The Passing of the Armies,* one of the most articulate and often quoted accounts in Civil War literature. In his many addresses to veterans' groups, he paid tribute to those who had tested their character in battle and proved worthy of the lofty ideals and visions for which they fought.

In 1889, Chamberlain shared these thoughts with old soldiers who gathered on Little Round Top at Gettysburg to dedicate a monument: "In great deeds something abides. On great fields something stays. Forms change and pass; bodies disappear; but spirits linger, to consecrate ground for the vision-place of souls." In generations to come, he added, people yearning "to see where and by whom great things were suffered and done for them, shall come to this deathless field, to ponder and dream . . . and the power of the vision shall pass into their souls." ★

"THE REGIMENTS PASSING TO THE FRONT MARCHED NOT BETWEEN FESTOONS OF LADIES' SMILES AND WAVING HANDKERCHIEFS. THEY WERE LOOKED UPON SADLY AND IN A CERTAIN AWE, AS THOSE WHO HAD TAKEN UPON THEMSELVES A DOOM. THE MUSTER ROLLS ON WHICH THE NAME AND OATH WERE WRITTEN WERE PLEDGES OF HONOR— REDEEMABLE AT THE GATES OF DEATH."

JOSHUA CHAMBERLAIN

Fighting for Maine *Joshua Chamberlain (top), assigned to hold the Federal far left on Little Round Top at Gettysburg on July 2, 1863, led the desperate charge of the 20th Maine that repulsed Confederates there (above). He was promoted to brigadier general in 1864 and commanded the Maine militia after the war.*

"With Malice Toward None"

A week after most presidential Inaugurations, few people can remember anything the chief executive said. Such was not the case with Abraham Lincoln. His two inaugural messages, along with the "few appropriate remarks" he made at Gettysburg, have become part of what one might term an American bible, filled with passages as powerful now as they were then.

March 4, 1865, was a terrible day for an inauguration. Nearly a week of rain had left streets slathered in mud up to 15 inches deep. Army engineers considered laying a pontoon bridge from the White House to the Capitol. Police told all pedestrians who could not swim to remain on sidewalks.

Lincoln was impassive and weary as he rode alone in a two-horse carriage through the muck to Capitol Hill. Four years of trying to keep the ship of state afloat had taken a heavy toll. His frame sagged; those who shook his hand remarked on the cold and clammy fingers. Lincoln was only fifty-six, but he looked twenty years older. Walt Whitman noted that day: "The lines, indeed, of vast responsibilities, intricate questions, and demands of life and death, cut deeper than ever upon his dark brown face."

After the swearing-in of Vice President Andrew Johnson in the Senate chamber, the presidential party moved to the platform erected on the east front of the Capitol. A drenched but enthusiastic crowd greeted the President. Below the platform sat abolitionist Frederick Douglass. In the crowd above Lincoln stood actor John Wilkes Booth.

As Lincoln stepped to read his address, the sun burst through the clouds. Many in the audience considered this a good omen. The clouds closed again, however, as Lincoln began to speak. His clear, high-pitched voice carried to the outer edges of the crowd as he delivered the shortest

> "WITH MALICE TOWARD NONE; WITH CHARITY FOR ALL; WITH FIRMNESS IN THE RIGHT, AS GOD GIVES US TO SEE THE RIGHT, LET US STRIVE ON TO FINISH THE WORK WE ARE IN."
>
> LINCOLN'S SECOND INAUGURAL ADDRESS

Inaugural Address in history, amounting to just 703 words. Lincoln prized brevity and did not think this occasion warranted a long speech. The past four years had delivered their own indelible message. A power greater than any army was deciding the outcome, Lincoln believed, and there was little he could add to that providential judgment other than to affirm that it was fitting and just.

The war was divine punishment for the sin of slavery, Lincoln stated, and God held both sides responsible for that sin: "He gives to both North and South, this terrible war, as the woe due to those by whom the offence came." America might suffer further for its long history of slavery, Lincoln warned. "Fondly do we hope, fervently do we pray, that this mighty scourge of war may speedily pass away," he declared. "Yet, if God wills that it continue, until all the wealth piled by the bond-man's two hundred and fifty years of unrequited toil shall be sunk, and until every drop of blood drawn with the lash, shall be paid by another drawn with the sword, as was said three thousand years ago, so still it must be said: 'the judgments of the Lord are true and righteous altogether.'"

After delivering that stern verdict, Lincoln ended his address with an appeal for mercy that reflected his compassion for all Americans and his hope that a forgiving God would redeem and heal the nation: "With malice toward none; with charity for all; with firmness in the right, as God gives us to see the right, let us strive on to finish the work we are in; to bind up the nation's wounds; to care for him who shall have borne the battle, and for his widow, and his orphan—to do all which may achieve and cherish a just, and a lasting peace, among ourselves, and with all nations."

Six weeks later, Lincoln was murdered. His gracious words lived on, however, and were recalled and recited by Americans ever after in times of trial. ★

Final Image *This portrait of Lincoln, taken on April 10, 1865, was the last photograph of the President before he died.*

Virginia Fire-eater

With white hair down to his shoulders and the countenance of an Indian warrior, Edmund Ruffin looked the part of a biblical patriarch ready to unleash fire and brimstone. He was such a fervent secessionist that he abandoned his native Virginia when it did not abandon the Union fast enough to suit him.

Ruffin was born in 1794 to a prominent family on the Pamunkey River. While managing his estate, he became an agricultural reformer and founded the *Farmer's Register,* which encouraged Southern planters to apply fertilizer and use other means to replenish the soil. His suggestions went largely unheeded, so the disgusted Ruffin abandoned agriculture in the 1850s and turned to politics.

Ruffin's overriding obsession became the preservation of slavery. Black bondage, he insisted, yielded enormous economic and cultural benefits while keeping the South's huge slave population firmly under control. Ruffin never recognized that slavery discouraged the very reforms he advocated to improve Southern farming. Like his hero, the late Senator John C. Calhoun of South Carolina, he believed that slavery was a "positive good" and that the federal government had no right to restrict it.

Ruffin became Virginia's leading "fire-eater," agitating for secession at a time when many in the South still hoped to avoid disunion through political compromise. Although he lacked oratorical skills and held state office only briefly, he crusaded for secession both in print and in public, arguing his case in hotel lobbies, steamboat parlors, and anywhere else he could find an audience.

Opening Shots *Edmund Ruffin, pictured at right in early 1861 when he was urging Southern states to secede, was on hand when the war began at Fort Sumter (above) in April and fired an early shot at that Union stronghold.*

John Brown's 1859 raid on Harpers Ferry put the venerable Ruffin into a frenzy. (Perhaps Ruffin saw in Brown an image of himself.) The old man somehow finagled an honorary appointment as a cadet at the Virginia Military Institute and accompanied its color guard to Harpers Ferry to watch the execution. Later, he sent one of the pikes that Brown had intended as weapons for rebellious slaves to each Southern governor as "a sample of the favors designed for us by our Northern Brethren."

South Carolina left the Union the following year. When Virginia held back, Ruffin renounced his state citizenship and moved to Charleston. Legend has it that the 66-year-old fire-eater fired the first shot in the bombardment of Fort Sumter. His shot may have been among the first, but Ruffin's military career with South Carolina's Palmetto Guards was otherwise brief and undistinguished. He appeared at the First Battle of Manassas and hoped soldiers would view him as an inspiration. Instead, they saw him as an ornament.

Infirmities of old age soon reduced Ruffin to a passive observer in the war he helped create. Union soldiers pillaged his property. Ruffin settled on a small farm in Southside Virginia. The more the military situation deteriorated, the more embittered he became. The collapse of the Confederacy, plus the deaths of six of his nine children within a decade, left him no reason to live.

On June 17, 1865, Ruffin wrote the last entry in his copious journal: "I have declared my unmitigated hatred . . . of the perfidious, malignant and vile Yankee race." Then he seated himself in a chair, placed the muzzle of a musket in his mouth, and used a hickory stick to pull the trigger. The gun fired on the second attempt. ✳

"I HAVE DECLARED
MY UNMITIGATED HATRED
. . . OF THE PERFIDIOUS,
MALIGNANT AND VILE
YANKEE RACE."
EDMUND RUFFIN

The Bishop-General

Leonidas Polk was proof that religion and war are separate professions, not easily combined. As a bishop he was comforting, but as a general this loyal Confederate offered less consolation to his own side than to the enemy.

A native of Raleigh, North Carolina, Polk formed a close friendship with Jefferson Davis at West Point in the 1820s. Polk was commissioned a lieutenant of artillery but soon resigned from the army to study for the Episcopal ministry. By 1841, he was bishop of Louisiana. Polk (portrayed at right by Mathew Brady) was an impressive figure in the pulpit and married into wealth, acquiring an extensive sugar plantation. He led a movement to create a college where Southern boys would be well educated without the "contaminating" influence of Yankee ideas. The University of the South was the result.

In 1861, Polk offered his services to the Confederacy. His old West Point comrade, now President Davis, appointed him a major general in command of a department comprising western Tennessee and eastern Arkansas—despite the fact that Polk had spent only six months in military service.

He wasted no time in demonstrating his incompetence. In September 1861, acting in direct violation of orders, Polk advanced into Kentucky and occupied the high bluffs overlooking the Mississippi River at Columbus. This move has been called "one of the most decisive catastrophes the Confederacy ever suffered." The bishop-general's intrusion drove the vital state of Kentucky—which was officially neutral—into the arms of the Union. That allowed Federal forces led by Ulysses Grant to enter Kentucky and advance up the Tennessee River. Polk squatted at Columbus until February 1862 when Grant's troops seized Forts Henry and Donelson and made his position untenable.

"POLK CHOSE TO OBEY A SUPERIOR ONLY WHEN IT PLEASED HIM TO DO SO. HE DEVELOPED A CONSUMING HATRED FOR HIS COMMANDER, GEN. BRAXTON BRAGG, WHO SOUGHT TO REMOVE HIM. BRAGG DESCRIBED POLK IN A LETTER TO PRESIDENT DAVIS AS 'UNFIT FOR EXECUTING THE PLANS OF OTHERS.' "

Thereafter, thanks to Davis's continued support, Polk served as a corps commander in the Army of Tennessee. His egregious error in Kentucky was only the first of many missteps, but he had an uncanny ability to shift blame for his failures to his lieutenants.

To the casual observer, Polk was a self-sacrificing clergyman who reluctantly buckled the sword over clerical robes from a sense of duty. In truth, he was a proud, ambitious troublemaker—stubborn, aloof, and quarrelsome. As a bishop, he had been trained to lead. As a soldier, he never learned how to follow.

Polk chose to obey a superior only when it pleased him to do so. He developed a consuming hatred for his commander, Gen. Braxton Bragg, who sought to remove him. Bragg described Polk in a letter to President Davis as "unfit for executing the plans of others. He will convince himself his own are better and follow them without reflecting on the consequences." Davis stood by the bishop-general, however. Bragg finally got Polk transferred—shortly before he himself was ousted.

On June 14, 1864, Polk rode with officers to the top of Pine Mountain in Georgia to survey the movements of General Sherman's opposing Federals. Union artillery opened fire on the party. Polk scoffed at the bombardment and stood fast. A cannonball killed him instantly. He was the second highest ranking Confederate to die in action during the war, after army commander Albert Sidney Johnston.

Leonidas Polk was widely mourned in the South, where few people knew of his deficiencies. Posterity was less kind to him. One historian assessed the damage Polk did to his own cause early in the war and called him the Confederacy's "most dangerous man." ✶

Brady, N.Y.

The Commander Who Fled

Gen. Gideon J. Pillow would rank high on any list of Civil War incompetents. He was the one Confederate for whom U. S. Grant voiced outspoken contempt.

Pillow owed much to the fact that he and James Knox Polk were once law partners in Tennessee. When war began with Mexico in 1846, Pillow was totally without military experience. That did not deter President Polk from appointing him a brigadier general of infantry.

Vain, ambitious, and easily offended, Pillow quickly displayed his lack of military knowledge by ordering his men to entrench by piling the dirt behind them rather than in front, leaving them no protection from enemy fire. As insolent as he was ill informed, Pillow was accused of insubordination by Gen. in Chief Winfield Scott. Young Lt. A. P. Hill wrote: "Pillow is as soft as his name and will no doubt be dismissed from the Army for barefaced lying."

In the 1850s, Pillow failed to win a U.S. Senate seat and twice sought the Democratic Party's vice presidential nomination without success. When Tennessee seceded, Governor Isham Harris named him commander of all the state's forces. An English journalist described Pillow at that time as "a small, compact, clear-complexioned man, with short grey whiskers . . . a quick eye, and a pompous manner of speech." Pillow clashed time and again with superiors, including Gen. Leonidas Polk.

In early 1862, Pillow was co-commander of Fort Donelson when Grant's forces hemmed in that stronghold on the Cumberland River in Tennessee. Pillow agreed to lead a

Notorious Troublemaker
An 1848 cartoon shows the esteemed Gen. Winfield Scott deflating his troublesome subordinate, Gideon Pillow. Portrayed at right early in the Civil War as a Confederate general, Pillow remained a problem for his superiors.

breakout attack that would open the road to Nashville for the besieged Confederates. After intense fighting on the morning of February 15, Pillow's men punctured the Union lines. "The day is ours," Pillow proclaimed. Instead of forging ahead, however, he unaccountably ordered his men to fall back. By evening, Grant's forces had rallied and the fort was doomed.

Pillow's battle cry had always been "Liberty or Death!" On this occasion, he chose liberty—for himself rather than his men. He feared being taken prisoner and thought he was so important politically that the Federals might hang him. Pillow abdicated his command and slipped away by boat across the Cumberland to safety, leaving 13,000 Confederates behind to face capture and confinement.

Pillow spent months explaining his failure to Jefferson Davis, who restored him to field service. At the Battle of Stones River at year's end, he hid behind a tree rather than lead his brigade against a strong enemy position. He received no more combat assignments.

The final word on General Pillow was pronounced by Grant, who told in his memoirs of receiving the surrender of Fort Pillow from Gen. Simon Buckner.

"Where is Pillow?" Grant asked. "Why didn't he stay to surrender his command?"

"He thought you were too anxious to capture him personally," Buckner replied.

"Why, if I had captured him I would have turned him loose," Grant said. "I would rather have him in command of you fellows than as a prisoner." ✭

"VAIN, AMBITIOUS,
AND EASILY OFFENDED,
PILLOW QUICKLY
DISPLAYED HIS LACK
OF MILITARY
KNOWLEDGE."

Butler's Beastly Order

Many inflammatory official pronouncements were issued during the Civil War. Few caused a greater furor among the public than Maj. Gen. Benjamin Franklin Butler's General Orders No. 28.

New Orleans had fallen into Federal hands in April 1862. Butler was in charge of securing the city. A prominent Democrat from Massachusetts, appointed by President Lincoln to help broaden political support for the war, Butler was fat, bald-headed, slovenly, unscrupulous, and cunning. He had already riled Confederates by claiming escaped slaves who sought refuge in territory his troops occupied on the Virginia coast as "contraband of war," or confiscated enemy property. That freed them to remain there and work for the Union without being officially emancipated, a step Lincoln was not ready to take.

Butler's reputation in the South went from bad to worse when he took charge of occupied New Orleans. Citizens there deeply resented Federal military rule and refused to comply with orders. When men gathered to protest, Butler used the threat of artillery fire to disperse them. Shopkeepers who denied business to Yankee customers found their stores seized and sold. Ministers refusing to pray for the United States were banished. "Very soon," Butler wrote proudly, "there was no uncivil treatment received by our soldiers except from the upper class of women."

In fact, most white women in New Orleans scorned the occupiers. One lady declared that they all were "in favor of resistance, no matter how hopeless." They wore secessionist badges, turned up their noses at Union soldiers, and exited streetcars or church pews when Yankees entered.

Butler Buffoon *A former Massachusetts politician, Benjamin F. Butler looked like a satirical version of a general even when photographed (right) and lost all dignity when portrayed on the bottom of chamber pots (above) by scornful Southerners.*

Initially, Butler was amused. Once, when a group of ladies turned their backs as he rode by, he said loudly: "Those women evidently know which end of them looks best." Then a housekeeper emptied her chamber pot on David Farragut's head as the Union naval commander walked beneath her balcony. Another woman spit at two Union officers. That was enough for Butler. On May 15, he issued General Orders No. 28, which stated that "when any female shall, by word, gesture, or movement, insult or show contempt for any officer of the United States, she shall be regarded and held liable to be treated as a woman of the town plying her avocation."

This so-called woman order hit hard. It clearly meant that women who publicly scorned Federal officers could be arrested as prostitutes—and seemingly suggested they could be harassed or even sexually assaulted by Union men with impunity.

Reaction was widespread and indignant. British prime minister Lord Palmerston called Butler's order "infamous" and added: "Any Englishman must blush to think that such an act has been committed by one belonging to the Anglo-Saxon race." Jefferson Davis declared Butler an outlaw in a decree that left any Southerner who captured him free to hang him on the spot. Butler surpassed Lincoln as the most detested man in the Confederacy. One diarist denounced him as a "hideous, cross-eyed beast."

Butler's decree proved crudely effective. A few women in New Orleans were arrested, but none was assaulted. Those who detested "Beast Butler" and his officers shifted from public insults to private expressions of contempt. Prostitutes in town had the last laugh. They got back at Butler for his uncouth reference to their "avocation" by painting his face on the bottom of their "tinklepots." ✱

"WHEN ANY FEMALE SHALL . . . INSULT OR SHOW CONTEMPT FOR ANY OFFICER OF THE UNITED STATES, SHE SHALL BE REGARDED AND HELD LIABLE TO BE TREATED AS A WOMAN OF THE TOWN PLYING HER AVOCATION."

BENJAMIN BUTLER

"BUTLER
SURPASSED
LINCOLN AS THE
MOST DETESTED
MAN IN THE
CONFEDERACY.
ONE DIARIST
DENOUNCED HIM
AS A 'HIDEOUS,
CROSS-EYED
BEAST.' "

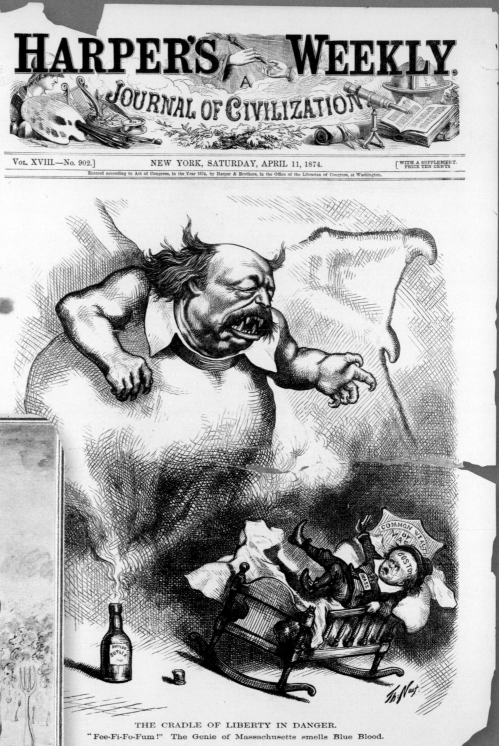

HARPER'S WEEKLY.
A
JOURNAL OF CIVILIZATION

VOL. XVIII.—No. 902.] NEW YORK, SATURDAY, APRIL 11, 1874. [WITH A SUPPLEMENT. PRICE TEN CENTS.

Entered according to Act of Congress, in the Year 1874, by Harper & Brothers, in the Office of the Librarian of Congress, at Washington.

THE CRADLE OF LIBERTY IN DANGER.
"Fee-Fi-Fo-Fum!" The Genie of Massachusetts smells Blue Blood.

Beast Butler.

Marks of the Beast *A satanic General Butler (left) is surrounded by looted household possessions in a cartoon that may have been produced in New Orleans. During the 1874 Massachusetts gubernatorial campaign, cartoonist Thomas Nast portrayed Butler as an evil genie (above), threatening the infant "Boston" in the Cradle of Liberty.*

"Good Old Dan"

He wore notoriety like a flowing cape. Whether he was politicking, fighting, or womanizing, Daniel E. Sickles always seemed to be running full throttle.

He gained early prominence as a lawyer and a stalwart of Tammany Hall, whose chiefs bossed New York City. In 1856, he won election as a U.S. congressman. His one notable act was to introduce a bill making George Washington's birth date a national holiday.

Ambition drove Sickles, but passion nearly derailed him. At 32, he wed the 16-year-old daughter of an Italian opera conductor. He was unable to confine himself to one woman. Yet when he learned in 1859 that his neglected wife was having an affair with the son of the man who wrote "The Star-Spangled Banner," Sickles killed Philip Key in cold blood on a street in Washington, D.C. The fact that Key was the city's district attorney did not bode well for Sickles. But Edwin Stanton, a future secretary of war, won acquittal for Sickles on the novel defense of temporary insanity.

Sickles saw the Civil War as a chance to demonstrate valor and fulfill his political ambitions, which reached all the way to the White House. Although he had no military experience, he was asked by New York's governor to raise a 1,000-man regiment. Sickles recruited a 5,000-man brigade, which brought him a brigadier's star. When the army was slow to supply him with tents, Sickles purchased a circus tent from P. T. Barnum and billed the government. The soldiers loved "Good Old Dan."

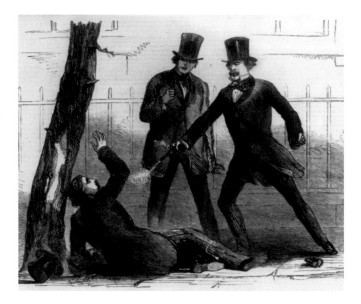

Murder in Washington *Daniel Sickles shoots Philip Key dead in a newspaper illustration of the notorious 1859 assault in the nation's capital.*

Commanding officers did not share that affection, for Sickles always interpreted orders loosely. Commanding a corps at Chancellorsville, he was told to move forward a short distance. Sickles advanced so far that the corps to his right, on the Union flank, was stranded when Stonewall Jackson attacked.

Two months later, Sickles did it again. In defiance of orders, he advanced his corps into an indefensible peach orchard at Gettysburg. A third of his men fell killed and wounded, and Sickles lost his right leg. A few days later, the Army Medical Museum in Washington received a box marked "With the compliments of Maj. Gen. Daniel E. Sickles." Inside was his amputated leg. The bone is still on display.

In 1865, President Andrew Johnson appointed Sickles to command the military district of the Carolinas. Sickles blasted Johnson's Reconstruction policies and was fired. He then lobbied to have Johnson impeached. Two years later, President Grant named Sickles ambassador to Spain, where he romanced former Queen Isabella. He returned to New York, where loving citizens reelected him to Congress.

"Good Old Dan" was not through. His long tenure as chairman of the New York State Monuments Commission came to an end when, at 91, he was accused of embezzling funds designated for battlefield memorials. Legend has it that he made off with the funds for his own monument at Gettysburg, where no statue of him was ever erected. At his death in 1914, however, he was given a hero's burial in Arlington National Cemetery. ✷

"A FEW DAYS LATER, THE ARMY MEDICAL MUSEUM IN WASHINGTON RECEIVED A BOX MARKED 'WITH THE COMPLIMENTS OF MAJ. GEN. DANIEL E. SICKLES.' INSIDE WAS HIS AMPUTATED LEG. THE BONE IS STILL ON DISPLAY."

BRIG. GEN'L DANIEL E. SICKLES.

Entered according to Act of Congress in the year 1861, by M.B. Brady, in the Clerk's office of the District Court of the U.S. for the So. District of New-York

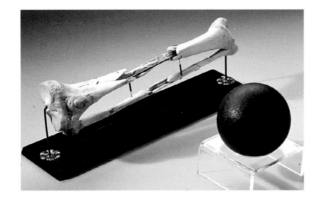

Wounded Veteran *Daniel Sickles, shown at top right as a brigadier general in 1861, stands above between two other former Union commanders, Joseph Carr and Charles Graham, near the site at Gettysburg where Sickles suffered the wound that cost him his leg. He donated his amputated limb (top left) to the Army Medical Museum and often brought friends to view it after the war.*

A Drill Sergeant as General

He was the most enigmatic and hated field commander in the Civil War. A strict disciplinarian, he never learned to control his own temper or hide his arrogant disdain for others. He fought a half dozen battles and mismanaged them all. Only one factor kept Braxton Bragg at the head of the Army of Tennessee: Jefferson Davis liked him.

Born in North Carolina, Bragg graduated from West Point in 1837 and fought gallantly as an artillery officer in the Mexican War. When Confederates chose Davis as their president in 1861, he called on his old friend and fellow officer Bragg to defend the South. In early 1862, Bragg joined Gen. Albert Sidney Johnston's army in the dual role of corps commander and chief of staff. At the Battle of Shiloh, which claimed Johnston's life, Bragg's corps fought tenaciously and boosted his reputation.

A few months later, he was named to command what became the Army of Tennessee. It needed a firm hand, but Bragg wielded an iron fist. He purged officers he disliked and cracked down on his troops, imposing harsh penalties for minor infractions. "He loved to crush the spirit of his men," one veteran complained.

Bragg's appearance was as forbidding as his manner. Bushy eyebrows and a heavy, grizzled beard lent him a feral look that some people thought apelike. Piercing, restless eyes gave the impression of intense, aggressive energy. Tall and lean, he carried himself like a warrior and often drew up audacious plans. What Bragg lacked was a fighting heart. In the heat of battle, his confidence often

> "HE HAD THE INSTINCTS OF A DRILL SERGEANT BUT NOT THE GENIUS OF A GENERAL."
>
> **AN ACQUAINTANCE OF BRAXTON BRAGG'S**

Lost Opportunity *Braxton Bragg (right) had Union troops pinned down at Chattanooga (above) and commanded the heights overlooking the town. But the Federals brought in supplies and reinforcements and broke his siege, forcing him to resign.*

wilted. Myriad illnesses plagued him. Migraine headaches, boils, dyspepsia, rheumatism—all aggravated by stress—left him irritable and moody.

Bragg's 1862 invasion of Kentucky was characteristically bold in conception and feeble in execution. He failed to coordinate troop movements and had only part of his army at hand when he attacked at Perryville and was beaten back. After his retreat to Tennessee, one general concluded that Bragg had "lost his mind." In a three-day battle at year's end along Stones River, Bragg again struck first but failed to press his advantage and lost a third of his army to no gain. His one notable victory, at Chickamauga in September 1863, cost him 6,000 more casualties than the Federals suffered and was squandered when he allowed them to regroup at Chattanooga. Two months later, with Grant in charge, Federals broke Bragg's siege by routing his troops on Missionary Ridge. Only then did Bragg gratify his many vocal critics—including most of the generals who served under him—by resigning as army chief.

Davis, faithful to a fault, then made Bragg his top military adviser and virtual general in chief. He had no chance of succeeding in that role amid an ever widening circle of military and political enemies. He ended up defending the Confederacy's last open port, Wilmington, North Carolina, which fell in early 1865 as much through Bragg's blunders as through Federal efforts.

After he died in 1876, an acquaintance summed Bragg up astutely: "He had the instincts of a drill sergeant but not the genius of a General." ✷

The Most Wanted Bushwhacker

In 1854, partisan warfare between pro-slavery and antislavery forces in Kansas and Missouri turned the area into a no-man's-land. It remained such through the Civil War years as gangs of horsemen called Jayhawkers rampaged for the Union while bushwhackers did the same for the Confederacy. Some of those border ruffians cared little for their cause and simply wanted an excuse to commit plunder and mayhem.

The bushwhacker most wanted by Federal authorities was William Clarke Quantrill. Born in Ohio, Quantrill drifted westward and lived for a while in Lawrence, Kansas, where he ran afoul of the law and absconded. In late 1861, he became a Confederate guerrilla and assembled a gang containing some of America's worst desperadoes. Gunslingers Frank and Jesse James, William "Bloody Bill" Anderson, and Cole Younger were among those who learned their trade under the tutelage of the slightly built, stern-faced Quantrill. Some of their forays were of military value to the Confederacy, and Quantrill won promotion to captain. Thereafter, he insisted on being called "Colonel."

In 1863, Union authorities arrested women related to Quantrill's raiders as accomplices. The building in which they were jailed collapsed, killing several of the women. Bent on revenge, Quantrill gathered 450 men and started toward Lawrence, a Unionist stronghold where he had some old scores to settle.

At dawn on August 21, 1863, he sent his raiders into Lawrence with the simple command: "Kill every male and burn every building." The first civilian to die was a clergyman, shot through the head while milking a cow. During the next three hours, Quantrill's band slaughtered 182 unarmed men and boys and torched nearly 200 buildings in the war's worst atrocity. One prominent target who escaped was Senator James Lane, a Jayhawker who had slain Confederate sympathizers in Missouri. Had he captured Lane, Quantrill said later, "I would have burned him at the stake."

Quantrill's murderous attack on Lawrence did the Confederacy no good and brought misery to thousands of people in western Missouri, who were forced to leave their homes by Union Gen. Thomas Ewing in a harsh reprisal against areas suspected of harboring bushwhackers. Jayhawkers then torched the homes those refugees vacated. The brutal raids and reprisals along the Kansas-Missouri border left scars that took generations to heal.

As the war drew to a close, the border ruffians were viewed increasingly as outlaws and lost support from civilians as well as military authorities. In late 1864, Quantrill sought refuge with his gang in Texas, where one disgusted Confederate officer likened his mode of warfare to "that of the wildest savage." He feuded with Bloody Bill Anderson—known for displaying the scalps of victims on his bridle—and other cohorts and the gang split up.

In May 1865, a Federal posse led by a hired killer tracked Quantrill down in Kentucky and mortally wounded him. Following his death in June, one old partner in crime stole his body from the grave. Today, the bushwhacker's bones are buried in three different states. ✶

> ### "KILL EVERY MALE AND BURN EVERY BUILDING."
>
> **WILLIAM QUANTRILL BEFORE SENDING HIS MEN INTO LAWRENCE, KANSAS**

Personal flag carried by one of Quantrill's partisans

Confederate Guerrilla
William Clarke Quantrill (left) cast his lot with the Confederacy at the outbreak of the Civil War. After brief service under Sterling Price, he left the army in December 1861 to organize partisan cavalry for raids in Kansas and Missouri. Quantrill's band attracted many ruthless individuals who, while they claimed allegiance to the South, fought largely for adventure and personal gain.

Jesse James

William "Bloody Bill" Anderson

Cole (left) and Jim Younger

Lincoln's Punishing Protégé

David Hunter was a Union general who came to personify Northern vindictiveness toward the Southern populace. Citizens in Virginia's Shenandoah Valley, where Hunter pursued a scorched-earth policy in 1864, considered him the very embodiment of evil.

Descended from a signer of the Declaration of Independence, Hunter graduated from West Point in 1822 but did not distinguish himself as an army officer. In 1860, he began corresponding with Abraham Lincoln on slavery and secession. Lincoln was impressed and appointed him chief of the White House Guard. When the war began, Lincoln showed little foresight in naming him the Union's fourth-ranking general.

Hunter was then 59, with sagging cheeks and a surly expression that matched his habit of writing ill-tempered letters to friend and foe alike. On one occasion, President Lincoln complained of the "grumbling dispatches" he was receiving from Hunter and warned him: "You are adopting the best possible way to ruin yourself."

In March 1862, while commanding Union toeholds along the Atlantic coast, Hunter on his own initiative issued an emancipation proclamation for all slaves in Georgia, Florida, and occupied South Carolina. At the time, Lincoln was trying to persuade border state leaders to accept gradual emancipation. He rescinded the order but did not reprimand Hunter.

In the spring of 1864, Hunter was assigned to replace bumbling Gen. Franz Sigel as Union commander in the Shenandoah Valley. One observer on hearing of Hunter's appointment said: "Mr. Lincoln certainly does hold on to his fourth-rate men."

Unable to halt raids on his supply lines by Confederate partisans, Hunter vowed to respond to any further attack by burning "every rebel house within five miles of the place." Not content simply to shut down the Virginia Military Institute, whose cadets had recently entered battle against Union forces, he torched the school and did the same to the Lexington home of Governor John Letcher. Hunter's soldiers looted and set fires indiscriminately. A Virginian surveying the damage declared that it could no longer be said that vengeance belonged solely to the Lord. Henrietta Lee, a cousin of the Confederate army chief who saw her home go up in flames, wrote a letter to Hunter declaring that "the curses of thousands … will follow you and yours through all time, and brand your name *infamy*."

When Confederate Gen. Jubal Early sent troops to challenge Hunter at Lynchburg, he withdrew to West Virginia. That left Early free to advance northward through the Shenandoah Valley into Maryland and threaten Washington. After the war, Hunter wrote Robert E. Lee, hoping that Lee would agree that he had acted properly. "I certainly expected you to retreat by way of the Shenandoah Valley," Lee replied, "and was gratified at the time that you preferred the route through the mountains to Ohio—leaving the Valley open for General Early's advance."

Discredited as a field commander, Hunter spent the rest of the war presiding over military courts, including the tribunal that judged the Lincoln assassination conspirators. Abandoning any attempt at impartiality, he was criticized by a fellow officer for favoring the prosecution. "The verdict was known beforehand," declared one defense lawyer. Four of the defendants were sentenced to death and quickly herded to the gallows.

A protégé of Lincoln, Hunter was lacking in the qualities the President later extolled when he urged Americans to act "with malice toward none; with charity toward all." ✴

> "HUNTER'S SOLDIERS LOOTED AND SET FIRES INDISCRIMINATELY. A VIRGINIAN SURVEYING THE DAMAGE DECLARED THAT IT COULD NO LONGER BE SAID THAT VENGEANCE BELONGED SOLELY TO THE LORD."

Bucking for Promotion
David Hunter, shown here before the war as a major with the First U.S. Dragoons, served as a paymaster before his friendship with Lincoln boosted him.

The Final Act *Surrounded by soldiers, government officials, and invited dignitaries, four conspirators condemned for involvement in the assassination of President Lincoln and an attack on Secretary of State William Seward—Mary Surratt, Lewis Powell, David Herold, and George Atzerodt—hang from a gallows in Washington's Old Capitol Prison on July 7, 1865.*

AFTERMATH

The guns ceased firing. The soldiers stopped fighting. Yet the repercussions of the Civil War continued to echo across a still divided America. Debris had to be cleared, and a new nation raised from the ruins. Mourning for the assassinated President Lincoln ended with the largest military parade in the nation's history. A political battle erupted in Washington over how to treat the defeated South in this new era of Reconstruction. One former Confederate officer went to the gallows in a miscarriage of justice, while others received pardons and helped reconcile North and South. Over time, chairs left vacant around dining tables in memory of the dead were filled with new generations for whom the war was an old story, told by aging veterans, who gathered on battlefields in remembrance, shook hands with their former enemies, and passed quietly into history.

Dedicated to Lieut.Col. B.B.Pritchard, 5th Mich. Cavalry.

JEFF DAVIS IN PETTICOATS

Jefferson Davis and his entourage were heading west and hoped to continue the war from beyond the Mississippi. Early on May 10, 1865, Union cavalry surrounded their encampment at Irwinville, Georgia. Davis mistakenly donned his wife's coat, and she hastily draped a shawl over him as they tried to escape. When captured, Davis gave the false impression of having disguised himself as a woman—for which he was ridiculed in Northern cartoons like this one. While Davis sought to prolong the war, Robert E. Lee accepted defeat and ultimately earned the respect of many Northerners who once considered him a traitor. (See "The Paradox of Lee," pages 338-9.)

From Slavery to Freedom

In 1865, with the adoption of the 13th Amendment, some 3.5 million black slaves in America suddenly found themselves officially free. The amendment gave them neither rights as citizens nor much freedom of movement. Many remained where they were, toiling on plantations like this one as they did before. "I works for Marse John just the same," one ex-slave remarked. In Washington, Radical Republican firebrands like Congressman Thaddeus Stevens enacted new amendments to grant freedmen citizenship and voting rights. But radical measures, enforced by keeping the South under military occupation, provoked a backlash that ended Reconstruction and left many freedmen less than free. (See "Reconstruction's Overseer," pages 330-31.)

Carpetbaggers

Among those who gave Reconstruction a bad name were Carpetbaggers: Northerners who settled in the postwar South. Their name originated from cheap luggage they carried, often made from carpet scraps. They included former Union soldiers, missionaries, politicians, and speculators. Some were idealists who sought to uplift free blacks, but too many were rank opportunists. The Carpetbag governor of impoverished Louisiana bossed a legislature that spent a million dollars one year for its own entertainment. Not until the late 1800s did Southern resentment toward Northern intruders ease enough to allow some Union veterans to settle amicably in Georgia. (See "A Model Community," pages 334-5.)

Mothers in Mourning

Reenactments can simulate war, but they cannot show its horrific impact—or the heartbreak it causes when a mother waiting at home learns that a son has perished in battle or died of wounds or disease. Every Johnny Reb and Billy Yank had a mother. Yet little attention has been paid to the millions of women who gave their "last full measure of devotion" when they lost boys to whom they gave birth.

Some young women welcomed the war and cheered when their sweethearts went off to fight, but few mothers did so. In the spring of 1861, Mary Anna Custis Lee, wife of the Confederate commander and mother of three sons who enlisted, told a daughter: "With a sad, heavy heart, my dear child, I write, for the prospects before us are sad indeed . . . there is nothing comforting in the hope that God may prosper the right, for I see no right in this matter."

Southern mothers bore a double burden. They had to endure separation from loved ones as well as danger and deprivation at home. Shortages of goods, galloping inflation, and the threat posed by advancing Union armies left women with loved ones at risk in a state of apprehension that was almost unbearable. Some of the hardest losses occurred at home, where the lack of medicines, made scarce by the Union blockade, resulted in deaths that could have been avoided. "Twenty grains of quinine would have saved our two children," a grieving Mississippi mother wrote her soldier-husband in Virginia. "They are now at rest, and I have no one to work for but you." She felt her husband's sorrow more deeply than her own, for she at least had the consolation of "their little graves near me."

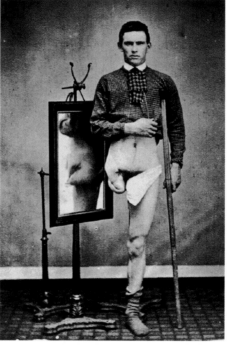

War's Toll *Crippled soldiers like this man were not the war's only victims. Women waiting anxiously at home like the Virginians at right suffered also.*

Heartache and misery intensified for mothers on both sides as the casualties mounted. Two months after the Battle of Gettysburg, Susannah Hampton of New York wrote authorities to ask if her son was alive or dead. "Oh pray let me know it and relieve my anxiety," she pleaded. "I have heard all kinds of rumors about him until they have left me in a state bordering on phrensy."

In September 1864, Henrietta Morgan of Kentucky learned of the death of her son, Confederate Gen. John Hunt Morgan. She had already buried one soldier-son, another was a prisoner of war somewhere, and a third was missing in action. To her remaining son, she wrote: "God seems to have fitted our backs to the burdens; the weight of mine is getting very heavy. I wish I could gather you all up and away to some far off place where there was no war . . . Excuse me, dear boy, I live in hourly dread of some other calamity."

Mothers who learned that their sons had been wounded or maimed in battle sometimes traveled far to comfort them where they lay. Others rushed to the bedside of loved ones, only to be told that they had arrived too late.

The toll on families was steeper in the South, where the wartime death rate among men was three times higher than in the North. Polly Ray, a North Carolina widow, lost all seven sons in the war. Catherine Cooper of Tennessee had five of her ten sons killed and four crippled. A mother in Georgia had four sons killed at Gettysburg.

Men waged war in haste and won or lost with their fellow soldiers. Women waited in quiet anguish and fought longer and lonelier battles. ★

"GOD SEEMS TO HAVE
FITTED OUR BACKS TO THE
BURDENS; THE WEIGHT OF MINE
IS GETTING VERY HEAVY.
I WISH I COULD GATHER YOU ALL
UP AND AWAY TO SOME FAR OFF
PLACE WHERE THERE WAS
NO WAR . . . EXCUSE ME,
DEAR BOY, I LIVE IN HOURLY
DREAD OF SOME OTHER
CALAMITY."

HENRIETTA MORGAN

Henry and Clara

April 14, 1865, was Good Friday. The mood in Washington was festive, as if Easter had already dawned. Not even the wet, chilly weather could dampen the exhilaration of victory. The Civil War was over, and the Union had prevailed.

That morning, President and Mrs. Lincoln decided to attend an evening comedy at nearby Ford's Theatre. It was a busy time in the capital, and they had some difficulty finding guests to accompany them. Fourteen people declined for various reasons before a young couple accepted the invitation.

Clara Harris was thrilled. The 20-year-old daughter of New York Senator Ira T. Harris, she was one of the few people in Washington society considered a friend of Mary Todd Lincoln, who called her "a superior woman." She had attended other functions with the Lincolns, but accompanying them to the theater was a special honor in this historic week.

Joining her would be her fiancé, Maj. Henry Reed Rathbone. The son of the mayor of Albany, New York, and a gentleman of means, Rathbone had spent the war uneventfully as a staff officer in the 12th U.S. Infantry. His widowed mother had married Senator Harris before the war, which made Clara Harris his stepsister as well as his bride-to-be.

The party arrived late at Ford's Theatre. Lincoln, his wife, and Clara sat on the front row in the presidential box. Henry Rathbone occupied a small sofa behind his fiancée. All four became absorbed in the play. None of them heard or saw the intruder until he fired a single bullet from his derringer into the back of Lincoln's head.

Caught Up in Tragedy *Maj. Henry Reed Rathbone and his fiancée, Clara Harris (above), were guests of the Lincolns at Ford's Theatre on the night the President was shot. A* Harper's Weekly *engraving (right) shows assassin John Wilkes Booth discharging his pistol at Lincoln, who sits beside his wife and Clara Harris, with Rathbone seated behind them.*

Rathbone lunged toward the assailant, who dropped the empty pistol and drew a large knife. John Wilkes Booth made a thrust; Rathbone parried with his left arm and received a long, deep gash from the blade, which cut to the bone. Rathbone grabbed for Booth, who jumped awkwardly from the balcony to the stage below. Although injured in the fall, Booth got away on horseback.

In the pandemonium that followed the shooting, Clara Harris tried to comfort the hysterical First Lady and stayed at her side through the night. Rathbone collapsed and was carried home, where a physician sutured the wound.

Tragedy awaited all those in the presidential box that night with Lincoln, who remained in a coma until he died early the next day. On April 26, Federal troops found Booth hiding out in Virginia and killed him when he resisted arrest. Mary Lincoln—who had grieved so deeply after losing a son in 1862 that Lincoln feared for her sanity—spent the remaining 17 years of her life after the assassination in what she called "intense misery." She passed her last months in a dark room, dressed in mourning, and died a virtual recluse in 1882.

Henry Rathbone and Clara Harris married two years after the assassination. Henry could never forgive himself for not somehow saving Lincoln's life. Perhaps it was guilt that drove him mad, or the shock he suffered in Ford's Theatre that night, or some hidden cause that lay deep in his tortured mind. At Christmastime in 1883, while serving as a U.S. consul in Germany, he killed Clara in a rage, attacked their three children, and tried to take his own life. He died in 1911 in an asylum for the criminally insane. ★

Booth's dagger

Booth's derringer pistol

"THE PARTY ARRIVED LATE AT FORD'S THEATRE.
LINCOLN, HIS WIFE, AND CLARA SAT ON THE FRONT
ROW IN THE PRESIDENTIAL BOX. HENRY RATHBONE
OCCUPIED A SMALL SOFA BEHIND HIS FIANCÉE."

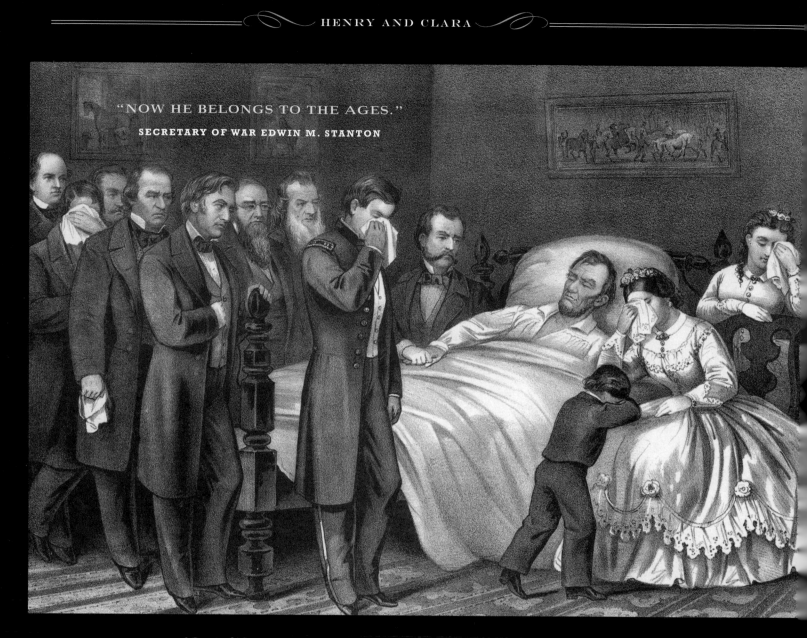

"NOW HE BELONGS TO THE AGES."
SECRETARY OF WAR EDWIN M. STANTON

Deathbed Scene *A Currier & Ives print depicts Abraham Lincoln's final moments, with his distraught wife and young son at his bedside and Clara Harris seated behind Mary Lincoln. In fact, Robert Lincoln, shown in uniform at the foot of the bed, was the only family member on hand when the president died. When Lincoln's clothing was removed by his doctors, his pockets contained the items shown at right, including a linen handkerchief, spectacles, a pocketknife, and a wallet containing a five-dollar Confederate note.*

SURRAT.   BOOTH.   HAROLD.

War Department, Washington, April 20, 1865,

$100,000 REWARD!

THE MURDERER

Of our late beloved President, Abraham Lincoln,

IS STILL AT LARGE.

$50,000 REWARD

Will be paid by this Department for his apprehension, in addition to any reward offered by Municipal Authorities or State Executives.

$25,000 REWARD

Will be paid for the apprehension of JOHN H. SURRATT, one of Booth's Accomplices.

$25,000 REWARD

Will be paid for the apprehension of David C. Harold, another of Booth's accomplices.

LIBERAL REWARDS will be paid for any information that shall conduce to the arrest of either of the above-named criminals, or their accomplices.

All persons harboring or secreting the said persons, or either of them, or aiding or assisting their concealment or escape, will be treated as accomplices in the murder of the President and the attempted assassination of the Secretary of State, and shall be subject to trial before a Military Commission and the punishment of DEATH.

Let the stain of innocent blood be removed from the land by the arrest and punishment of the murderers.

All good citizens are exhorted to aid public justice on this occasion. Every man should consider his own conscience charged with this solemn duty, and rest neither night nor day until it be accomplished.

EDWIN M. STANTON, Secretary of War.

DESCRIPTIONS.—BOOTH is Five Feet 7 or 8 inches high, slender build, high forehead, black hair, black eyes, and wears a heavy black moustache.

JOHN H. SURRAT is about 5 feet, 9 inches. Hair rather thin and dark; eyes rather light; no beard. Would weigh 145 or 150 pounds. Complexion rather pale and clear, with color in his cheeks. Wore light clothes of fine quality. Shoulders square; cheek bones rather prominent; chin narrow; ears projecting at the top; forehead rather low and square, but broad. Parts his hair on the right side; neck rather long. His lips are firmly set. A slim man.

DAVID C. HAROLD is five feet six inches high, hair dark, eyes dark, eyebrows rather heavy, full face, nose short, hand short and fleshy, feet small, instep high, round bodied, naturally quick and active, slightly closes his eyes when looking at a person.

NOTICE.—In addition to the above, State and other authorities have offered rewards amounting to almost one hundred thousand dollars, making an aggregate of about TWO HUNDRED THOUSAND DOLLARS.

Manhunt *A War Department poster offers a reward for information leading to the arrest of John Wilkes Booth and two of his accomplices, whose names are misspelled here: John Surratt, who aided Booth and escaped to Canada; and David Herold, who abetted an attack on Secretary of State William Seward and was later convicted and hanged. The poster warns that "all persons harboring" them or "assisting their concealment or escape" will be treated as accomplices in the President's murder and the attempted assassination of Seward and subject to the death penalty.*

Wreck of the *Sultana*

When the luxury British liner *Titanic* sank in 1912, it was a tragedy that shocked the world. Yet the loss of life on *Titanic* was less than another maritime catastrophe that has no equal in the history of American shipping. It occurred not on the high seas but on the flooded Mississippi River. Because it happened in the dark days following the assassination of Abraham Lincoln, the accident did not receive great attention at the time.

The *Sultana* was a two-year-old paddle-wheel steamer that regularly worked the Mississippi. It was of medium size, with limited power. On April 21, 1865, the vessel departed New Orleans with 200 passengers plus animals and cargo. When it docked at Vicksburg, thousands of Union soldiers just released from prisoner of war compounds at Andersonville, Georgia, and Cahaba, Alabama, were awaiting passage to the North. The army offered five dollars per private and ten dollars per officer for those taken as passengers. That appealed to financially troubled Cass Mason, captain of the *Sultana*, who packed his boat with every man it could hold.

On April 26, the *Sultana* left Memphis, Tennessee, with 2,500 soldiers and 80 other people on board. That was more than six times its legal capacity, but military necessity and the profit motive took precedence. An Indiana soldier was not exaggerating when he wrote: "We were huddled together like beef for the slaughter." Still, the soldiers were happy. They were going home.

The *Sultana*'s boilers had been straining against the current ever since the boat was overloaded at Vicksburg. They needed

Funeral Train *The loss of the* Sultana *received little coverage as the press focused on the progress of the funeral train carrying Abraham Lincoln's body home to Illinois through some of the nation's largest cities.*

repair but received little attention before the *Sultana* left Memphis. Seven miles above that city, at 2 a.m. on April 27, three of the four boilers exploded at once with volcanic force.

The blast nearly cut the *Sultana* in two. Soldiers and wreckage were hurled into the darkness. Hundreds of men were killed by the explosion. Hundreds more were scalded to death by escaping steam. The remaining passengers—many of them sick or weakened by confinement in prison camps—found themselves on a burning wreck that would not long remain afloat. Men either jumped or were swept into the swift floodwaters of the Mississippi.

For days thereafter, one observer reported, lifeless bodies were seen floating downstream. Other dead victims were found wedged amid boulders or hanging on low-lying tree limbs.

The *Titanic* was the largest vessel afloat in her day, nearly 300 yards long. She carried 2,200 passengers and lost 1,800 of them. The *Sultana*, barely the length of a football field, lost as many passengers as the *Titanic* carried. Among the dead was the negligent Captain Mason.

The *Sultana* disaster has long been considered little more than a curious footnote to the Civil War. Yet its victims had much in common with those who died of neglect or ill treatment in camps, hospitals, or prisons during the war. A Union soldier who lost many friends in the disaster later commented: "There in the bosom of the Mississippi they found their last resting places. No stone or monument marks the spot . . . There is no tablet with their names, or even [the word] 'unknown' for them. There is not even a hillock to which friends and survivors can go and drop a tear of remembrance of these noble defenders of the Union." ✳

"THE BLAST NEARLY CUT THE *SULTANA* IN TWO.
SOLDIERS AND WRECKAGE WERE HURLED INTO THE DARKNESS.
HUNDREDS OF MEN WERE KILLED BY THE EXPLOSION.
HUNDREDS MORE WERE SCALDED TO DEATH BY ESCAPING STEAM."

Doomed Passengers *The side-wheel steamer* Sultana, *her decks crowded with newly liberated Union prisoners of war, leaves Helena, Arkansas, on April 25, 1865. The* Sultana *continued upriver to Memphis, the last stop before her faulty boilers exploded in the early hours of April 27.*

The Grand Review

May 23, 1865: Washington, D.C., bustled with pomp and enthusiasm. Black crepe for the assassinated Lincoln had shrouded the national capital for a month. In its place now were flags and miles of red-white-and-blue bunting. Pennsylvania Avenue, the city's main thoroughfare, had been swept and watered to a spanking cleanliness it had never known before.

Some 100,000 Union soldiers were bivouacked in and around the city. A like number of civilians had poured into town from near and far. Even the trial of those charged with murdering Lincoln and attacking Secretary of State Seward was put on hold. About to take place was the last and greatest pageant of the Civil War: a grand review of the victorious armies of the North.

At dawn that Tuesday, crowds swelled by government employees and schoolchildren who had the day off began packing the sidewalks. Spectators, clutching bouquets and waving flags and handkerchiefs, occupied porches, balconies, and rooftops. At the elaborate viewing stand in front of the White House were President Andrew Johnson, his Cabinet, and a host of dignitaries.

A signal gun sounded at 9 a.m. First to swing into sight on the broad boulevard, holding his saber aloft, was Gen. George Meade—the hero of Gettysburg, who had remained in charge of his forces since then under General in Chief Grant. Behind Meade marched the Army of the Potomac, which had shielded Washington, marched on Richmond, and fought many a desperate battle before finally claiming victory.

For nearly six hours, the steady, even lines of men 60 abreast, stretching from curb to curb, marched up Pennsylvania

Last Parade *Spectators pack bleachers to watch the grand review of the Union armies. At right, Gen. Henry W. Slocum and his staff lead troops who marched through Georgia under Sherman.*

Avenue. A young girl in the crowd thought that "glorious old army" must be "eighteen or twenty miles long, their colors telling their sad story. Some regiments with nothing but a bare pole, a little bit of rag only, hanging a few inches to show where the flag had been."

People shouted until they were hoarse. Soldiers smiled and marched with the assurance of those who have won their war.

That night, while marchers caroused, another 100,000 soldiers moved into town and bedded down in the streets. These were the Western fighters: men of the Army of the Tennessee and the Army of the Ohio who had conquered Georgia and the Carolinas.

The next day, the pageantry began anew as the Westerners paraded. At their head was stern, stoic Gen. William Sherman. Regimental bands played "Marching Through Georgia" as soldiers he called "ragged, dirty, and sassy" trooped to the White House.

Sherman had apologized in advance to Meade for the poor showing he expected his boys to make. However, when Sherman reached the crest of the avenue and looked back, he saw his regiments faultlessly aligned and keeping step like the polished soldiers of Frederick the Great. Sherman later confessed that it was the happiest moment of his life.

As the soldiers paraded those two days, many of them cheered as well. They had marched countless weary miles in the past four years, in and out of battle. They had done what they had to do. Now, with the knowledge that nothing could erase their deeds and memories, they were marching for pure joy.

That night, Sherman's boys had a celebration of their own, as wild as any Washington had ever seen. No one complained. The city was intact, as so too at last was the nation. ✶

"A YOUNG GIRL IN THE CROWD THOUGHT THAT 'GLORIOUS OLD ARMY' MUST BE 'EIGHTEEN OR TWENTY MILES LONG, THEIR COLORS TELLING THEIR SAD STORY. SOME REGIMENTS WITH NOTHING BUT A BARE POLE, A LITTLE BIT OF RAG ONLY, HANGING A FEW INCHES TO SHOW WHERE THE FLAG HAD BEEN.'"

The Hanging of Henry Wirz

Vengeance is mine, saith the Lord" is a lesson often repeated in church and rarely practiced in war. Cries for vengeance made one ill-fated Confederate officer a scapegoat for a sin committed by both sides during the Civil War—the shameful neglect of prisoners of war.

Heinrich H. Wirz was born in 1823 in Switzerland. He claimed later to have obtained a medical degree, but no verification exists. In 1849, after being jailed for debts, the divorced Wirz migrated to America. He wed a Kentucky widow and settled in Louisiana, where he practiced as a doctor.

Wirz enlisted as a Confederate sergeant in 1861 but suffered a wound at Seven Pines the following year that rendered his right arm useless. Wirz was then assigned to the military prison system, commanded by Gen. John Winder, who promoted him to captain.

For much of 1863, Wirz was on a diplomatic mission to Paris and Berlin. He had been back in the South for only a month when in March 1864 he was placed in command of the uncompleted military prison at Andersonville, Georgia (pages 144-47). Wirz tried to put Andersonville in proper order, but his authority was limited and his superiors in Richmond were indifferent to his needs. The prison population swelled to over 30,000 men, many of whom fell sick and died in squalid conditions.

No prisoner likes his jailor. Inmates came to blame Wirz personally for their ordeal. His foreign origins, heavy accent, hot temper, and martinet-like insistence that all those in this "hell hole" obey his rules made him an easy target for the prisoners' rage. Wirz was labeled "an inhuman wretch," "the infamous captain," and "the Andersonville savage."

By war's end, Wirz and his superior, General Winder, were viewed in the North as the two most notorious Confederate prison officials. Winder escaped punishment when he died in February 1865 of a heart attack. A proposal to try high-ranking Confederates for mistreating Union prisoners of war—which could have raised embarrassing questions about the neglect of Southern prisoners of war by Federal authorities—was vetoed by President Andrew Johnson. That left Wirz alone to face the wrath of his former inmates.

He went before a military tribunal in Washington in August 1865 on charges of murder and conspiring with Jefferson Davis and others to harm prisoners. Survivors of Andersonville accused Wirz of killing men whose names were never given. Evidence was manufactured, including testimony from a star witness using an assumed name who was later revealed as a perjurer. Motions by defense counsel were denied, and defense witnesses were either not allowed to testify or badgered from the bench.

The outcome was a foregone conclusion. Wirz was declared guilty on all counts. On November 10, 1865, he mounted the scaffold (right) in a lot where now stands the U.S. Supreme Court building. Maj. C. B. Russell, who presided over the execution as provost marshal, told Wirz that he "deplored this duty."

"I know what orders are, Major," Wirz replied. "And I am being hanged for obeying them." ✶

> "I KNOW WHAT ORDERS ARE, MAJOR. AND I AM BEING HANGED FOR OBEYING THEM."
>
> **CAPT. HENRY WIRZ TO HIS EXECUTIONER**

Capt. Henry Wirz

Reconstruction's Overseer

For some politicians, the Civil War never ended. One of the most powerful men in postwar Washington was Congressman Thaddeus Stevens, who would not let up on those he considered rebels and fought to impose radical terms on the South during the turbulent era known as Reconstruction.

Born clubfooted in 1792 in Vermont and abandoned by his father in childhood, Stevens grew up adoring his mother. In 1815, he moved to Pennsylvania and became a prominent lawyer and owner of an ironworks, which was later torched by Confederates on their way to Gettysburg. An ardent foe of slavery, he entered Congress as a Republican in 1858.

During the Civil War, Stevens chaired the influential House Ways and Means Committee. He clashed frequently with Lincoln and defended his harsh criticism of the President by saying: "Faithful are the wounds of a friend, while the kisses of an enemy are deceitful."

Even before Lincoln was buried, Stevens began lashing out at President Andrew Johnson of Tennessee. In late 1865, he and his fellow Radical Republicans scrapped Johnson's Reconstruction plan—which they considered far too kind to former secessionists and slave owners—and launched their own. They enacted historic legislation, including the 14th and 15th Amendments, which granted former slaves citizenship and the right to vote. Yet their efforts to impress those laws and other measures on the South by force of arms met with considerable resistance. Reconstruction ended in 1877 with the Radicals in retreat.

THE SMELLING COMMITTEE.

Chief Radical *The 1868 political cartoon above satirizes the failed impeachment proceedings of President Andrew Johnson instituted by Radical Republicans, including Pennsylvania Congressman Thaddeus Stevens (right). Stevens was the congressional leader of Radical Reconstruction.*

Stevens was a study in contradictions. He was as charitable as he was combative and defended fugitive slaves as a lawyer for free. He lived in Washington with a mulatto housekeeper who may have been his mistress. Stevens could not legally have married her, but he defied other color barriers. He insisted to the last that he would be buried only in a cemetery that barred no one on the basis of race. In the end, he got his wish.

To those who did not share his views, Stevens was a terror. His perpetual scowl and ill-fitting black wig gave him a villainous look. A fondness for gambling took him almost nightly to Washington's casinos. His biting sarcasm was legendary in the House, where he once said of a colleague: "I now yield to the gentleman from Massachusetts, who will make a few feeble remarks." Stevens's words were often so scurrilous that they were deleted from congressional records.

Always he was zealous and uncompromising. When Andrew Johnson dared to dismiss Secretary of War Edwin Stanton, a powerful ally of the Radicals, Stevens orchestrated Johnson's impeachment. The President was acquitted by the Senate in 1868.

The verdict came as a blow to Stevens, who died soon after. Republicans renominated him in tribute to represent his district, and he won in a landslide—a few months after his burial. Detractors joked that he had campaigned as "Corpse for Congress." That was not kind to his memory, but then Stevens had never spared his foes ridicule. Once when a fellow congressman described Andrew Johnson as "a self-made man," Stevens snapped back: "Glad to hear it. It relieves God Almighty from a heavy responsibility." ✴

"FAITHFUL ARE THE
WOUNDS OF A FRIEND,
WHILE THE KISSES OF AN
ENEMY ARE DECEITFUL."
THADDEUS STEVENS

The Confederados

The Confederacy expired in 1865, but its seeds dispersed and ended up as far away as South America, where they took root.

In the first weeks of defeat after Appomattox, most Southerners heeded the call of Gen. Wade Hampton of South Carolina, who urged them to "devote their whole energies to the restoration of law and order . . . and the rebuilding of our cities and dwellings which have been laid in ashes."

Thousands of Southerners, on the other hand, could not accept defeat, or feared living under Federal occupation. Associations were formed with the aim of finding territory abroad for colonization by Confederate expatriates. Small Southern settlements sprang up in Mexico, Venezuela, and British Honduras. The largest colonies were established in one of the few nations that had granted belligerent rights to the Confederacy and allowed Southern ships safe entry to its ports: Brazil.

Among the country's attractions for the refugees were the fertility of the soil, the availability of slave labor, and the potential for a new cotton boom. Emperor Dom Pedro II provided help with transportation and offered Southerners citizenship as well as promises of a semi-independent agricultural commune in southeast Brazil. Prominent families like the Calhouns and the Yanceys in the South and the Campos Sales in Brazil promoted emigration from both ends.

New settlements arose with names such as Santa Barbara and Americana. A steady influx of displaced Southerners

> "A STEADY INFLUX
> OF DISPLACED
> SOUTHERNERS SWELLED
> THE EXPATRIATE
> POPULATION IN BRAZIL
> TO NEARLY 4,000.
> THEIR BRAZILIAN
> NEIGHBORS CALLED THEM
> CONFEDERADOS."

Émigrés *Former Confederate soldier Walter S. Scofield—seen above with his wife, Celia—arrived in Brazil in May 1867 in his early 20s with 154 fellow Southern expatriates.*

swelled the expatriate population in Brazil to nearly 4,000. Their Brazilian neighbors called them *confederados*.

The émigrés prospered, worked harmoniously with Brazilians, and adapted successfully to the abolition of slavery in Brazil in 1888. They established Baptist, Methodist, and Presbyterian churches there as well as a number of missionary schools.

Remarkably, the confederados are still there. What was long described as "the lost colony of the Confederacy" remains part of the state of São Paulo. As often as four times a year, descendants of Southern expatriates gather at a small church and cemetery near Santa Barbara. Dressed in costumes of mid-19th-century America, farmers and owners of small businesses sing old revival hymns and listen to sermons like those heard at services by the first confederados. Afterward, they share a communal dinner consisting in the main of fried chicken and biscuits with gravy.

Many still speak a quaint English dialect at home. Such features as red hair, blue eyes, and freckles are visual evidence that these people are not Brazilian natives. Some have been baptized Juan, Carlos, or Benito, but their surnames are Carlton, Cobb, Moore, and Smith—common family names in the Deep South whence their ancestors came.

Those ancestors lie in the small cemeteries of the colonies they founded. Having lived in a war-torn country, they achieved something here of inestimable value. As the epitaph on one tombstone reads: "Died in Perfect Peace." ✶

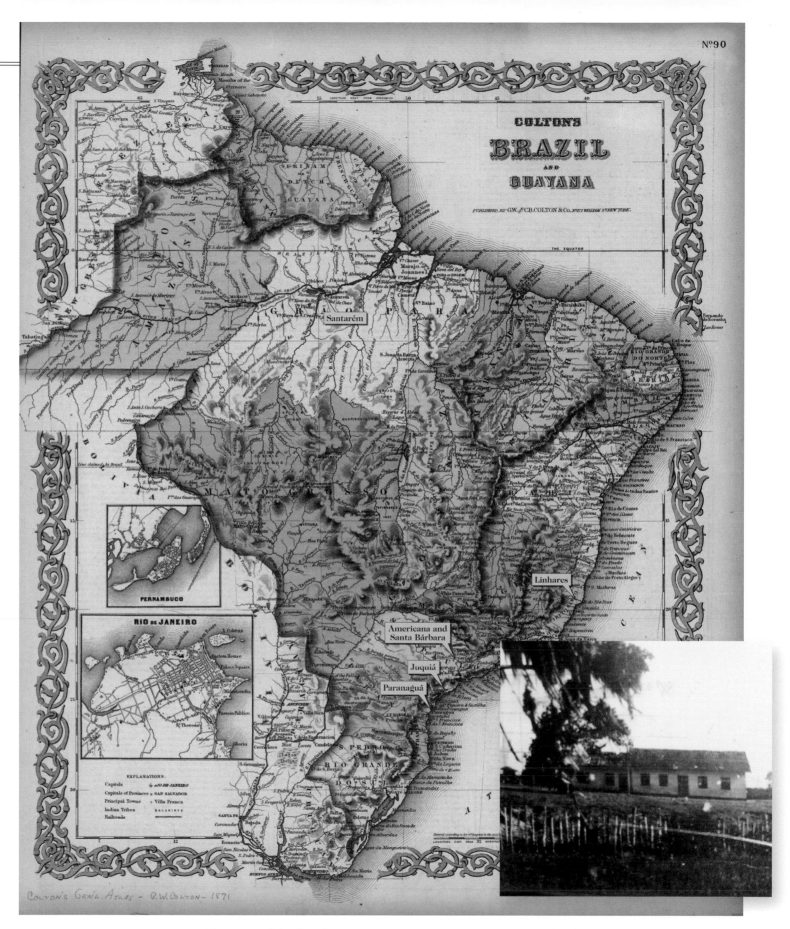

Rebel Towns *The major confederado settlements, containing houses like the one shown here (inset), are marked on this 1871 map of Brazil and Guyana. The towns include Americana, Santa Barbara, and Juquiá in São Paulo, Santarém in Pará, Linhares in Espírito Santo, and Paranaguá in Paraná.*

A Model Community

I n the 1890s, as an economic depression gripped America, farmers in the Midwest suffered another cruel blow when drought blighted their fields. A nationwide call for help went out. Georgia responded quickly and generously by sending trainloads of food and other supplies to the needy in Indiana, Illinois, and Iowa. Union veteran Philander H. Fitzgerald was an Indianapolis attorney and editor of the *American Tribune,* a veterans' magazine. Georgia's acts of mercy inspired him to pursue a dream he was nurturing. Fitzgerald envisioned a Southern colony where aging Northern veterans might spend their final years in warm comfort.

Fitzgerald contacted Georgia Governor William J. Northen. The governor liked the idea and invited Fitzgerald and his friends to visit the state. The delegation learned of some abandoned Creek Indian territory in south-central Georgia that was now public property. Ironically, the parcel was only ten miles from Irwinville, where Jefferson Davis had been captured, and not too far from Andersonville, site of the Confederacy's most notorious prison camp.

Fitzgerald publicized the project in his magazine. Even before surveys could be completed, the race for settlement began. People came by railroad, by wagon, and on foot. Settlers quickly claimed the 50,000 acres set aside for them. Another 50,000 acres of private land in the vicinity were needed. Some Georgians stubbornly refused to sell to Yankees, but good prices in hard times for land that was not worth much induced others to do so.

Founded in 1895, the colony was open to "all good people." Union veterans made up the overwhelming majority of settlers. Where weeds and scrub pines once grew, a town

> "UNION VETERANS MADE UP THE OVERWHELMING MAJORITY OF SETTLERS . . . TO PROMOTE FRIENDLY RELATIONS WITH THEIR SOUTHERN NEIGHBORS, TOWN PLANNERS NAMED SEVEN STREETS TO THE WEST OF MAIN STREET AFTER CONFEDERATE GENERALS SUCH AS LEE AND JACKSON, AND SEVEN STREETS TO THE EAST OF MAIN FOR GRANT, MEADE, AND OTHER UNION GENERALS."

emerged. The first dwellings were tents, shanties, or wagons covered over to provide makeshift lodgings. Shacktown, as it was called initially, took on a more orderly appearance as streets were laid out in a grid. Main Street ran north-south, Central Avenue east-west. To promote friendly relations with their Southern neighbors, town planners named seven streets to the west of Main Street after Confederate generals such as Lee and Jackson, and seven streets to the east of Main for Grant, Meade, and other Union generals. The east-west avenues bore the names of Georgia rivers, trees, and plants.

A year after settlement began, the community opened the first schools in Georgia to offer a nine-month term, free tuition, and free textbooks. Children from 38 states were taught there by 12 teachers, only 1 of whom hailed from the South. Before long, the community had a railroad station, neatly built homes, churches, and businesses. The town's first hotel was called Grant-Lee, until grumbling from Southern neighbors resulted in its being renamed Lee-Grant.

By the turn of the century, Shacktown had 9,000 residents. It celebrated two Memorial Days: Georgia's on April 26 and the national holiday on May 30, which was not widely observed in the South until after the First World War. The Georgia Division of the United Confederate Veterans once held its annual reunion in the town—with entertainment provided by the local post of the Grand Army of the Republic.

The town is now called Fitzgerald, in honor of the Union veteran whose dream gave birth to the place. It stands as a living memorial to the capacity of Americans to overcome conflict and division and build a true community. ✶

Thriving Colony *Planned as a refuge for aging Union veterans, Fitzgerald, Georgia, developed into a prosperous Southern town, as evidenced by the bales of cotton, valued at $16,000, shown here on Central Avenue. A bird's-eye view of Fitzgerald (below), published in 1908, reveals a neatly designed community, with vignettes illustrating public schools, businesses, churches, and factories.*

The Stained Glass Window

In the autumn of 1855, Maj. Thomas J. Jackson of the Virginia Military Institute organized a unique class at the Lexington Presbyterian Church. Meetings were held on Sunday afternoon. Major Jackson was the principal teacher. The "students" were mostly slaves but also included some free blacks.

The Virginia code of that day permitted blacks to gather in daylight for religious services, but the statutes forbade whites from teaching slaves to read or write about any subject. Although Jackson was within the law by leading Bible services, such instruction was also educational and could motivate slaves to learn to read the Bible.

The service began with all in attendance singing the first stanza of "Amazing Grace." It was Jackson's favorite hymn. Included in the hour-long class were Bible readings by Jackson, prayers, and instructions from the Presbyterian children's catechism. The service closed with the remaining stanzas of "Amazing Grace."

By 1861, more than 100 people were regularly attending the Sunday school. Jackson knew each one personally. The major left that spring for war and never returned. His celebrated career as Gen. Stonewall Jackson ended with his death from wounds in 1863. His dying words were "Let us cross over the river and rest under the shade of the trees."

Two of the slaves who attended his meetings married early in the war. Lylburn Downing and his wife, Ellen, had a son, born the day after Jackson died. The parents never let young Lylburn Liggins Downing forget what a spiritual inspiration

> "LET US CROSS OVER THE RIVER AND REST UNDER THE SHADE OF THE TREES."
>
> **THE DYING WORDS OF THOMAS J. "STONEWALL" JACKSON**

Spreading the Gospel *Thomas J. Jackson, shown in 1857 as an instructor at VMI, was honored by the memorial window at right for his service to slaves and free blacks as a Sunday school teacher.*

Jackson had been in their lives. In the 1870s, the son attended the Sunday class begun by Jackson. Downing matured, completed theological training, and became minister of the Fifth Avenue Presbyterian Church in Roanoke, Virginia.

In the course of the Reverend Downing's 42 years as pastor of that congregation, it became necessary to replace the window behind the chancel. Downing designed the new stained glass memorial that dominated the sanctuary. It depicted an army camp, a wide stream of water, and a clump of woods. At the bottom, he placed the words: "In memory of Stonewall Jackson. Let us cross the river and rest in the shade of the trees."

Downing himself crossed the river in 1937. Twenty years later, fire destroyed the Fifth Avenue Church. Flames and smoke heavily damaged the window. The black congregation restored the memorial and installed it above the altar at its new church on Roanoke's Patton Street. The chancel window is still there.

Not all wounds of the Civil War have healed. Some people still view that conflict as a morality play, in which right triumphed over wrong. They see no redeeming graces in the Old South and believe that its leaders bequeathed nothing of value to modern generations.

One preacher who was born a slave in Virginia and grew up free felt differently. On Sunday mornings, at a church in Roanoke, one can still see black worshippers praising God as sunlight streams through the stained glass window he dedicated to the memory of a Confederate general. ★

The Paradox of Lee

Robert E. Lee is America's most perplexing hero. To his many admirers, he belongs in the company of his fellow Virginian George Washington. Yet Washington founded the nation, and Lee became the most dangerous opponent the young United States ever had. Historian Charles Roland concluded: "Robert E. Lee is America's great tragic hero . . . He was a marvelously gifted soldier and an ardently devoted patriot, yet he defended the most unacceptable of American causes, secession and slavery, and he suffered the most un-American of experiences, defeat."

For a military commander of a failed revolution to be held in such high esteem by citizens of the nation he defied is unprecedented and paradoxical. One explanation is that Lee was a great soldier and recognized as such even by his foes in wartime. Officers in the Army of the Potomac held such a high opinion of Lee's generalship after battling him for two years that Ulysses Grant grew tired of hearing him touted as a magician, who could "turn a double somersault and land in our rear and on both flanks at the same time." Grant told one anxious brigadier to go back to his command and "try to think what we are going to do ourselves, instead of what Lee is going to do."

Lee described his generalship in deceptively simple terms. His task as commander, he said, was to "bring the troops to the right place at the right time; then I have done my duty. As soon as I order them into battle, I leave my army in the hands of God." Lee had faith in God, but he also had confidence in his gifted commanders and freed them to execute his daring plans as they saw fit.

Lee possessed inspirational qualities that set him apart from generals who were shining figures only in battle. Viscount Wolseley, commander in chief of the British

> "ALTHOUGH HE WON SOME OF THE MOST SMASHING VICTORIES IN MILITARY HISTORY, LEE WAS SO VOID OF MALICE THAT HE CUSTOMARILY REFERRED TO THE ENEMY AS 'THOSE PEOPLE' AND 'OUR FRIENDS ACROSS THE RIVER.' "

armies, wrote near the end of his career: "I have met many of the great men of my time, but Lee alone impressed me with the feeling that I was in the presence of a man who was cast in a grander mould, and made of different and of finer metal than all other men." Others described Lee (pictured at right late in the war) simply as a true gentleman. Although he won some of the most smashing victories in military history, Lee was so void of malice that he customarily referred to the enemy as "those people" and "our friends across the river." A true gentleman, Lee wrote, "can not only forgive, he can forget; and he strives for that nobleness of self and mildness of character . . . to let the past be but the past."

What ultimately secured Lee's position as an American hero was the manner in which he met defeat and put the past behind him. When his army no longer had any hope of victory, he scorned the idea of dispersing his troops to fight as guerrillas. When he surrendered, the Confederacy died. He never sought to resurrect that Lost Cause as some ex-Confederates later did by defying federal authority.

Lee signed an oath of loyalty to the United States in late 1865. He was pardoned along with other former Confederates by President Johnson in 1868, but he did not regain American citizenship. He spent the last years of his life as president of Washington College (later Washington and Lee University), where he welcomed students from the North and encouraged those from the South to be true and useful Americans. At his death in 1870, he was mourned in the South and honored in the North as one who stood for reconciliation.

Great in war, Lee was ultimately greater in peace. After leading Southerners to battle, he led them home to the nation Washington founded. ✶

The Final Reunion

The last joint reunion of Federal and Confederate veterans occurred in July 1938 at Gettysburg. It was a moving scene, sometimes humorous but often heartbreaking.

In 1937 a Pennsylvania commission established to observe the 75th anniversary of the great battle mailed out questionnaires to 12,500 living Union and Confederate veterans, most of whom had not fought at Gettysburg. A few who responded opposed a joint reunion, but ten times as many were in favor of the idea. Typical of the positive replies was that of a 92-year-old Union veteran: "Since the war was over, I have never had any hard feelings toward the boys in gray, and I think a reunion of soldiers from both sides is a fine thing." An Alabama soldier responded: "I'll be there if I have to crawl!"

Gettysburg had accommodated more than 50,000 former soldiers for the 50th anniversary of the battle. Fewer than 2,000 were expected for the 75th anniversary. Since most of the honored guests were in their 90s, much professional care was needed. Officials built a tent city on the campus of Gettysburg College. A staff of 7,000 people stood by, including medical personnel, attendants, police, Boy Scouts, cooks, and waiters.

Each veteran's tent had luxuries unknown to those old soldiers when they went to war—a cot and mattress, pillow, sheets changed daily, four blankets, electric light, water pitcher, wash basin, cabinet, two canvas armchairs, umbrella, rubber seat pad. The camps of Union and Confederate veterans were separated, but eight miles of lighted wooden walks connected them.

In the last week of June 1938, special trains unloaded 1,845 veterans from 47 states. Yanks outnumbered Rebs by four to one. The average age was 94; one man was 112. Only 65 of the veterans had fought at Gettysburg.

Most of the men had unsteady legs and fading memories. Yet the event lit some sparks in the old soldiers. Former Confederate Johnny Claypool detrained with the statement: "Since the Lord has put up with the Yankees all this time, I guess I can also for a few days." A century-old veteran observed: "I haven't been in Gettysburg since I fought here in '63, and if it's like it was then, I'm gonna scram out of here!"

On July 1, three days of ceremonies began. Veterans listened to speeches, hands often cupped to their ears. They watched parades and withstood the heat. In the evenings they sang some old songs and traded barbs with former foes of long ago. An ancient Georgia veteran joked: "We ran those Yankees all through Georgia, only we were in front of them!"

The climax of the reunion came late on the afternoon of July 3. An estimated 400,000 people were in attendance as President Franklin Roosevelt dedicated an eternal beacon of peace on the battlefield to commemorate the soldiers' gathering and the nation's reunion. Roosevelt called the veterans "a fragment spared by time," and added: "All of them we honor, not asking under which flag they fought then—thankful that they stand together under one flag now."

Only 77 of the veterans required hospitalization during the three days of excitement. Two died during the reunion, and five others passed away on the way home. One man spoke for many when he said he wished they could remain at the encampment until "Gabriel shall call us."

The last call came soon for many of those old soldiers, who waged war, found peace, and entered history. ✴

75th anniversary Gettysburg reunion program

> "I HAVEN'T BEEN IN
> GETTYSBURG SINCE
> I FOUGHT HERE IN '63,
> AND IF IT'S LIKE
> IT WAS THEN,
> I'M GONNA SCRAM
> OUT OF HERE!"
>
> **A CENTURY-OLD VETERAN**

Comrades-in-Arms *The 1938 Blue and Gray Reunion featured many scenes of comradeship, including two former adversaries side by side (above), Union veterans standing together near "The Angle" where Pickett's Charge culminated (above right), and William D. Welch, a veteran of the 140th Pennsylvania, embracing young Annie Laurie of Atlanta (right).*

Children of War

When the nation split apart in 1861, family ties remained strong. America was a fast-growing country, and a third of its population were youngsters. Most soldiers who went to war had children of their own or little siblings who doted on them. Children who were old enough to know what war meant often reacted with adolescent patriotism or stoic acceptance. Yet few were left with hearts unbroken when a father or brother departed for the army.

For many soldiers, that moment of separation was just the beginning of a struggle to keep memories fresh and remain close to their loved ones in spirit. A common fear among fathers who went to war was that their children would forget them. In letters home, they often reminded youngsters of how much they cared for them and imagined being back home with them. One lonely Alabama cavalryman, John Cotton, wrote to his wife and seven children: "I would bee glad to see little ginny and give her a kiss and see the rest of the children frolic around and play on my lap and see babe suck his thumb."

A soldier's delight was to have children forward messages to him through their mother. In 1863, Mary Neblett of Texas wrote to her husband: "Billy says send him a cannon ball Bob says write to him some. Buddy walter says send him some candy Kate says howdy."

The death of a child could be devastating to a soldier far from home. When Louisiana Sgt. Edwin Fay's oldest son died at the age of five, he sent a stream of grieving letters to his family. "My heart is bursting," he wrote at one point. "I almost fear I shall go crazy—I don't see how I can stand it."

Many soldiers kept memories of home alive by carrying with them framed photographs of children. Portraits of sons or daughters were the proudest possessions of fathers in uniform. They held such mementos close to their heart and sometimes carried them into battle.

Those images are timeless and haunting. Some have dramatic stories behind them.

Three days after the Battle of Gettysburg, an unidentified body was found in a secluded spot. Clutched in the Union soldier's hand was a photograph of his three children (left). They were his last vision and final thought before he died. The photograph, labeled "Children of Gettysburg," was distributed throughout the North in a search for the father's family. Newspaper articles described the image in detail. "The youngest boy is sitting in a high chair, and on each side of him are his brother and sister," one article related.

Philanda Hamiston of Portville, New York, who had been waiting four months to hear from her husband, read of the photograph with a sinking heart and obtained a copy. The picture confirmed her fears: Those were her children and the dead soldier was their father, Sgt. Amos Hamiston of the 154th New York.

Each loss in battle was felt several times over at home. These children of war, beloved and too often bereft when the fighting was over, remind us today never to forget what war costs. ★

"I WOULD BEE GLAD TO SEE LITTLE GINNY AND GIVE HER A KISS AND SEE THE REST OF THE CHILDREN FROLIC AROUND AND PLAY ON MY LAP AND SEE BABE SUCK HIS THUMB."

ALABAMA CAVALRYMAN JOHN COTTON, IN A LETTER TO HIS WIFE AND SEVEN CHILDREN

Lost in Battle *These "Children of Gettysburg" were identified. But another such memento (right), found between dead Confederate and Union soldiers after the Battle of Port Republic in 1862, portrays an unknown child.*

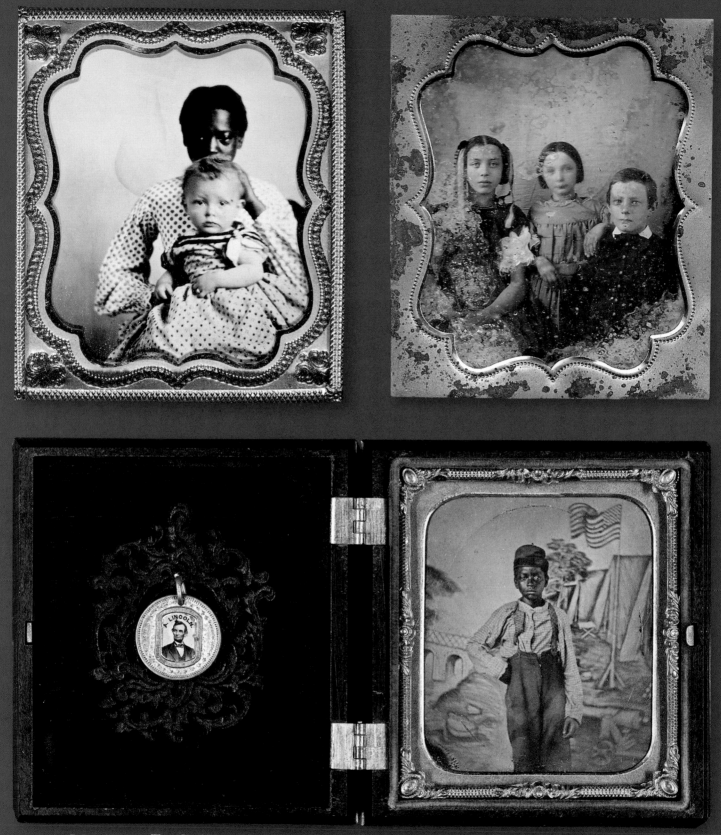

Beloved Images *These Civil War–era family portraits include a Union boy shown against the backdrop of an American flag (above, displayed alongside a Lincoln campaign button); three siblings; and an infant held by a house slave. At right, a somber girl in mourning dress grasps a picture of a Union cavalryman, who may be her deceased father.*

ABBREVIATION KEY:

LC: *Library of Congress, Prints and Photographs Division*
LCMD: *Library of Congress Manuscript Division*
LCGMD: *Library of Congress Geography and Maps Division*
MHIB: *Military and Historical Image Bank*
MOLLUS-MASS: *Military Order of the Loyal Legion of the United States-Massachusetts*
MOC: *Museum of the Confederacy, Richmond, Virginia*
NARA: *National Archives and Records Administration*
USAMHI: *United States Army Military History Institute*

FRONT MATTER:

1, MHIB; 2, LC, 27528; 4 (UP LE), National Museum of American History, Smithsonian Institution; 4 (UP CTR), National Park Service, Historic Graphic Collection, Harpers Ferry Center; 4 (UP RT), LCGMD, CW0011000X; 5 (UP LE), Courtesy of George Eastman House, International Museum of Photography and Film; 5 (UP CTR), LC, 0657; 5 (UP RT), Children's Museum of Indianapolis; 7, LC, 26871; 8, Courtesy of the Collections of the Louisiana State Museum; 9, Boston Athenaeum; 10, LC, 00193; 11, C. Paul Loane Collection; 12, MHIB; 13, MHIB; 14, LC, 01187; 15, LCGMD, CW0049A00; 16, From the Collections of The Henry Ford; 17 (UP CTR), LCMD; 17 (UP LE), LCMD; 17 (UP RT), LCMD, MMC 3160.

CHAPTER 1:

18-19, LC, 01192; 20, LC, 01192; 21 (UP), LC-DIG-cwpb-04402; 21 (LO), LC, 19470; 22, David H. Jones; 23 (LE), LC, 27133; 23 (RT), David Wynn Vaughan Collection; 24 (LE), LC, 19195; 24 (RT), LC, 3a09984; 25, Courtesy of the Burton Historical Collection, Detroit Public Library; 26 (UP), Courtesy of the Trustees of the Boston Public Library/Rare Books; 26 (LO), Collection of the New-York Historical Society; 27, Underground Railroad Museum and Center, Cincinnati, OH; 28 (UP), Harvard University, Peabody Museum, 35-5-10/53040; 28 (LO), MHIB; 28 (UP RT), Natchez Trace Collection NTC-0305a, The Dolph Briscoe Center for American History, the University of Texas at Austin; 28-29, www.sonofthesouth.net; 30, National Museum of American History, Smithsonian Institution; 31 (UP LE), LC, 3c07588; 31, LC, 3a48697; 32, MHIB; 33 (UP LE), Virginia Historical Society, Richmond, VA; 33 (UP RT), LC, 3b30026; 33 (LO), NARA; 34, MOC; 35 (UP), MHIB; 35 (LO), LC-USZ62-65663; 36, MHIB; 37 (UP), LC, 00972; 37 (LO), Virginia Historical Society, Richmond, VA; 38, MHIB; 39, Courtesy Stonewall Jackson House, Virginia Military Institute, Lexington, VA; 40 (LE), Wikipedia; 40 (RT), Wikipedia; 41 (UP RT), Wikipedia; 41 (LO), The Atlanta Journal-Constitution; 42, MOC; 43 (UP), William Dickinson Washington (1833-1870), *The Burial of Latané*, 1864, Oil on canvas, 38 x 48 in., The Johnson Collection; 43 (LO), Courtesy USAMHI; 45 (LE), LC, 02995; 45 (RT), LC, 01025; 46, LC, 00518; 46-47, LC, 01590; 48, MHIB; 49 (UP RT), LC, 3g12604; 49 (LO LE), Virginia Historical Society, Richmond, VA; 50, The Library of Virginia; 51 (UP), LC, 20592; 51 (LO), LC, 20497; 52, NARA; 53 (UP), LC, 01099; 53 (LO), LC, 01109; 54-55, LC, 04352; 56, Camden Archives and Museum; 57, Mort Kunstler; 57 (LO), MHIB; 58, LC-USZ62-5962; 59 (UP RT), Courtesy North Carolina Museum of History; 59, LC, 3a42351; 60, LC, 3a08013; 61 (UP), LC, 3b49856; 61 (LO), Patrick Walsh/Grace Episcopal Church, St. Francisville, LA; 62, Dr. Michael Echols; 63 (UP), National Museum of Health and Medicine, CP1043; 63 (LO), LC, 3g01826; 64, West Point Museum/MHIB; 65 (UP RT), Getty Images; 65, LC, 01294; 67, LC, 07523; 68, LC; 69 (UP), LC, 3g12949; 69 (LO), LC, 15768; 70, LC, 10900; 71, www.sonofthesouth.net; 72, MOC; 73 (UP), LC, 07546; 73 (LO), LC, 23730; 74, MHIB; 75 (UP RT), LC, 22395; 75 (LO), LC, 03543; 76-77, LC, 04324; 78, MOC; 79 (UP), Abraham Lincoln Presidential Library & Museum; 79 (LO), LC, 05369; 80, Pennsylvania Historical and Museum Commission, Pennsylvania State Archives; 81, State Museum of Pennsylvania, Pennsylvania Historical and Museum Commission; 82, LC, 00468; 83, LC, 02688; 84, Courtesy of Appomattox Court House National Historical Park, Photo by Joe Williams; 85 (UP), LC, 12910; 85 (LO), Tom Lovell/NG Stock.

CHAPTER 2:

86-87, NARA; 88, MHIB; 89 (LE), MHIB; 89 (RT), MOC; 90, MHIB; 91 (UP LE), © 2005 The Children's Museum of Indianapolis; 91 (RT), Picture History; 91 (LO LE), C. Paul Loane Collection; 92 (CTR), MHIB; 92 (LE), MHIB; 92 (RT), Massachusetts State Archives/MHIB; 93 (UP), Kansas State Historical Society; 93 (LO), LLCMD, Papers of Charles Wellington Reed, Volume 3, "Absolution in Wheat Field"; 94, Courtesy Georgia Archives, Vanishing Georgia Collection, #gor517; 95 (UP), LC, 3g06189; 95 (LO), LC, 04324; 96, MOC; 97, MHIB; 98, David Wynn Vaughan Collection; 99 (UP), LC, 3b53061; 99 (LO LE), Fredericksburg and Spotsylvania National Military Park; 99 (LO CTR), David Wynn Vaughan Collection; 99 (LO RT), David Wynn Vaughan Collection; 100 (UP LE), David Wynn Vaughan Collection; 100 (UP CTR), MOC; 100 (CTR), MOC; 100 (RT), MOC; 100 (LO), MOC; 101 (UP), LC, 26862; 101 (UP RT), C. Paul Loane Collection; 101 (LE), C. Paul Loane Collection; 101 (RT), MHIB; 101 (LO LE), C. Paul Loane Collection; 101 (LO), MHIB; 102, LC, 07584; 103 (UP), MOC; 103 (LO), MOC; 104, MHIB; 105, LC, 01680; 106, MOC; 107 (UP), LC, 21215; 107 (LO), LC, 01144; 108, LC, 07136; 109 (UP RT), Wisconsin Veterans Museum; 109 (CTR), MOC; 109 (LO), LC, 3c05798; 110, LC, 3g02724; 111 (UP), LC, 20740; 111 (LO), LC, 22444; 112, MHIB; 113, LC, 20740; 115, LC, 3c09737; 116, MHIB; 117 (UP), MHIB; 117 (LO), LC, 00323; 118-119, LC, 20518; 119 (UP), LC, 02637; 119 (CTR), MHIB; 119 (LO), LC, 03882; 120, MHIB; 121 (UP), Courtesy USAMHI, MOLLUS-MASS vol. 32, page 1557; 121 (LO), LC, 20585; 122, Ken Turner Collection; 123 (UP), LC, 00163; 123 (LO), LC, 20747; 124, McLellan Lincoln Collection, John Jay Library, Brown University; 125 (UP), LC-USZC2-499; 125 (LO), Old Court House Museum Collection, Vicksburg, MS; 126, Dr. Michael Echols; 127 (UP), C. Paul Loane Collection; 127 (LO), LC, 01887; 128, LC, 00367; 129, LC, 01663; 130, LC, 3a09814; 131, Dr. Michael Echols; 133 (UP LE), LC, 26461u; 133 (UP CTR), LC, 26960; 133 (UP RT), LC, 27231; 133 (LO), www.sonofthesouth.net; 134, MOC; 135 (UP RT), Courtesy USAMHI; 135 (LO), LC, 21047; 136, Pennsylvania Capitol Preservation Committee; 137, Richard F. Carlile Collection; 138 (UP LE), Ohio Historical Society; 138 (UP RT), MOC; 138 (CTR LE), MHIB; 138 (LO RT), www.sonofthesouth.net; 138 (LO LE), New York State Military History Museum/MHIB; 139 (UP LE), MHIB; 139 (UP RT), MOC; 139 (CTR LE), MHIB; 139 (CTR RT), Military History, Smithsonian Institution; 139 (LO LE), MOC; 139 (LO RT), MHIB; 141, LC, 02539; 142, LC, 01227; 143 (UP), Chicago Historical Society; 143 (LO), Abraham Lincoln Presidential Library & Museum; 144, Virginia Historical Society, Richmond, VA; 145, NARA; 146-147, NARA; 147 (UP), Bettmann/CORBIS; 147 (LO), NARA; 148, National Park Service, Historic Graphic Collection, Harpers Ferry Center; 149, Courtesy USAMHI, MOLLUS-MASS vol. 28, page L1389.

CHAPTER 3:

150-151, NARA; 152, Chicago Historical Society; 153 (UP), LC, 03792; 153 (LO), Courtesy Bill Turner; 155 (UP), MHIB; 155 (CTR), LC, Geography and Map Division, CW0024000; 155 (LO), LC; 156-157, LC, Geography and Map Division, CW0003000; 159 (UP), Courtesy of Picture History; 159 (LO), NARA; 161, West Point Museum Art Collection, United States Military Academy, West Point, NY; 162, LC, Geography and Map Division, CW0011000X; 163, LC, 3a01815; 164, LC, 07970; 165 (CTR), Photo by Meg M. Eastman, Virginia Historical Society, Richmond, VA/Artifact courtesy of West Point Museum, United States Military Academy, West Point, NY; 165 (LO), www.sonofthesouth.net; 165 (UP), Courtesy of West Point Museum, United States Military Academy, West Point, NY; 166, MOC; 167 (UP LE), The W. S. Hoole Special Collections Library, the University of Alabama; 167, LC, 02740; 168, Bill Turner; 169, Courtesy of the Siege Museums, City of Petersburg, VA; 170, Jedediah Hotchkiss Papers, Stewart Bell Jr. Archives Room, Handley Regional Library, Winchester, VA; 171, LC, Geography and Map Division, CWH00089; 172 (UP), LCGMD, CA000001; 172 (LO), Photo by Neil Kagan/Courtesy of the Winchester-Frederick County Historical Society/Stonewall Jackson's Headquarters Museum Collection; 172-173, LC-DIG-cwpb-04406; 174, Cook Collection, Valentine Richmond History Center; 175 (UP), Virginia Historical Society, Richmond, VA; 175 (LO), LC, 02695; 176, MHIB; 177, LC, 3g01829; 179 (UP), LC, 00277; 179 (LO), LC, 21006; 180, The Gilder Lehrman Collection, courtesy of The Gilder Lehrman Institute of American History; 181 (LE), The Gilder Lehrman Collection, courtesy of The Gilder Lehrman Institute of American History; 181 (LO RT), LC, 11196; 182 (UP), Robin Stanford; 182 (LO), LC, 26454; 182-183 (LO), LC, 02004; 184, David Wynn Vaughan Collection; 185 (UP), www.sonofthesouth.net; 185 (LO), LC, 21740; 186, MOC; 187 (UP), State Museum of Pennsylvania, Pennsylvania Historical and Museum Commission; 187 (LO), Stratford Hall; 188, MOC; 189, MHIB.

CHAPTER 4:

190-191, NARA; 192, LC, 3g03598; 193 (UP), MOC; 193 (LO), Courtesy Naval Historical Foundation; 195 (UP), LC, Geography and Map Division, CW0014100; 195 (LO), LC, 08273; 196, LC, 05227; 197, LC, 10325; 198, LC, 10408; 199 (UP), LCMD; 199 (LO), LC, 21453; 200 (UP), LC, 3g12112; 200 (LO), MOC; 201 (UP), C. Paul Loane Collection; 201 (LO), MHIB; 202, LC, 3b09802; 203 (UP), LC-USZC2-1985; 203 (LO), Courtesy Vicksburg National Military Park; 204, LC, 01061; 204-205, LC, 3b50939; 205, LC, 04058;

206, LC, 04811; 207 (UP), Virginia Historical Society, Richmond, VA; 207 (LO), NARA; 208, Courtesy of the Collections of the Louisiana State Museum; 209 (UP), Courtesy Naval Historical Foundation; 209 (LO), MOC; 211, National Archives-digital vers/Science Faction/CORBIS; 212 (LE), LC, 3b37307; 212 (CTR), LC, 3b08292; 212 (RT), LC, 3c37591; 213 (UP LE), LC, 21335; 213 (UP RT), LC-DIG-cwpb-00074; 213 (CTR), LC, 21334; 213 (LO), NARA; 214 (UP), LC, 3a05727; 214 (LO), LC, 3a11882; 214-215, LC, 3a42878; 216, Dr. Michael Echols; 217 (UP RT), U.S. Army Medical Museum; 217 (CTR), NARA; 217 (LO), LC, 3g07974; 218 (LO), Courtesy of the National Library of Medicine; 218 (UP), U.S. Army; 219 (UP), Dr. Michael Echols; 219 (LO LE), Dr. Michael Echols; 219 (LO RT), Dr. Michael Echols; 220, Courtesy National Library of Medicine; 221, Pray, Maiden, pray!: a ballad for the times (M1.S445 v.170 no.29), Special Collections, University of Virginia Library; 223 (UP), LC, 3c10261; 223 (LO), LC, 04061; 225, Fanny U. Phillips/The Civil War Times; 226, Clara Barton National Historic Site/Bruce Douglas; 227 (UP), LC, 3g06307; 227 (LO), Dr. Michael Echols; 229 (LE), St. James Episcopal Church, Richmond, VA, LC, 10813; 229 (RT), MOC; 230, Courtesy of George Eastman House, International Museum of Photography and Film; 231 (UP LE), LC, 00915; 231 (UP RT), LC, 04337; 231 (LO), NARA; 232 (UP LE), Courtesy USAMHI; 232 (UP RT), LC-B8184-558; 232 (LO), LC-B8171-152-A; 233 (UP), LC-B8171-1084; 233 (LO), LC, 04734; 235, LC, 04326; 236, NARA; 237, LC, 04849; 239, LC, 01988; 240, LC, 3g06811; 241 (LO LE), The Library of Virginia; 241 (UP), Virginia Historical Society, Richmond, VA; 241 (LO RT), from *On Hazardous Service* by William Gilmore Beymer, Harper & Brothers Publishers, 1912; 242, The Gilder Lehrman Collection, courtesy of The Gilder Lehrman Institute of American History; 243 (UP LE), MHIB; 243 (UP CTR), LC, 27014; 243 (UP RT), LC, 26880; 243 (LO), LC, 04294; 244, LC, 11280; 244-245,

NARA; 246, West Point Museum/MHIB; 247 (UP LE), LC, 199111; 247 (UP RT), Courtesy USAMHI; 247 (LO), Chicago Historical Society; 248, LC, 05423; 249 (UP), Jari Villanueva/www.tapsbugler.com; 249 (LO RT), LC, 21154; 249 (LO LE), New York State Military Museum/MHIB; 250, Washington Custis Lee Collection, Washington and Lee University; 251 (UP), NARA; 251 (LO), LC, 03111; 253 (UP LE), LCMD; 253 (UP RT), Richard's Free Library, Newport, NH; 253 (LO), LC, 3g04237; 254, www.sonofthesouth.net; 255 (LE), www.sonofthesouth.net; 255 (RT), LC, 3b17823.

CHAPTER 5:

256-257, LC, 04758; 258, Wisconsin Historical Society, WHI-4502; 259 (UP), The W. S. Hoole Special Collections Library, the University of Alabama; 259 (LO), LCMD; 260, LC, 3b37282; 261 (UP), State Historical Society of Missouri, Columbia; 261 (LO), LC, 05690; 262, Military History, Smithsonian Institution; 263 (LE), LC, 03240; 263 (RT), LC, 06346; 265, LC, 03218; 266 (LE), Virginia Historical Society, Richmond, VA; 266 (RT), LC, 3b01783; 267, MHIB; 268, Old State House Museum, Little Rock, AR; 269, Tennessee State Museum; 270, LC, 3g11456; 271, Courtesy Naval Historical Foundation; 272-273, Virginia Historical Society, Richmond, VA; 273 (UP), LC, 3b51001; 273 (LO), NARA; 275, LC, 04844; 276, The John Bell Hood Historical Society; 277, NARA; 278, Wikipedia; 279 (LE), Connecticut Historical Society/MHIB; 279 (RT), Info + UNC at Chapel Hill; 280-281 (RT), LC, 2033; 281 (UP), LC, 0657; 281 (LO), LC, 3g02974; 283, Collection of the New-York Historical Society; 285 (LE), Courtesy *The Atlantic;* 285 (RT), LC, 3a10837; 287, LC, 3b29434; 288, LC, 3a02045; 289, CULVER PICTURES; 291, Courtesy Louisa May Alcott's Orchard House/L.M.A. Memorial Association; 292, MHIB; 293 (UP), LC, 03163; 293 (LO), MHIB; 295, LC, 3a11366; 296, LC, 3b52027; 297, LC, 3c23816; 299, LC, 06716; 300, LC, 3a13799;

301, Valentine Richmond History Center; 302, The W. S. Hoole Special Collections Library, The University of Alabama; 303, LC, 00894; 304 (LE), MOC; 304 (RT), LC, 3c32827; 305 (RT), LC, 3g10511; 306, LC, 3b02612; 307 (UP LE), National Museum of Health and Medicine/Norman Watkins/NCP003675; 307 (UP RT), LC, 08355; 307 (LO), LC, 3b17266; 308, Medford Historical Society Collection/CORBIS; 309, LC, 3g07984; 310, Kansas State Historical Society; 311 (UP), Courtesy of Picture History; 311 (LO LE), LC, 3a07301; 311 (LO CTR), State Historical Society of Missouri, Columbia; 311 (LO RT), State Historical Society of Missouri, Columbia; 313, LC, 08362.

CHAPTER 6:

314-315, LC-B817-7798; 316, LC, 3b38181; 317 (LO LE), Children's Museum of Indianapolis; 317 (UP RT), Collection of the New-York Historical Society; 318, LC, 10106; 319, LC, 00204; 320, From the Lincoln Financial Foundation Collection, courtesy of the Indiana State Museum; 321 (LO LE), LC, 04709; 321 (LO RT), LC, 04711; 321 (UP), www.sonofthesouth.net; 322 (UP), LC, 19484; 322 (LO), LC; 323, LC, 3g05341; 324, LC-USZ62-11964; 325 (LO), LC, 3a48909; 326, LC, 00595; 327, LC, 02941; 328, Louisiana Historical Association Collection, Manuscripts Collection 55-FF, Louisiana Research Collection, Tulane University; 329, LC, 04194; 330, LC, 3a17588; 331, LC, 00460; 332, Anne Raugh Keene; 333, LCGMD, br000023; 333 (LO RT), Anne Raugh Keene; 335 (UP), LC, 3c01968; 335 (LO), LCGMD, pm001260; 336, Courtesy Stonewall Jackson House, Virginia Military Institute, Lexington, VA; 337, Richard Boyd, Fifth Avenue Presbyterian Church, Roanoke, VA; 339, LC, 04406; 340, Courtesy USAMHI, RG206S-GAR POST 201,49; 341, Photo by U.S. Signal Corps/The Horse Soldier of Gettysburg, PA; 342, National Park Service; 343, MOC; 344 (UP LE), LC, 3g05251; 344 (UP RT), David Wynn Vaughan Collection; 344 (LO), LC, 26463; 345, LC, 26863.

ADDITIONAL READING

The following books are the author's top ten Civil War titles that focus on the human side of war.

Davis, William C. *Jefferson Davis: The Man and His Hour.* New York: HarperCollins, 1991.

Freeman, Douglas Southall. *R. E. Lee: A Biography.* 4 vols. New York; London: Charles Scribner's, 1937–1940.

Glatthaar, Joseph T. *General Lee's Army: From Victory to Collapse.* New York: Free Press, 2008.

Long, E. B., and Barbara Long. *The Civil War Day by Day: An Almanac, 1861–1865.* Garden City, NY: Doubleday, 1971.

Nevins, Allan. *The War for the Union.* 4 vols. New York: Charles Scribner's, 1959–1971.

Oates, Stephen B. *With Malice Toward None: The Life of Abraham Lincoln.* New York: Harper & Row, 1977.

Robertson, James I., Jr. *Stonewall Jackson: The Man, the Soldier, the Legend.* New York: Macmillan, 1997.

Time-Life. *The Civil War.* 28 vols. New York: Time-Life Books, 1983–1987.

Wiley, Bell Irvin. *The Life of Billy Yank.* Indianapolis: Bobbs-Merrill, 1952.

———. *The Life of Johnny Reb.* Indianapolis. Bobbs-Merrill, 1943.

The Untold Civil War

James Robertson | Edited by Neil Kagan

Published by the National Geographic Society

John M. Fahey, Jr., Chairman of the Board
and Chief Executive Officer
Timothy T. Kelly, President
Declan Moore, Executive Vice President; President, Publishing
Melina Gerosa Bellows, Executive Vice President;
Chief Creative Officer, Books, Kids, and Family

Prepared by the Book Division

Barbara Brownell Grogan, Vice President and Editor in Chief
Jonathan Halling, Design Director, Books and
Children's Publishing
Marianne R. Koszorus, Director of Design
Lisa Thomas, Senior Editor
Carl Mehler, Director of Maps
R. Gary Colbert, Production Director
Jennifer A. Thornton, Managing Editor
Meredith C. Wilcox, Administrative Director, Illustrations

Staff for This Book

Neil Kagan, Editor, Illustrations Editor
Stephen G. Hyslop, Text Editor
Carol Farrar Norton, Art Director
Harris J. Andrews, Contributing Writer
Judith Klein, Production Editor
Lewis Bassford, Production Manager
Marshall Kiker, Illustrations Specialist

Manufacturing and Quality Management

Christopher A. Liedel, Chief Financial Officer
Phillip L. Schlosser, Senior Vice President
Chris Brown, Technical Director
Nicole Elliott, Manager
Rachel Faulise, Manager
Robert L. Barr, Manager

Created by Kagan & Associates, Inc. Falls Church, Virginia
Neil Kagan, President and Editor in Chief
Sharyn Kagan, Vice President and Director of Administration

Founded in 1888, the National Geographic Society is one of the largest nonprofit scientific and educational organizations in the world. It reaches more than 285 million people worldwide each month through its official journal, *National Geographic,* and its four other magazines; the National Geographic Channel; television documentaries; radio programs; films; books; videos and DVDs; maps; and interactive media. National Geographic has funded more than 8,000 scientific research projects and supports an education program combating geographic illiteracy.

For more information, please call 1-800-NGS LINE (647-5463) or write to the following address:

National Geographic Society
1145 17th Street N.W.
Washington, D.C. 20036-4688 U.S.A.

Visit us online at www.nationalgeographic.com/books

For information about special discounts for bulk purchases, please contact National Geographic Books Special Sales: ngspecsales@ngs.org

For rights or permissions inquiries, please contact National Geographic Books Subsidiary Rights: ngbookrights@ngs.org

This 2013 edition printed for Barnes & Noble, Inc. by the National Geographic Society.

ISBN: 978-1-4351-4751-5 (B&N ed.)
ISBN: 978-1-4262-0812-6
ISBN: 978-1-4262-0832-4 (deluxe ed.)

Printed in China

14/RRDS/2

CONTRIBUTORS

JAMES ROBERTSON, author, is one of the most distinguished names in Civil War history. A nationally acclaimed teacher and lecturer, he has written or edited two dozen books on the Civil War era. His award-winning biography of Stonewall Jackson was hailed as "a book every student of the war should read and every chronicler should emulate." Early in his career, Robertson was appointed executive director of the U.S. Civil War Centennial Commission by President John F. Kennedy. He is an Alumni Distinguished Professor Emeritus at Virginia Tech.

NEIL KAGAN, editor, heads Kagan & Associates, Inc., a firm specializing in designing and producing innovative illustrated books. Formerly publisher/managing editor and director of new product development for Time-Life Books, he created numerous book series, including the award-winning Voices of the Civil War. Recently he edited *Great Battles of the Civil War, Great Photographs of the Civil War,* and for National Geographic the best-selling books *Concise History of the World, Eyewitness to the Civil War,* and *Atlas of the Civil War.*